P9-CCO-874

THROWING STONES
AT THE MOON

SANTA FE PUBLIC LIBRARY

THROWING STONES AT THE MOON

NARRATIVES FROM COLOMBIANS DISPLACED BY VIOLENCE

COMPILED AND EDITED BY

SIBYLLA BRODZINSKY
AND MAX SCHOENING

FOREWORD BY

ÍNGRID BETANCOURT

Research editor
ALEX CARP

Appendix essay writers
NADJA DROST, ADAM ISACSON,
WINIFRED TATE

VOICE OF WITNESS

Transcribers
MAURO JAVIER CARDENAS, ABNER MORALES,
AMANDA PALOMARES, ALBERTO REYES,
NYDIA SERRANO, AND THE TRANSCRIPT CO-OP.

Copyeditor
MEGAN ROBERTS

Fact checker
MARÍA FERNANDA RAMÍREZ

Additional assistance
KYLIE BYRD, NAOKI O'BRYAN,
ANN READING, ANGELENE SMITH

To the book's narrators, who courageously and generously shared their stories, often at risk to their own lives, and to the millions of other displaced Colombians, whose stories remain untold.

VOICE OF WITNESS

MᶜSWEENEY'S BOOKS
SAN FRANCISCO

For more information about McSweeney's, see www.mcsweeneys.net
For more information about Voice of Witness, see www.voiceofwitness.org

Copyright © 2012 McSweeney's and Voice of Witness

Front cover photo by Stephen Ferry
Maps by Julien Lallemand

All rights reserved, including right of
reproduction in whole or part in any form.

McSweeney's and colophon are registered trademarks
of McSweeney's Publishing.

ISBN: 978-1-936365-91-3

VOICE OF WITNESS

Voice of Witness is a non-profit book series that seeks to illuminate human rights crises by humanizing those most closely affected. Using oral history as a foundation, the series explores social justice issues through the stories of the men and women who experience them. These books are designed for readers of all levels—from high school and college students to policymakers—interested in a reality-based understanding of ongoing injustices in the United States and around the world. Voice of Witness also brings socially relevant, oral history-based curricula into U.S. schools with independent educational programming, and in partnership with Facing History and Ourselves. Visit www.voiceofwitness.org for more information.

VOICE OF WITNESS BOARD OF DIRECTORS

DAVE EGGERS
Author; Co-founder of
826 National, the Valentino
Achak Deng Foundation,
and the Zeitoun Foundation

LOLA VOLLEN
Visiting Scholar, Institute of
International Studies, UC
Berkeley; Executive Director,
Life After Exoneration Program

JILL STAUFFER
Assistant Professor of Philosophy;
Director of Peace, Justice, and
Human Rights Concentration,
Haverford College

VOICE OF WITNESS FOUNDING ADVISORS

STUDS TERKEL
Author, Oral Historian

ROGER COHN
Former Editor-in-Chief,
Mother Jones

MARK DANNER
Author, Professor, UC Berkeley
Graduate School of Journalism

HARRY KREISLER
Executive Director, Institute of
International Studies, UC Berkeley

MARTHA MINOW
Dean, Harvard Law School

SAMANTHA POWER
Author; Professor, Founding
Executive Director, The Carr
Center for Human Rights Policy

JOHN PRENDERGAST
Co-chair, ENOUGH Project;
Strategic Advisor, Not On Our Watch

ORVILLE SCHELL
Arthur Ross Director,
Asia Society

WILLIAM T. VOLLMANN
Author

VOICE OF WITNESS SERIES EDITORS: Dave Eggers, Lola Vollen.
EXECUTIVE DIRECTOR/EXECUTIVE EDITOR: mimi lok.
DEVELOPMENT AND COMMUNICATIONS DIRECTOR: Juliana Sloane.
EDUCATION PROGRAM DIRECTOR: Cliff Mayotte.
EDUCATION PROGRAM ASSOCIATE: Claire Kiefer.
PUBLICITY & OUTREACH ASSOCIATE: McKenna Stayner.

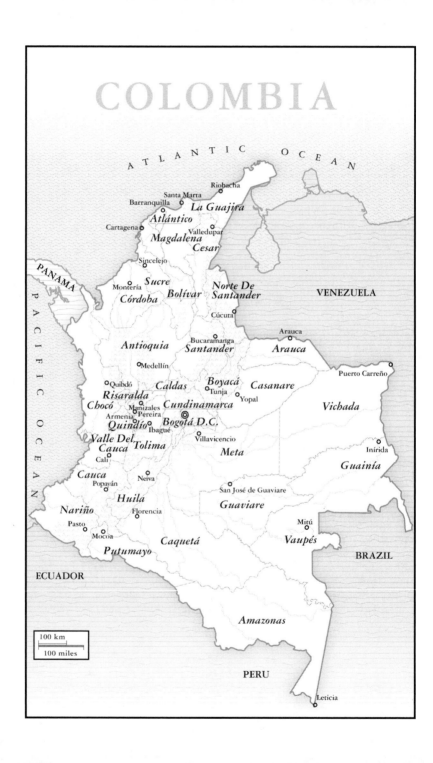

COLOMBIA

ATLANTIC OCEAN

PANAMA

PACIFIC OCEAN

Riobacha

Santa Marta
Barranquilla
La Guajira
Atlántico
Cartagena
Valledupar
Magdalena
Cesar

Sincelejo

Sucre
Montería
Córdoba
Bolívar
Norte De Santander

Cúcuta

VENEZUELA

Antioquia
Bucaramanga
Santander
Arauca
Arauca

Medellín

Puerto Carreño

Quibdó
Caldas
Boyacá
Tunja
Casanare
Risaralda
Choço
Manizales
Yopal
Cundinamarca
Vichada
Armenia
Pereira
Quindío
Ibagué
Bogotá D.C.

Valle Del Cauca
Tolima
Villavicencio
Inírida
Cali
Meta
Guainía

Cauca
Neiva
Popayán
San José de Guaviare

Nariño
Huila
Florencia
Guaviare

Pasto
Mitú
Mocoa
Vaupés

Putumayo
Caquetá

BRAZIL

ECUADOR

Amazonas

100 km
100 miles

PERU

Leticia

CONTENTS

THE SILENCE
OF SHAME

by Íngrid Betancourt

When you live through the trauma of having your most basic rights violated, the experience becomes ingrained in your genetic makeup. What you lived, and how you lived it, is your new identity.

Remembering is painful. And telling your story involves submerging yourself deeply and intensely in your own past, bringing forth a flood of uncontrolled emotion. You become conscious of your most glaring vulnerabilities. But sharing is also your way out. Every time you tell your story, you can distance yourself from it, take a step back. You learn to remember without reliving, and begin to recover.

The guerrillas of the Revolutionary Armed Forces of Colombia held me hostage for six and a half years in the jungle. I lived with a chain around my neck, locked up in a cage. Subjected to every humiliation, I was a direct witness to, and victim of, remorseless power, abuse and domination.

But I survived—I became stronger, with newly acquired lucidity. I discovered that whatever happened to me, I could protect the essence of who I was. Therefore, nobody could damage the "inner-me." On the other hand, I also understood that I needed to change. Surviving meant learning how to act and how not to react. It meant choosing to be what I wanted to be. That became for me, in the midst of captivity, the revelation of what true freedom is.

The narrators in *Throwing Stones at the Moon* have also been brutalized and dispossessed in Colombia's armed conflict. And from their immeasurable loss, a beautiful, human fortitude has emerged. This book is a window into the indomitable essence of each narrator, and also into the war that has driven them and four million other Colombians out of their homes.

Colombians who have been forcibly displaced have escaped massacres, murders, threats, rape, and an endless list of other abuses. They face a situation of life or death; they flee because there is no alternative. It is a calamity of world proportions, that we discover through the words of anonymous men and women, sharing with us what it meant for them, in the midst of atrocities, to remain truly human.

However, their stories are hidden by the silence created by our indifference. Many of us have hardened our hearts to their stories because it is impossible to witness their suffering and continue living with our unbearable lightness of being.

A worldwide survey conducted some years ago showed that Colombians assessed themselves as being the happiest people on Earth. This survey was conducted through phone calls, and could only reach people living in the security of Colombian cities. The result proved the existence of an immense gap between the suffering of half of the population and the turning-a-blind-eye of the other half.

In fact, this is part of a defense mechanism. Colombia has lived centuries of repeated cycles of violence. When there are so many victims of so many atrocities, people often feel uncomfortable when they hear the details of cruelty and violence. They don't want to be touched by the pain of others, fearing it could become their own fate.

This is why we so often see people pointing fingers at the victims, accusing them of being responsible for their own suffering. They are accused of being part of the guerrilla, paramilitary or drug trafficking organizations that targeted them. If the suspicions are proven to be wrong, the same people will conclude that it was nevertheless the victim's fault for being in the wrong place at the wrong time.

The lives of those so quick to judge rarely cross paths with those who live in the "other Colombia," where it is guerrillas, paramilitary armies or drug traffickers who, in effect, rule the daily lives of civilians, and where those who try to remain neutral are seen as the enemy or a snitch.

If the conflict and human rights crisis are invisible within Colombia, they are even more so on the international front, where the country is seen as having largely overcome its war. It is true that leftist rebels have been relegated to remote areas of Colombia, and officially, the paramilitaries have been disbanded. But there are still more than 100,000 civilians fleeing their homes because of violence each year.

There is no better way to heal the wounds of human rights victims —and of society—than for them to receive the recognition of equals: to have their neighbors, their boss, their friends, and their loved ones, understanding what happened; to know that people they may never meet, including political leaders, and even citizens abroad, are being informed on how and why they have suffered. It is the first step to recovering their dignity.

When Colombia's displaced ask to be heard, they are not begging for economic support or looking for a handout. They are seeking to transform their ordeal into social wisdom. They offer the intimacy of their pain to enrich our lives and to make us reflect. The men and women who tell their stories in this collection are helping us to become better humans in a world that lacks humanity. They are examples of survival, perseverance and courage, who should be admired and respected. This is why I believe they are the true heroes of our times. This book offers them the recognition they need and deserve.

Íngrid Betancourt, a Colombian politician, was kidnapped in February 2002 by FARC rebels while campaigning as a candidate in the Colombian presidential elections. She was held in jungle camps for six and a half years until she was rescued, along with fourteen other hostages, in July 2008. Her book about her experience, Even Silence Has an End, *has been published in eighteen languages.*

INTRODUCTION

DESPLAZADOS

by Sibylla Brodzinsky and Max Schoening

We sat in gloomy silence as our taxi wound around 8,000-foot-high mountains from the southwestern city of Pasto to the airport for our one-hour flight home to Bogotá. The sun seemed too bright, the mountains too lush.

We had just come from the apartment of a local human rights activist, where we met Felipe Aguilar and Mariana Camacho. A quiet, gentle man, Felipe described to us how a group of paramilitaries gunned down his ex-wife and three children a few months before. Leftist rebels had previously driven him off three different farms. "Everything I've loved, my God has taken away," he said, summing up a life of loss.

We then turned to Mariana, who had been waiting to talk to us. A plump, meek-looking woman, she surprised us with the ferocity of her pain and anger. Right-wing paramilitaries killed two of her sons, and disappeared her husband in 2001. A decade later, she learned that he had been cut into three pieces with a chainsaw while still alive, and then buried in a clandestine grave.

Felipe's and Mariana's stories had overwhelmed us. Even more overwhelming is the reality that, for the four million Colombians who have been uprooted from their homes, there are similar tales of loss, cruelty and violence, equally matched by determination and defiance. Fleeing from murder, massacres, threats, forced recruitment and countless other abuses, Colombia's forcibly displaced—los desplazados—make up one of the largest populations of internal refugees in the world.

Colombia's armed conflict pits left-wing guerrillas, right-wing paramilitaries and government forces against one another; drug mafias battling over smuggling routes add to the general violence. The country's last remaining Marxist rebel groups, the National Liberation Army (ELN) and the Revolutionary Armed Forces of Colombia (FARC), rose up against the state in the mid 1960s. In the 1980s, right-wing paramilitary groups mushroomed throughout the country, representing a loose alliance of the Colombian military, cocaine traffickers, and wealthy landowners, all set on eliminating guerrillas and suspected supporters.

The conflict peaked at the end of the 1990s, when regional paramilitary militias joined forces under the United Self-Defense Forces of Colombia (AUC), and the FARC reached its pinnacle of strength, controlling as much as 40 percent of the national territory with some 20,000 fighters. Both groups, fueled by the drug trade, were designated foreign terrorist organizations by the United States and the European Union.

The year 2002 marked a watershed moment in the war: peace talks between the government and FARC collapsed, and Colombians elected President Álvaro Uribe, who started a massive counter-insurgency campaign against guerrillas. By the time Uribe left office in 2010, the tide had turned in the conflict. The AUC had agreed to disband and between 2003 and 2006 more than 30,000 supposed paramilitaries turned themselves in, in exchange for pardons or reduced sentences for confessing to atrocities. The government had driven guerrillas from Colombia's main cities, towns and highways, halved their troops and declared the paramilitaries extinct. Colombia began to project itself internationally as a country that had largely overcome its conflict, an apparent success story in the War on Terror.

This turned out to be more wishful thinking than reality. Without a doubt the number of massacres, murders and kidnappings dropped sharply. But in its zeal to fight the guerrillas, Colombia's army murdered innocent civilians and presented them as members of illegal groups killed in combat; thousands of cases of alleged extrajudicial killings by the military are currently under investigation. The paramilitary demobilization ceremonies turned out to be filled with stand-ins rather than actual fighters. Many former AUC members reorganized into neo-paramilitary groups, which are far less ideological than their predecessors, but continue to target civilians. The FARC, after suffering crushing military blows to its leadership and rank and file, regrouped and kept up its relentless attacks on both civilians and the military.

As an observer and chronicler of Colombia's conflict, Sibylla witnessed many of the events of the past decade unfold. But it was not until she began interviewing narrators for this book and hearing their stories that she understood the tragic magnitude of each episode. A vague sense of remorse overcame her when she realized that she'd been on a reporting assignment just five kilometers from Mariana Camacho's farm in Putumayo province days before Mariana's husband was disappeared in February 2001.

Max had just moved to Colombia when we started to research this book. He knew about the war's dramatic scale, its different players and the theories of its causes—and that he wanted to tell the story. But until he began interviewing narrators, he had no idea how often the ideological, political, and economic contours of the conflict are eclipsed by its deeply personal nature. It was a one-on-one battle of wills with a guerrilla commander that ultimately drove Rodrigo Mejía to flee his farm, and María Victoria Jiménez worked side by side in a hospital with the man she suspected of ordering her assassination.

Both of us feel honored to have been welcomed into each one of the narrators' lives, and we were amazed at their capacity to give after having lost so much. They offered us beds in their homes, steaming sancocho soup, their friendship, and their stories, despite the renewed pain caused by the retelling. We never felt we could fully reciprocate the generosity with which they shared their lives—many lacked food, decent jobs, and protection, and all we could offer was the opportunity to make their stories public. Keenly aware of the limitations of our undertaking, we hope that these personal perspectives in *Throwing Stones at the Moon* will add depth and complexity to readers' understanding of the country, and draw attention to a war that remains largely unknown abroad.

We also hope to highlight how Colombia's conflict and human rights crisis is ongoing: during the two years that we worked on this book, more than 250,000 Colombians were newly displaced by violence. Over the course of multiple interviews with each of the narrators, we witnessed how several of them had suffered a new atrocity or threat since our previous encounters. When we first met Felipe he told us he couldn't take any more suffering after losing three of his children in the massacre. By the time we caught up with him again, we learned that an unidentified armed group had nearly chopped off the hand of one of his two surviving sons.

The narratives in this book also reveal how far back this war goes in the country's history, and how deeply ingrained it is in the national psyche. Its deep roots are reflected in the premonitions of impending violence that many narrators experienced. One felt a tingling in his body before being attacked by guerrillas; another felt a sudden need to turn back just before stepping on a land mine. Emilia González recalled how the village dogs howled the night before the 2000 El Salado massacre, one of the bloodiest mass killings in Colombian history: "People say that when dogs howl, something bad is about to happen." Episodes of violence are remembered as if they should have been foreseen.

We do not pretend to provide explanations for Colombia's human rights problems. The Colombian conflict is messy, and there is no overarching analysis that can explain its causes and motives or even its consequences. The country has long led the world in cocaine production, and profits from the trade fund guerrillas, paramilitaries, and violent mafias, while also corrupting politicians and members of the armed forces. But the drug trade is only part of the equation. Colombia has one of the most unequal land and income distributions in the world. Its Andean mountains, Amazonian jungle and two coastlines have produced a splintered society where regional political barons, guerrilla commanders, and warlords control daily life. The conflict has also been fueled and motivated by the fight for land, gold, bananas, coal, oil, emeralds, and palm oil, as well as by vengeance, political power, and ideology.

Rather than attempting to tell *the* story of Colombia's conflict, this book depicts the many ways it plays out in the everyday lives of the people it has displaced and dispossessed. The narrators are black, white, mestizo, and indigenous, poor and wealthy; they are peasant farmers and urbanites; they have been driven from their homes by guerrillas, paramilitaries, army abuses, and the random violence of drug traffickers. Their common experience is having been caught up in a seemingly inescapable spiral of violence. While some seem to accept their fates in the face of incessant brutality, others confront their abusers and seek justice for their crimes. Whether with quiet stoicism or with tears of rage, nearly all of the brave men and women we talked to show a will to maintain their dignity, to protect their families and to rebuild their lives. The title of the book, *Throwing Stones at the Moon*, which speaks to an apparently impossible task, refers to that tenacity to persevere and survive against the odds.

EDITORS' NOTE

The narratives in this book are compiled from interviews conducted over a two-year period in different regions of Colombia and Ecuador. The interviews were conducted and transcribed in Spanish, then translated and edited in English. In each case we tried as best we could to maintain the narrator's unique voice, though it was often challenging to approximate certain slang or idiomatic words in English. Many of the people we interviewed shared their story with us at great personal risk. To ensure their safety, we have honored their request that their real names not be used, and that certain identifying details of their stories be changed. We have indicated name and location changes in each narrative.

WHEN DOGS HOWL

The Caribbean Coast

Colombia's Caribbean region is the inspiration for Gabriel García Márquez's magical realism. It boasts the elegant cobblestoned streets of colonial Cartagena, the raucous Carnaval of Barranquilla, and the pristine beaches of Parque Tayrona, near Santa Marta. The Costa, as most Colombians call the region, extends far beyond the shimmering coastal cities, through the rugged mountainous terrain of the Montes de María, the fertile savannahs of Sucre and Córdoba, and high mountain peaks in the Sierra Nevada de Santa Marta. It is in this other part of the Costa that the Colombian conflict has played out, while cities like Cartagena receive hundreds of thousands of the region's displaced.

The savannahs of Córdoba were once beset with guerrillas of the Popular Liberation Army (EPL) and the Revolutionary Armed Forces of Colombia (FARC), who extorted large cattle ranchers, kidnapping those who refused to pay. By the mid-1990s right-wing paramilitary groups were fighting back, and the Peasant Self-Defense Forces of Córdoba and Urabá (ACCU) were created under the command of Fidel and Carlos Castaño, who set up a hierarchical structure with fifteen different blocs, mostly in the Costa.

In 1999 a statue was erected in Montería, the capital of Córdoba, showing a peasant and a man in uniform each holding the wing of a dove with the figure of Jesus Christ looming behind the two. Carlos Castaño, who by then was the head of a nationwide paramilitary federation called the AUC, said in his 2001 authorized biography that the monument "invites citizens to become paramilitaries." Despite the demobilization of the AUC blocs in the province in 2005, the statue still stands, and new paramilitary groups have emerged and made Córdoba one of the most violent provinces in all of Colombia. They were blamed for many of the 562 murders reported in Córdoba in 2010.

To the east of Córdoba are Sucre and Bolívar provinces, where the low-lying Montes de María mountains stand. For decades, these mountains provided shelter and important movement corridors to FARC guerrillas. They also gave their name to the paramilitary group that was created there, the Héroes de los Montes de María bloc of the AUC, responsible for some of the bloodiest massacres in the country, including those in the villages of El Salado, Chengue, Macayepo, and Mampuján.

Further east lies the Sierra Nevada de Santa Marta, the world's highest coastal mountain range, soaring from sea level to an altitude of 5,700 meters, just forty-two kilometers from the Caribbean. Its northern foothills saw the marijuana boom of the 1970s, known locally as la bonanza marimbera. By the mid-1980s the illegal crop of choice was coca, the leaves of which are used to make cocaine. This fuelled the growth of the FARC and National Liberation Army (ELN) guerrillas in the area, and two separate paramilitary groups who fought for control of the mountain, considered sacred by the indigenous people who live there.

EMILIA GONZÁLEZ

AGE: 59
OCCUPATION: *Farmer*
HOMETOWN: *El Salado, Bolívar*
INTERVIEWED IN: *El Salado, Bolívar*

Depending on the weather, it can take anywhere between one and six hours to travel the thirty-two kilometers of dirt track separating the bustling town of El Carmen de Bolívar and El Salado village. El Salado was once a thriving community. It had a population of seven thousand, offered education through high school, and had a well-equipped health clinic. Tobacco companies had pressing and rolling plants there, which gave jobs to the women in the village.

On February 18, 2000, a right-wing paramilitary group called the Héroes de los Montes de María circled the village, gathered all its residents on the micro-soccer court and committed one of the most gruesome massacres in Colombia's bloody conflict, killing sixty people over the course of four days. Between 1999 and 2001 in the Montes de María region of northern Colombia alone, 354 people were murdered in forty-two separate massacres, according to the country's Center for Historical Memory.

Emilia González is a native of El Salado. From her front door, she can see the soccer court where many of the killings occurred. In her narrative, she describes life before and since the massacre, and her family's attempts to rebuild their lives. As she talks, Emilia chain smokes and sometimes paces around the open-walled hut that serves as her kitchen. Here, she shells peas and pounds corn into meal as stray chickens scratch in the yard.

Names in this narrative have been changed at the request of the narrator.

WHEN EL SALADO WAS EL SALADO

I thank God I'm a native Saladera through and through. When El Salado was El Salado, it was a wonderful village. We used to say that, as soon as anyone tasted the water here, they felt at home. Today it's not one fourth of what it was then. Now we are ruined. The town was never like it is today, lost among the weeds.

When it was still our town, everyone here had a way to make a living. We didn't have to live from hand-outs. We had tobacco companies here, and we women worked in the plants, smoothing out the tobacco leaves. Every Saturday we left with our pockets full of money. On weekends, people came in from the countryside with loads of tobacco to sell to the tobacco companies, and we made pots of peto[1] to sell to them. People also brought in merchandise from other towns and they'd decorate the park with goods for sale.

It was a happy town, and people were always waiting for the next celebration. There was the bull festival in January, and Carnival was celebrated in February, where we had beauty pageants and dressed up in costumes. For Easter Week, we'd make pots of chicha and bollos;[2] everyone would go out with plates, and neighbors would hand out food and sweets. In June, it was horse races for the festival of San Juan, and on the day of Santa Rosa de Lima on August 30, we'd take the statue of the saint out from the church and carry her in a procession. In November, everyone would start fixing up their houses and cleaning up the streets to welcome the New Year. We'd put up Christmas trees and holiday lights everywhere.

---

[1] A corn-based drink.

[2] Chicha is an alcoholic drink made of fermented corn. Bollos are cornmeal tamales.

In those days, a priest would come regularly to the village. But since the violence, it's rare. A priest only comes on February 18, for the commemoration of the massacre victims, and for first communions in October. Otherwise, the church stays closed.

I LIKE THE MACHETE AND I WORK LIKE A MAN

My family and I are close. I have two sisters, and we all went to school here. I'd study during the week and help my parents on the farm on the weekends, cutting tobacco. Since I was little, I've always liked farming. I'd say, "I want to use a machete, just the same as my father." My dad would get angry and say, "That's not for women," but finally he gave me a small one and showed me how to use it. I dreamed of continuing my studies, but I didn't get beyond sixth grade; my parents didn't have the money. By then, I was fourteen years old and I was stuck, so I helped my parents on the farm.

When I was seventeen, I met my husband, Alberto. He was a cabinetmaker and a carpenter. At one point I went to work as a maid in El Carmen and then in Barranquilla, but I'd come back every month and he was there, waiting. We never had any problems, no fights, nothing.

We got married in 1973, when I was twenty-one. It was wonderful; I was so happy. We went for a honeymoon at my in-laws', in a town called Villanueva. We stayed there for two weeks, and when we came back to El Salado, Alberto went to work in the fields. Even though he had learned the art of carpentry, he said he was going to try his hand at farming to see how it went.

In 1975 we bought a small plot of land in the village and he built our house there. In 1977 I got pregnant and I had my first daughter. We named her Amelia. I was so happy, because having a child is the most precious thing. My husband celebrated by partying for two days. Things went well for the next few years, and in 1984 I had a boy named Carlos. After that, I had three other girls: Katerine in 1988, Mayerli in 1993, and Carolina in 1997.

During that time, I would always get up at four, make my first coffee, sweep the patios, and make breakfast for the kids. Then I'd make
breakfast for me and my husband, and then I'd get to work: washing
clothes, making lunch or dinner. I'd spend some days working in the
tobacco plants, and some days in the fields, pulling tobacco or yams with
my husband. If wood needed chopping, I'd chop wood. If yucca had to be
harvested, I'd harvest it. I was used to it. I like the machete and I work
like a man.

IT'S A MIRACLE THEY DIDN'T KILL US ALL

In the 1980s and '90s, the guerrillas were always coming into the village.[3]
They walked around like they owned the place. A guerrilla would knock on
your door and "invite" you to a meeting in the park. You couldn't refuse;
you had to go. Or they'd come and tell the men, "Sunday you have to clear
the road to San Andrés." If you said no, they'd say, "Okay, but just wait and
see what happens." If someone didn't go, the guerrillas would note it down
in a book. So they got us used to doing things by the barrel of a gun.

I say that where the guerrillas are and have people collaborating with
them, nothing good can happen. That's what happened here. In El Salado, the guerrillas had many people cooperating with them, so what else
could we expect but that the paramilitaries would eventually come?[4] It's
a miracle they didn't kill us all.

The paramilitaries first came to El Salado in February 1997. A few of
them came one day, dressed as civilians. They called a meeting and said

---

[3] The Revolutionary Armed Forces of Colombia (FARC) and National Liberation Army
(ELN) are the two largest guerrilla groups in Colombia. Founded in the 1960s and claiming to represent the country's rural poor in the fight against Colombia's wealthy classes
and U.S. imperialism, both groups commit widespread abuses against civilians, including
killings, threats, and recruitment of child soldiers.

[4] Right-wing paramilitary groups began to form in Colombia in the early 1980s with the
purported aim of fighting left-wing guerrillas. Backed by the military, landowners, drug
traffickers, and political and economic elites, they murdered tens of thousands of civilians.

they would no longer allow stores in the village to open because guerrillas got their supplies there. The police inspector[5] was at the meeting, and she argued that this was a small town; she asked where we were going to buy things if they closed the stores. The paramilitaries just said that they'd be back in two weeks. No one took it very seriously. Among my family and friends, we just asked ourselves why they were trying to close the stores, and wondered if they'd really come back.

Then, on March 23, at 5:30 a.m., I heard villagers yelling, "The paras have come to El Salado!"[6] I grabbed my children and we hid under the bed. We could hear gunshots for about two or three hours. When we didn't hear any more shots, we crawled out.

Later, the villagers learned that the paramilitaries had killed five people in the park. They'd killed a teacher who was still in her nightgown, a man and his son, and another boy. They took another man away and killed him later.[7] The paras had killed and left.

My family and I left the next day in one of the Jeeps that come and go from El Carmen, which is the nearest big town. Everyone in the village left. My family and I stayed with a cousin for three months, and then we were back. Most people from the village also returned.

We went back to our homes and started to work again. It was March when the paras had come, and around here, that's the month when people start preparing the tobacco fields for planting. So when we got back, we continued the work we had left behind. We thought the worst was over.

WHEN DOGS HOWL

After we returned to El Salado, every once in a while there would be killings on the road to El Carmen. We lived with a lot of anxiety.

---

[5] The highest civilian authority in Colombian villages.

[6] "Para" is conversational shorthand for paramilitary.

[7] The dead were professor Doris Mariela Torres, José Esteban Domínguez and his son, and Néstor Arrieta. Álvaro Pérez, then president of the Community Action Board, was disappeared.

One day in December 1999, a helicopter flew over the village. It passed and passed again, and then it dumped leaflets onto the village. The leaflets said, "Enjoy yourselves on New Year's Eve. Kill a turkey, make sancocho,[8] be happy—because later on, just wait." Everyone talked about it, but again, no one left. Even though we'd seen what had happened in 1997, we remained sort of ignorant. That Christmas we had parties, we celebrated normally. But on January 9, 2000, as my family and I were getting to my cousin's birthday party, a helicopter flew over and opened fire. Everyone ran back to their houses and hid. There was no party that year.

Then, on February 16, 2000, we started to suffer. On that day, word got around the town that the paramilitaries had blocked the road to El Carmen. We thought the paramilitaries were on their way to El Salado, but we waited and waited to see if someone brought news. At four in the afternoon we still hadn't heard anything, and by six, most people had decided to leave El Salado, fleeing to hide in the surrounding countryside. My husband refused to go—he said he hadn't done anything to anyone— and my son Carlos, who was sixteen, stayed with him. I left with my four daughters, who were twenty-three, twelve, seven, and three at the time.

My daughters and I spent the night in a small hut, on a farm about fifteen minutes outside of town. We were there with a bunch of friends, one of my sisters, uncles, and cousins. There were about fifty people there altogether. That night, the young children slept, but the adults didn't. We were so nervous, we stayed up drinking coffee and smoking cigarettes. That's when I started smoking. I was worried about my husband and son, wondering what could happen to them.

Early on the next morning, on the seventeenth, a boy from the village rode up on a horse. He had come to milk the cows in the pasture. As soon as we saw him coming, we ran up to him and asked, "What's happened in El Salado?" And he said, "Nothing's happened." The boy milked the

---

[8] A hearty Colombian soup of chicken, beef, or fish with plantains and yams.

cows, and when he was leaving all of us in the hut told him we'd go with him back to town. As we were setting off, a boy in our group pointed to a nearby farm and said, "Look, look over there at the flames. The paras are burning down the huts." When we saw that, the people in the group said, "No, we're not going back to El Salado."

That's when the group split up, running through the countryside, fleeing to areas we'd never been to. I was with my four daughters. I cut my leg, but I didn't pay attention to the cut or the blood or anything. We ran for about an hour, until we got to a kind of ditch. By then we had lost the others. As we sat there in the ditch, little ants started biting us, and we were swatting them off our bodies.

At ten that morning, a helicopter went by, and we threw ourselves onto the ground under some trees until it passed. Our feet were so swollen. We hadn't eaten since lunch the day before. My girls, the younger ones, started to cry at noon, saying, "Mother, I'm hungry. Mother, what are you going to give us?"

And all I thought was, *God give my daughters strength. I have nothing to give them.* The little ones cried, and I said, "Be quiet, be quiet," because we didn't know if the paras could come up on us.

By four in the afternoon we were lost; we didn't know the way out of the bush. Then we heard a donkey braying, and we decided to follow its sound. When the donkey fell silent, we stayed still. When the donkey brayed, we went forward, one in front of the other, afraid. By six in the evening we made it out of there.

We arrived at a hut in a field. There was no one else around. Then suddenly a boy we knew from the village came and asked me, "What are you doing out here? Go back to El Salado, your family is looking for you. They're desperate because no one has seen you." But when we got to the village, a neighbor asked me why we'd come back if the paramilitaries were here. We didn't have the strength to run anymore. I told myself, *If they're going to kill us, they're going to kill us.*

My daughters and I got home and found my husband and son still there. Our house was on the edge of town, and I thought it would be safer to spend the night on the main street. So I went with my daughters to a friend's house on the main street. Most of our neighbors from the neighborhood were there too. My husband and son stayed at our house because Alberto didn't want to leave the house abandoned. I tried to convince him and Carlos to come with us but Alberto insisted on staying. At about nine that night, the "ghost plane"[9] flew over really low. It sounded like it was going to take off the roofs of the houses. Everyone was scared. I kept worrying about my husband and son. People say that when dogs howl, something bad is about to happen. That night, the dogs were howling, and we were awake all night. I thought, *Now they're really going to kill us.*

YOU, TOO, ARE HUMAN

The day dawned on the eighteenth and I headed home with my daughters. As we were going into the house I heard shots from the hills outside town, *pra, pra pra*, and I said, "Run my children, they're here! Run!" So with my daughters and son, I went running again to my friend's house on the main street. My son told me that Alberto had gone out to buy some yucca for breakfast so he was out when the shooting began. I just hoped he'd found a place to hide.

At my friend's house we stayed in the living room with other neighbors, waiting to see what would happen. For a while, everything was quiet, but everybody was still scared. Then a village boy came by and said everyone should go up to another neighborhood that we call the upper neighborhood. Carlos decided to stay at another house with friends and some of his cousins instead of going to the upper neighborhood. I fought with him and told him to come with me but he refused. So my daughters and I ran to the upper neighborhood, and when we were near the health clinic there, I fainted. At that point, I hadn't eaten in three days.

---

[9] Avión fantasma, or "ghost plane," is a name given by civilians to the Douglas AC-47 "Spooky," a U.S.-made Vietnam-era airplane retrofitted for use in the Colombian Air Force.

When I came to, I was in a house with about fifty other people, mostly women and children, including my daughters. The sun beat down; it was hot, very hot. We heard shots, and people crawled under the three beds that were in the room. I hugged my daughters and tried to calm them. They were crying because they still hadn't eaten anything. All they'd had was juice.

A few hours later, at about ten in the morning, the paras came into the town. From the moment they came in, they started yelling, "We've come to El Salado, come out you guerrilla bastards!"

I lay on the floor and looked out under the front door. Through the gap, I was able to see the paras kick in a neighbor's door and take him away. Some babies that were in the room started to cry, and one of the paras out on the street said, "Hey, there are people in there! Kick in the door!" One of them kicked the door off its hinges.

When I saw that, I ran out to face them. My body was trembling, and I said to myself, *My God, give me the courage to defend myself, because if they kill me, they kill me unjustly*. When I came out to confront them, an elderly gentleman also came out with me, and the paras grabbed him and kicked him, and threw him down on the ground. I said to them, "Oh my God, please have mercy on that old man! You, too, are human beings. Don't kill this poor guy!" And they said to me, "Shut up, guerrilla bitch! Shut up. Don't talk so much, you have no idea what's about to happen. We don't want any crying." They grabbed me and the others and pushed us down the street. "We want everyone on the soccer court," they said. When I looked around I saw that my seven-year-old daughter Mayerli and my sister weren't with us and I panicked. But the paras pushed us down to the court.

THEY WENT ON KILLING
AND KILLING AND KILLING

When we got to the soccer court, the paras already had my son Carlos sitting there along with four other people. When I saw him there I thought,

Oh my Lord, don't let them kill my son. Carlos saw me and called out "Mami!" and I said to him, "Have faith in God, my son." I looked at him and he looked at me. I didn't see my husband Alberto, and I wondered what could have happened. I thought maybe they'd killed him.

There were something like two hundred paramilitaries all in uniform on the court. Soon, more villagers started coming from different parts of the village. One neighbor came up to me to tell me that my sister and Mayerli were hiding and that they were okay. Eventually there were about three hundred villagers on or around the court.

The paramilitaries split us up: the men were on the court, and the women were sent to stand in front of the church, which is right in front of the court. Some of the women stood, and others sat on the curb. I stood with my daughters. The paras started asking questions. For example, they asked us if we were guerrillas, or which of us were guerrillas, or if the guerrillas spent time here, where the weapons were hidden, and so on. They also said things like, "Today is the day you die. Our orders are to finish off all of you." At one point, they started taking jewelry from the women. They would take a person's earring and put it on someone else; if you had a chain they'd take it and put it on another person. I don't know why they did that. I never wear any jewelry so they didn't bother me with that.

And then, they started killing, right there in front of us. There was a girl with a long mop of hair, standing with the rest of the women by the church. One of the paras came up to us and asked, "Is she Camacho's woman?" Camacho was a guerrilla commander. We knew the girl, but how would we know if she was his woman? So we said no. The man who was asking the questions went to talk to a group of paras and then they came back. One of them grabbed her long hair and wrapped it around his hand, like you wrap a towel, and they dragged her away. They took her to an orange tree away from the court and killed her. Afterwards, they came back to us and said, "See how she died? Those who don't speak the truth here, die." Later, when neighbors went to look at her body, they said that the paras had put a stick in her private parts.

My oldest daughter Amelia, who was twenty-three, was with me. One of the paras came up to us and asked her if she'd been the girlfriend of a guerrilla member. I said, "No, my daughters have never been the girlfriends of guerrillas." He said, "You old bitch, why do you talk so much?" And I said, "Because I answer for my daughters. Because I know they have never been girlfriends of guerrillas."

Then the paras came and pointed to my twelve-year-old daughter Katerine, and told me, "We need this girl to cook for us." I said, "I'll let her go, but only if I accompany her." One of the paras said, "No we don't want you, we want her." Then Katerine said, "Mom I'll go," because she saw that they were fighting with me every few minutes and she was afraid they'd do something to me. So she went. I saw the paras take her to a house nearby, and about ten minutes after they left, I followed. When I got to the house, I looked through a window and saw that they had stripped her naked. There were ten men surrounding her. Some paras standing outside pushed me away. I stayed crying on the curb for a while, but then they made me go back and stand in front of the church. I was mortified thinking about what they were doing to my daughter.

At about one in the afternoon the paras really started killing. All the men in the town who hadn't fled were sitting on the court. The paras had them count off from one to thirty. They said that whoever the number thirty landed on would be killed. I could see my son Carlos, and when I saw the paras start to count off, I thought, *Don't let thirty land on him.*

The first to be killed was a friend of Carlos, who was sitting next to him. The paras grabbed him and lopped off his ear, and then they put a black bag over his head and started stabbing him and asking questions. When he died, he fell into my son's lap.

And the paras went on killing and killing and killing.

One woman was tied up with a red rope around her neck. One of the paramilitaries would pull the rope and then pass it on to another, who'd pull it again and then pass it on to another. After they choked her, they shot her.

They celebrated each killing. They danced, they sang, they played the drums and the accordion. They turned on a stereo and danced on the court. Here in the village, many people liked to raise parrots and fine fighting cocks. The paras took the parrots and put them to fight the roosters. They killed donkeys too. They did all that in front of us.

It was cruel. From about ten that morning we'd been standing in front of this armed group, who went on killing and saying atrocious things. At about three in the afternoon, we began asking the paras if they planned to keep killing. They said, "You will not move from here until we give the order to go home. But before we leave here, we're going to empty this M60[10] on all of you. We don't want anyone to live."

Some time before six in the evening, Katerine came back to the church. She told me she had been raped. I hugged her, crying, and then she fainted. Some other paras caught her and put her in a house next to the church. I went with them. When she came to, I hugged her as she cried and I cried. She kept saying, "Mother, they're going to kill us." For a while, she kept saying that and passing out; she passed out four times, and the paras would splash cologne on her to get her to come to. Finally, she got up and we went back to the church. There, she sat on the curb, crying.

Then, at six, the paras said, "Okay, everyone go home, but leave the doors open. No one can leave town, because we're staying here." The dead were still lying there on the court.

I went with my daughters and my son to a house with cousins and neighbors; there were about thirty people there, men and women. There, I was reunited with my sister and Mayerli. The children asked me about their father and I wondered too what might have happened to him. We spent the whole night with the doors open, as the paras had told us to. We talked about what had happened, tried to account for other villagers and count the dead but we spoke quietly since the paras were passing

---

[10] The M60 is an American-made machine gun widely used by paramilitaries in Colombia.

by all the houses. The paramilitaries came by the houses and threw live chickens at us and said, "Here, eat this, it's yours." We asked ourselves, *What will become of us? Where will we go?* We knew we couldn't stay in the village. The paras told us that when we left town we shouldn't go to El Carmen, and that we should never come back here.

YOU'LL SAY YOU DON'T KNOW WHO DID THIS

The paras partied the next day, on the nineteenth; it was a binge. We saw them walking around with bottles of beer and rum in their hands. We stayed in the houses as the sun beat down.

At around three in the afternoon, some paras came by the house I was in and said, "We're going to go, and then government security forces are going to come here. They'll ask you about what happened here, and you'll say you don't know who did this." But the owner of the house we were in said, "Of course we know. What are the AUC armbands for, then? If they ask we will say it was the paramilitaries." We were surprised that they didn't do anything to him for saying that. But some of us who were at the house had been reading the Bible, Psalm 91, which talks about God's protection and so I think maybe that saved him.

The paramilitaries finally left at about five in the afternoon. Once they had all gone, we cried hard.

I went home with my children. We found my husband sitting in the house, crying. We hugged each other and he said, "Mi'ja,[11] I thought you'd all been killed," and I said, "I thought the same about you." He told me that when the paras had fired the first shots on the eighteenth, he and a cousin of mine had run out of town into the hills and had spent the whole massacre up there, hearing the shots.

---

[11] A contraction of "mi hija," (in English, "my daughter"), which is used affectionately for female friends and relatives.

The marines showed up at around six that night.[12] A lot of people here said that, among the marines who arrived, they recognized men who had participated in the massacre.[13] But they helped the families of the dead put the bodies on tables and carry them inside the church. Because the sun had been so strong that day, they were already decomposing. Some people decided to bury the bodies two and three to a grave in a small plot near the court. My husband helped bury the bodies, and he told me that when he lifted them, the skins slipped off in his hand.

That night, some neighbors found a cousin of mine, Alicia, in a house tied to a chair. She had been raped. The paras had made her eat barbs; her whole mouth was full of barbs and blood, and she was all scratched up.

That's also when I found out that another cousin of mine, Pablo, was killed on the eighteenth. His wife had escaped with their two children. She told me that when the paras were ordering everyone to go to the court, there was a knock on their door and it was a lone para who was making his way through the neighborhood. When the para opened the door, my cousin chopped off his arm and the para went off screaming. I remembered at one point on the soccer court I'd seen a para run by us with blood gushing out of the stub of his arm. My cousin's wife told me that another para came and opened fire at my cousin's house and Pablo was killed. But my cousin had got his man.

Many villagers left on the twentieth because they had relatives in other towns who'd sent in trucks for them. Others, like us, had to stay until we figured out a way to leave.

People from the Attorney General's office came on the twentieth and started taking stock of all the dead. They dug up the bodies for identifica-

---

[12] Marines arrived in response to reports about the paramilitary incursion in El Salado.

[13] Former paramilitary José Vicente Gamboa, alias Pantera, has testified that a group of twenty-five marines participated in the paramilitary operation that concluded in the El Salado massacre. According to the *New York Times*, "not only did the armed forces and the police not come to the aid of the villagers here, but the roadblock they set up prevented humanitarian aid from entering the village."

tion. We couldn't stand the stench. When they reburied them, many of the niches[14] in the cemetery weren't sealed well, and the dogs went in and ate the bodies. We could see the bones. Then it rained, and donkeys that had been killed swelled up, and the smell was awful.

LEAVING EVERYTHING BEHIND

My husband and I couldn't find a car to take us out of El Salado because we didn't have enough money to pay the fare, so we had to sit and wait. The village was a wreck, and many of the houses were shot up. The days that we stayed in El Salado, no one slept. My son Carlos was traumatized; he didn't eat or speak.

Luckily, I had a brother-in-law in Cartagena who brought in a Jeep on the twenty-third. We packed my family and what few things we could take into the Jeep. It was me, my husband, our five children and my brother-in-law, who was driving. We didn't all fit in the Jeep, so some of us were standing, and others were sitting on the front bumper. We left that day for El Carmen de Bolívar, the main town in our municipality. It took about two hours to travel the thirty-two kilometers. The road wasn't in such a bad state, but there was a long caravan of cars and mules taking people out.

Leaving was painful. My family and I were crying; we were leaving our village and we didn't know what torments lay ahead.

There were people at the entrance to El Carmen, just waiting for the displaced to arrive so they could buy things cheaply. As we rode into town, the people would yell out at us, "Are you selling?" They knew that, as displaced people, we needed cash. I had brought some of our chickens with me, and I ended up selling them for 200 pesos[15] each—I practically gave them away! But I had nowhere to put these animals.

---

[14] In much of Latin America the caskets of the dead are traditionally interred in niches built into concrete walls in cemeteries, rather than being buried in the ground.

[15] About 10 U.S. cents.

We moved in with a cousin of mine. About a month after we arrived, two displaced guys from El Salado were killed in El Carmen. Everyone got scared. We had escaped from the paramilitaries in El Salado, and now they were killing the displaced in El Carmen.

So my family went to my husband's hometown, Villanueva, Bolívar, which is about 140 kilometers north. What little we'd been able to take to El Carmen, we had to leave at my cousin's because we couldn't afford a truck to take all of it. We lasted six months in Villanueva. My husband didn't feel at home there, even though it's his hometown. So we decided to go back to El Carmen.

We rented a house for 70,000 pesos[16] a month, and there were months when we couldn't pay because we had no income. My husband couldn't manage to get work, so to pay the rent I had to sell the TV, I had to sell the iron. Sometimes I'd look into working as a cleaning lady in some family home, but they always said they needed a recommendation, which I didn't have.

While we were in El Carmen, my oldest daughter Amelia went off with a boy and ended up having twin girls with him. I had to take one of them in because they couldn't afford to take care of them both. We had to buy her milk on credit, and we'd get the bienestarina[17] free. Sometimes I had to feed that child with just milk and salt, because I didn't have enough for sugar.

When you're displaced, people look at you badly. People would scowl at us for being displaced, and for being from El Salado. Because it was a "red zone"[18]—that's what they called it—many people saw us as guerrilla collaborators. And when we went to collect relief kits from the Red Cross and the mayor's office, we heard people comment, "They're probably bad people."

---

[16] About U.S.$36 at the time.

[17] A powdered nutritional drink handed out by government agencies for poor children and pregnant women.

[18] "Red zone" is a term for an area with persistent guerrilla activity and intense conflict.

YOU COULD HEAR THE SOLITUDE

One day, in March 2001, my husband decided to go back to El Salado to see how it was. He went with my cousin Pedro. Pedro was on a donkey and Alberto went on foot; walking, the journey takes four hours. That was a day of torment for me, and I didn't sleep that night. But they came back the next morning at about eleven, and I was so happy, I said, "Thank you, God."

When other displaced people from El Salado heard that Alberto and Pedro had returned, they came to our house to ask about the village. Alberto and Pedro told them that El Salado was nearly buried under the weeds. It had been empty for a year. They couldn't see the houses, and the church wasn't visible under the bush.

Even though the village was a mess, our neighbors from El Salado started talking about returning. They'd say, "What are we doing here in El Carmen? We have no work; we have no way to pay the rent." So we decided to go back. It was our home, and there didn't seem to be any danger.

We applied for government assistance to organize our return to the village. Government officials called a meeting of the displaced from El Salado and it was decided that seventy men from the village would go there to clean it up. That was in November 2001. But once they got there, only thirty men had the courage to stay. The others came back to El Carmen when they saw the loneliness, the village overrun by weeds.

In February 2002, the men started to return to El Salado permanently. I first came back in March with my daughter Katerine, because I'd got word that Alberto had food poisoning. The day we arrived, I let out a scream. Chairs were scattered around the streets. The houses were destroyed. You could hear the solitude; the only sound was the birds singing.

Alberto had occupied a neighbor's house because the house he'd built had been washed away by a stream that had flooded. He told me that just a few days after the men had arrived to reclaim the village, the guerrillas came back again as if nothing had happened. The guerrillas invited the men to a meeting at six in the evening. Seven guerrillas came, including

Camacho, the commander. But people got pissed off. At the meeting, the villagers told the guerrillas that we didn't want them there. Alberto said the men told the guerrillas that what happened with the paramilitaries was because of them, and that if the guerrillas were going to continue bothering the people of El Salado, that they'd leave again. Camacho said that the guerrillas wouldn't be coming here, that they knew that the massacre was their fault because they had not faced up to the paramilitaries themselves.

During the three nights I stayed there with Alberto, we made a fire at the door for light, and to fight off the mosquitoes. I couldn't sleep. I heard things. I thought I heard gunshots.

MY MISSION WAS TO FIX UP THE VILLAGE

After three days I went back to El Carmen with my daughter. But by then I'd decided I would eventually return to the village for good, to try to recover it from the abandonment. I came back several months later with my daughters, but my son Carlos, who was eighteen by then, stayed in El Carmen. He was too afraid to come back.

The first months back were pure suffering, because we found nothing, nothing. We ate rice with oregano, because we had no salt. Eventually, my family got government assistance. We were given some groceries and tools to work the tobacco, and we also got help moving our things back. My mission when I returned to this town was to fix up the village. With another woman here, we went house to house on Fridays telling people, "Let's work two hours on Sunday cleaning the village." We'd make juice and cook sancocho for people who helped. For a month, that worked well. But then people started saying, "No, I've already cleaned." That happened because we didn't come together as a community. We shouldn't have to have some government agency or NGO come clean the village—we ourselves have to clean our town, especially the cemetery. The cemetery is an embarrassment.

WE COULDN'T SLEEP AT NIGHT

The house where my family lives today belongs to a woman who hasn't returned from the displacement. I talked to her and she gave me permission to live in it. But any day she can tell me to vacate, and we'll be out on the street. My family also has no land to cultivate tobacco; we work the tobacco on someone else's land.

After we returned we found a lot of minefields. People find them working in the fields. There is still some land that farmers don't dare go on because there are parts where people know the guerrillas used to be. Thank God there haven't been any land mine accidents.

For the first six months I didn't sleep at night, I was too on edge. I had panic attacks. I spent three months pressing towels to my ears at night to try to stop hearing what I thought were gunshots. I thought I was going crazy. My husband told me to leave; he said I was going to have problems here. My daughter Mayerli, the one who hid in the bathroom the day of the massacre, also couldn't sleep. She was nine years old. Whenever a helicopter passed over the village she'd say, "Mother, they're going to kill me, let's get under the bed."

My son Carlos came here about a year after I returned with my daughters. He started painting dragons on the walls of abandoned houses. One house near mine was covered in dragons inside and out. Everyone who saw it said it was evil because he was drawing death. One day he went out and came back with a piece of wood and carved it into the shape of a hand. He says it's the hand of the paramilitary who had his arm chopped off. He painted it blood red. The massacre traumatized him, and today he still sees psychologists. He now works in Cartagena, and he almost never comes back to El Salado. When he does, he gets discouraged and says, "Mom, our village is finished."

I CAN'T FORGET WHAT I WITNESSED

Although the guerrillas had promised not to bother El Salado again, they didn't stay away. In early August 2003, María Cabrera, the village nurse, set off for El Carmen. She stayed two days and headed back on August 7 in a car filled with passengers. The guerrillas stopped the car, pulled her out and killed her there on the road. After that, the guerrillas would pull people from their homes and kill them, accusing them of being collaborators of the paramilitaries or the government.

We thought we'd have to flee again—no one knew who'd be next. Then, on October 4, 2003, the government sent in the marines, and they've been here ever since. Most of the villagers don't want them here because they say the marines are to blame for the massacre. But I think, *That was in 2000, and the boys who are here now, this is the first time they've come here.* I even asked a corporal once, "How long have you been working for the government?" and he said, "Two years." Then he said, "You ask me that question because a lot of people say we were to blame for the massacre. When that happened I hadn't even dreamed of holding a gun."

I haven't heard of the paramilitaries still being around, but the guerrillas, well, in a small town people start to talk. People tell you that they saw two guerrillas in the bush, or in another part of the village. But I go into the fields with my husband and I haven't seen anything out there. It's quiet. I haven't been harassed or anything, and the marines are always out there patrolling.

I'm glad to be back, because I'm in my hometown. I get discouraged, though, because of the loneliness in this village, the sadness. There were seven thousand people here before the massacres, and today there are only three and a half thousand. I miss the people, the bustle. There are days I sit there at the door and look up the street and I don't see anyone, just solitude. But where else can I be if not here?

My hope is to keep going, fighting and keep things the way they are: quiet. And I hope that the government gives us what it owes us, because they have to give us something. Different government agencies call meetings all the time and they make promises about reparations and compensation. I don't go to meetings anymore, I'm tired of them. We returned 2002, and here we are in 2010, and what have we seen? Meetings and more meetings. The only thing they've come through on is security.

However, I say that no matter what we get, we still cannot recover what we lost. Life cannot be bought with money.

As much as I would like to, I can't forget what I witnessed. I don't like to walk by the soccer court; it makes me sad. And every February 18 it's like reliving the massacre. It starts on February 16. I feel that something changes in me; I lose my appetite, I can't sleep. And on the eighteenth, it's like seeing what I saw again. I cry all day. I say, "God give me the strength to overcome it with time."

Sometimes I dream that the paramilitaries have all the villagers together as a group. They shoot at us and we go running, or we kneel in supplication, pleading. I wake up crying from nightmares like that. When that happens, I get up and drink a glass of water and begin to pray to God.

JULIA TORRES

AGE: *42*
OCCUPATION: *Farmer, president of farm cooperative*
HOMETOWN: *Tolú, Sucre*
INTERVIEWED IN: *La Alemania Farm, San Onofre, Sucre*

Sucre province, on Colombia's northern coast, experienced a powerful, peasant-led land reform movement in the 1960s and 1970s. The movement made important gains in land redistribution until a violent backlash in the 1980s from landowners and ranchers. By the mid-1990s, paramilitarism began to take hold, and within a few short years completely permeated local politics, the economy, and the daily lives of residents. The Héroes de los Montes de María bloc, under the command of a man who went by the name Cadena, was one of the most ruthless and powerful of the county's right-wing militias. The group was responsible for scores of murders, massacres, and forced disappearances, as well as rape and torture. In Sucre province, they enjoyed the support of politicians, ranchers, and power brokers, and were the main force behind the illegal transfer of titles to approximately 37,000 hectares of land in the region.

Just as paramilitaries were securing their grasp on the region, Julia Torres and her husband Rogelio Martínez were among fifty-two families that used government subsidies to cooperatively purchase a vast farm known as La Alemania. For them it was a dream come true. But by 2001, the men under Cadena's command had installed themselves on the farm as a permanent, menacing presence.

Julia and Rogelio at first resisted fleeing with other members of the cooperative, but eventually escaped to the nearest city, where they struggled to make ends meet. Once the paramilitaries demobilized in 2005, Julia and Rogelio, along with other cooperative members, went back to La Alemania to try and recover what they'd lost, only to find the farm had been foreclosed. Rogelio led the cooperative's fight to hold onto the farm until members of a neo-paramilitary group called the Paisas gunned him down in 2010. Today, Julia continues fighting for the cooperative and demands justice for her husband's murder.

I SAW A MAN AND HE SAW ME

I was a mischievous, pampered tomboy when I was little, because I grew up with six brothers. I loved climbing trees and swimming in the stream that ran near our house. My family lived on a small farm, in a village in Sucre province. There, my father planted yucca, yams, corn, and rice, most of which was for our own consumption. I studied up to the fifth grade. I was eleven, and from then on I stayed at home to help my mom around the house.

One day, when I was fourteen, I went to see a baseball game in town with a friend. At the game, I saw a man, and he saw me. He was ten years older than me but he had this mischievous look in his eyes that I liked. My friend knew the man because she was dating a friend of his, so she introduced us: his name was Rogelio. He later told me that once he saw me, he told his friend that he was going to have me. A few days later, I was at my friend's house and Rogelio's friend came and gave me a letter from him. In the letter Rogelio said he loved me, that he wanted me to be his wife and the mother of his children. I answered it, and that's how things started.

My mom and dad eventually found out about my relationship with Rogelio. Since he was older than me they told me, "We won't permit you to go out in the street to talk to him. When you need to talk, tell him to come here to the house." He did, and from then on he began a great relationship with my dad.

When I was fifteen, I went to live with Rogelio and his parents on a little farm in the municipality of San Onofre. I had my first baby in 1986 soon after I turned sixteen. Rogelio was so happy to have a boy. We named him Luis, and three months later Rogelio and I got married. Three and a half years later I had another boy, who we named Álvaro. And two years later a girl came, Mabel. I said, *Okay, this is where I stop*, and I decided I was going to have my tubes tied. But the doctors didn't want to do it because at that time I was barely twenty years old. I had my last daughter, Kelly, in May 1992, and at twenty-two years old I finally decided to have a tubal ligation.

OUR OWN PIECE OF LAND

I spent my time caring for my children while Rogelio worked on the farm with his father. At the same time, Rogelio was working on acquiring a piece of land for us. It was what he'd always dreamed of. His dad was a member of the ANUC peasants' movement,[1] and when Rogelio was thirteen years old, he would go on land invasions[2] with him. That was in 1973, and back then they'd get a group of two or three hundred peasants together and squat on the land. They'd set up shacks and plant plantains and other crops. The IN-CORA[3] officials would come, and if the landholder had 2,000 hectares the

---

[1] ANUC stands for Asociación Nacional de Usuarios Campesinos (National Farm Workers Association), whose creation was encouraged by Liberal Party president Alberto Lleras in the 1960s to kickstart a land reform process.

[2] In the 1960s Colombia attempted to promote land reform, but by the end of the decade little had been achieved. In 1968, Liberal Party president Alberto Lleras signed a law that allowed for the expropriation of private lands worked by share croppers or tenant farmers. This prompted large groups of peasants to occupy fallow land on vast estates and work it until the government land reform agency would expropriate it and grant titles to the farmers. While it was applied nationwide, the peasant movement in the provinces of Sucre and Córdoba were the most active in land takeovers.

[3] Instituto Colombiano de Reforma Agraria (The Colombian Institute for Agrarian Reform). Now known as Incoder, it is the government institution in charge of agricultural policy and rural development.

INCORA would expropriate two hundred and give it to farmers. Sometimes the police came and arrested people, but the others would stay, and they managed to keep a lot of land that way. That's how my father-in-law got his land. So Rogelio was always interested in the land reform process, and as our family grew he was looking for ways to get his own land.

Around 1996, the owner of a farm called La Alemania decided to sell. The farm is about twenty minutes from the town center of San Onofre. I think the old man had a problem with the FARC guerillas because they asked him for money and he didn't want to pay.[4] He wanted to organize a group of peasants to go to the INCORA so the government would buy his land to then sell to the peasants.

He was selling 558 hectares with everything: five houses, the cars that were used to transport the milk, the corrals, and even the scales where the cattle were weighed. My parents told Rogelio about a new co-operative in their village that they and two of my brothers had joined to try and get the farm. Rogelio also joined, and in all there were fifty-two families who were members of the cooperative.

One day, in December 1997, Rogelio told me that he'd achieved what he'd always wanted: our own piece of land. The government paid 70 percent of the price for La Alemania and the cooperative had to pay the other 30 percent. We had three years to start paying, and in addition to that, the cooperative took out loans to buy the cattle that was already on the land. To celebrate, the families in the cooperative slaughtered and roasted two or three sheep, and people gave speeches. Everyone was so happy because we'd achieved our goal.

La Alemania has a beautiful landscape because it has different climates; due to the terrain, it has areas that are hot and areas that are cool.

---

[4] The Revolutionary Armed Forces of Colombia (FARC) and National Liberation Army (ELN) are Colombia's two main guerilla groups. Founded in the 1960s and claiming to represent the country's rural poor in the fight against Colombia's wealthy classes and U.S. imperialism, both groups commit widespread abuses against civilians, including killings, threats, and recruitment of child soldiers.

There are hills and pasturelands, and there are lakes, streams, and many trees. This farm is rich, because there are areas that are good for livestock and others that are good for planting. We can harvest everything here: plantain, yucca, corn, yam, rice, coconut, avocado, and guama.[5]

Rogelio and I arrived with the children, and we chose to live in one of the houses that were already on the farm. One of the cooperative members, Nilson Herrera, stayed at our house too. Our house had three rooms and an outside kitchen. There was an open-walled hut with a thatched roof, which is where we often sat. It was like our living room.

The farm was very organized. Each one of the families had their own plot to farm for food, but the rest was for the whole community. The milk was sold by the cooperative, and that money was used to maintain the farm. Every week, we all had to dedicate one or two days to keeping up the cooperative property, like clearing the brush for pasture. If for some reason you couldn't do the cooperative work, you could pay someone to do it for you.

I looked after the house and began to raise pigs and chickens. Rogelio would set out early to work in the fields, and I would make a breakfast of yucca, yam, cheese, suero,[6] eggs, coffee with milk, and fried fish, and take it to him in the fields.

A few months after we started living there, about six guerrillas arrived and there were five or six of us farmers sitting there under the hut next to my house. They came in green uniforms, like the police, and one of them said, "We're from the thirty-fifth front of the FARC. We have no problem with working farmers. But we don't like snitches."

They told Rogelio that they were hungry, and told him to sell them a chicken and some plantains. When one of them asked me for water, I was so scared that my legs froze and I couldn't stand up. One of the cooperative members saw that I couldn't stand, so he went and gave the guerrillas

---

[5] Guama, or ice cream bean, is a legume that looks like a large green bean. The beans themselves are inedible but the pulp surrounding them in the pod tastes sweet.

[6] A Colombian style of sour cream that people from the Caribbean coast use on their food.

some water. Rogelio cut a bunch of plantains and gave them a chicken. He said, "I'll give this to you but go somewhere else to eat it, not here in my house." They said, "Sure, no problem, relax." Several times after that, two or three guerrillas came by. On those occasions, I didn't panic like I did the first time.

I'M NOT GOING TILL ROGELIO GETS BACK

One day in late September 1998, I saw that Rogelio was sad. I kept asking him what was wrong until he finally told me that Nilson Herrera had been killed. Nilson and his brother had been drinking, and were on their way by mule to San Onofre when a pickup nearly sideswiped them on the road. Nilson apparently cursed at the pickup, the truck stopped, and paramilitaries pulled Nilson and his brother in.[7] The brother escaped but Nilson was murdered that night.

That was the arrival of the paramilitaries. The commander was supposedly a man who went by the name Cadena.[8]

We had the first paramilitary incursion onto the farm on March 30, 2000. That morning I made breakfast, and for some reason, instead of going out really early to the fields like they usually did, Rogelio, my brothers and the other men sat around the hut chatting. Then, at about seven, we heard a few shots near the house. They seemed to come from our neighbor Ismael's house.

Then we saw a group of twenty-five or thirty men about fifty meters away. A few were in uniform and others were in plain clothes. One of my brothers said, "Those are neither guerrillas nor the army. Those are the

---

[7] Right-wing paramilitary groups began to form in Colombia in the early 1980s with the purported aim of fighting left-wing guerrillas, and spread throughout various regions of the country. Backed by the military, landowners, drug traffickers, and political and economic elites, they murdered tens of thousands of civilians.

[8] Rodrigo Mercado Peluffo, who went under the nom de guerre Cadena, which means chain, was the top-level commander of the Héroes de los Montes de María bloc and led the massacres of peasants in El Salado, Chengue, Macayepo, and Mampuján.

paramilitaries." I think he had already seen them in other parts of the region. When he said that, I was overcome with an immense fear because of what we'd heard about these people—that they committed murders and massacres. I said to everyone, "Let's run, let's not stay here." No one got up. I prayed, *Oh dear God don't let those people come to my house.* And they didn't; they walked right by.

A boy came running down from the hills above my house and told one of our neighbors at our hut that his brother had been killed. The boy said, "Those guys said they were from the paramilitaries, and that when they return they won't leave anyone standing." It was then that Rogelio decided to go and see what had happened to our neighbor Ismael.

Then we started seeing other farmers coming down from the hills. I thought, *Oh, my daughters!* My two little girls were in school in a nearby village, and I asked my brother to pick them up and take them to my mom's. So he left with some of the others and I stayed with Rogelio's nephew and a niece. But at one point I went into the kitchen, and when I came out no one was there. Everyone had gone and had left me alone. Despite the fear, I found strength and told myself, *I'm not going until Rogelio comes back.*

THE DOG'S TONGUE DRAGGED IN THE SAND

Rogelio appeared two hours later. I was shaking and alone in the doorway of the house. He told me he had run into Ismael on the path, and that the paramilitaries had killed some other guy, a day laborer who they'd apparently grabbed on the road and killed in front of Ismael's house. They killed the day laborer's brother too.

Rogelio said, "I don't want to leave, because if they had come to kill me, they would have killed me. But I see you're shaken up. Let's go."

Rogelio had a turkey that he was very fond of, and that was all we took: the turkey and a radio that I had. Rogelio got on a donkey and I got on a bicycle. We had a tiny puppy, and he followed behind us. He was panting, trying to keep up so much that his little tongue dragged in the sand. We ran into some other people who were leaving and they were with a blind man, so Rogelio put him on the donkey. I gave Rogelio the bike and I walked, carrying the dog. We were nervous and worried that we'd run into the paras.[9] It took us two hours to reach the main road. As we were walking on the main road we had a scare. A car passed and suddenly stopped. I thought, *We're dead.* But it was a friend of Rogelio's, and he took us to Rogelio's mom's house about twenty minutes away. Later that night we got to my mom's place and reunited with my children.

That day the paramilitaries killed three people.[10] No one from La Alemania, but people from neighboring farms. There was the day laborer and his brother who they killed in front of Ismael's house. Rogelio and I learned about the third as we headed out to the main road with other people who were fleeing. That day, there was a massive displacement of the whole community, not just of La Alemania but of the surrounding villages of Las Pavas, Las Lomas, Las Luchas, and Rollo Arena.

The next day Rogelio went back to the farm to see what was going on. He'd told me, "If I see that things are complicated there, I'll come back here. If I don't come back, it's because everything is normal there." I was so anxious. Back then there were no cell phones, unlike now when everyone has one. I thought, *What if the paramilitaries catch him and kill him?* The day after Rogelio went back to the farm, one of my brothers also went there with one of Rogelio's brothers. The three of them were there alone for about a month. At the end of April, I also went back to La Alemania, but left the children at my mom's. I'd see them on the weekends, and during school vacations they'd come to the farm. In all, only seven members of the cooperative went back to La Alemania. The others came to work on the farm during the day from San Onofre and other nearby towns.

---

[9] "Para" is conversational shorthand for paramilitary.

[10] That day paramilitaries led by Uber Martínez, alias Juancho Dique, Cadena's lieutenant, killed Vidal Martínez, Oscar Martínez, and Orlando Fernández, according to press and NGO accounts.

THEY WERE OWNERS OF THE WORLD

A couple of months later, the paramilitaries returned to the farm. But they came and went; they just passed through. Then, on August 8, paramilitaries stopped Prisciliano Herrera, one of the cooperative members, at the entrance to La Alemania. Prisciliano was coming from the main town of San Onofre to pick up some milk. Other farmers said that they saw the paramilitaries stop him and accuse him of being a guerrilla informer, and then they took him away. The next day, Prisciliano's body was found on the road to Tolú.

After that we didn't see the paramilitaries again for about five months, when they came back to the farm and became masters of it. There were about fifty of them, all in uniform, and they took over our house. I think they chose my house because it's at the top of a hill, so you can see all around. They took over the kitchen and the hut right next to my house, so that we couldn't sit there anymore.

I think they arrived around the time of the Chengue massacre[11] because I remember hearing them talking about it. The paramilitaries called one of their members "Mataviejos" because he'd cut off the heads of some old people.[12]

They forbade us and the other families in the area from buying large amounts of supplies in town. We were only allowed to buy what we needed for three days, because if we bought more, the paras thought we were bringing it to the guerrillas that were still around. So we had to go into town constantly. The paras once brought in a truckload of food, but it was just for themselves.

One day they wanted to eat chicken and they told me to sell one of mine to them. I told them my hens weren't for sale, and one of them said, "If you sell it to me, I'll eat it. And if you don't, I'll eat it anyway."

---

[11] On January 17, 2001, approximately eighty members of the Héroes de los Montes de María bloc of the paramilitaries stormed the village of Chengue, killed at least twenty-seven men with sledge hammers, and then cut off some of their victims' heads.

[12] Mataviejos roughly translates to "old people killer."

Another time one of them told me, "You have to cook for me because I'm not eating food made by a man if there's a woman around to cook." They were the owners of the world at the time.

Eventually I told Rogelio, "We can't stay here any longer. We have to go." By that time, three of the seven cooperative members had already left. But Rogelio said, "I'm not going. They're the ones who have to leave. This is my house, it's not theirs."

My mother was very nervous about us being there, and she didn't understand why we stayed. My mom even asked me once if I was also a paramilitary. She actually said that to me.

Rogelio and I stayed on the farm, but it wasn't because we wanted to live with the paramilitaries. We, as the owners, were humiliated by them; the situation was really screwed up. We didn't even sleep in our bed. Instead, we threw the mattress under the bed and slept there, because I thought that if there were a sudden gun fight with the guerrillas, that would be our salvation. The paramilitaries didn't allow us to light a lamp at night, so from six in the evening we locked ourselves inside. But even inside we didn't have any privacy because the house was surrounded. So it was hard for us to even talk about what was going on. We had no moments of intimacy.

Once, when my son Luis was visiting, one of the paramilitaries ordered him to run an errand. Luis, who was about fifteen years old at the time, refused to do it, and the para was going to hit him. I got really angry and I said, "You have no right to hit him! He's my son and I don't hit him." And the para said, "That boy is spoiled. He's very rude." I said, "What right do you have sending him on errands? You're neither his father nor his mother. And you can't hit him either. If you do I'll tell your boss." His boss was Cadena. It was impossible living with those people, hearing them brag about the terrible things they did. I'd hear things like, "That woman was on her knees, begging us not to kill her son, and we killed him there in front of her." "We cut one of their heads off and used it as a soccer ball." "We took out his heart and it was still pumping." It's traumatic to hear all that. It's a sheer miracle that I haven't gone crazy from it.

TODAY IS THE DAY WE LEAVE

Once, one of the paramilitaries told Rogelio, "You can't leave because you already know too much about us." But there was another one who said, "What are you still doing here? Get out of here, don't be an ass. Don't you see that everyone has a gun? And what do you have? Nothing. If the guerrillas ever come back you're the one who'll have to pay."

It became unbearable living with those people, so Rogelio finally agreed to leave. I started taking our things over to my mom's when I visited the children. I'd take the pots filled with food and then just leave them there, and when I took my laundry over there, I'd leave some clothes behind. I even managed to take the beds. We also sold off some of the chickens, the turkeys, and the pigs.

On August 5, 2001, a truck came to pick up the paramilitaries. I heard them say that they were headed to the south of Bolívar province to clash with the guerrillas. After they'd left that time, I said to Rogelio, "Today is the day we leave here."

EVERYONE SWALLOWED
THEIR BITTER PILL ALONE

I left La Alemania and went to stay with my mother. Rogelio left the same day, but he went to the city of Sincelejo, about eighty kilometers from La Alemania. He had family there, and he went there so that he could find us a place to live. I joined him after a few days, and when the children finished school that year, we took them all from my mother's to Sincelejo.

We lived in a neighborhood where Rogelio's brother and cousin lived. There were a lot of displaced people there. It's very near the center of Sincelejo but it has no paved roads, has no legal electricity, no gas. And that's where we went to live, in a small rundown shack of wood planks and zinc. We didn't say anything about what we'd seen or heard or what had happened. At that time no one talked about anything. Everyone swallowed their bitter pill alone.

Because here in Sucre everyone was a paramilitary: the governor, the mayors, the police, the marines, the senators. It was like that everywhere, but here it was especially putrid.[13] The paramilitaries in Sucre had a lot of support from the people. Anyone who didn't agree with them had to leave, and if they didn't leave they were killed.

When we fled the farm, Rogelio had left a rice crop in the ground. He left our neighbor Ismael in charge of harvesting it. Ismael picked the crop and took it to my mom's, so rice was something that we didn't have to buy in Sincelejo. And I would take the two-hour trip from Sincelejo to my parents' farm and bring back yucca, plantains, milk, and eggs for the children.

Rogelio bought an old motorcycle with the money we had made from selling the livestock, and went to work as a motorcycle taxi driver. I would work cleaning other people's houses when I could, not all the time. Rogelio didn't like me to work and leave the girls alone in the house, because there were a lot of drugs in that neighborhood.

In September 2001, a month after we arrived in Sincelejo, I registered my family with the government agency Social Action, and they gave me a certificate that said we were displaced. Social Action coordinates humanitarian aid to the displaced but I wasn't born to ask for hand-outs, to go begging for things, or to have people pity me. That's something that's very hard for me. It's not my style.

That month, the president of the cooperative came to Sincelejo to get the deeds to the property in La Alemania. We handed them over but didn't know what it was for. Some time later, the cooperative president told Rogelio that some lawyers from Barranquilla needed them because Cadena was going to buy our debt and keep the farm. The cooperative president had allied with the paras. He asked Rogelio what he thought about it, and Rogelio said, "As long as I don't end up with debts, they can do what they

---

[13] Sucre department was at the heart of the "parapolitics" scandal in which more than 120 members of Congress came under investigation for ties to paramilitaries, with approximately forty convicted as of September 2011. In 2009, the governor of Sucre province from 2001 to 2003, Salvador Avana, was sentenced to 40 years in prison for his role in the murder of a local mayor who was assassinated by paramilitaries.

want." He knew he couldn't say anything else or he'd be killed. It hurt him to know we could lose the farm, but he felt it was futile to try to fight it.

I don't think the kids understood much of what was happening at the time. But I remember one day, my youngest daughter Kelly, who was nine years old, sat on her father's lap and asked him to make a house out of iron, all closed up so that bullets couldn't come in and kill us. Rogelio told her it was impossible.

Around March 2002, two of the paramilitaries who'd been at La Alemania showed up at our house. I don't know who told them we were there. They asked me for Rogelio but I said he was out. After Rogelio arrived a few hours later, they came back and told us that everything was fine, but that we had to stay quiet. They said, "You have to be as silent as a tomb." Rogelio told them that it was fine, that we weren't going to say anything about them. I think they had no reason to kill us because we didn't pose a threat to them. Still, I was very scared.

WE STARTED OVER AGAIN

In 2003, paramilitaries all over the country started demobilizing.[14] At first, the paramilitary commander Cadena didn't demobilize, but then he went to Ralito, in Córdoba province, and in 2005 we heard on the news that he'd been killed or disappeared. His body was never found. On the one hand I felt relief, but on the other hand, I thought if he were alive he could reveal a lot of information about politicians and leaders in the region who had collaborated with them.

In January 2006, the paramilitaries were all supposedly demobilized. By that time, I was sick of living in Sincelejo, and Rogelio was killing himself to make enough money. Although I worked sometimes and my mom would send us things from my parents' farm, the kids were in

---

[14] In a deal struck with the government of Álvaro Uribe, paramilitary militias began gradually demobilizing by blocs between 2003 and 2006. The mid-level and top commanders were confined to an estate in Córdoba province known as Ralito.

school, and we had to buy uniforms, books, and food. In the city, everything is about money.

I got the idea to go back to the farm, so one day I went back there with a friend. Rogelio didn't know I was going. I didn't find anything we'd left behind: the crops, the corrals, plantations of coconut trees, the cattle. They were all gone. We went to my house and it was a mess. It was overgrown with weeds. There were blood stains on the floor of the hut and the garage. It looked like the paras had tried to scrub them out with dust or ashes. The fields looked terrible. We went back to Sincelejo the same day but then returned to the farm a few days later. Afterwards, I told Rogelio about it.

He went back to La Alemania with me and we began to clean up our old house. We started by sweeping and washing things down with soap and bleach. We'd come for a few hours and then go back to Sincelejo. We agreed that we wouldn't come back permanently until it was all clean. We were going back and forth until one day, after washing the floors again, we spent the night. On February 16, 2006, in sowing season, we came back for good. We started over again. We started to plant corn, rice, yucca, yams, and plantain. Five other families from the cooperative came back at the same time.

ROGELIO LOST HIS FEAR

Trouble began at the start of 2007, when Rogelio started to speak out and file complaints about how the paramilitaries had stolen the cooperative's cattle. By then he was the president of the cooperative. I didn't like that he was doing that; our idea had been to keep quiet. But he said he couldn't any more.

On April 11, 2007, Garibaldi Berrío Acosta, one of the cooperative members, was found murdered two hours from the farm. The day before, he'd been forcibly removed from his home. Later that year we learned that La Alemania was going to be auctioned off. The court was already setting a date for the auction. Supposedly we had been notified through ads in the newspapers but we peasants aren't used to looking at the papers every day.

The authorities said that the former president of the cooperative had been notified, but since he'd joined the paramilitaries, he obviously didn't inform the other members. And that's when Rogelio's struggle really started.

It was Cadena who had requested the foreclosure back in September 2001, a month after most of us had left. The farm had been foreclosed on, before the cooperative had even missed a payment. The cooperative had made two payments on the loan for the cattle before we were displaced in 2001. After that, there was no way to make the payments. Also, we'd been given three years before we had to start making the payments on the farm, but we hadn't even been on the farm for three years. Cadena must have seen that he was never going to get fifty-two families to sign over the deeds to him, so he wanted to buy off our debt. But he could never formalize it because the authorities started going after the paramilitaries and things got complicated for them. In 2007 the Banco Agrario sold the debt to a private collection agency called CISA, which then sold it to another one called Covinoc.[15]

Rogelio filed a tutela, which is a writ for the protection of constitutional rights.[16] The court ruled against us. He appealed and lost again. The court said that because the cooperative members as a group weren't registered as displaced persons,[17] and because we hadn't made the loan payments to the Banco Agrario,[18] we were liable for the debts. The debt is something like 1.6 billion pesos.[19]

Rogelio lost his fear. He kept trying to stop the auction of the farm, filing legal papers. After staying quiet for so long he said, "There's no one

---

[15] Covinoc, a Colombian debt collection company, has been identified in several press reports as having placed pressure on indebted displaced peasants to sell off their land in the Montes de María region.

[16] A tutela is is a widely used legal tool allowing citizens to file for judicial injunction against public authorities and private parties who they claim have violated their constitutional rights.

[17] Under Colombian law, displaced persons can register their lost land in order to block it from being sold.

[18] A government-owned rural development bank.

[19] About U.S.$842,000.

who can shut me up now." He spoke to the press, both the local papers and the national ones. And then the threats started. Everyone, including our children, tried to convince him to not say anything, but it was no use. He'd just say, "If they kill me, they kill me, but I am not leaving here again and I will not stay quiet."

In 2008 Rogelio joined a group called the Movement of Victims of State Crimes, Movice,[20] because they offered support for the process he was leading.

On December 24, 2008, he got his first death threat. A demobilized paramilitary threatened him directly. Rogelio knew him—his alias had been El Garrapata[21]—because he was one of the paras who had been on the farm. El Garrapata told Rogelio that the paramilitaries in the area had demobilized, but that they were still working. The guy told Rogelio that he'd been sent to kill him by former paramilitary commanders who were now in jail. He told Rogelio that he wouldn't kill him because he knew that he was a good man. But he told him to be careful because the Águilas Negras was a large organization and that if *he* didn't kill him, someone else might.[22]

Rogelio got scared and filed a criminal complaint. Then others from the Águilas Negras started calling him and telling him to shut up, that they were going to kill him. One time they called and said that they were following his steps, that they were at his heels.

They told him that he shouldn't try to be a hero because "heroes end up dead." He took the threats seriously. Every time he got a threat he told me about it and then he reported it to the police. I told him he should

---

[20] Movice supports victims of state security forces and paramilitaries.

[21] Garrapata translates to English as "tick," the blood-sucking insect.

[22] Neo-paramilitary groups such as the Águilas Negras, Urabeños and Paisas are armed groups that emerged in 2006 in the wake of the demobilization process of the AUC national paramilitary coalition. Led largely by former paramilitaries and often employing the same criminal, political, and economic networks as their predecessors, neo-paramilitary groups have a powerful presence in many regions throughout the country.

leave, that if he didn't want to leave the land unoccupied, the kids and I would stay. He didn't want to hear it. He said, "If they kill me, stay here. This is yours. You have no reason to leave here."

We continued to work the farm and Rogelio kept fighting to keep it and getting more involved in the victims' movement. The threats kept coming and I was worried for him. I worried that he might be killed.

I FEEL SOMETHING IN MY HEART

In March 2010, the Constitutional Court finally ruled that the community of La Alemania cooperative members had to be recognized as displaced, and they stopped the foreclosure process. But the threats continued. Because of the threats, the marines were supposed to patrol the farm, but the truth is they came very rarely because the roads are so bad here.

On the afternoon of May 18, 2010, I was at a well, bathing with my daughter Mabel. We heard a sharp noise. Mabel said, "Hey Mom, what was that?" I told her it was probably nothing, that it was probably someone chopping down a tree. She said, "No, I feel something here in my heart." I said, "Let's finish bathing and go back to the house." But it wasn't a tree, it was gunshots.

One of our neighbors called me while we were still at the well. He said, "Ms. Julia, Rogelio has just been killed. The motorcycle taxi driver who was driving him just came to my house and told me." Rogelio had gone to the town of San Onofre that day and was on his way home. The taxi driver got on the phone and told me that the killers had been waiting for Rogelio on the road. They'd pulled him off the motorbike and shot him three times in the head.

Rogelio's death was so hard on our family. I haven't been able to accept it yet. On the eighteenth of every month I still get depressed, I miss him so much. My oldest son, Luis, still cries over his father. He's grown up now but no matter how old you are, you miss your father. My granddaughter Sofía wasn't born yet when Rogelio died but when she sees a photo of him she says, "Papá."

I didn't leave the farm when they killed Rogelio, though people from the government's human rights office told me I should. I don't think I'll ever leave, even though we don't know what his killers have in mind for the rest of us. There were supposedly six or seven men who were involved in Rogelio's murder. One of them was captured a couple of months after the murder. In September 2011 I went to Bogotá to testify in court against the man. He had demobilized as a paramilitary and then was a member of the Paisas.[23] A few months later the authorities released him because the judge said there wasn't enough evidence to hold him.

That same month, the Constitutional Court ruled on our case and the foreclosure order was lifted. It's been our only victory in the cooperative. We still have the problem of paying the debt.

When Rogelio took the job as president of the cooperative, I didn't like the idea because I knew that it carried risks. But today I am the new president, since March 2011. I am doing it out of the love I had for Rogelio and the love that he had for La Alemania. I don't care about the risk. I'm doing it for him so that his dream is accomplished: to see La Alemania free of debt and so that people can say, "La Alemania is ours." That's what Rogelio would have wanted.

In March 2012, a Bogotá appeals-court judge convicted Mario de Ávila Díaz, the same man who had been released in 2011, of Rogelio's murder, and ordered his arrest.

---

[23] One of the neo-paramilitary groups that sprung up after the demobilization of the paramilitaries.

SERGIO DÍAZ

AGE: *21*
OCCUPATION: *High school student*
HOMETOWN: *El Jobo, Bolívar*
INTERVIEWED IN: *Bogotá*

From the time he was a small child, Sergio Díaz dreamed of playing soccer professionally. But his dream ended at the age of thirteen, when he stepped on a land mine and lost his left leg. The Colombian government has reported 9,755 civilian and military land mine victims between 1990 and March 2012. Most mines— often homemade contraptions made of plastic syringes and beer bottles—are planted by leftist rebels to block the advance of government troops, but more than one third of all mine victims, like Sergio, are civilians. We met Sergio at a rehabilitation center in Bogotá, where he was waiting for a new prosthesis.

Names in this narrative have been changed at the request of the narrator.

WHEN I HEARD THE FIRST BOMB

When I was little, what I loved most was to play soccer. I was good. I was on the school team, and every afternoon after school I'd kick a ball around with my two little brothers. My dad promised me that he'd support me in becoming a professional player, or if not a player, at least a coach. That was my goal.

I first realized that there was conflict in Colombia when I was eight years old. It was 1999, and my family and I were at the farm where my dad worked, near El Jobo, in Bolívar province. At about one in the afternoon we heard an explosion in the surrounding hills, and then immediately after, we heard shots being fired, bombs going off, and then a plane came and opened fire. I was excited when I heard the first bomb, when the combat started. I don't know why—maybe it was because I liked action movies. But then the combat went on and on, and I realized that it was serious. I got so scared that my face changed from this color to that, and I was given sugar water to drink to calm me down.

At first my dad told us all to gather in the living room. Then he decided it was too dangerous there, so he took us to hide under a concrete ledge at the back of the house. He wanted to get our minds off what was going on, so he tried to distract us by telling us jokes, and stories about his childhood.

Things calmed down about three hours later, and my dad took us back to the house but told us not to speak loudly or run around. Then, at about eight in the evening, a group of guerrillas came to the property.[1] That made me more nervous. I recognized them as guerrillas because they had a yellow flag on their armbands. They said that they'd clashed with the marines and that there hadn't been any casualties among the guerrillas. They told us we had no reason to worry because nothing had happened, and then they went on their way.

The next morning, the marines came to the property. They crossed the farm on the same trail that the guerrillas had used, but they didn't stop. We didn't have any serious problems with the marines because by then a light rain had fallen that had erased any trace of the guerrillas' footsteps. If the marines had known that the guerrillas had come by, my

---

[1] The Revolutionary Armed Forces of Colombia (FARC) and National Liberation Army (ELN) are Colombia's two main guerilla groups. Founded in the 1960s and claiming to represent the country's rural poor in the fight against Colombia's wealthy classes and U.S. imperialism, both groups commit widespread abuses against civilians, including killings, threats, and recruitment of child soldiers.

dad would've been mistreated. At that time, the marines said that all farmers acted as front men for the guerrillas, that the peasants snitched to the guerrillas when the troops went by.

Generally, the marines always treated my dad like a guerrilla. When they passed through the farm, they'd cut the barbed wire and my dad's cattle would wander onto other properties. He had to stop doing whatever he was doing to go and fix the fences again. One time, in September 2003, he asked the marine commander not to damage the wire fence there, and to make a single gate where the troops could cross. So the commander called him a guerrilla, and said that all farmers in that region were guerrillas. My dad just stood back and didn't answer him. Whenever they called him aside I would try to sneak up and listen to how they treated him badly just for living in the countryside, just for being a peasant.

My dad always told me and my two younger brothers, "If one day you catch the fever of going off with an illegal group or serving in the military, keep me as a father in your heart, but do not visit me." He'd tell us, "I don't want to have a child in any group, anywhere. Neither to one side nor to the other."

Every time my dad left the farm, I'd get scared. I was afraid he'd get caught out there and get mistreated, or that he could be hurt or killed. I'd stand at the gate and look constantly to see if he was coming. When I'd see him coming, I'd get so happy that I'd run up and hug him. He would hug me back and tell me, "You're a fool. Nothing's going to happen to me." I would say, "No, it's not that I'm worried, I was just watching." But he knew.

I GOT AN IDEA THAT I SHOULD GO BACK

In January 2004, I was thirteen years old. I was on school vacation, so I was helping my dad on the farm. Early on January 9, my dad sent me to get some mules from the pasture to carry milk into town. I went with my two younger brothers. We had to walk one kilometer up a hill to the pasture where the mules were. While we were walking, I had a premonition. I got an idea in my head that I should go back, that I needed to go back. I was going to turn around but it was my duty to go to the pasture, so I didn't. I kept going, and chatted with my brothers to keep my mind off that feeling.

We arrived at the pasture where the mules were grazing. My youngest brother Michael, who was ten years old, grabbed the first mule. My other brother Tito, who was twelve, went after another mule, and I went for the other. When I went up behind the mule to grab it, he ran off to the right. I tried to cut him off and I stepped on his rope. Suddenly, I heard an explosion on the ground. I'd fallen to the ground, my ears were ringing, and I felt this heat wash over me. I didn't feel pain, really. I was so disoriented that I wasn't sure whether it was a dream or reality. I even managed to stand up but I fell down again. I tried again and fell. I didn't understand why I kept falling. That's when I looked down and realized I'd lost my left leg. It was destroyed.

My brothers had jumped up on a big rock and were crying. It was very hard for me when I saw my leg, but I told them calmly to come get me and take me home. They were afraid to come close. They yelled for my dad, and in a matter of minutes he came running with a cousin of mine. I remember seeing him coming and that's when I started crying. But I was relieved to see him. He picked me up, and then I passed out. He says that when I was in his arms, I said, "Don't let me die." I don't remember that.

MY LEG TOOK WITH IT ALL THE HAPPINESS

I woke up two weeks later in a hospital in the city of Cartagena, about two and a half hours away. I couldn't move anything in my body. My head was bandaged, my hands were bandaged, the leg that was still half good was bandaged. I had shrapnel in my head. My dad told me that when he found me, he'd taken me to the village, and from there I was taken to the municipal hospital in El Carmen de Bolívar. There, they amputated my leg. I was in a coma at the time, and since there was no improvement they took me to Cartagena.

While I was in a coma the nurses had tied me up. It was the hospital director's idea. I didn't understand why I was tied up, since I couldn't move anyway. She told me that it was in case I got overwhelmed by what had happened when I woke up. But I knew I'd lost my left leg. I told her, "No, untie me. What has already happened has happened."

When I woke up I actually felt my two legs; I could wiggle my toes and everything. But I looked down and saw the space where my leg should have been. My mom cried when I did that, but I didn't cry.

I felt that my leg had taken with it all the happiness that I'd had. I spent forty-five days at the hospital, and during that time they made me see psychologists. But they said the same stupid things all psychologists say. The best psychologist I had was my dad. He's my role model, and he knows how to cheer me up. He would make me laugh and try to get me out of my depression.

IN THE BLINK OF AN EYE

My father left the farm, afraid that there were other mines on the property. I was the first mine victim in that region, but two days after my accident a man also stepped on a mine nearby. I think it was the guerrillas who'd laid the mines, because even though the military commit the worst abuses, they don't lay mines.[2] My family moved to the main town of El Carmen de Bolívar, and my dad sent a nephew to the farm to collect what he had there—all the chickens and cows. He went back himself once, to hand over the land to the owner. After that, he worked on other farms, but he never recovered the prosperity he once had. It was all so hard for him. He couldn't get over my accident, and that everything he'd achieved over so many years of hard work was gone in the blink of an eye.

---

[2] The FARC utilizes land mines more than any other armed group in Colombia, according to the Colombian Campaign Against Land Mines, the preeminent NGO monitoring the issue. In 1997, the Colombian government signed the Mine Ban Treaty, which imposes an absolute ban on antipersonnel land mines, and by 2004 the military had completed the destruction of its arsenal of more than 18,000 mines. Although there have been reports of land mines laid by the military since, these reports are scarce, and have been refuted by the government.

My dad once said, with all the pain in his soul, that it was best that it had been me who stepped on the mine. I asked him, "Why do you hate me so much?" And he said, "Had it been a member of the marines that stepped on it, maybe I wouldn't be alive—maybe none of us would be alive." The truth is that there would have been so much anger that the marines would have taken it out on him. They would have immediately said that he knew the mine was there and hadn't warned them. So it was better, then, that it wasn't a member of the marines who'd stepped on the mine, because then they would have finished off every last one of us.

While I was recovering in El Carmen, my little brothers would play soccer, and when they saw I was watching, they would change games and do other things, so they wouldn't see me sad. Sometimes they played soccer far from where I was so I couldn't see them.

In July 2004, I went to a Red Cross rehabilitation center in Bogotá, where I got my first prosthesis. I'd promised my mom that the next time she saw me I would be walking. I learned to use the prosthesis very quickly—I'm very agile with it—and when I went back to El Carmen in December, I was walking.

Soccer is what I miss the most. I've tried to play soccer with the prosthesis, but it's too hard to move my body the way I need to. It's really heavy, and my back hurts. I did work as assistant coach for a neighborhood team though, and in 2009 we were the league champions. Then I said I didn't want to be assistant anymore, that I wanted my own team. The coach who I was working with said, "Let's change roles. You'll be the coach and I'm the assistant." And we were champions again! That motivated me.

I really enjoyed it until I had a problem with one of the players. He yelled at me a lot, because I'd tell him how to play. He said things like, "You don't even play soccer, and now you come and teach *me* how to play." So I decided not to continue with the neighborhood league. I heard my team was champion again, twice.

I'm finishing high school now. I'd stopped studying because of the rehabilitation, but I'm now in eleventh grade.[3] I've thought of maybe studying medicine but chemistry is my worst subject, and chemistry is important for medicine, I think. So I don't know. I don't know what comes next.

---

[3] The Colombian high school system goes up to the eleventh grade.

AMADO VILLAFAÑA

AGE: 56

OCCUPATION: *Director of indigenous media group*

HOMETOWN: *Guatapurí basin, Sierra Nevada de Santa Marta*

INTERVIEWED IN: *Santa Marta, Magdalena*

Colombia is home to at least eighty-seven indigenous groups that speak sixty-four different languages. The 1991 Colombian Constitution recognized special territorial, political, and social rights for the indigenous peoples, but these groups have nevertheless been vulnerable to the violation of such rights and the violence of Colombia's conflict. According to the National Indigenous Organization of Colombia (ONIC), more than 1,500 indigenous people were murdered between 2002 and 2010. In 2011 alone, 111 murders were reported. A 2009 Constitutional Court ruling stated that at least thirty indigenous groups in Colombia are in danger of "cultural or physical extermination" due to armed conflict and displacement.

The Sierra Nevada de Santa Marta is the world's highest coastal mountain range, soaring from sea level to an altitude of 5,700 meters, just forty-two kilometers from the Caribbean Sea. The Sierra Nevada is home to four indigenous groups that all descend from the Tairona people. They consider the Sierra Nevada the "heart of the world," and that their mission is to protect it. Over the years, they have had to deal with the presence of evangelizing Capuchin priests, white colonists, drug traffickers, leftist guerrillas, right-wing paramilitaries, and the army. Amado Villafaña is a member of the Arhuaco people, one of the main indigenous

groups in the Sierra Nevada. In his narrative, he recalls how his people got caught
in the crossfire between paramilitaries, guerrillas, and the army.

WE CAN'T SAY THERE WAS A TIME OF PEACE

In the Sierra Nevada de Santa Marta there are the Kogi, the Wiwa, the Kankuamo, and the Arhuacos. I belong to the Arhuaco people. The traditional Arhuaco territory extends from the city of Valledupar in Cesar province to Mamatoco, just outside of the city of Santa Marta, Magdalena province. The four peoples share a territory, a vision of creation, and a responsibility to the conservation of land through spiritual offerings.

A Mamo is a sage, the spiritual authority of the Tairona people. This person gives children their Arhuaco names, identifying the mission each person comes to the world with. My name in Arhuaco is Sei Arimaku. Sei means "before seeing the light," Ari means "activity," and Maku means "the Mamo," the sage. Translated it means: "Activity defined before seeing the light close to the Mamo."

Indigenous peoples in Colombia have been hit hard by the conflict, but for us, we can't say that there was a time of violence and then a time of peace, no—there has been no "good period" for the indigenous people of the Sierra. For us, the conflict begins with Christopher Columbus. Ever since the conquistadors arrived we have been mistreated. But we're not resentful. We live trying to share the knowledge that we have to make people more sensitive to nature.

SON OF THE GUATAPURÍ RIVER

I am a son of the Guatapurí River basin on the southwestern side of the Sierra. My dad had about thirty children, but just two with my mother: me and my brother Vicente, who is three years older than me.

When I was a child, my dad would build a house and establish it as a property, but he wouldn't stay there long. He would go and establish another and another. He was one of the first Arhuacos to begin getting personal land titles, but in a way it was to protect the territory from white colonists who were buying up our traditional lands.

My dad had a lot of dealings with white people. He was a great Mamo, and people would seek him out to consult with him, and ask him to act as a translator for them. Back in 1916, he had acted as the interpreter for a mission that went to Bogotá to ask the president for education for indigenous people. That year, Capuchin friars set up schools, but my father told me that he later realized they had come to destroy the Arhuaco culture. The Capuchin friars took the children to their orphanages and schools and cut their hair, and they prohibited the Arhuacos from speaking our language.[1] Around the late 1920s, my dad was put in jail in Bogotá for protesting against the Capuchins. He told me he was held in a prison building that's now the National Museum.

My father died of natural causes when I was nine years old. At the time I was living with my mother and my brother Vicente in Valledupar, the capital of Cesar province. After my father's death I became very close to my mother and I liked to be spoiled by her. She was very loving with me.

I MANEUVERED BETWEEN
EXTERNAL AND INDIGENOUS

In 1972, when I was sixteen, I went to a white public school in Valledupar. I dressed in civilian clothes[2] but my upbringing had been totally indigenous. So I accepted things from outside the Indian traditions, but as a complement to them. In '75, there was a long teachers' strike because they hadn't been paid and there were no classes for about six months. I was nineteen years old then, and I decided to stop studying and return to the Sierra with my mom to work on our family farm.

---

[1] Capuchin friars had been present in the Sierra since 1888, but in 1916 they built the Nuestra Señora del Carmen de la Sierrita orphanage and took over the education of the Arhuacos.

[2] The term Arhuacos use to refer to Western-style clothing.

About a year later, I married an Arhuaco woman named Cecilia. When you get married in the Arhuaco tradition, both the man and the woman have to do a spiritual cleansing. It's the union of two beings who each have a history, so that needs cleansing, because no one is a saint! When you join together, you have to start from scratch.

In 1978 I started working as a teacher while I continued to work my family's farm. I hadn't studied much, but in the land of the blind the one-eyed man is king. At that time, education in the Sierra was still run by Capuchin friars, so I was employed by the priests. But the indigenous organizations there had demanded that the teachers be bilingual, so that the local education could reinforce both the Arhuaco traditions and the outside knowledge. There was also an indigenous opposition to teaching religion, and I had to maneuver between external and indigenous elements.

As an Arhuaco teacher, you become a sort of leader because you're responsible for the future generations.

THE PARTY LASTED FOR THREE DAYS

In 1981 I gave up teaching and devoted myself entirely to agriculture. I decided to do that because every year I had to teach in January, February, and March, which is when you have to be preparing the ground for planting. And at the time of the coffee harvest in October, I was still caught up in school. I dedicated myself to harvesting coffee and sugar cane. I also produced panela,[3] which I enjoyed a lot. In the Sierra you don't need much, just the basics. It's not like in the city where at the end of every month the bills come like little goat turds!

For years, many indigenous leaders had been fighting to drive the Capuchin friars from the Sierra. In 1982, Arhuaco leaders organized a huge mobilization against the Capuchin friars, and about a thousand Arhuacos

---

[3] Panela is an unrefined food product made by boiling sugarcane juice into a hard, crusty block.

took over the mission, the orphanages, and the schools in Nabusimake, which is considered the capital of Arhuaco territory, and stayed there until they managed to expel the friars from Arhuaco land. I had stayed on my farm as part of the logistical backup, providing food for those who were participating in the occupation. On August 7, 1982, the friars agreed to leave, and the Arhuaco leaders sent a messenger to our settlement and told everyone. I went to Nabusimake to join the celebration. Everyone was happy, dancing. The party lasted for three days.

NOW THE FARC ARE HERE, THINGS HAVE GOTTEN BETTER

In the eighties, there was a lot of crime in the Sierra. We Arhuacos and the white peasants who lived there would often get robbed when we went to sell coffee to the white towns. There were cattle rustlers, and mules were stolen. There was no police presence and there was no army presence; it made for a very difficult situation. And that's when the FARC guerrillas arrived.[4] At first I think the FARC moved in secret. They would have contact with certain people among the peasants, but many of us didn't see them around. Then the FARC began to drive out the criminals. They'd grab the rustlers and the thieves and they would kill them. That gave peace to the area, and with that, the FARC began to win people over, especially the peasants. It got to the point where people would go to the FARC commanders to complain about robberies and such. People would say, "I think so-and-so stole my mule," and then the guerrillas would seize the suspect, tie him up, and conduct a sort of investigation. If the accusation was true, they killed the suspect. So that was seen as a solution at the time. I heard people say, "Now that the FARC are here, things have gotten better." The people were happy to be friends with several armed

---

[4] The Revolutionary Armed Forces of Colombia (FARC) is the country's largest and strongest rebel group.

groups; it wasn't just the FARC. There was the ELN[5] and the EPL[6] as well. But the FARC was a little more disciplined, a little more respectful. When they came to a farm they were more courteous, not like the Elenos—the ELN—who would waltz in like it was their own house.

Personally, I never wanted to be good friends with the guerrillas. I wanted to be neither friend nor foe. I lived on the edge of the road, and sometimes a guerrilla would show up and say, "I'm going to rest this tired mule here." And I'd say, "Oh well, okay. Leave it." Once a small group of guerrillas arrived and one of them said, "I need you to sell me two hens, but I have no money. I can pay you later." And I told him, "The chickens belong to my wife. But I have fish that I brought from Valledupar. I'll give you some fish." That's how I handled things.

At the same time that the guerrillas showed up, coca started being planted in the Sierra for drug trafficking. Before, there was coca but it was for our own use, because for indigenous people it is a sacred plant.[7] Coca is used by the Mamos to make offerings, and is like a key to enter the spiritual world for baptisms, weddings, or for making offerings to Mother Nature. It is also custom for the men to chew coca leaves mixed with quicklime, so when a boy becomes a man he receives a poporo[8] and coca, because coca will always be his companion. When two men meet, they exchange a handful of coca leaves as a greeting.

But the little brothers—non-indigenous people—are always looking for ways to destroy their bodies and the environment. The illegal coca was

---

[5] Founded in 1964, the National Liberation Army (ELN) is Colombia's second-largest guerrilla group.

[6] Ejercito Popular de Liberación (Popular Liberation Army), a small rebel group created in 1965. Most of its members demobilized in 1991.

[7] The leaves of the coca plant are the raw material used in making cocaine. Coca is also used by indigenous peoples as a ritual plant in Andean countries such as Colombia, Bolivia and Peru. In Arhuaco language it is call "ayu."

[8] Poporo is a gourd that is filled with quicklime. Arhuaco men insert a stick into a hole in the gourd and it comes out covered in lime. They then rub the lime on their gums while they chew the coca leaves.

mostly planted on the Santa Marta side of the Sierra by the white peasants; on the Valledupar side there weren't any large extensions of coca.

THE SOLDIERS PRETENDED TO EXECUTE ME

In 1985 I separated from my wife Cecilia. We'd had two children, but we had problems. When we split up, I had many problems with the Arhuaco authorities because they don't allow married couples to separate when they have children. I turned a deaf ear to their protests.

When I left Cecilia I moved to Valledupar to live with a white woman, Amarilys. In March 1990 we had a baby boy. His name is Amado too. My brother Vicente was also living in Valledupar, just around the corner from us. By that time he was a well-known indigenous rights leader who was trying to recuperate traditional lands that had been colonized by whites in the Guatapurí basin.

On November 28, 1990, three Arhuaco leaders set out from Valledupar to Bogotá to talk to government officials about land issues. It was an important meeting to explore ways the indigenous people of the Sierra could recover traditional lands. Vicente didn't go because he worked specifically on the Guatapurí issues and other leaders were dealing with broader issues.

Then, that night, at about eleven, someone knocked on the door. I'd been sleeping, and I thought, *Who could it be at this hour?* I asked my wife[9] to see who it was, and when she came back into the room, she said, "It's the army." I said, "Oh well, open the door. We have nothing to fear." But once she opened the door, the soldiers came in and began searching the whole house. One of the soldiers told me, "You have to come with us." I was wearing only shorts at the time, so I said, "Let me go and put on my clothes." As I was getting dressed, I told my wife, "Go and tell Vicente that the army's taking me to the La Popa army base," which was in Valledupar. The soldiers

---

[9] In Colombia, a couple becomes common-law spouses after living together for two years.

let her leave and she went out to Vicente's house, which was just around the corner. When she came back, she told me, "They're taking Vicente away too and beating him." She had seen soldiers dragging Vicente out of his house by the hair and beating him as they put him in a truck.

The soldiers didn't mistreat me in my house. But once we reached the La Popa base, the soldiers tied my hands behind my back, put a bag over my head, took me to a water channel, and began to drown me. They had Vicente and me together at that point.

The reason they detained us was because the soldiers thought we were involved with the kidnapping of a wealthy rancher named Jorge Eduardo Mattos, who the FARC had kidnapped in May. They'd grabbed him close to the Indigenous House[10] in Valledupar. Neighbors of our family farms had told us that the FARC took him to the Sierra, near a town called Sabana Crespo, about an hour from Valledupar. And above Sabana Crespo is where our family's farms were. The army thought Eduardo Mattos had been held on my brother's farm. As the soldiers beat us they kept asking us where the hostage was.

They told me I had to tell the truth. And I said, "But what am I going to say if I don't know anything?" At one point the soldiers separated me from my brother, but apparently he could see me. I couldn't see anything because I had a hood over my head. The soldiers pretended to execute me by firing gunshots over my head. They did it so my brother would think they'd shot me.

I'M GOING TO START KILLING INDIANS
AS IF THEY WERE FISH

The first night, I got kicked, beaten, dunked in water, and I had a gun put in my mouth. That was terrible. The next day they took me and Vicente to a small room with a desk. There, Vicente told me that when

---

[10] A community center for indigenous people in the city.

the soldiers were pretending to execute me, he could see the flame of the bullet going over my head, and he knew it was pure show.

The next day, the brother of the kidnapped rancher came and sat down at the desk and slapped down a wad of cash. He said, "Here's this money. You'll take me to where the hostage is." Vicente said, "Where am I going to take you if I don't know where he is?" The man said, "Well, my brother had better show up, or I'm going to start killing Indians as if they were fish. I have the money to do it."

After that, the soldiers took my brother in a helicopter. I thought, *I'll never see him again.* But a while later they brought him back. He told me they had taken him and flown him over the Sierra, demanding that he point out where the FARC were holding the hostage.

We were held for six days. I think they held us that long to give the bruises a chance to heal so then we couldn't prove they'd tortured us. On the sixth day we were handed over to the Arhuaco community.

That was when Vicente and I learned that the Arhuaco leaders who set out for Bogotá on November 28 had never arrived. The army had seized them in a town called Curumaní, about 170 kilometers from Valledupar, and brought them back to a farm near the town of Bosconia. They kept them there for several days and then killed all three of them. They were buried in unmarked graves. But by asking around, the Arhuaco community had been able to find them, dig them up and bury them in the Sierra.

Vicente called a meeting in an auditorium in Valledupar about six days after we were released. Representatives of the government and the battalion commander responsible for the Popa were there. My brother said publicly that we had been tortured, and he blamed the commander for the deaths of the three Arhuaco leaders.

The only result of that was that the danger increased for my brother. He had to go to Bogotá for several years because both the army and the guerrillas wanted him. The guerrillas had it in for him because, since we hadn't been killed like the others, people wondered if we had collaborated with the army.

A HUGE PSYCHOLOGICAL PROBLEM

We consulted the Mamos and they told me it was safe for me in the Sierra, so I decided to leave Valledupar and go back there. I told my wife, "I can't live here, it's very dangerous. Let's go." But she said, "If you go to the Sierra, don't come back." She was a white woman, and she saw it as a backward step to live in the Sierra, out in the country. She stayed with my eight-month-old child and eventually I lost contact with them.

For a year or two after I returned to the farm in the Guatapurí basin, I was in bad shape, psychologically. I couldn't see anything that resembled army camouflage, because it reminded me of what happened at the army base, and it would set me off. Sometimes, in a bunch of banana trees, there are leaves that look like army camouflage, and I'd see that and get scared. It was a huge psychological problem, but eventually, with the help of the Mamo, I got over it.

The Arhuaco community began to resent the FARC and blamed them for the deaths of the three leaders at the hands of the army. It was the guerrillas who'd kidnapped the rancher and brought him into our territory, putting us in danger. So they were responsible for those deaths. It was then that the community leaders began to reject the FARC presence in the territory.

The guerrillas had started gaining more and more power. They began to challenge the traditional authorities of the territory because people would seek out the guerrillas instead of going to the Mamos. Gradually they were also trying to gain members for their organization, trying to recruit young people, and even some leaders began to work for their cause. Pressure on the Arhuaco leaders began when the FARC saw that we wouldn't go along with them.

In 1991, I met an Arhuaco woman named Edilma. We decided to start a family, and our first son was born in 1992. My relationship with the community and our territory became stronger. That was when I decided to start wearing the traditional manta.[11] For me it was natural to do it; it was my right, and the Mamos at the time were trying to get the community to recover its identity. Up until that point, I had always dressed as a civilian. But I never understood why my dad, being a Mamo, had dressed me and my brother that way. I guess it was because we used to go to Valledupar a lot. But I thought, *That was never my choice.* So since then, that's what I wear.

My relationship with the Arhuaco community and with the land was so strong that I said to myself, "I'm going to learn more from the Mamo." So I started to train in spiritual aspects of our traditions. I wanted to handle spiritual matters, especially for my family. By 1998, I was deeply involved in traditional life and working in agriculture. I don't consider myself a Mamo, because for that you have to have the recognition of a settlement or a community. But I have the knowledge.

OTHERWISE WE WOULDN'T BE TALKING

People kept telling me that the FARC questioned whether Vicente and I had cut a deal with the army because we'd survived our detention. So one day, around the end of 1993, I sought out the guerrilla commander and said, "I've come to clear things up with you, because there are rumors that you say we may have sold out the leaders who were killed by the army. So what's really happening?"

The commander said, "Those comments come from your own people. They are the ones who accuse you. But we investigated and we know it's not true. Otherwise, we wouldn't be talking." I immediately felt that what the guerrillas were trying to do was to drive a wedge in the community, trying to divide us. At different meetings of the Arhuaco governing council I talked about that issue and tried to make clear that we had nothing to do with it.

---

[11] Traditional Arhuaco clothing. The men wear loose-fitting, thick-woven cotton pants and a woven cotton poncho-type garment tied at the waist by a sash. Their hats are knitted into a particular flat-topped shape.

After that, life continued more or less calmly. Edilma and I had two more children, one in 1994 and another in 1998.

It was around 2000 when the paramilitaries started making a presence in the Sierra.[12] They started off by killing white people who worked or did business in the Sierra, like shop owners, bus drivers, and some farm owners. Then the paramilitaries set up roadblocks on the roads that lead up to the Sierra. They had complete control of the roads while the FARC guerrillas still controlled things on the mountain. The paramilitary presence around the foothills also pushed the ELN guerrillas higher up the mountain than they usually were.

A MILITARY TARGET

In August 2002, a few days before Álvaro Uribe[13] took office, there was a clash between the ELN and the army about five or six kilometers from my house. My wife and I didn't hear anything, but we saw people fleeing from that area. It was unusual because I couldn't remember ever seeing the guerrillas and army clash like that before.

Three days later, a small group of ELN guerrillas came to my house. They said that they were fighting for us, the indigenous people, and that we had to give them a contribution. They said I had to give them a bull. I refused. I told them that I belonged to the indigenous community and said, "Any contributions I make would be to my own community." Their only reaction was to tell me, "Well we're going to take an animal, and you keep your mouth shut."

From then on they would just take things from the farm; they were like a dog pissing on a tree trunk. They took about ten cows, bunches of plantains, and they'd let their mules trample through the fields.

---

[12] Right-wing paramilitary groups began to form in Colombia in the early 1980s with the purported aim of fighting left-wing guerrillas. Backed by the military, landowners, drug traffickers, and political and economic elites, they murdered tens of thousands of civilians.

[13] President of Colombia from 2002 to 2010.

The ELN would call meetings and I wouldn't go, but friends who did told me that the ELN had declared me a military target. I lived in fear that they would kill me. Around that time the FARC suggested I work with them, and I considered accepting so they could be my protection against the ELN. But I refused. I said, "No, I'm fine just as I am."

I went to consult a Mamo up in the páramo about my situation.[14] I made offerings for my safety. When I returned I heard that the ELN had started a rumor that I'd been seen in Valledupar at La Popa, and that I was working with the army. That was a total lie; it was a justification to kill me.

I spoke to another Mamo and made other offerings. Both the Mamos told me that after the offerings I'd made, I didn't need to leave the Sierra, that spiritually I was healed and could continue my farm work with no problems in the Sierra.

WE TOO ARE RESPONSIBLE

But I kept hearing about killings of peasants and of indigenous people every day and so I was very scared. In December I grabbed my wife and three children and we left. I told my wife, "Yes we'll lose everything, but let's go. What is lost can be recovered, but we can be with our children and we will be at peace." I lost everything. Ten years of work on the farm: the panela mill, the cane crops, the houses.

I am not registered as a displaced person anywhere.[15] The Arhuaco people always maintained the idea that we shouldn't register as displaced because we hold the vision that if this was happening it was because we were failing at something, and these are the consequences. Spiritually,

---

[14] The páramo is the ecosystem of the northern Andes of South America that lies above the continuous forest line but below the permanent snowline.

[15] To receive government aid, a displaced person must register their status with the government. Some humanitarian organizations supply aid to people who are unregistered, or whose applications have been rejected.

things need to be repaired and replaced. So we don't see it just as someone else's fault. We too are responsible.

I came to Santa Marta, a city on the northern coast, in December 2002 and started working with the Gonawindua Indigenous Organization that groups the Arhuaco, Kogi, and Wiwa people of the Sierra. One of the Mamos I had consulted in the Sierra had told me that I should dedicate myself to letting the world know what was going on in the Sierra: our vision of creation, and the importance of our territory to us; the threats we were living with, and the danger we were in.

So I left the mountain with the idea of making a documentary and a book. I didn't know anything about how to do that, but one day in 2003 I was in Valledupar and I saw a gringo there taking pictures. His name is Stephen Ferry. I approached him and I told him about my project, and he told me he wanted to do a story on the Sierra. So he taught me photography and I helped him gain access to the Sierra.

PRESSING A LITTLE BUTTON IS EASY

When I first picked up a camera, I thought, *Using a machete is work. Pressing this little button is easy.* I didn't take an artistic view of photography. I took as many pictures as I could. I was on a mission. Gradually, I formed the Zhigoneshi Media Center as part of the Gonawindua Organization. Zhigoneshi means "mutual aid" in the Kogi language. Through the center we could do what the Mamo in the Sierra had told me to: let the world know what was happening in the Sierra.

We would get word through Gonawindua that the situation was getting worse in the Sierra. The guerrillas were attacking more and more indigenous people. In November 2004, the FARC murdered Mamo Mariano. They had accused Mamo Mariano of working with the army, and said that he'd served as a guide for the soldiers to kill a FARC commander. No one believed that, because Mamo Mariano didn't even speak Spanish.

Guerrillas and paramilitaries had killed around twenty-five Arhuacos, but it was Mamo Mariano's murder that finally prompted a reaction from the Arhuaco authorities. They started calling meetings with the guerrillas. Four or five hundred of them would get together with the FARC and ELN commanders in the different river basins of the Sierra. They'd complain to them, and tell them that they wouldn't allow them to continue killing their people or recruiting their young men.

In one such meeting in 2006, I was able to clear up my situation. The ELN commanders said, "No, see, there was some misinformation, and so we made mistakes. We apologize."

After that, it was safe for me to return to the Sierra. But I didn't move back. My three eldest children were studying here and Edilma and I had just had our fourth child.

I continued with the idea of making a documentary. In 2005 I had met Pablo Mora, an anthropologist and documentary filmmaker, and I told him about the project I had. By then there were three others on the media team. He said, "If you allow me to film alongside you, I will advise and help you. But you have to let me make a movie, and you have to take me to all the sites where you film."

The media team learned a lot with him and he also learned a lot from us. Our first production was "Palabras Mayores," a documentary based on interviews with the Mamos. Even I learned many things about the Sierra and the spiritual world through the interviews. We produced the film in English, French, and Spanish. Then we made another film called "Memorias de una Independencia," about how we got rid of the Capuchin friars.

The media center is the good that has come out of all this violence. The Mamos say that difficult situations teach us how to behave and how to build strategies. At the media center, we are building an advocacy tool for our territory and our culture.

So I feel that my Arhuaco name has a certain logic to it. Sei Arimaku: "Activity defined before seeing the light close to the Mamo." I'm not a Mamo, but I am close to a Mamo, and I am passing on the Mamo's words.

LINA GAMARRA

AGE: *41*

OCCUPATION: *Teacher*

HOMETOWN: *La Apartada, Córdoba*

INTERVIEWED IN: *Cali, Valle del Cauca*[1]

Lina Gamarra raised her family in Córdoba province. As a primary school teacher in Tierra Santa, a small rural town in the municipality of Buenavista, she strove to protect her students from being ensnared by the conflict between paramilitaries, guerrillas, and the army. But in 1998, the chronic violence proved unbearable, and Lina and her family abandoned their home and fled to the nearby city of La Apartada, Córdoba, where her mother and eight siblings also lived. In the wake of their displacement, Lina managed to pursue an advanced degree, send her daughters to college, and establish herself as a respected teacher. Yet, as neo-paramilitary groups formed in the region, threats and assassinations returned to pervade daily life. More than a decade after Lina's first displacement, one such group, called the Águilas Negras, killed her husband Roberto. After seeking justice for the crime, Lina had to flee once again—this time to the city of Cali, Valle del Cauca province.

Names in this narrative have been changed at the request of the narrator.

---

[1] La Apartada, Tierra Santa, Buenavista, Cereté and Cali are false locations that have been employed here to protect the narrator's identity.

ROBERTO

I met my husband Roberto when I was fourteen years old. He was the only boyfriend I ever had, and the only husband I ever had. He was short, chubby, and a little fairer skinned than I am. I loved his physique. He was tender and loving, and treated me very nicely from the very beginning. At fifteen, I went to live with him, and after six years we had our first girl, who we named Alexandra. Two years later we had another girl, Jenny. Roberto and I loved each other, and we got married in the church in Tierra Santa.

After we got married he was even more loving, sweet and tender. He always told me, "Mi'ja,[2] I don't know why, but every day I love you more."

My dream was always to be a teacher. I began teaching even before graduating from high school, but in 1995 I started pursuing a degree in primary school teaching at a university. However, when my dad died in 1997, I wanted to withdraw from the university because my family was struggling to pay for a lot of expenses. I felt pretty disheartened, and I told my husband, "I want to withdraw, even if it's just for a year." He said, "Even if we have to eat dirt, you're not going to withdraw; you're going to continue." Whenever I'd become disheartened over something, it was my husband who'd push me to continue forward. I have now been a teacher for over twenty years.

DAY IN AND DAY OUT

Between 1997 and 1998, the paramilitaries would come to Tierra Santa and kill three or four people almost every day.[3] It's always been the same there, day in and day out: maybe they'd stop for a month or two, but then they'd come back.

---

[2] A contraction of "mi hija," (in English, "my daughter"), which is used affectionately for female friends and relatives.

[3] Right-wing paramilitary groups began to form in Colombia in the early 1980s with the purported aim of fighting left-wing guerrillas. Backed by the military, landowners, drug traffickers, and political and economic elites, they murdered tens of thousands of civilians.

It affected the schools a lot. As a teacher, you'd be in class and one of the students' relatives would show up and say, "Seño," because there they call teachers seño, "let little Jonny leave class because they just killed his dad," or, "They just killed his brother." Back then, I had a student who was about eleven years old when the paras[4] killed his dad. I tell you, that boy could no longer listen in class. You'd always see him crying. He was a little white kid, and you'd see him turn red, red, red. I'd ask him, "What's wrong?" And he'd say, "Seño, what's wrong is that I have to avenge my father's death." So, that's a lot of work that's needed there: an eleven-year-old kid saying, "I have to avenge my father's death." I'd hug him, sit him down on my lap and tell him, "God gives life and God should take it away. But it's also necessary to forgive. Because we can't condemn someone who's already condemned."

THEY'VE COME TO FINISH OFF THE TOWN

During that time, the army was in Tierra Santa, but they would leave town so that the paramilitaries could enter.[5] Up to one hundred uniformed paramilitaries would stay in town for a week or two, and after they'd killed a lot of people, they would leave and the army would return. The guerrillas also had a presence in the area,[6] but less than the paramilitaries.

Both the paramilitaries and the guerrillas would use the town priest's megaphone to call the entire community to meetings. It was scary to me. I'd think, *While we're in the meeting, the other group will come and kill everyone who's there.* Once, when the guerrillas called a meeting, I thought, *I'm not*

---

[4] "Para" is conversational shorthand for paramilitary.

[5] The army and AUC, a paramilitary coalition, collaborated closely throughout the country, often coordinating their movements and operations.

[6] The Revolutionary Armed Forces of Colombia (FARC) and National Liberation Army (ELN) are Colombia's two main guerrilla groups. Founded in the 1960s and claiming to represent the country's rural poor in the fight against Colombia's wealthy classes and U.S. imperialism, both groups commit widespread abuses against civilians, including killings, threats, and recruitment of child soldiers.

going to that meeting, and I stayed at home, cleaning. I started mopping and singing, and then I heard someone say, "Hey, you're not planning on going to the meeting?" I looked up and saw a really ugly, bearded guerrilla at the window. I said, "No, it's just that I'm finishing cleaning, and then I'll go." And I ended up having to go.

In June 1997, the paramilitaries killed a shopkeeper and the town inspector. The town inspector was named Carlos, and he was my cousin's husband. It was a Sunday, and there was going to be a graduation for a typing course that Carlos had organized. My family lived close to where the ceremony was going to be, and I was with my husband and my seven-year-old daughter Alexandra, getting ready to take some loudspeakers to the graduation. As my husband lifted up one of the speakers, we heard the shots.

My sister came to the house, crying, "They killed Carlos!" Alexandra took off running from the house. I tried to stop her, but nobody was able to grab her. I ran after her because I didn't want her to see Carlos lying there dead. After running for about seven minutes, I saw my cousin by the ice-cream parlor, kneeling over Carlos's body. Alexandra was hugging her from behind, crying and screaming.

I think the paramilitaries killed Carlos because he was a candidate for the municipal council. They said he was a guerrilla accomplice since he used to go to the villages in the area and take sick people into town by boat.[7]

The community was so frightened after those two murders that about 70 percent of the people ended up leaving—on foot, by car, by horse. The day after the murder, I left with my family to the nearby municipality of Cereté, where some of my husband's sisters lived. Classes in Tierra Santa were suspended for a week, but at the end of that week we had to go back because I had to teach. Other families didn't return to town for months.

---

[7] People who travel or work in Colombia's remote rural areas where guerrillas maintain a presence are sometimes baselessly labeled as guerrilla collaborators.

After the shooting, I had to take Alexandra to six sessions with a psychologist. During that time, she would often cry, and she wouldn't let a man enter the house, even if he were a friend; she said he was going to hurt her dad. She overcame it, but she still remembers that day and says, "I never want to return to that town."

That year my husband ran as a Liberal Party candidate for the municipal council. A few months before the local elections in October 1997, someone knocked at our door at six in the morning and said, "Seño, let me in!" I opened the door and it was the mother of one of my students. When I saw that she was scared, I said, "What happened?" And she said, "Last night a friend stayed at my house. He said the guerrillas are going to kill Roberto." I said, "What do you mean? What has Roberto done?" She said, "I don't know, but he said they're going to kill him." I immediately made Roberto leave for the city of La Apartada, where I was born. I stayed in Tierra Santa. Later, locals told me that the guerrillas thought Roberto was allied with the paramilitaries because he'd campaigned with a mayoral candidate who was said to sponsor the paramilitaries.

Roberto didn't return to Tierra Santa until May 30, 1998, the night before the presidential elections. When I saw him arrive at the house, I got really scared, and asked him why he'd come back. He said, "I came to vote, and I'm going to leave tomorrow."

Later that night, I was sleeping when I heard a sound like *pan*! It was about two in the morning, and I said to my husband, "Do you hear that?" Then I heard the shots coming clearly. I said, "What is that? My God, the guerrillas have come to finish off the town. They're going to kill you!"

Then the army helicopters arrived and began bombing very close to the town. The combat between the guerrillas and the army was the most horrific thing I'd ever heard in my life—the bombing, the shots, the gunfire. There were people fainting from fright in the middle of the street. I could see the fire from the explosions. I said to Roberto, "I've been shot." I was so scared I thought I could see the blood on my arms and hands. I said, "They've shot me in the head, look! I'm dripping with blood!" but Roberto told me he didn't see anything. Then I said to him, "I'm not living in this town a minute longer. Either you come with me or I'm going alone."

When the bus passed in front of the house to pick up voters, I grabbed my two girls, who were eight and six years old at the time. I said, "Let's go, let's go," and we boarded the bus with my husband. That day, we left without anything. When we arrived in the town center of Buenavista and were about to get off the bus, my daughter Alexandra told me, "Mami, look I didn't bring my shoes." So I immediately bought her some shoes, and then we took off for La Apartada, Córdoba.

We'd left our house just as it was, and later our family members who'd stayed behind sent us our things—the things that hadn't been lost. A large part of what we left there was stolen. You always have to start from zero when these displacements happen to you.

YOU HAVE TO STRUGGLE FOR THOSE KIDS

For me, my home has always come first. So after Roberto and I came to La Apartada, we took out a loan from a foundation and bought a piece of land in town. Then my husband began to work as a mechanic's assistant for a consortium that belongs to the Cerro Matoso nickel mine. But one of the problems is that even though the Cerro Matoso mine is in Montelíbano, close to La Apartada, they don't hire people from the area as workers; they always bring in people from other places. So my husband's work only lasted two and a half years, and then there was nothing more. But it was enough, thank God, to build a very nice house.

Life in La Apartada was tranquil then. People were caring and hospitable. You could fall asleep on the terrace and nothing would happen. I was very happy there. All of my family lived in La Apartada, and I come from a very united family of nine brothers and sisters. They lived opposite my house, and sometimes we'd all get together.

In 2000, I had my third daughter, Luz Adriana, and the following year I graduated from college. I was thirty-three years old, and I was the first in my family to finish college. I was happy because I'd achieved what

I wanted to, and God had given me someone who supported me. Because a lot of times a woman gets married and then the husband wants her to stay in the house. But it wasn't like that. My husband was very loving, he helped me continue forward, and he was committed to his home. Roberto helped me finish high school and go to college. But he didn't want me to stop there. He said, "Mi'ja, what are you going to do now? You've finished college, so why don't you do a specialization?"[8] So in 2002, I began a specialization in ecology and finished it in the middle of 2003.

The teachers union I belonged to helped to relocate my job to La Apartada. You have to struggle a lot for those kids, because many of them become disheartened easily, and the first thing they do is take off for the armed groups. That's where the role of the teacher comes in. Thank God that, up until now, I take a group of students and the group doesn't want to leave my side. Even though I'm academically demanding, I'm very affectionate and understanding with my students. I don't want to leave their side either.

I taught the fourth grade, which is normally nine- and ten-year-olds. But there was a fifteen-year-old boy in my class named Navi. His dad had been killed, and I'd already spoken with the boy about a series of problems he had at home. Then, six weeks after classes started, I heard that the school was going to kick him out for being a troublemaker. So I visited his house, and realized that it was completely unlivable; it was small and falling apart. You could see his embarrassment when I arrived and there wasn't anywhere for me to sit. There was a dirt floor, no bathroom, and he and his mom had to get their water from the street. As soon as the boy got home from school he'd grab a cart to go sell watermelon.

Afterwards, I went to the principal to talk about Navi. I said, "I want you to tell me if you know about his living conditions." He said, "No," and I told him about how the boy didn't have enough notebooks for school and didn't have a uniform. I said, "They killed his father. Why

---

[8] A specialization is an advanced degree that is typically less formal than a Master's degree.

are we going to kick him out onto the street? So that he becomes a criminal? As long as I have that boy in my classroom, no one's taking him away." As I spoke to the principal, tears began to fall from his eyes. He said, "Seño, if you say so, we won't remove him." He gave Navi the school uniform and I gave him the notebooks. The boy had had every expectation of dropping out, but decided against it. After that, I always tried to help him out the most I could. I didn't give him gifts, because sometimes that's bad. Instead I gave him 10,000 or 5,000 pesos[9] to clean my yard. The boy started getting along excellently.

A TICKING TIME BOMB

In 2004, Roberto and I had my son Álvaro. The following year, my husband went back to Tierra Santa to look for work. But I never agreed with it. I always told him that the town was dangerous. The paramilitaries had handed in their weapons and demobilized,[10] but the demobilized paramilitaries took their payments from the government and started forming other paramilitary groups, like the Águilas Negras.[11]

My husband would tell me, "But there isn't any work here in La Apartada." He didn't like to sit around because people would say, "Look, the wife's working and he's sitting around." The economic situation in La

---

[9] About U.S.$5 or U.S.$2.50.

[10] The government sponsored a demobilization process for paramilitary groups between 2003 and 2006 in which more than 30,000 supposed members participated in demobilization ceremonies. Many demobilized paramilitaries entered government reintegration programs that provided benefits, including a monthly stipend.

[11] Neo-paramilitary groups such as the Águilas Negras, Urabeños and Paisas are armed groups that emerged in 2006 in the wake of the demobilization process of the AUC national paramilitary coalition. Led largely by former paramilitaries and often employing the same criminal, political, and economic networks as their predecessors, neo-paramilitary groups have a powerful presence in many regions throughout the country. While human rights groups have documented the existence of the Águilas Negras, a name that is also adopted by the Urabeños neo-paramilitary group in certain areas, the Colombian government does not recognize their existence.

Apartada is very difficult, and there are a lot of people like my husband who have to leave because the living conditions there don't allow them to stay.

The separation wasn't difficult because he didn't spend very long in Tierra Santa. For example, after five days he'd return by motorbike, which took two hours. First he worked as a mule driver. Then, since a relative of his had a motorboat, he began to work as a boat driver, taking cargo and passengers down the San Jorge River.

My mother became gravely ill on a Friday in the middle of March 2010. At her gravest hour, she told me, "Mi'ja, check that calling thing"— that's what she called my cell phone—"that calling thing that you're holding onto all the time. If your husband calls and tells you to go with him to Tierra Santa this weekend, don't go." She said, "Don't go there, mi'ja, because it's a ticking time bomb. Something could happen to you, and I'm very worried."

Three days later, on Monday morning, at about seven, I was lying in bed when I heard my phone ring. It was Roberto. He told me he was going on a trip that day. He said, "We're going to take some plantains down river, and early tomorrow I'll send you some." He'd often send me a sack of plantains and say, "Give it to someone in La Apartada who needs it."

He asked me about the kids and I said, "They're all well." He told me, "Take good care of them." I said, "But I always take good care of them, why do you have to tell me that? Take care of *yourself*, and may the Virgin be with you. My mom's delirium has got me worried." He said, "But I haven't done anything, I'm just working. I'll call you when I get back, and tomorrow I'll send you the plantains."

I got up and brushed my hair, but I didn't feel like going in the kitchen at all. So I sat down on the terrace. I never do that in the morning, but it was the Monday of a long weekend, and I didn't have to go to school. Then at about eight, my cousin called. She was crying. I said, "Why are you crying, what happened?" At first she didn't say anything to me, and as I listened to my cousin with that despair, I told myself that something had happened. I started crying too. Then my daughter Jenny, who was nineteen years old at the time, grabbed the cell phone. When she received the news, she began to cry. She said that my cousin had told her, "Ten boat drivers were called to a meeting. Of the ten, four went. Of the four, three were killed. One escaped, but we don't know who."

I said to myself, *I hope they tell me that it was Roberto who escaped.* But about ten minutes later, Roberto's sister called me and told me that Roberto had been killed. One of my husband's relatives was the one who'd escaped. Once he felt safe, he called his wife on his cell phone to tell her what had happened.

The Águilas Negras had called the boat drivers from the area to a meeting in a village outside of Tierra Santa. They said they were going to change the boss of the Águilas Negras, and that they had to introduce them to him so that he'd let them work.

Roberto's relative who escaped says that he, Roberto, another of his relatives, and a guy from town went to the meeting on three motorbikes. When he got there he didn't like the malicious look on the paramilitaries' faces, so he didn't get off the motorbike but parked it at a distance. My husband, on the other hand, jumped right off the motorbike. He'd talk to everyone, he was very friendly, and he used to say that he didn't owe anything to anybody. When he went to shake the guy's hand, *tras*! He was the first one they shot. His other relative took off running, but the Águilas Negras killed him and the other man too.

The army had a checkpoint at the same place on the road where the three were killed. They were killed on a Monday, and people from the area say that the army had left the area that Sunday night. I think it was so that the Águilas Negras could go there and kill them.

My brothers didn't let me go and pick up Roberto's body. He was there from eight in the morning until around four in the afternoon, when his body was picked up by the authorities. Today, I regret not having gone because it saddens me that those bodies stayed there on the ground for so long. The authorities brought the bodies to the town center of Buenavista. There had been another massacre the same day in another town, where another seven people had been killed. So there were ten bodies in the morgue, and it took a while to perform an autopsy.

A funeral home from La Apartada brought my husband to me at about eleven in the morning on Tuesday. The burial was the following day. A ton of people showed up—colleagues, neighbors, students, a lot of people from Tierra Santa. The community was very hurt by the deaths. The people who died had never done anything to anybody. They didn't work in illicit businesses. It was honest work. What people say is that as boat drivers they transported the guerrillas. That's the argument you hear, that's what people imagine. They labeled Roberto as something that he wasn't. My husband wasn't a thief, he wasn't a drug trafficker, he wasn't any of that. You have a boat, I get on the boat, and you don't know who I am. That's how their work was. If you live in that area and a paramilitary arrives at your house and asks for water, you have to give it to him. If not, *tras*. If a guerrilla comes and asks for water, you also have to give it to him, because if not, *tras*.

At that point, I was furious at the injustice of being left without Roberto, of being left with four kids, of being left alone. But later I asked God to take away my anger. I don't want to be condemned because of someone else. I asked him to help me so that my heart doesn't fill with bitterness.

PARAMILITARISM NEVER ENDED

In May, I placed a request with the government agency Social Action[12] asking for reparations for my husband's death. About a month later I was at a workshop at school with all the teachers when the wife of one of the men who'd been killed the same day as Roberto called me. She said that Social Action had responded to our request and said they couldn't provide reparations for their deaths because the incident had been a settling of scores between common criminals.

I retreated to the bathroom so that no one could see my pain. If Social Action doesn't want to pay me, they don't have to pay me, but the

---

[12] The government entity entrusted with coordinating assistance to the displaced population, to the poor, and to victims of violence. Social Action was replaced by the Department for Social Prosperity in 2012.

memory of my husband has to be pure, like he was. I won't rest until his memory is restored.

Social Action also said that my husband wasn't a victim of the paramilitaries because the Águilas Negras weren't recognized as such by the government. But they are paramilitaries because they're the same people who are paid salaries for demobilizing. They're the same ones who went to Tierra Santa before and they're the same ones who keep going. In Tierra Santa, everyone knows they're the same. It's the same thing, the same evil deeds. Paramilitarism never ended. The army knows who the paramilitaries are and they don't do anything. On the contrary, they give them free rein to carry out their massacres.

LET EVERYTHING HAPPEN WITH
YOUR MOUTH SHUT AND ARMS CROSSED

In June 2010 I filed a legal request and took it to the Attorney General's office in La Apartada so that they would change the official report of my husband's death. A prosecutor there told me, "I can't investigate anything. Whatever you hand me I'll give it right back to you." I told him, "Whatever the case, I beg you to clarify this situation because otherwise, I won't be able to rest and it will be bad for the memory of my husband. And that's what I don't want." They told me that they couldn't do anything, that there would be no investigation. So, bad people appear as good, and the good appear as criminals.

I went to Cartagena for two weeks during school vacation and returned to La Apartada on July 19. At three in the afternoon, a little boy showed up at my house and said, "Seño, we came to say that you have to leave." I hadn't even taken my suitcases out of the living room yet. I said, "Papi, come here." But he began to run and turned the corner.

I thought, *What have I done? I go from school to my house, and from my house to church. Those are the places I visit. Why this problem?* The only thing I'd done was go to the Attorney General's office and ask them to clarify the facts about my husband's death. You're not allowed to protest anything here. You have to let everything happen with your mouth shut and arms crossed.

The other reason for the threat could be that I know it was the paramilitaries who killed my husband. Maybe they're afraid that I'm going to denounce them. They want to shut up everyone who knows about their evil deeds. The truth is, one of the risks I see is that the paramilitaries don't want to leave any evidence. Roberto's relative who survived the massacre is still in hiding, because the paramilitaries tell people in town that wherever they find him, they're going to eat him alive.

By that time, the paramilitary presence in La Apartada had grown, so the threat made me very afraid. There are groups called the Águilas Negras, Paisas, and Rastrojos, and you don't know who's who. The army and the police have a presence in La Apartada, but they don't do anything. The people there are afraid to go out onto the street. You used to be able to go out at any hour, and now there isn't a soul on the street at five in the morning. But if you lock yourself inside, they'll knock down your door when they want to kill you. It means nothing to them. You have a house there, they threaten you, you leave, and they take the house.

WHO'S GOING TO GIVE ME THAT KISS NOW?

I told my mom about the threat and she got very scared. She said, "Mi'ja, you'd better leave here. They've already begun." The day after the threat, I threw my clothes in a bag and left with Álvaro and Luz Adriana for the city of Montería,[13] where Jenny was studying at a technical school. At the time, Álvaro was six, Luz Adriana was ten, Jenny was nineteen, and Alexandra was twenty-one, and going to college in the city of Barranquilla.[14] In Montería, I filed a complaint in the prosecutor's office and with the

---

[13] Montería is the capital of Córdoba province, and is a hundred kilometers from La Apartada.

[14] Barranquilla is the capital of Atlántico province, and is about three hundred kilometers from of Montería.

police. The police were in charge of evaluating what level of risk I had, and they gave the report to the teachers' union. The Special Committee of Threatened Teachers[15] met and gave me the status of "extraordinarily threatened." In other words, I had to leave the province of Córdoba.

I left by bus right away with Álvaro, Luz Adriana, and Jenny for the city of Barranquilla, where Alexandra was studying. I went to the Secretary of Education in Barranquilla and told them everything that had happened to me. By that time, I was falling apart. My weight had dropped from sixty-eight kilos to fifty-two. I stayed in Barranquilla for two months trying to get relocated to a teaching job there, but it never happened. An official from the Secretary of Education told me that they didn't take teachers from other provinces. I thought, *There's nothing for me here.* I sent Jenny back to Montería, because she only had four more months left before she graduated.

Then, in September 2010, I took the bus back to Montería. Based on my risk evaluation, the police commander in Montería told me that I should leave because I had the right to be relocated as far away as possible. My union and the police sent me to the city of Cali. Roberto's relative's wife was waiting for me and the kids at the bus station when we arrived. She had gone to Cali after the massacre.

We stayed at her house with her four kids for about two weeks while I searched for a place to live. There was only one bedroom and one bed, and it was quite uncomfortable. The kids slept on the floor, and we ate badly. There were days when we only ate rice. The Red Cross helped us, though. They gave us 67,000 pesos[16] per person each month for about

---

[15] Special Committees on Threatened Teachers are made up of different government agencies, and are designed to assess the risks that individual teachers face and determine protection measures—including job relocation—on a case-by-case basis. Colombian teachers often face threats, displacement, and assassination: twenty-seven teachers—about 60 percent of whom were unionized—were killed in 2010, according to government figures.

[16] About U.S.$38.

four months. Social Action didn't give us any help. They still say that the paramilitaries don't exist.[17]

We found our own apartment in October, and Jenny came to live with us in December after she graduated from technical school. I missed my friends, my school, and my loving students. I asked my God that he reassign me to work in a school in Cali. I really missed being in the classroom. For me, my students are my other children. I have four children, and if they give me forty students, I say I have forty-four children.

I started to think, *If they don't reassign me, should I go back to La Apartada? Could it be that they'll kill me? Could it be that if I go to my house they'll do something to me?* Around November, my cousin's son was killed in La Apartada. I didn't know what happened—people are very afraid to talk over the phone—but I was worried that it had to do with my case.

I thought it was better to stay in Cali. If the paramilitaries do something to me, my kids will be left with no one; it would just be more suffering for them.

There were nights when I would put my kids to bed and then sit down and cry. My kids are affected. It's been hard for them. They were so accustomed to their father's warmth, his affection. Roberto used to come home and give Luz Adriana a kiss on the forehead. Sometimes she says, "Mami, now who's going to come home to give me that kiss?"

I didn't tell Álvaro that the paramilitaries killed his dad because he started becoming a little aggressive. He'd come up with some strange things, like, "I'm going to kill," or "I'm going to leave," or, "I don't want you to talk to me. When is Dad going to come?"

Since his dad had a motorbike, I'd tell him that he fell from the bike and hit his head. So every time he got furious, he'd say things like, "Papi, I told you not to get on that bike. Why did that bike have to kill you?" Every night I'd pray with my kids, and one night Álvaro said to me,

---

[17] In many cases, when victims of neo-paramilitary groups have tried to register as displaced people with Social Action, the agency has denied their claims under the argument that they are not party to the conflict.

"Mami, you always tell God to have Dad basking in His glory, but you've never asked Him to have Dad stand up from his tomb and come to live with us again."

THE BOY DROPPED OUT

In February 2011, I was reassigned to teach at a school in Cali. The teachers union in Valle del Cauca spoke with an official from the Secretary of Education in Valle del Cauca and he promised them that he'd place me at a good school. I feel good at the school where I now teach second grade. I'm also finishing a specialization that I'd started in Córdoba. So I teach Monday through Friday, and I go to class on Saturdays.

After I came to Cali, I'd always call and talk with Navi, my student from La Apartada. I'd tell him, "Navi, don't drop out. If you do, it will be detrimental to you, and you're a good person, a good student." He'd call me and talk for almost a half an hour with me. He'd even talk with my kids. He'd say, "Pass me to Luz Adriana, to Álvaro, to Jenny."

It turns out that the boy dropped out. He called me and we talked for about twenty minutes. He said, "Seño, I regret being stuck here in the countryside." He's working as a farm laborer in the country far outside the town. "I regret it so much," he said. I keep worrying about his situation because I know that this boy could get lost. Sometimes I'm tempted to tell him to come live with me, because I worked hard for that boy. I'm afraid that he'll go off with the paramilitaries.

Other students still call me and say, "Seño, when are you going to come back?" I wanted to push them to get ahead, for them to become professionals. Some students that have passed through my hands are now professionals, thank God. A doctor passes through the hands of a teacher. In fact, any professional has to pass through the hands of a teacher, who should have a better-paid salary. While the government pays those bandits a salary for doing their evil deeds,[18] a teacher has to struggle for healthcare.

One Saturday evening in November 2011, I received a telephone call at my house. The man on the end of the line asked if I was Roberto's wife. I asked, "Why?" and he said that Roberto owed him 3.5 million pesos.[19] He said, "You have to give it to me next week, and if not, I already have the order to kill you." I asked who he was and he said he was Rodolfo. Rodolfo is the name of one of the paramilitary commanders from Tierra Santa. It scared me, but I'm not going to run, I'm not going to flee. I haven't done anything bad to anyone. My only sin is working and getting my children ahead. And where would I get 3.5 million pesos to pay him?

I SEE MY ENORMOUS SOLITUDE AND PRAY

I never thought I would leave La Apartada. I told myself that I would stay there, fix my house up nicely, put my children through college, and retire there. Now, my life will never be the same. I don't think I'll ever feel joy again after sharing so many years with a person, and having him taken away like that, leaving me with such great agony. He was the only man I loved my whole life. It's like you're dying every day, fading more. Sometimes I say to myself, *Oh God, why don't you remember me?* The little ones make me persevere. If not for them, I would want to die. I feel like a living dead person.

Your land is your land, but here I feel like an outsider, always a stranger. In La Apartada I lived surrounded by family and friends, and here I have nothing. Every night when I lie down in bed I see my enormous solitude and I pray, "God, take charge of this solitude and judge the killers yourself. Don't allow me or my kids to condemn ourselves because of them."

---

[18] Lina is referring to the fact that the government provides demobilized paramilitaries with economic benefits, and many of the demobilized paramilitaries returned to arms in the neo-paramilitary groups.

[19] About U.S.$1,940.

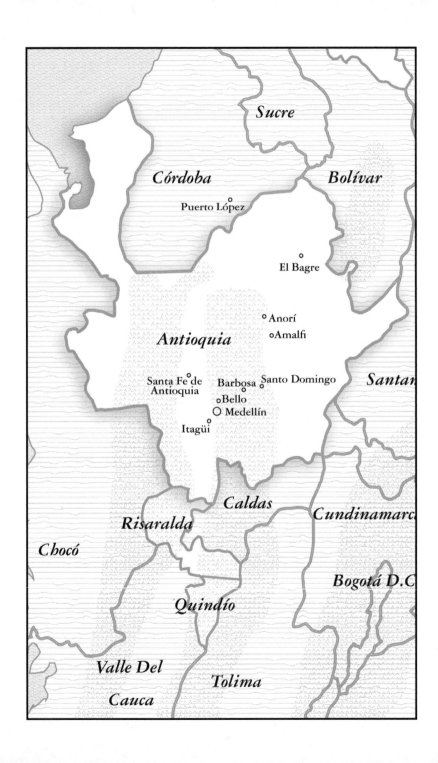

THE LESS YOU KNOW, THE MORE YOU LIVE

Antioquia

One of Colombia's largest provinces, Antioquia stretches from the Caribbean coast down through the Andean mountains, and east into the lush Magdalena Medio Valley. Antioquia's inhabitants, known as paisas, talk with a distinctly singsong accent and are famously vivacious and entrepreneurial. There's a joke in Colombia that any town you go to in the world, there will always be a paisa with a business there. This ambition has manifested itself with world famous artists like painter Fernando Botero and writer Fernando Vallejo. It has also produced the most famous drug trafficker in world history: Pablo Escobar, chief of the Medellín cartel.

Escobar was based out of Medellín, Antioquia's capital, the second largest city in Colombia. Beginning in the late 1970s and early 1980s, Escobar and his Medellín cartel associates invested their fortunes from the drug trade in vast land holdings throughout the country, including the Magdalena Medio Valley. They organized private armies to protect their riches and eliminate guerrillas, who threatened them with kidnapping and extortion. The creation of one of these death squads in 1981—Muerte a

Secuestradores (Death to Kidnappers)—marked the beginning of Colombia's modern day paramilitary movement.

By the early 1990s, Escobar was on the run from rival traffickers, paramilitaries, Colombian security forces, the U.S. Drug Enforcement Administration, Delta Force commandos and the CIA. Escobar was ultimately gunned down in Medellín in 1993, and his former business associates-turned-enemies—including Fidel, Vicente and Carlos Castaño, and Diego Murillo, alias Don Berna—inherited the capo's criminal enterprise and expanded paramilitary operations throughout Antioquia and the country. Between 1996 and 2007, fighting between paramilitaries, guerrillas, and government forces, as well as the atrocities committed by all three, displaced more than 300,000 people in Antioquia—more than any other province during that period. Many of the displaced flocked to Medellín, populating the poor neighborhoods—known as comunas—that hug the hills overlooking the city. By the late 1990s, the FARC's urban militias and paramilitaries had converted Medellín's comunas into fiercely contested battlegrounds.

In 2003 and 2005, nearly 3,000 supposed members of Medellín's main paramilitary blocs participated in disarmament ceremonies. The city's homicide rate dropped precipitously. Medellín, the one-time murder capital of the world, was heralded as emblematic of Colombia's success in overcoming conflict. However, the Medellín demobilizations were essentially a media show. The relative peace established in Medellín appears to have actually been the result of Don Berna's monopoly on crime in the city following the demobilization. When the Colombian government extradited Don Berna to the U.S. to face drug trafficking charges in 2008, rival armed factions fought to fill the power vacuum, and the number of homicides spiked.

Meanwhile, in other regions of Antioquia such as Bajo Cauca and Anorí, in the north, guerrillas and neo-paramilitaries, fuelled by coca production and gold mining, have contributed to the province becoming the nation's leader in forced displacement. In 2011, the government reported more than 29,170 newly displaced in that year alone.

CARMEN RODRÍGUEZ

AGE: *50*

OCCUPATION: *Cook*

HOMETOWN: *Anorí, Antioquia*

INTERVIEWED IN: *Cúcuta, Norte de Santander[1]*

A single mother, Carmen Rodríguez raised her five children in a Medellín neighborhood built by world-famous drug trafficker Pablo Escobar. Beginning in 2005, a neighborhood gang linked to one of Colombia's most powerful criminal organizations started harassing her college-student son and his friends. The threats escalated until 2009, when Carmen's entire family—along with dozens of other community members—were forced to flee the neighborhood. After the gang tracked down one of her sons and murdered him, Carmen spearheaded a criminal investigation against the killers who had terrorized her neighborhood for years. She and her family now live in hiding under the Attorney General's office's witness protection program.

All names in this narrative, except those of the narrator and other central figures, have been changed.

---

[1] Cúcuta is a false location employed for the safety of the narrator.

LOVE AND TRANQUILITY REIGNED

My life began in 1961 when I was born in Medellín into a poor home with a lot of love. My mom was a teacher and my dad was a farmer. As I understand it, I brought a lot of happiness to the family, since I was the first child.

Soon after I was born, my mom's teaching post was transferred to a town called Anorí, in Antioquia province. I love that town. If people ask where I'm from, I say Anorí. My dad got a farm there and also ran a bar in town. My parents adopted a girl when I was seven years old and had another girl the next year. Even though we were very poor, love and tranquility reigned.

When I was about twelve years old, a guerrilla war flared up in town. Anorí became completely militarized; it was full of army soldiers, and there were helicopters in the sky. I thought it was the best—being twelve years old and seeing yourself surrounded by so many men. In order to talk with the soldiers I would tell my mom that I was going to the noon mass, when I really was going straight to the ice cream parlor to talk to soldiers.

A lot of people died. Around that time the army killed the Vásquez Castaño brothers, who were the top leaders of the guerrilla group there.[2] The army brought the mother of the two into town to identify the bodies of her sons. But out of pure pride, the mother said that they weren't her sons. Everyone in the town said, "How valiant of that woman, what pride!" But I thought, *Even if my son was a bad man, if they brought him to me dead, I would say he was mine and cry over him.*

The army didn't bury the Vásquez Castaño brothers. They tied them up, hung them from a helicopter and dropped them into the jungle. That was in 1973 and I can still see in my mind how the helicopter took off with the two cadavers tied to it. I told my friend, who was a sergeant in the army,

---

[2] Manuel and Antonio Vásquez Castaño were commanders of the National Liberation Army (ELN), Colombia's second largest left-wing guerrilla group. They were killed by the army in 1973.

"How horrible. What would it have cost to take a few planks and bury them there in the cemetery?" I still have the memory of war.

THE QUEEN OF A PALACE

In 1977, when I was sixteen years old, I ran away with a boyfriend to Medellín, which was about eight hours away by car. I started living at my aunt's house there, and my boyfriend left me to seek adventures in Portugal. After he left I found out that I was pregnant and had my son Jonatan. My mom asked for a job transfer to Medellín and I went to live with my mom and dad at my grandparents' house with my mom's brother's family.

When Jonatan was about seven months old, his father returned to Medellín. He called and asked me if I had a baby and I said yes. He said he wanted to meet him, and that day I became pregnant with my daughter Lorenza.

My family supported me a lot and around 1979 I graduated from a technical training program in secretarial work. Then I entered the SENA[3] and took a course where I learned how to make shoes. When I finished the course, a friend found me work at a shoe factory. I started to work there and made the minimum wage.

There were a lot of people living in my grandparents' house because my uncle lived there with his wife, mother-in-law, and four kids. So we started having problems. One day when my uncle's kids saw my son walking towards my uncle's room, they slammed the door and crushed all his fingers. That was awful for me; I lived for my children.

Soon after that incident, I was sweeping outside of the house and heard some neighbors talking. They were saying that a government program was going to give money to the people who lived in Medellín's trash dump so that they could buy a house. I told my cousin Clara, "Let's go live in

---

[3] The SENA is a public technical training school in Colombia.

the trash dump so that they give us a house." She said, "Ay, no! I couldn't do that." I said, "Let's go Clara! You want to stay here struggling your whole life? When are you going to have the opportunity to buy a house?" The next day we went to see the trash dump. It was a hill of pure garbage. About five hundred families were living there in houses made out of wood or plastic sheets. They were people who had been displaced from their towns during other eras and who had come to Medellín with nothing, nothing, nothing. There wasn't a place where you could stick a shovel and dig out dirt. Black water that looked like petroleum flowed by. Flies, rats. My cousin was more delicate than me and said, "Ay! We're not going to bring our kids to live here." I encouraged her, "The kids won't die here. Look at that kid over there. He's chubbier than our kids! I've been taught that people are creatures of habit. There are people capable of living here, and we're no different than them."

I pawned a gold necklace the father of my children had given me, and we used the money to buy two housing lots at the trash dump for 3,000 and 2,000 pesos[4] each, hire two workers, and build two houses for me and my cousin. My house was lovely. I felt like the queen of a palace in that shack. I had a place where I could invite my friends and I was never embarrassed to say that I lived among the trash. Jonatan and Lorenza stayed with my parents during the week when I worked at the factory, and I would take them to stay with me on Saturdays and Sundays.

One Thursday around 1982, two shacks burned down at the trash dump. A lady had gone to work and locked her three kids inside. The kids burned to death. At around seven at night trucks arrived with blankets, cooking pots, groceries, and potable water. People said a man had sent the trucks, but we thought, *What man?*

On Friday someone said over a megaphone that there was an urgent meeting on top of the trash dump, and that a man was going to speak to us. At the meeting, a man in a T-shirt and blue jeans said that he had seen

---

[4] Approximately U.S.$64 and U.S.$42 in 1980.

the tragedy the day before, and that he hadn't been able to sleep since. He told us that it had broken his heart to see that there were a lot of people with money in Medellín, and in the entire world, but that there were also people who didn't possess anything. He said that the trash dump was going to disappear. It was the man that a lot of people don't love, but who I adore. His name was Pablo Escobar.[5]

About two weeks later, Pablo's representative came back with cars and buses and took us to the place where we were all going to live. It was a farm in the hills of Medellín. At the time there were only two houses there. I said, *This is the paradise that God promised*, because it was a beautiful farm. A month or two later they took us back to the farm and showed us the model of the house that we were going to live in. It was six meters by sixteen meters and had two big bedrooms, a big dining room, kitchen, bathroom, and backyard.

When they were building the houses, we were told that the elections were coming up for Congress, and that the man who was helping us—Pablo—was going to run to help the poor.[6] They asked if we could help with a vote. I asked my dad, "Can you help me by voting for a guy who's going to give me a house?" He said, "I hope you're not going to make me vote for a Conservative."[7] Later the news came on and said that Pablo Escobar was running for the Liberal Party. So my dad agreed to vote for him.

---

[5] Colombia's most famous drug trafficker, Pablo Escobar co-founded and ran the Medellín Cartel.

[6] In 1982, Pablo Escobar was elected as an alternate member of the House of Representatives.

[7] The Liberal and Conservative parties were Colombia's two main political parties until the 2000s. Between roughly 1948 and 1958, the rival parties had fought in a civil conflict known as La Violencia, which took some 200,000 lives, and evolved into the modern day conflict.

When the Community Action Board[8] from the trash dump selected which families would go to live in the new houses, I was told that I couldn't go. Someone had told the board that I didn't need a place because my mom already lived in a house and the father of my children owned a car, and the homes were supposed to be for poor people. There was a man on the board named Iván who always used to flirt with me. He had a wife and I've always avoided married men. But the day that they told me I couldn't have a house, I went to Iván's store and told him that I wasn't going to be given a place. He told me, "If someday we get houses, you're going to get one."

About two years later, in May 1984, the board gave me a card saying that they'd give me house number 185. I went and when I saw 185 on the door, I sat down on the ground to cry. I said, "My God! When was I ever going to be able to buy a house like this?" My mom and dad had worked their whole lives and didn't even own a house, so I knew that it was impossible to have one when you're only twenty-three years old. That's where my life started. My life split in two—before I had my house and after.

PEOPLE STARTED TO MODERNIZE

Iván didn't give me the house for free. He "charged" me for it: our daughter Emma was born in January 1985. Three months after Emma was born, Iván was killed in Montelíbano, Córdoba. I met another man who was a relative of a friend of mine who lived in the neighborhood. He moved into my house quickly and I had my son Reinsson in October 1986. My son Carlos was born in 1989 and I got married in 1991.

There's been violence in the neighborhood ever since it was founded. We lived through the gang of "macheteros." They were called that be-

---

[8] Community Action Boards are small civil organizations that represent villages, communities, and neighborhoods. Each board has a president who is elected to a three-year term.

cause they didn't have revolvers then and killed with machetes. Then other gangs starting killing with traucos, which are homemade guns. In the end, people started to modernize and would go around with machine guns. There were FARC[9] guerrillas and paramilitaries[10] in other parts of Medellín, but never in our neighborhood.

I worked as a cook in restaurants and kept busy with my kids. In 1996 I had two hard blows: my dad died and I got separated from my husband because he had a little girlfriend who lived close to our house. From that year on I've been alone with my five kids and focused on raising them and having them study.

THAT'S WHERE THE PROBLEMS BEGAN

Around 2004 Medellín's mayor's office started a program called Plan Disarm. My son Reinsson was about seventeen years old then and told me, "Mom, if you hand in a weapon, the mayor's office will help you go to college. What do you think?" I said, "But did you check that you just hand over the weapon, and that it doesn't hurt your record?" He said, "You don't have to be a paramilitary, you don't need to belong to a gang, you don't need anything. You just need to hand over the weapon and you have the right to a scholarship."

Stupidly thinking that I was looking out for his interests, I told him, "Pawn the television and buy a weapon." We bought a revolver at a pawnshop. Reinsson and some of his friends went to the Plan Disarm ceremony and handed over the guns. The church and bishop were there and it was a very nice ceremony. Two months later, Reinsson had a spot and full scholarship at Remington College.

---

[9] The Revolutionary Armed Forces of Colombia (FARC) is the largest left-wing guerrilla group in Colombia.

[10] Right-wing paramilitary groups began to form in Colombia in the early 1980s with the purported aim of fighting left-wing guerrillas. Backed by the military, landowners, drug traffickers, and political and economic elites, they murdered tens of thousands of civilians.

That's where the problems began: when the real members of the Pablo Escobar neighborhood gang became aware of the program, they went to the mayor's office to look for benefits. And an official at the mayor's office told the gang members that they couldn't have the benefits because there were some guys from Pablo Escobar neighborhood who had already received them. The person from the mayor's office read the names of Reinsson and his friends to the gang members one by one. The gang members were furious and went to look for them.

The guy who looked for Reinsson was a policeman by day and a member of the Pablo Escobar gang by night. I was with Reinsson when the policeman told him, as if he were about to hit him, "You're getting benefits from the mayor's office for being from the gang? When have you picked up a gun? When have you fought for this neighborhood?" So Reinsson told him, "I'm not interested in taking over the neighborhood or fighting for the neighborhood. The only thing I did was make use of the program so that I can go to college. And in fact, I already started studying." The policeman left, but Reinsson and his friends got scared.

In 2005, right after my son started studying, the gang members participated in the Héroes de Granada[11] paramilitary bloc demobilization ceremony. They went to demobilize in the municipality of San Roque and came back even fiercer because the government paid them and they could arm themselves even more.[12]

In Pablo Escobar neighborhood, it used to be that the bad people would only kill each other. But this gang decided to kill all the young workers, all the good boys who studied, everyone, just because they wouldn't join them. The gang members had been my children's class-

---

[11] The Héroes de Granada was a paramilitary group that operated in the Medellín area and had close links to neighborhood gangs in the city.

[12] The Héroes de Granada demobilized in August 2005. Demobilized members received benefits from the government, including monthly stipends, in exchange for participating in demobilization ceremonies, pledging to cease criminal activities, and entering reintegration programs.

mates. They didn't like to work, they didn't like to study, they liked the easy life.

Someone who used to belong to the gang says the Envigado Office[13] used to pay them to kill people. The gang would look for the people, take them to an abandoned school in the neighborhood, chop their bodies into pieces, and bury them there. It's also said that the gang would take girls to the school and rape them. They were usually girls they liked—or the girlfriends of the guys they had it in for. The gang was bad, bad, bad.

WE DON'T WANT YOU IN THE NEIGHBORHOOD

Reinsson studied public accounting at Remington College and was doing excellently; the dean of the college always congratulated me. Reinsson had to maintain a B+ average to keep the scholarship, and he got an A- average. They raised the requirement to an A- and he got an A average. They never took the scholarship away.

Reinsson bettered himself and bettered himself, and he liked to save and save and buy things. The young girls in the neighborhood liked that a lot. My mom gave him a car and he would give rides to people, including the gang members' little girlfriends. So there started to be distrust and it fed his problems with the gang.

In 2008, during his last semester of college, Reinsson got a job working as an accountant at a hospital in Medellín. At that point, we were living in a house with eight separate apartments. I lived in one, my mom had one, my sister had one, Carlos and Reinsson each had one, my eldest son Jonatan lived in one with his wife and five-year-old son, and my daughter Lorenza lived in one with her husband and eight- and nine-year-old girls. Emma had left to live in Spain around January 2008 and we rented her apartment out.

---

[13] The Envigado Office (Oficina de Envigado) is an organization that provides assassination and enforcement services to organized crime in Medellín. It has maintained close ties to paramilitary groups and neo-paramilitary organizations.

When Reinsson started studying at Remington, he had also started a dance club in the basement of our house. A lot of people would go and he was very good at managing money; he knew how to spend each peso. We took in about 2 million pesos[14] every weekend, which is a lot of sales for a poor neighborhood.

The gang members wanted to go to the club as well, but didn't want to pay. And they wouldn't take their girlfriends or wives to the club. Rather, they wanted to go the hard way—they wanted to dance with and share the women that the other clients were with. I'd always be there and wouldn't go to bed on Saturdays and Sundays because I knew that there was a latent danger. I'd let everyone know when the gang was showing up and we'd put Reinsson in the DJ room and I would attend to the customers with Lorenza and Reinsson's girlfriend.

One time some gang members went to the club to show their machine guns. They were going to kill my son's friend Jackson there—I don't know what it was over. I stood between the gang leader who everyone called Tabique, with his machine gun, and Jackson. They said, "We're going to kill Jackson." I said, "Ay, no, no, no, you're not going to kill him, you're not going to kill him." I grabbed Tabique and took him outside. He said that it wasn't me he had problems with and got on his motorcycle and left.

About three weeks later, when Reinsson came home from work at the hospital, he asked me, "Mom, where's Carlos?" Carlos was about nineteen at the time. I said, "I saw him going to the park." He said, "Mom, go get him." I could tell that he was worried. I told him, "I'm not going until you tell me what happened." He told me, "They just killed Jackson's little brother. They thought he was Jackson because he was riding on Jackson's motorcycle." I went to get Carlos at the park, where he was exercising. About eight gang members were there with scarves covering their faces and hats on, but they didn't do anything. I got Carlos and took him home.

---

[14] About U.S.$1,000.

I was so worried about my sons that I sent Reinsson to go live with my aunt in another neighborhood in Medellín, and Carlos to live with my brother-in-law in a different neighborhood. Reinsson would call me every day, crying, "Mom, my aunt's food is doing me harm. I miss you so much, Mom." We started looking and looking to see where we could all move.

On February 28, 2009, after living with his aunt for about two weeks, Reinsson found a house for our whole family to move into in Castilla, a different neighborhood in Medellín. The day he found the house, he was waiting for me with his girlfriend downtown. He was going to hand me the keys to the place so that I could clean it. He told me that as he was waiting, one of the heads of the gang passed down the street in his car and saw Reinsson. He stopped the car and said, "What?" Reinsson stood up to him and said, "What do you mean, 'what'?" and the gang leader drove on.

After cleaning the new house, I went back to our house in Pablo Escobar neighborhood. I had packed everything in the house into bags to get ready to move to the new house. I didn't tell anyone in the neighborhood that we were going to leave.

That evening a neighbor of mine came to the house and told me, "Someone who I respect a lot had me tell you to watch out for Reinsson, because the head of the gang knows where he hangs out. He saw him four hours ago." I thought, *This is really serious.* I called the movers to have them pick us up at six in the morning the following day to take us to the new house. That night I told my mom, softly, "Mom, we have to leave here tomorrow." She said, "I'm not leaving." I said, "Mom, things are very serious, we really have to leave." She said, "Let them kill me here." I cried with sadness, *I have to leave my house and my mom's not going to leave.*

At eleven at night we were all in bed when I heard a little noise at the front gate. I thought, *Oh my God, they're coming in.* I got out of bed and saw that there was a piece of paper underneath the front door. I picked it up: SONS OF BITCHES. LEAVE UNLESS YOU WANT US TO KILL YOU. WE DON'T WANT YOU IN THE NEIGHBORHOOD. WE'LL HAVE NO MERCY ON KIDS OR THE ELDERLY. It was signed by the Envigado Office.

I heard a knock at the door at about 1:30 a.m. It was Jonatan's wife, who lived in the apartment next door. She had just gotten home from work and said, "Carmen, Carmen, look what I found under my door." It was the same note. I called Reinsson, who was at my aunt's house. He told me, "When the moving van arrives tomorrow morning, call the police so that they give you protection to leave the house."

At six in the morning my sister showed up and said, "Look what I found underneath my door." It was the same threat. A little later the moving van arrived. Since each one of us had our different apartment in the house with their own things, we had seven refrigerators, seven stoves, and seven dish sets. We chose the newest one of each to take with us in one trip.

Reinsson called and asked if I had asked for protection. I told him that two policemen had shown up. He said to check their vests to see if they came from the Villatina police station. I told him that they came from there and he said, "Ay, no Mom. They're all friends with the gang. We can't show them where we're going to live." So he called the head of the Villatina station and told him that the police from Villatina couldn't escort me, because all of them are bought off by the gangs. We ended up having the police escort us halfway to the new house, and then waited for them to leave before we drove to the house.

The house we moved to in Castilla had five rooms for Reinsson, Carlos, Lorenza, her husband and two daughters, Jonatan, his wife and son, and me. My mom had stayed in our other house, but two weeks after we moved she got scared because someone knocked at her door during a shootout in the neighborhood. So Reinsson found her a different apartment in Medellín that she moved into. When I went to the house to help her move, the guys from the gang died of laughter. They saw the moving truck and said, "Those were the last ones left to leave."

I WON'T HAVE TIME TO CRY

We filed a complaint for threats at the Attorney General's office in Medellín. I told the prosecutor that the people responsible were a gang of demobilized paramilitaries, gave him their addresses, and brought him a picture of one of the leaders. We went to the office every day to see how the investigation was going, because they wouldn't call us. They didn't call any of the other people from the neighborhood who had been displaced either. One day I told the prosecutor, "This is horrible. These threats aren't just some little thing, they were sent by the Envigado Office. Do you know the strength that they have? We're hiding and we know that at any moment they'll find us because the office rules all of these neighborhoods. Where can we hide where they won't find us?" He responded, "Ask God to make sure they don't find you." That was the solution that the prosecutor gave us.

Many of Reinsson's friends had also been forced to leave the neighborhood. When we started living in the new house, Reinsson would tell me, "My friend called to tell me that he's sitting in the park and has no place to go. What can we do, Mom? Should I tell him to come live with us?" I'd say, "Ay, my son, okay." His friends were boys I had known since they were in their mothers' wombs. I ended up taking in five of his friends to live with us.

The gang kept looking for Reinsson because they knew that more than forty young men had left the neighborhood. And in the neighborhood there's a custom that a gang makes a ton of people leave, and those people get together, arm themselves, and return to kill the people who had made them leave the neighborhood. It's something historic that's happened for years. The gang leader thought that the young men followed Reinsson and that he was going to lead them to take revenge against the gang. Reinsson had friends from the neighborhood who would tell him, "I'll get your enemy off your back and whack him." But Reinsson would always say, "No man, we're not going to stoop to their level."

We had been living in the new house for two months, when Reinsson came home one day and I could see on his face that something had happened. He told me that the doorman at the hospital where he worked had told him that some people had gone to the hospital twice to ask for the owner of Reinsson's yellow motorcycle. Someone had also asked what time the owner of the motorcycle left work. The doorman told him not to leave work on the motorcycle because he was being followed. So Reinsson left his motorcycle there, exited through a different door from the hospital and took a taxi home.

Reinsson sold his motorcycle and bought another bigger one. When he came home with that motorcycle I told him, "Reinsson, how could you think of buying such a showy bike? Can't you see the problems that we're in?" He told me, "No one will catch me on this bike." He said that after selling his first bike he had to buy a better one. I told him, "That's what's killing us. That's what's caused the envy and ire of everyone in the neighborhood." My son had that flaw, he would always tell me, "Mom, you can't be mediocre, you can't descend."

By early May 2009, Reinsson had three weeks left until he graduated from college. He would tell me, "Mom, let's move to Cali. But give me a month so that I have my diploma, and I know that wherever I go I can look for work as a professional." He became so worried that his hair began to fall out. He couldn't even tolerate having a scar; he was so proud, proud, proud. He went to see a dermatologist, who told him that it was because of stress. Reinsson didn't like telling anyone what was going on so he told the doctor, "I'm in the last semester of college." The doctor said, "You have the stress of having to write a thesis, it happens to all of us." He prescribed him some creams.

On May 7, 2009, I went to show our old house to someone who was interested in renting it. As I was going out I saw my son sitting on his bed, reading through the phonebook, and calling pharmacy to pharmacy to see where he could buy the cheapest cream for his scalp. I left, and my cell phone rang as I was arriving at my house in Pablo Escobar neighborhood. It was Lorenza's husband. He said, "Carmen, where are you? Reinsson is wounded." I got in a taxi and thought, *My God, my boy's going to have a horrible scar. He'll be so frustrated with his scar.* My daughter Emma was still living in Spain then and I thought, *Emma will take him to Spain and he can have the surgeries there.*

We were arriving at the corner of our block when I saw yellow tape surrounding my house. That's when I got a sinking feeling: *They don't block things off like that for a wounded person.* But then I went back to thinking, *They must have done it so that they can investigate.* When I got to the house, all the neighbors were watching me from their balconies. I went into the house and asked, "What happened?" My grandchildren came up to me and said, "They killed Reinsson."

I said, "No, they wounded him." My daughter-in-law said, "No Carmen, they called from the hospital to say that he died." That's when I grabbed the policemen and asked, "Where's my son? Where'd you take him?" They told me what hospital he was in so I got in a taxi and went. The whole time I didn't think about how much I was going to miss Reinsson, because you don't know what you haven't lived. What I had was a thirst for vengeance that invaded me and invaded me and invaded me.

When I got to the hospital, I asked the doorman where the morgue was. I was relaxed. I don't know why I had so much strength, I didn't cry like other mothers who scream with despair. He said, "The morgue's over there but you can't go in because the CTI[15] police investigators haven't come yet." I said, "The CTI didn't give birth to my son." I went towards the door to the morgue and he tried to grab me. I told him, "I don't want to see him cold, I don't want to see him cold. I'm going to see him now." I grabbed the door to the morgue, gave it a push, opened it, and my son was there on a counter.

I felt him still warm. I hugged him and kissed him and told him, "My son, I promise you that I won't cry. I won't have time to cry, because I promise you right here that the people who did this to you are going to pay. You didn't deserve this, you were a very good son, a very good brother, and a very good friend. I promise you, son, that the rest of the days that God gives me I'll use to make sure that the people who did this to you pay, but not with blood."

I looked at his face and his head and didn't see blood anywhere. His clothes were clean, his shoes were clean; he didn't have a drop of blood.

---

[15] The Technical Investigative Corps (CTI) is an entity attached to the Attorney General's office, and charged with providing investigative and forensic support in criminal cases.

I thought, *What'd they do to him? Why's he dead if he's so clean? Could it be that he's not dead?* Then I lifted up his shirt and saw an enormous hole in his heart.

SHE COULDN'T SHUT THE DOOR

Later, my family told me how it had happened. After I had left for the house, Reinsson left for the university at 5:30 p.m. He used to mount his motorcycle in the living room with his helmet on so that no one would see his face outside. So Lorenza's nine-year-old daughter had to open the front door for him. She says that when he went outside he ducked his head. She looked toward the street and saw a taxi with some guys. And that's when the shooting started.

Lorenza grabbed her daughter and told her to go into the back room of the house, which was farthest away from the window. But instead she went up to the window in the first room that looked out onto the street. My granddaughter says that she saw when Reinsson fell off his motorcycle, and that when he fell, the motorcycle fell on top of him. She was able to see Tabique, the gang leader. My son Jonatan and his wife took their kids to the back room and were yelling at Lorenza to shut the front door. But Lorenza couldn't shut the door. She'd shut it and open it because she knew that they were shooting at her little brother outside.

THIS WAS A DEATH FORETOLD

After Reinsson's murder, the family started to see where we could hold the wake. The place that seemed safest to us was in the vigil room at the cemetery. My daughter Emma sent me money from Spain so that we could keep him in the vigil room for three days until she arrived and we could bury him.

We arrived at the vigil room on May 8, the day after Reinsson was killed. I called the police to see if they'd provide us with protection while we waited for my daughter to arrive from Spain. They said that they couldn't because there was a lot of work to do and they couldn't have a policeman stay in one place the whole night. So we said, "Fine, you can't provide us with protection? Then we'll lock ourselves in." I had the people who ran the vigil room give us the keys so that we could lock ourselves inside.

My kids, mom, sister, and some of Reinsson's friends who had already fled Pablo Escobar neighborhood, were there with us. The gang warned people in the neighborhood that whoever went to Reinsson's wake would have to leave the neighborhood, so the few people who went were the ones who were ready to leave. People from the neighborhood called to tell us that the gang was celebrating there. And we also received calls in the vigil room from the gang telling us that my son Jonatan was next, that Carlos was next, that we were all next.

We spent the night locked in there. Early the next morning a factory owner died. He was a personal friend of the president at the time, Álvaro Uribe, so the cemetery filled up with truckloads of soldiers and policemen and armored cars. The vigil room for the factory owner was right next to my son's.

That day Emma arrived from Spain and more of our friends and family began to show up. The people who were visiting the dead factory owner started to see people arrive in our vigil room who weren't very high class. Five policemen came and said that the people next door felt threatened because there were strange people in our room. They started searching all of the women's bags. When I saw them lifting up the top of Reinsson's casket to see if there were weapons inside, I stood up and said, "Don't touch the casket. We're from a different class, but the dead person in their room and the dead person I have here deserve the same respect. Last night when we called to ask for protection—for you to send just one policeman to watch out for us here—you didn't send any. But today there are enough police for protection and even to search us."

A psychologist from the mayor's office was at the wake. She had worked with Reinsson after he participated in the disarmament program. She told me, "Carmen, I'm very sorry. Know that you have a friend and support in me." I told her, "Eva, don't feel sorry. You know how you can feel sorry?

Since you work with the mayor, get me a meeting with him tomorrow. I need to talk to him." That night everyone slept in the chairs in the vigil room.

The psychologist called me on Sunday, May 10, when we were still in the vigil room, and told me to go to the mayor's office the next day at eight in the morning. I said, "I'll be grateful to you for the rest of my life." I told everyone who was there at the vigil room: "I'll be waiting for everyone who's been displaced tomorrow at the plaza of the mayor's office at eight in the morning. Because things can't go on like this." We were all used to having two people killed every week in the neighborhood, and nothing would happen.

We buried Reinsson at four in the afternoon on Sunday. People started to leave, but I said, "Where are we going to sleep?" The young men who had stayed with me in the house in Castilla had already found an apartment. One of them told me, "Carmen, we're living in a tiny apartment. But even if we have to all sit, we'll all fit in there." So we all went to the apartment and that night about eighteen of us slept on the floor of one room.

Forty-seven people showed up outside of the mayor's office at eight in the morning the next day. The mayor didn't show his face, but the mayor's assistant and representatives from the Inspector General's office, police, and Social Action[16] were there.

My son's friend Antonio showed up with a black trash bag and said to the officials, "This little plastic bag has been with me for two months since they made me leave my house. I have three pairs of socks and this underwear. It's everything I have and every night I have to hug it so that it's not stolen from me, because I have no place to sleep. I have a three-story house in the neighborhood and have no place to sleep because those people won't let me go there."

---

[16] The government entity entrusted with coordinating assistance to the displaced population, to the poor, and to victims of violence. Social Action was replaced by the Department for Social Prosperity in 2012.

I asked everyone who was there, "Raise your hand if you're willing to denounce what you've seen, what you've lived." Everyone raised their hands. Right then an official from the Personería[17] of Medellín told the police, "Never have I seen a community so prepared and dedicated to having peace and justice in their neighborhood."

I said, "We're going to trade information in exchange for protection." At eight at night the Personería official told us that he'd take us to a shelter to stay in while the Attorney General's office looked for a place for us to go into the witness protection program.

That night forty of us arrived at the shelter for displaced people. There were one hundred people there in total, including many displaced people from Urabá. The first night they put all forty of the people I arrived with in a three-by-two-meter room. After a few days, some buses came and took the other displaced people to a different shelter, and we each got our own room.

The one good thing about the shelter is that we had police standing at the door. At the plaza of the mayor's office I had told the head of the police, "I don't mean to generalize, but I know that various members of the police are complicit with the gangs. Please give us protection with a group of police that is from outside of Medellín." And they did send us a group of police that had recently graduated from police school.

About three days after Reinsson's death I went back to the Attorney General's office where we had reported the threats. I was furious with the prosecutor because he had told me to pray to God that they wouldn't find us. So I told him, "Well, our prayers didn't work, they found us and they killed my son. Could it be that now you can pay attention to what I'm denouncing?" The Attorney General's office changed the prosecutor for the case.

The SIJIN[18] set up an office in my room in the shelter. In spite of their fear of the gang, my neighbors from Pablo Escobar neighborhood sup-

---

[17] The Personería is a municipal entity charged with monitoring human rights and citizens' rights.

[18] The Sectional Judicial Police (SIJIN) is a branch of the national police force.

ported me and the SIJIN agents when I asked them to come to the shelter to give a statement. We got forty-five people to give testimony against Tabique, the head of the gang. People from the neighborhood would call and tell me where he was. And I'd call the police investigator with that information.

About two, three weeks after being in the shelter, I had a lot of free time. I thought, *At the house there's a paper Reinsson wrote in college. It was so nice, I'm going to go look for it.* The police accompanied me to my house and I found the papers. When I began to read them, I realized, *This was a death foretold.*

It was an autobiography that he had written in 2005 during his first semester in school. It read, "I love my neighborhood so much, maybe because it's the only one I know... The only way I'll leave this neighborhood is in four planks of wood... I'm going to show some poetry from one of my greatest idols. He's the deceased rapper Tupac Shakur. I identify with him because ever since I was a kid I've always looked for the truth, liberty, and above all else, respect for others and myself. My ideals and goals have always been very clear to me." The poem that he liked is called *And 2morrow.*

I'M GOING TO CUT YOU UP INTO PIECES

The authorities put Tabique on the Colombian police's most wanted poster,[19] with a reward of 50 million pesos[20] for information about his whereabouts. That's a lot of money in a poor neighborhood; even your own mother will turn you in for that much. In June 2009, Tabique turned himself in to the authorities. Lorenza's nine-year-old daughter testified at the trial. She said that she remembered the men shooting at her uncle and that she saw when Reinsson fell off the motorcycle. When she went

---

[19] Jhon Jairo Jaramillo Pérez, alias Tabique, was included in the Colombian police's list of the forty most wanted criminals in the Medellín metropolitan area.

[20] About U.S. $25,000.

to go pick him up, they shot at her as well. The prosecutor asked her if she knew who shot at him, and she said, "Yes, Tabique." Then she started to cry. The prosecutor asked why the loss of her uncle had affected her so much and she said that she loved her uncle a lot.

Tabique threatened us during the middle of the trial. He said, "We're going to kill all of you, all of you." His lawyer told him, "Be quiet, this could bring repercussions." But he said to my daughter Lorenza, who was right in front of him, "No, we're going to kill all of you."

My son's friend Antonio had helped a lot by testifying. Around July 2009, the gang saw him when he was leaving the shelter, followed him and killed him that night. He left a two-year-old daughter behind. We used to call him Toño and the whole night of his wake his daughter stayed below his casket saying, "Toño, Toño, Toño, Toño."

On September 18, 2009, there was a massive arrest of twenty-two members of the gang. The police investigator told me to go to the neighborhood to help him find the people who had arrest warrants out against them. Once the people from the neighborhood saw me there, they'd call me and tell me where the gang members were hiding. That's how the police were able to make many of the arrests.

At one point, the police entered a house twice to look for one of the gang members. The police investigator told me, "He's not there, Carmen." But people were calling me and telling me that he was still in the house. So the investigator said, "You go in and look." When I entered the house, the mattresses were on the floor, the beds were destroyed. They'd searched everywhere and he wasn't there. I went to the kitchen with a SIJIN agent and saw a trash can flipped upside down. I thought, *How strange,* and grabbed the trash can. The guy was inside of it.

The SIJIN took the guy down to the street and he was really mad. He kicked at me and kicked at me and said, "When I get out I'm going to kill you, I'm going to cut you up into pieces."

The arrest that made me most proud and happy was of one of the leaders of the gang. He's the one who had kidnapped a twelve-year-old girl from school, brought her to an apartment and kept her as a sex slave.

He had had her locked up there for a week and would take clients there who raped her. The girl later told me, "Sometimes they brought me food, and sometimes they didn't. But they'd bring me clients every day."

VERY FEW MOTHERS IN THIS COUNTRY

On October 10, 2009, after living at shelters for five months, my family was accepted into the witness protection program—me, my children, their spouses, and my grandchildren. The SIJIN didn't tell us where they were going to take us. We didn't know whether to bring clothes for warm weather or cold weather.

The protection program officials took us to Bogotá. Most people from Medellín live with their doors open. If we're going to have a coffee, we call our neighbor, "Come on over and have a coffee." One of my first days in Bogotá I went to sweep outside of our house and one of our neighbors passed by. I said, "Good morning." She didn't respond.

I started to work at a restaurant that sold grilled chicken. The woman who owned the place paid me well. Working there was one of the few things I liked about Bogotá, because life isn't good there. It's horribly cold, and people don't like to talk there.

I asked many times for the program to move us to a different location, and on April 1, 2010, they sent us to Cúcuta. The people from the witness protection program check in on us twice a week at our house where I'm living with Emma, her daughter, and Carlos. Everyone has to be in the house by six at night.

I feel fortunate compared to other families that have had their losses or who have been displaced, and who may have to beg at traffic lights to survive. What weighs down on me most is knowing that I don't have my own house. I've tried to rent out our house in Pablo Escobar neighborhood many times. But the twenty-two gang members who've been arrested have brothers, sons, and uncles who are furious with us. The only way that they have to get revenge is to not let us rent the house. So people have gone to the house and wanted to rent it, but a neighbor will go up to them and say, "Aren't you afraid? A bomb will be placed in that house."

On June 17, 2010, Tabique was sentenced to fifty years in prison for Reinsson's murder. That was the day I cried most, when I cried like I should have cried when I saw my son in the morgue. Tabique's reign had lasted for ten years, until we got him. A lot of time will pass in which nobody will die at his hands. A lot of time will pass in which a mother doesn't have to suffer what I suffered.

Knowing that my son's death didn't go unpunished has given me a lot of strength. There are very few mothers in this country who can say that less than a month after the death of their son, there were two people captured and others to be convicted.

When we get out of the witness protection program I don't know where we'll go to live. I watch the news to see which Colombian city doesn't seem very violent, and I haven't found it yet.

MARÍA VICTORIA JIMÉNEZ

AGE: *40*
OCCUPATION: *Bacteriologist*
HOMETOWN: *Medellín, Antioquia*
INTERVEIWED IN: *Bello, Antioquia*[1]

Colombia has long led the world in the killing of trade unionists. Since 1986, more than 2,900 trade unionists have been murdered, according to the National Labor School, the preeminent Colombian NGO monitoring labor rights.[2] While no one has been convicted for over 90 percent of the killings, it is widely believed that right-wing paramilitaries are the principal perpetrator of the slayings.

In 2007, María Victoria Jiménez was elected president of the hospital workers union in Santa Fe de Antioquia, a town just outside of Medellín. In 2008 and 2009 she reported a series of irregularities at the hospital, including labor harassment. As a member of a prominent family from Santa Fe, María Victoria felt shielded enough to make the complaints before the hospital's board of directors. Then, in September 2009, assassins tracked her down outside of her home and stabbed her seven times, slicing off part of her nose and upper lip. María

---

[1] Some locations in this narrative have been changed to protect the security of the narrator.

[2] This figure includes forty-seven in 2009, fifty-one in 2010, and thirty in 2011.

Victoria has had ten facial reconstructive surgeries since the attack. Neither the paramilitary-linked assailants nor the person she suspects of ordering her murder have been brought to justice. Today, she remains the president of her union, but lives in hiding because of constant fear of reprisals.

All names in this narrative, except María Victoria and Jaime Henao, have been changed.

WELL-BEHAVED AND STRAIGHT

Maybe if I'd participated more when I was a student, I'd have had a well-formed outlook about who people really are, and I would have better grasped evil. I wouldn't have committed as many errors as I have. I knew that people in Colombia killed, but I never thought that people I knew would be capable of going so far.

I was born in Sopetrán, Antioquia province, but I grew up in Medellín because my dad got a job there as a school treasurer. I have an older brother and a younger sister. I went to a convent school and I was well-behaved and straight. I was the one who the nuns loved.

In 1987, when I was sixteen, I began studying bacteriology at the University of Antioquia. University was terrifying to me—I was just a girl, and I didn't know anything about life then. The students there were always going on strike. Even though I was a leader among my friends, I tried to stay away from the strikes and student organizing. I'd often hear that the student assembly was meeting to discuss the university's problems, but for me, there weren't any problems there. I simply wanted to work hard and graduate.

I was twenty-one years old when I graduated from college as a bacteriologist. There were 120 students ahead of me on the waiting list for the mandatory rural internship in Antioquia province. So first I worked for a private blood lab in Puerto Berrío, Antioquia for seven months. In September 1993 I started writing letters to the health departments in Caquetá, Putumayo and Amazonas provinces. It was easier to get an internship in those places because they were considered dangerous; they had the reputation of being guerrilla[3] areas where you could get killed or kidnapped. A week after sending the letters, I received a call from the Caquetá health department asking if I wanted to go there. I was in a hurry to begin working and get ahead, so I told them I would go. I was assigned to do an internship in a little town called Belén de los Andaquies. I moved there in October 1993.

I went to Caquetá expecting to find a ton of guerrillas. And in fact, the guerrillas took siege of the town three times while I was there. They'd take over the park, and from the hospital you could hear their shootouts with the police. During Easter Week, about six months after I'd arrived, my sister came to visit me. On Thursday of Easter Week a rattle sounds off at church, and they turn the lights off. We went to church that day, and when they turned off the light and the rattle went off, we threw ourselves under our chairs. When they turned the lights back on we were so embarrassed!

Since Caquetá is considered a conflict zone, I was only required to do a six-month rural internship. But I ended up staying for a year and three months, until January 1995. I left Caquetá and in April 1995 I started working at the San Juan de Dios hospital in the town of Santa Fe de Antoquia.

NO ONE COULD SAY ANYTHING

Santa Fe de Antoquia, or Santa Fe, is where my mom's family is from, so when I first arrived, I lived at my grandfather's house with him and my Aunt Lilia. Several months later, my mom moved to Santa Fe, and she built a house two blocks from my grandfather's place. When it was finished, I started living there with her.

---

[3] Caquetá is a province in southern Colombia that has historically had a large guerrilla presence. The Revolutionary Armed Forces of Colombia (FARC) and National Liberation Army (ELN) are the two largest guerilla groups in Colombia. Founded in the 1960s and claiming to represent the country's rural poor in the fight against Colombia's wealthy classes and U.S. imperialism, both groups commit widespread abuses against civilians, includings killings, threats, and recruitment of child soldiers.

When I started working at the hospital, I joined the social welfare committee, which is in charge of the welfare of the employees, the staff parties at the end of the year, and classes that aren't related to work. At that time, the Santa Fe chapter of the National Association of Hospital Workers of Colombia (ANTHOC) union had more or less seventy members. But around 1997, paramilitaries[4] started threatening the members. The intention was for the workers to leave the unions and to lose all the rights they'd won in bargaining agreements. In 1998, the leader of the ANTHOC chapter in a nearby municipality was killed. When that happened, the president of the Santa Fe chapter quit the union; she told me she had to resign before she got killed too. By 2002, only three people remained in the union, and the Santa Fe chapter of ANTHOC was dissolved.

From then on, everything began to change. Management started taking away a lot of workers' bonuses, and they wouldn't let us take breaks. When we had staff meetings, no one could say anything; we had to listen to what the hospital manager had to say, and that was it. If you complained about something, the manager would immediately say, "Whoever isn't with me has to leave." He'd even get red if someone raised his hand. I was one of the two or three people who'd speak out.

In 2005 I met a man named Iván and I started a relationship with him. On Mother's Day in 2006 I realized I was pregnant. I was very happy because I really wanted to have a child. I remember looking up at the sky and saying, "I didn't know I could be so happy in life." Everyone at the hospital spoiled me and bought me food. I put on twenty-five kilos, but it was nice. I saw myself as the picture of health.

My son was born prematurely, six months into my pregnancy. He weighed just over a kilo and was born crying, so I thought his lungs were fine. When I held him I understood what mothers call the greatest joy in the world. It's something you can't explain. On the third day after he was

---

[4] Right-wing paramilitary groups began to form in Colombia in the early 1980s with the purported aim of fighting left-wing guerrillas. Backed by the military, landowners, drug traffickers, and political and economic elites, they murdered tens of thousands of civilians.

born, the doctor told us that he'd had a brain hemorrhage overnight. But he was still moving, and he was responsive. We baptized him on the fifth day and the doctor removed the respirator to see how he would react. On the sixth day the blood clot began to move and he started to choke. And on the eighth day, on November 1, 2006, he died.

I entered into postpartum depression. Living together with Iván became very hard. By December Iván was telling me that he wanted to leave. I told him not to, but in January 2007 he finally left me.

I THOUGHT, I CAN TALK AND TALK AND TALK AND NOTHING WILL HAPPEN TO ME

Eventually I began to recover from my son's death and see it in another way—that I'd been so fortunate to have had an angel. In March 2007, a co-worker at the hospital told me, "María Victoria, we need twenty-five workers to reactivate the union." People had doubts. They said that they'd been threatened before, and that maybe the same thing would happen again. It took us until October 2007 to get twenty-five people, and the Santa Fe chapter of the union was finally reactivated in December 2007. I was elected president of the chapter. I accepted, because my son's death made me feel very strong. I had overcome the greatest pain that I'd ever felt, and I thought, *Now nothing can knock me down.*

That year, I learned through several patients that a colleague of mine named Luis had been taking blood exams for people outside of the hospital, processing the samples at the blood lab, and then charging the patients and keeping the money for himself. I made various complaints during the hospital's board meetings but no action was taken. In November, I had also been elected to represent workers from the scientific sector before the hospital's board of directors. A few months later the hospital director finished his term, and the mayor decided to appoint a woman named Rocío to be the director of the hospital for a three-month period. By June 2008, when the three months were almost up, there was a hospital board meeting. At the meeting I asked the mayor, "When are we going to take applications for the position of hospital director?" The mayor said that he didn't want to take applications for the post because there was a lot of pressure over who to appoint. He said that the governor's office had even offered him money so that he'd choose the person they wanted. So I said, "Tell us who's been offering you money, and we can denounce them for bribery." But he said, "No, no, no, I can't do that." He said that he'd already told them he wouldn't accept the money.

In September 2008, we had another hospital board meeting. Again, the mayor said that he didn't want to take applications for the post because there was still a lot of pressure, and it was better to keep Rocío as the director until a transparent application process could be held. The mayor called a vote to decide whether Rocío would stay as interim director. All my other colleagues from the board of directors voted in favor, but I voted against her.

In early 2009, I came into work one Monday and noticed that the racks where you process patients' blood samples were completely full. I went to the registry book and saw that only six exams had been recorded for the whole weekend. So the tray should have had six samples, but it had ninety-eight. I said to myself, *Here I have proof*. When I saw the tray of blood samples that morning, I thought, *Now the board of directors will have to pay attention to me*.

I went to the next board meeting on June 11, 2009 with a packet of information describing the irregularities in the lab. I handed the packet over to the mayor and asked him to deliver it to either the Inspector General's office or the Attorney General's office. Instead, the mayor handed the packet over to Rocío and said, "Doctor, you're in charge of the investigation."

On August 15, I left for vacation and returned about twenty days later to find that I'd been assigned the on-call shift for an entire week. It bothered me because I'd have to work my regular shift and also be on-call all night. I knew I'd be overworked. So on September 14 I filed a complaint of labor harassment at the Ministry of Health and Social Protection. The harassment had started since I voted against Rocío's interim management in September 2008, and the complaint described my stigmatization at the hospital for belonging to the union, because each time we had a board meeting, the director would say that I was the only one in the hospital who caused problems. The board members would also say that I was a thorn in their side, because I often voted against them.

I've always thought that you have to denounce bad things; that's always been clear to me. I loved the hospital because it was my first job after my rural internship and it's in my mother's hometown. I didn't like the fact that the director and board were destroying the hospital. I said to myself, *Where are we headed? All these people are going to be left without work.* I wanted to protect what little there was, and because of this, the workers began to trust me.

At that time, I felt very protected, too protected, by my family's position in the town. My grandfather was a local councilman for forty-five years, and had sold his farm to finance the then-mayor's first campaign in 1995. I thought that the mayor had a lot to be grateful for, and during his first term, he'd actually helped me get my job. So I felt safe because of this, and because I was the president of the union and I felt the support of all my colleagues.

And the other thing is that the government couldn't catalog me as a member of an illegal group. For a long time the government has said that trade unionists are related to the FARC,[5] that they're guerrillas or leftists. And I'm not a leftist trade unionist, by God. My family is Conservative.[6] I even voted for President Álvaro Uribe[7] the first time.

So everything around me was like a protective shell. I thought, *I can talk and talk and talk and nothing will happen to me.* I didn't imagine that

---

[5] The Revolutionary Armed Forces of Colombia (FARC) is the largest left-wing guerrilla group in Colombia.

[6] The Liberal and Conservative parties were Colombia's two main political parties until the 2000s.

[7] A hard-line conservative, Álvaro Uribe served two terms as president between 2002 and 2010.

people were so bad. I never felt that evil would reach me. And it turns out that the shell wasn't such a shell because they didn't even threaten me; what they came for was to kill me.

I WAS COMPLETELY COVERED IN BLOOD

On Thursday September 24, 2009, I left work at around 9:15 p.m. and went to my Aunt Lilia's house, where my mom usually waited for me. When I got there, my aunt told me that my mom had already left for her farm. So I began walking down the street to my mom's farm, which is two blocks away. It's an unpaved road with no public lighting, and there are other farms along the side.

As I was approaching my mom's farm, I noticed that everything was dark. I thought that my mom had probably turned off the house lights thinking that I was going to stay at my Aunt Lilia's house.

Then I had a very strange premonition. I thought, *What if I were here and two guys came and grabbed me?* Right as I was opening the farm gate, two guys attacked me, one covering my mouth and the other hitting me. I thought that they were going to kidnap me, and I started biting their fingers. Then I freed up my mouth and began screaming, "Help! Help!" I dodged their blows and I kicked and screamed really loud until I fell on the ground. Then I looked up and saw the guys had masks on; they covered their faces until below their noses. As I looked up I felt the last blow against my face. That's when my mom turned on the house lights and ran out screaming, and the attackers took off.

I stood up, and when I touched my face I felt my nose dangling by a thread. That's when I thought, *By God, what were they hitting me with?* When I looked down at myself I was completely covered in blood. I saw a knife lying on the ground. I began screaming, "They killed me, they killed me, they killed me!" My mother yelled out desperately, "Ay, they're killing my girl!" We walked to the house, which was about a hundred meters from the gate. The whole time I held and covered my nose with my hand so that my mom wouldn't see that it wasn't attached. I was bleeding horribly from my waist so I told my mom to get a sheet and tie it tight. Then I grabbed the wireless phone and we called the hospital. We called twice until it finished ringing and still no one answered, so we left the house. I told my mom, "Keep dialing, keep dialing, we'll see who can take me to the hospital."

The whole time my mom was screaming, "They killed her! They killed her! They killed her!" The caretaker of the farm next door saw us and asked what had happened. He was going for his motorcycle to take me to the hospital when a guy and a girl on another motorcycle started coming toward us. The girl got off and told the driver, "Ay! It's the bacteriologist, pick her up!" So I got on the motorcycle and the guy drove me up to the hospital.

When I entered the hospital, Rocío and the doorman were both at the reception desk next to the phone. I don't know why they hadn't answered when my mom and I called. I entered the emergency room and said that I'd been stabbed. My colleagues were shocked to see me there, covered in blood, just twenty minutes after I had left work. The nurses laid me down on a stretcher and tried to stop the bleeding. At that point, I started to feel dizzy and cold. I said to myself, *If I die, I'm going to where my son is.* Then my mom arrived at the hospital and I heard her screaming, "My girl died! Tell me the truth! She's dead!" When I heard her I felt horrible; I stopped thinking about being with my son, but rather that I was going to leave behind a family that was suffering because of me.

A technician took X-rays, which showed that none of the wounds had penetrated my vital organs. They sutured up my chest and hooked me up to fluids. I said, "My nose—send me to a plastic surgeon." Rocío called Juan Carlos, a surgeon in Medellín who had worked at the hospital. I left in an ambulance at 12:30 a.m. and I arrived in Medellín at two in the morning. Everyone at the clinic was touching my nose and I didn't want them to. When they lifted it I said, "You're going to take it off, you're going to take it off!" It was hanging by a thread.

THE SILICONE HAD DEFLECTED THE KNIFE

I woke up after the operation at six the next morning, and my surgeon, Juan Carlos, told me that he had reattached my nose. He also said that the silicone—I'd had breast implants at the time—had deflected the knife towards my ribs. If not, the knife would have entered my lung. The knife was so long that I'm now missing a piece of my first rib.

I had felt the attackers stabbing and stabbing and stabbing. But there's an explanation for why the stabs didn't all enter my body. I generally dress in tight clothes, but that day it was really hot, so I'd put on a loose dress. Because of this, many of the stabs landed in the air, and many of them broke through the dress but nothing else. In total I'd been stabbed seven times: twice in my left side towards my kidneys; twice in my back, close to my lungs; once close to my spine; once in my breast, and once in the face. I lost the tissue in my breast and it looked crushed, as if I had breast cancer. The stab to my face cut my nose, upper lip, and left cheek. My upper lip had also been left dangling, but I hadn't realized it when it happened.

On Tuesday, five days after the attack, Juan Carlos, my doctor, told me, "I need to check you because there's a 50 percent chance that your nose will die." That day, my nose did die from necrosis—it had gone too long without receiving blood. When that happened, Juan Carlos told me, "You'll never return to being the same as you were." When he said that, I thought about my mom. I thought, *She's going to cry.* I remembered her screams when she arrived at the hospital the night of the attack.

A few days later I had the first reconstructive surgery on my nose. I left the surgery with everything covered but my eyes. I told my mom that the surgeons had just fixed a little piece of my nose, but in fact, they'd reconstructed half of my nose with flesh from my forehead. The flesh has to have blood, because if not, it dies. So they made a tube and buried it against the veins in my eye, since it's a very irrigated area. The tube passed the blood to my nose so that the tissue wouldn't die.

After surgery I stayed at another aunt's house in Itagüí, a city outside of Medellín. I couldn't sleep because I kept thinking that someone was going to come after me. I was taking a lot of antibiotics and other drugs to make me sleep, but I couldn't sleep.

Iván, my son's father, called me after the attack. He was nervous because he thought that the attackers might go looking for him. We'd started going out with each other again in October 2008, and the relationship had been growing, growing, growing. Things were starting to go well again. And then this happened to me. After the attack, he told me that he realized there were two kinds of people in the world: pretty people and ugly people. He said he categorized me among the pretty people, but I didn't feel pretty. I thought I was disfigured, and I categorized myself among the ugly people. How was I going to believe that he meant it?

Even though he showed interest in the beginning, it became less and it was very difficult because I thought, *He's really seeing me as ugly, so how must the rest of the world see me?* I even told him, "Pretty people and ugly people? What about pleasant people and unpleasant people?" Eventually, our relationship ended.

THEY WERE SURE THEY'D LEFT ME DEAD

The attackers began to call my Aunt Lilia's house in Santa Fe. They said that they were going to finish me off. They told her, "We're going to kill that bitch. Tell us where she is."

Finally one of my cousins answered the phone and said, "How can we settle this?" She proposed a deal to them. The attackers called back and said, "Pass the phone to the girl who said she'd give us money." So my family began to talk with them. My family told the Sectional Judicial Police (SIJIN)[8] that the attackers were going to call again. My family had wanted the SIJIN to take over the matter, and record the phone conversations so that they could use them as evidence. But the SIJIN responded that it was up to us to settle this.

---

[8] The Sectional Judicial Police (SIJIN) is a branch of the national police force.

So my cousin talked to the attackers again and wired 3 million pesos[9] to their account in exchange for them telling us who'd hired them to kill me. My family recorded the phone conversation where the attackers described everything. I haven't personally listened to the recording, but my family tells me the attackers said that on the night of the attack, someone from the hospital had alerted them five minutes before I left work. They said they arrived at the farm five minutes before I did, and that my mom was there, but they didn't kill her because they "felt bad for the old lady."

They couldn't explain how I was still alive, because they'd stabbed me so many times, and had used a knife that cuts through bone. They were sure they'd left me dead. They mentioned Luis, the colleague who I'd denounced to the hospital board. They also said that Luis's daughter was the one who'd driven them to my house, and that the order was for them to kill me using whatever means they wanted.

Your body has premonitions, but what happens is that you don't pay attention to them. A week before the attack, I thought that Luis was going to order someone to do something to me. And about three weeks before the attack, while I was on vacation, I looked at myself in the mirror and saw myself without a nose, and without my breasts. At the time, I just said to myself, *Could it be that I'm going to get a nose job?* And, *Could it be that I'm going to have my silicone changed?* Because it wasn't long before I was going to have to get a touch-up.

One of my cousins found a bag that the attackers had intentionally left at the scene of the crime. In order to be sure that it was really the attackers they were talking to, my cousin asked them what was in the bag, and the attackers described everything correctly. In the bag there was a Bible, with a paragraph about the adulterous woman highlighted. The intention was for me to die and for that page in the Bible to spread the false idea that I'd been killed because I'd been going out with a married man.

---

[9] About U.S.$1,500.

After I found out, I asked my mom, "If I'd died, would you have believed what that page from the Bible said?" My mom had always gone around with me—we went to the gym, to church, to my aunt's house, almost everywhere together. But she looked at me and said, "Ay, I don't know. You don't know what your kids do." My own mother told me that. So if your own family, the people you share the most with, would have believed this, what can you expect from everyone else? If the attackers had killed me, I think the adulterous woman story would have been the version that stuck, even if the lover had never appeared.

I FELT I WOULD DIE IF I WERE ALONE

The day after the attack my brother had filed a complaint at the Attorney General's office. After that, some SIJIN investigators had gone to Itagüí to take my statement and some photos of me. I told the investigators that I thought it was Luis who'd ordered the attack. A week after the prosecutor from the Attorney General's office started investigating my case, she was transferred to a different municipality. After that, Santa Fe was left without a prosecutor for two months. And ever since they brought a new prosecutor to Santa Fe, the case has been reassigned eight times. My brother said, "We wasted the money paying the attackers for the confession."

The first time I returned to Santa Fe after the attack was in December 2009. My brother drove and I hid in the back of the car underneath some sleeping pads for the entire hour-and-fifteen-minute ride from Itagüí. We entered my brother's house from the garage. Nobody in town knew that I was in that house.

My family couldn't leave me alone because I felt I'd die if I were alone in the house. Any noise I heard, I thought the attackers were going to come in. The most horrible thing was being stuck in the house on December 22. Santa Fe is very festive, and on that day there's a parade that I used to participate in and dance in. That day, it was so hot outside and I could hear all the music. It was hard to know that I couldn't be there.

Everyone was calling me on my cell phone, saying, "Merry Christmas, María Victoria!" I stayed in town until January 1, but besides my family, no one knew I was there.

I left Santa Fe and went to live in Bello, another city outside of Medellín. Even there I didn't feel safe, and I'd change houses about every three days. I didn't go out alone. I'd call my neighbors before leaving my house and ask them to see if there was anyone strange outside.

I stayed with cousins or friends. It was very uncomfortable. At the beginning everyone says, "Whatever you need, María Victoria." But when I'd stayed at their house for the third or the fourth time, I'd start to feel very bad. I felt that I was getting in the way, even though people don't express that. I put myself in their shoes and thought, *But how much longer?* I imagine everyone thought it was going to be for just a while, but now it's been a long time.

I BEGAN TO FEEL GUILTY FOR CONFRONTING THINGS

Santa Fe is a town where there are still a lot of paramilitaries because they didn't demobilize there.[10] That creates a lot of pressure, because when people see their lives threatened they keep quiet. Above all it's because everyone has families, and I realized that the family is most affected when you confront things.

I began to feel guilty because I saw that my mom couldn't go down to her farm after the attack. So I say to myself, *What right did I have to ruin her life?* I also have two nephews studying in Santa Fe. Luciano is twelve, and all his life he's been by my side. I've always watched out for him. Now my nephews can't go to school alone; an adult has to take them and pick them

---

[10] Between 2003 and 2006, approximately 30,000 supposed members of the AUC paramilitary coalition participated in demobilization ceremonies and pledged to cease criminal activity. Many of these demobilized paramilitaries rearmed into neo-paramilitary groups, which the government labels "emerging criminal gangs" (BACRIM).

up. They can't even be alone in their house. The kids were used to me taking them to the movies. In the beginning, soon after the attack, they would beg me, "Come on, let's go." But the first time I went out with Luciano I felt that any person I saw who looked like the attackers—men with hoods, hats and skinny hands—were going to grab both of us. I looked at him and thought, *Something's going to happen to him because he's with me.* So I tried to distance myself from him and my other nephew because of all that.

Even though we tried to keep everything hidden, Luciano understood everything. It's sad to see a kid feeling violence. And above all when I know that he loves me a lot and he asks, "Why did they do that to you?" It's an explanation that I can't give him. And when I do try to explain, my mother says, "They did that to her for joining that union and talking. And look what happened to her."

AS IF THE SOUND WERE IN YOUR EARS

I went back to work in Santa Fe from May 24, 2010, when my sick leave ended, to July 3, when I had the right to take my first vacation of the year. It was obligatory to return to work because if I hadn't gone the hospital would have fired me. I was only getting paid 65 percent of my salary because I was on sick leave, but I couldn't stop working because my debts were increasing. I had an apartment that I'd bought months before the attack, credit card debt, creams for the scars on my face, and medical bills.

When I came back to town after such a long time away, former patients often stopped me in the street to tell me, "I've prayed a lot for you." Their affection was immense, and for me it was one of the nicest things a human being can feel. It was very gratifying to know that the people who like you are many compared to those who don't like you. And it's even more gratifying to know that those people realize you inspire so much in other people.

On my first day back at the hospital, I went into work with my brother, my aunt, my cousin, some guys my cousin had hired to watch out for me, and some SIJIN agents. I was in the lab talking with my aunt, brother and cousin when Luis walked in. I had my back to him so I didn't see him at first; later my aunt told me that his face had turned pale when he saw me. He didn't even say hi, but my aunt signaled to me that he was there, so I turned around and said, "Good morning, Luis. How are you?" I said it to him just like that. He didn't respond. He just left, and for the next two weeks he tried to not be in the same space as me. If I was in the front part of the lab, he'd go to the back.

In the beginning Luis couldn't even look me in the eyes. Then, after twenty days, he said to me, "Could you lend me your pen?" I think he was trying to get closer to me, maybe because he'd been told not to be so obvious. But he still didn't look at me. Rocío, the hospital director, tried to be nice to me, but I haven't seen any remorse from either her or the mayor about my attack.

Soon after I started working, two guys went up to the window of the lab and were looking at me. I asked them what they were doing and they told me that they were observing me. I let the authorities know, and from then on a police officer went around with me at work.

During that time, I stayed at my Aunt Lilia's house again. It's one of those old houses from Santa Fe that has a huge yard. We'd checked the entrances and knew it would have been difficult for someone to enter, but not impossible. One of my cousins lent me a revolver that I didn't even know how to use. I was afraid that it would go off without me wanting it to, so at night I put it in a box under my bed.

I didn't sleep for that whole month and a half. If I heard a leaf rustle, I thought that the attackers were climbing down into the house from the palm tree outside. There are bats in Santa Fe, and I felt the flutter of their wings. I heard everything, and everything became as if the sound were in your ears, as if it roared and roared. All night I'd be watching out; I thought that the attackers were going to knock down the door and break into the house. I could only sleep in the afternoon when I returned from work, from five in the afternoon until eight at night, because I knew that there were other people awake. During that time, I got horribly sick. My lymph nodes started to swell and I couldn't swallow. I had a headache the entire time I was in Santa Fe.

Around June 25, a nurse came up to me at work and said, "Don't go to your mom's farm. My friend has passed by there on many occasions and seen four masked men nearby." I was afraid for my mom, because even though she didn't sleep at her farm, she stayed there during the day.

When I went back to Bello in July, the government assigned me a bodyguard. Around that time, an investigator from the Technical Investigative Corps (CTI)[11] in Medellín was also assigned to work on my case. His name was Jaime Henao. In the following months, he found out that money had been wired from Luis's bank account to the same account that my family had wired money to for the attackers' confession. That was a big link, a big piece of evidence.

Jaime spoke with one of the attackers implicated in the investigation, and the attacker told him that they belonged to the Envigado Office.[12] But Jaime didn't believe that. From what he could tell, the attackers were demobilized paramilitaries who were now in gangs. Demobilized paramilitaries also work in the hospital, and Luis is good friends with many of them. By December 2010, Jaime told me he was able to obtain arrest warrants for four suspects, including Luis.

I DIDN'T FEEL LIKE DANCING

Since the attack, I've had twelve surgeries: nine on my face and nose, one on my mouth, and two on my breasts. My face and breasts are nice, but when I see myself in the mirror it's as if I were another person.

Thank God I didn't end up looking like a monster. The surgeries have been a success and I know that in the end I won't have that many scars.

---

[11] The Technical Investigative Corps (CTI) is an entity attached to the Attorney General's office, and charged with providing investigative and forensic support in criminal cases.

[12] The Envigado Office is an organization that provides assassination and enforcement services to organized crime in Medellín and that has close ties with paramilitary structures.

Anyhow, beauty isn't what's important. Now I look at someone's nose and it could go from ear to ear, but for me it's still a pretty nose because the person was born with it. I can't feel the same way about my nose. I magnify it more. And when I talk I feel the scar tissue inside my face; I think that it's reflected on the outside and that I look like a monster.

I'm a very good dancer. I'm an expert in porro,[13] and I also dance salsa and merengue. But I'm not the same person as before. Since the attack two years ago, I've gone out partying three times. The first time I went out it was horrible. I was sitting at a table with three of my best friends, and at one point everyone was saying, "Dance, María Victoria!" I told them "No, no, no!" I felt that everyone was watching me and I was in a terrible mood. They began to bring me drinks and so I drank and drank and drank. But as tipsy as I got, I didn't feel like dancing. Then my friend Federico said, "María Victoria, I thought that what happened to you had passed, but what they really killed was your spirit." He said it just like that. I felt like crying. I stood up and danced to the last song, but I felt that everyone was looking at me, and that I looked horrible.

Another thing that comes to mind a lot is the idea of having a partner. I'll say to myself, *Now I'm going to be left without anyone.* But then I'll think, *Fine. If that partner isn't able to see what's inside, why do I want him?* But you also see that what's inside isn't important to other people. It's like a contradiction. I say to myself, *I'm a good person but people don't see that in me.* In any case, no one's exempt from suffering an accident or some sickness that disfigures him.

For my birthday in October 2010, my friends and I had another night out. This time I partied better, and we danced until four in the morning. I have a godfather who's a policeman in Bello. He saw me all distressed and he organized the night out. The police watched out for us at the bars we went to. First we went to a bar with some soft music and talked. Then we went to a place where they played crossover music and we danced to

---

[13] Porro is a musical style from Colombia's Caribbean coast.

everything. At three in the morning we finished off the night at a reggaeton bar. We had a great time, and my friend Federico said to me, "I'm so happy to see you returning to the person you used to be."

NO ONE HAD BEEN ARRESTED

At the end of February 2011, I went to Santa Fe for a union assembly at the hospital. Even though I don't work at the hospital anymore, I continue to be the president of the Santa Fe chapter. I have "union permission," which allows me to do my union-related work and continue to be paid by the hospital. I arrived in Santa Fe at night with two bodyguards and went straight to my aunt's house. My family sleeps on the first floor and my bodyguards sleep on the second floor, where they can see the farm outside.

The next morning I walked to the hospital with my two bodyguards. As we were walking up the hill to the hospital, we saw two guys on a motorcycle at the top of the hill watching us. I said to one of my bodyguards, "Look at those guys. They're not moving; they're just watching us." He said, "María Victoria, things are bad up there."

Then the guys started slowly coming down the hill on the motorcycle. I stood behind my bodyguard and used him as a shield. The two guys passed right next to us and kept going.

When we got to the hospital, one of my colleagues told me that he'd seen some guys on the same motorcycle pass by the hospital several times. As soon as the meeting ended that day, I left with my bodyguards for Bello.

In the beginning of May 2011 I called Jaime to see what was going on with my case. Months had passed since he'd told me about the arrest warrants for the four suspects, but no one had been arrested yet. It turns out he'd been removed from my case at the beginning of the year because he'd been appointed to be the head of the CTI's anti-BACRIM unit.[14] After that, I didn't even know the investigator who was in charge of my case. Jaime asked me, "What do you mean they haven't captured anybody? I left four arrest warrants ready to be executed. If you want, I'll check what's going on." I said, "Of course, that's why I'm calling you." He said that he'd check on my case that Monday, May 16.

One of my bodyguards always buys *La Chiva*, which is a sensationalist newspaper. On Tuesday, May 17, I picked up the paper and saw a little photo of Jaime with the headline, "CTI INVESTIGATOR KILLED." I said, "Jaime!" He'd been killed as he was entering his house on Monday night. It scared me a lot. It also made me really sad. I'd known Jaime for a year, and we were very friendly with each other. I'd even invited him to my birthday the year before, but he couldn't go because he had kids and he spent his little free time with them. Whenever he talked to me about his colleagues who'd been killed, he'd say, "This job is very dangerous, but I watch out for myself."

MY LIFE IS FOUR WALLS

In July 2011, I was elected to be the vice president of ANTHOC for Antioquia province. I've proposed to my union in Santa Fe to elect a different president, but no one else wants to take the position. After my attack, who else would want to be the president of the Santa Fe chapter? The environment in the hospital has become worse since the attack because people keep totally silent. Everyone at the hospital thinks that I'll make all the complaints on their behalf. So I tell them, "Well, why don't you write a letter, and we'll all sign it?" They say, "No María Victoria, we were waiting for you."

---

[14] "Emerging Criminal Gangs" (BACRIM) is the label the Colombian government gives to neo-paramilitary groups that emerged from the paramilitary demobilization process between 2003 and 2006. The "anti-BACRIM unit" is a group of prosecutors and police investigators dedicated to investigating the groups.

I don't want to move to another part of the country because that would be quitting. And if I quit, everyone will do the same, and we won't get anywhere. The fact is that if people stay silent, what future will my nephews have, and what future will their children have? I continue to move around from house to house in Bello. I go to work and then I go straight home. I don't have a life. I stay in my room by myself and I sleep with a kitchen knife, pepper spray, and a bulletproof vest next to my bed. Outside of work, my life is four walls. Sometimes I think that maybe it would have been better to have died.

Before, I didn't have that much time to read literature, but now I read a lot. I'm currently reading stories by Edgar Allen Poe. I dance by myself at home. I'll also have a bottle of wine, olives, and cheese, and get a little tipsy by myself in bed. It's risky though, because sometimes I'll start weeping.

I try not to cry, because it seems horrible to me that people would feel sorry for me. My mom and dad and my siblings have never seen me cry. But at night the need to cry comes over me, so I cover myself with pillows so that nobody can hear me. Sometimes the tears come because of my impotence, because I think, *Man, why can't I say, "It's those people, get them!"* Sometimes the impotence is seeing everything I used to have. I think to myself, *I came from an environment surrounded by affection and now I'm alone.*

ZULLYBETH ZAPATA

AGE: *42*
OCCUPATION: *Teacher*
HOMETOWN: *Anorí, Antioquia*
INTERVIEWED IN: *Bogotá*[1]

Zullybeth Zapata was born in Anorí, Antioquia province, a historic stronghold for left-wing guerrillas. When her time as a missionary was cut short by the sudden murder of her father, she returned to her hometown and found work as a schoolteacher. In the late 1990s, she witnessed how a right-wing paramilitary group took over her town, killing her friends and family members. After about five years, when the paramilitary violence began to subside, a state-owned company started to build a road through her husband's farm as part of a large-scale hydroelectric project. Zullybeth recounts that she and her husband disputed the company's purchase of part of his land, and subsequently endured threats and intimidation by the army, the police, and unidentified armed civilians. The pressure mounted until 2010, when she had to flee to the nearby city of Medellín. Zullybeth continues to wait for justice, as no one has been prosecuted for her displacement or the events leading up to it.

Names in this narrative have been changed at the request of the narrator.

---

[1] Bogotá and Amalfi are false locations employed to protect the narrator's identity.

SHADOWS

There was a guava tree right outside the window of my first-grade classroom. It was so nice for me to be able to see that little tree grow. I saw its first flowers, I saw its first tiny little guavas, and I ate its first fruit. I watched over it and protected it. If a classmate got close to scratching their name in it, I fought with that kid, and the teachers took me to the principal's office.

That little tree cast shadows; it was delightful to take shade under it. There are shadows that astonish, that really give you satisfaction, that generate well-being. There are also shadows that astonish, but negatively. I remember that when the school built some new classrooms, they took that tree, cut it down, and threw it out. It was just like a little skeleton, all sad. I saw it decompose. It became a ghost. And for my whole life I've related that event to what's happened to me.

My dad was a lumberjack, but with the technology of the era—he used a saw, not the modern equipment we have today. He worked tirelessly his whole life in multiple trades, because both he and my mom came from low economic conditions and had to struggle to make a living. He used to tell me stories of La Violencia[2] in Anorí. The stories were of the guerrilla groups from La Violencia called the chusma that emerged from the huge rift between the Liberals and the Conservatives. He said that the chusma would take the kids, throw them in the air and catch them with the kind of forks that the devil uses. If they came upon a family from the opposing political group, they would kill them all.

People had to sleep in the coffee plantations in case someone came to them and asked, "Liberal or Conservative?" And without knowing who the person was, if you guessed right and said, "I'm a Conservative," and they were Conservatives, you saved yourself. And if not, there you would end. But in Anorí more than anything they killed you for being a Conserva-

---

[2] La Violencia (The Violence) refers to a period of civil conflict fought between the Liberal and Conservative parties from roughly 1948–1958, during which an estimated 200,000 people were killed, and as many as two million were internally displaced.

tive. You had to be a Liberal. My dad's family was Conservative, and the Liberals killed his uncle, his uncle's wife and their four-month-old baby. My dad had to live through that whole period of violence when he was little.

In my own story I have much to tell because, despite my forty-two years, I've lived through many things. My life has been an adventure since I was a girl. Anorí is the cradle of the guerrillas.[3] In 1973, when I was four years old, I lived through Operation Anorí.[4] I would see the army helicopters take dead guerrillas and place them at the foot of a big pomo tree in front of my school. It was an exhibition of the trophies that they'd brought from the war.

I saw soldiers torture the guerrillas after they'd caught them. There was an army base right next to my house, and outside of the base there was a water tank where they'd dunk the guerrillas' heads. They would stick them in there so that they'd drown. I imagine that they were asking them for information, and when they were about to die they'd pull them out and they'd be in horrible despair.

As a child, a disconcertedness and sadness grew in my mind and in my heart. However, in family life, with my four sisters and two brothers, we were happy in the midst of absolute poverty.

THE BIBLE SAYS, WHEREVER
YOU GO, EAT WHAT'S THERE

For me, to feel useful was to be able to do something for others. Although my family was poor like the rest of the population in Anorí, I saw there

---

[3] The Revolutionary Armed Forces of Colombia (FARC) and National Liberation Army (ELN) are the two largest guerrilla groups in Colombia. Founded in the 1960s and claiming to represent the country's rural poor in the fight against Colombia's wealthy classes and U.S. imperialism, both groups commit widespread abuses against civilians, including killings, threats, and recruitment of child soldiers.

[4] Operation Anorí was a military offensive carried out by the Colombian army against the National Liberation Army (ELN) guerrillas in 1973.

were kids who were even more in need. Some of my friends only had panela water[5] for breakfast, so when rice was being prepared at home, I would
steal a little and give it to them.

Around 1986, when I was about seventeen years old, I had the opportunity to study at a convent about five hours' drive from Anorí. I'd
heard that going there would lead to a missionary life. I thought, *This is
for me! This is what I like*, because it meant going to work with indigenous
people and vulnerable groups that otherwise had little access to education
and other opportunities. I had just finished the ninth grade when I left for
the convent. There, I studied pedagogy for two years in a teacher training
college and became a teacher. After three years, I took vows of chastity,
poverty, and obedience, and I became a nun. Around 1989, when I was
twenty years old, I went on a mission to Ecuador.

I think that if I'd stayed in Anorí there may have been fewer opportunities for me. There wasn't a pedagogy program in Anorí, and generally,
girls who finished school in Anorí stayed there, went off with a man and
got married. I'd always dreamed of doing something different.

Over the next few years, I traveled through almost all of Ecuador
with groups of three or four missionaries. I loved it because I got to work
with indigenous people, and in border areas where the people were really
poor. We'd bring them sewing machines and teach them how to sew, or
show them how to raise chickens or rabbits that they could eat. If there
was no food, we starved with the people, because the Bible says: "Wherever you go, eat what's there."

THEY WERE ALL AMONG US

Around 1992, when I was about twenty-three years old, I took a vacation
from Ecuador and visited Anorí. During my visit, there was a guerrilla
siege of the town. The atmosphere in the town was very tense because

---

[5] Panela is an unrefined food product made by boiling sugarcane juice into a hard, crusty
block. It can then be dissolved in hot water to make a drink.

when there's going to be a siege, the guerrillas generally let the population know by telling a few people in town first.

That day, I was at my house with some of my family members. I was on the second floor of the house with my aunt and her family, and my mom was on the third floor with my siblings. At about six that evening, three men and a woman showed up at the house. They entered the house without knocking, went to the third floor and said, "Good afternoon," to my mom. Like a typical Antioquian, my mom asked them if they wanted something to drink. They said no. They told her that they were going to stay the night, but not to worry because they wouldn't be there in the morning. My mom got scared because she assumed they were guerrillas.

Soon after the visitors had arrived, a group of police came and walked around the outside of the house. Someone must have alerted them that there were suspicious people around. My mom says that the guerrillas looked out of the bedroom window, took their pistols and threw them under the mattresses. They told my mom that if the police came upstairs, she should tell them that they were her relatives.

The police never went up to the third floor. After they left, the guerrillas sat down to watch television as if nothing was going on. Anyone who arrived would have thought that they were members of our family. My mom gave them food, but they hardly ate anything. That night, everything was silent, and around midnight they lay down to sleep. Then, at one in the morning there was a sound like fireworks in the mountains. It sounded like a whistle, like *eeeeeee*... and then it exploded. As soon as that sound went off, the guerrillas were all on their feet and went downstairs.

We heard the sound of gunshots as the guerrillas went up through the cemetery shooting at the police. It was horrible.

Everyone who was on the second floor lay on the floor, dead with terror. We stayed in the same place all night because we were in shock. It was also best for our safety. No bullets entered the house, but you could feel them whistling by. The shootout lasted until about six in the morning, and by that time, because there was no bathroom in the room we were in, we were all lying in puddles of our own urine.

We left our house at around nine in the morning. It was sad to go into the town, to see the desolation and the blood spilled. Many of the shop doors were perforated with bullet holes. There were a lot of dead people. The guerrillas had killed about six policemen, and the strangest thing was that they took most of the bodies away with them. As they were leaving town, they shot and killed a young woman, who left a little baby behind. They also killed an old man and an old woman, supposedly because they'd informed the police about the operation.

Later, I understood why the guerrillas had gone into our house. One of my brothers told me that they'd made my dad store weapons for them in the first floor of our house. They told him that they'd kill him and my family if he alerted anyone about the siege.

I SMELLED BLOOD

I was in Ecuador for another two years. It was a stage of my life when I was really happy. Then, in 1994, the religious community superiors selected me to go to Africa the following year. So in November 1994, when I was twenty-five, I left Ecuador by bus to go to Bogotá, get a visa, and take a course in French. On the trip back I bought gifts for my dad.

At one point during the trip, I smelled blood. I didn't sleep. I had that feeling: *Ay no, something bad is happening. There's going to be an accident.*

When I arrived in Medellín to change buses, a missionary told me that my dad had been killed. My pain was so great that I wasn't even able to cry. My brother and aunt had been waiting for me in Medellín, and from there they drove me to Anorí. My other brother was convicted for my dad's homicide. My dad was a womanizer, and it hurt my brother a lot to see my mom suffer. When I visited him in jail, he said he was capable of killing our dad, but he swore that he hadn't done it.

After my father's death came a stage in my life that was another shadow; things changed. I knew that sooner or later I had to go to Africa, but I started to think, *Africa is too far away from my family.* My father's death had left them financially destitute. There's a part of the Bible that says, "Whoever starts to plow and looks back is not fit for the kingdom of God." I think I'm one of those people. For all that I wanted and desired to continue my work as a missionary, I couldn't. I quit in January 1995.

I already had my degree in pedagogy, so I started knocking on doors looking for work. Almost no one knew me in Anorí anymore, because I'd left nine years earlier. The municipal school was looking for a teacher, but didn't have the budget to pay for one. So I told them, "I'll give classes in the meantime, even if it's for free." And that worked out because eventually they hired me, and I kept on climbing the ladder as a teacher.

THE LESS YOU KNOW, THE MORE YOU LIVE

The paramilitaries entered Anorí around 1997, when I was in my late twenties. Soon after their arrival, they began killing townspeople who they said were guerrilla collaborators.[6] They killed merchants, transporters, anyone. My family lived close to the cemetery, and there was a time when there were so many massacres and deaths in Anorí, that the smell of the rotting cadavers was intolerable.

Many times the paramilitaries would kill people and then go to their funeral, dying with laughter. The townspeople would leave the church with the coffin and pass by the shops. If the deceased person was well known, the shops would put on that person's favorite record. That's a very nice tradition in Anorí that still exists. But the paramilitaries would be standing on the park corner, saying, "There goes the big son of a bitch."

They took over the town; they were the authority. For a time, everyone in Anorí shut themselves up in their houses by five in the afternoon. There was a general anxiety and sadness, and you couldn't do anything. But the paramilitaries had their parties, and the music stayed on as late as they felt like it. They would take over houses by saying to the owner,

---

[6] Right-wing paramilitary groups began to form in Colombia in the early 1980s with the purported aim of fighting left-wing guerrillas. Backed by the military, landowners, drug traffickers, and political and economic elites, they murdered tens of thousands of civilians.

"This house here, you have to vacate. Now." And you had to vacate.

The paramilitaries in town generally went around dressed as civilians and almost never went around uniformed. The most regrettable part was that they were really friendly with the army and the police. I'd see them getting drunk together on the corners. I used to think that the mere fact of being a policeman, a soldier, a councilman or a mayor guaranteed that a person was honest and ethical in their work. But when you see that it's not like that, it's like when you're a child and discover that your mom or dad is a human being with flaws.

Over the next few years, a lot of people I knew died. One of them was a friend I had who fixed motorcycles. He was an incredible salsa dancer and very handsome. One night, at the beginning of 1999, he knocked at the door of my apartment. He said, "Profe, profe, open the door. I have to hide because they're going to kill me." It was around one in the morning—how was I going to open the door for a man that late at night, as much as he was my friend? Not me. At that time I was living by myself, and the next day people would have said that I lived with him or something. I told him that we'd talk the next day. The following night I heard he'd been killed.

I have this sadness, this moral dilemma. I don't know if I was very wrong to not have opened the door to him. And I don't know if I would have made a mistake by opening the door, because the less that you know, the more you live. I've always thought that, and unfortunately, it's true.

IF GOD EXISTS, WHERE WAS HE?

Between 1996 and 2000 I was getting a degree in natural sciences, and I was also working at the Educational Institute of Anorí. There, I taught high school students social sciences, philosophy, economics, and natural sciences. The local kids who hung out with the paramilitaries and worked for them would insult the teachers, and no one could say anything to them. Then one day, one of them threatened a teacher. When the paramilitary bosses found out about this, they investigated the situation. They put the student in a pickup truck and took him away. When the student returned to town, he fainted on a corner in front of some houses. They must have threatened to kill him. Afterwards, the paramilitaries called us teachers to a meeting and told us that their kids had to be the best students, and that if we had a problem with any of them, we should let them know. And furthermore, the paramilitaries said that we should control the kids' girlfriends, because they had gotten out of hand. If someone looked at their boyfriend, they would grab them and beat them up.

One of my students was a former guerrilla, and had become the girl-friend of one of the top paramilitaries. She told me that the guerrillas took her away when she was about seven years old, and that she didn't remember her mother, didn't remember anyone. She spent about six years in the guerrillas until she deserted. She said that one of her dreams was to study and graduate. One time, when I presented a video of the solar system that showed the planets in movement, she was amazed. She asked me, "Profe, if God exists, where was he? He didn't appear in the camera shots they took at the time?" She was very ignorant, but also had an in-credible desire for knowledge. One of the students that makes a teacher say, *It's so great that students are surprised by knowledge!*

AS POOR PEOPLE WE HAD EVERYTHING

Around 2000 I entered into a serious relationship with a man named Fer-nando. He was my first boyfriend; I knew him from before I left for the convent. He's a beautiful person with incredible morals and ethics. He had a farm in a rural part of Amalfi, a municipality that neighbors Anorí. I moved to the town center of Amalfi, and I visited him on his farm on the weekends. It was about seventy hectares, planted with fruit and timber. Even as poor people, we had everything we needed there.

The farm is located in the area of a hydroelectric project run by a state-owned company. The company first arrived on our farm around the end of 2000. They wanted the land on the farm so they could build a modern road between the dam and the place where they were going to process the energy.

One day Fernando and I saw the company's workers on his property, cutting down avocado trees, tangerine trees, commercial woods, everything. They damaged the three wells we had, demolished plots of land. They channeled the water that the humans and cattle survive off of and damaged the lagoon. And there on the farm, your life depends on water.

The majority of the people in the area stayed quiet because there's an idea that fighting against a company is a sure failure. But Fernando and I began to make a series of complaints. We called and wrote to the Personería.[7] Unfortunately, they shelved the complaints there. We complained to the mayor. We went to the Inspector General's office.[8] We filed many complaints but none of them came to anything.

At that point Fernando had owned his farm for twenty years. He was born there, grew up working there, bought the farm, made all of the improvements to it and says that he'll die there. I had always dreamed of having my children with him. We had our first daughter in 2003 and named her Esmeralda.

In 2004, we realized that the company was negotiating for our property with its former owners, who said that Fernando was just the farm administrator. Two of the previous owners and an investment company began to argue that they owned the property. That November, the situation was brought to conciliation in the Chamber of Commerce in Medellín. Conciliation is an arbitration where they bring all the implicated parties together and try to negotiate so that the matter doesn't have to go to the courts.

I wasn't allowed to enter the conciliation session. I had to wait outside for Fernando, who didn't know the city and had never been to the Chamber of Commerce. By six in the evening, a representative of the company told him that whether or not he signed over the land, they

---

[7] A government entity charged with monitoring municipal administrations and defending citizens' rights.

[8] The state office that conducts most disciplinary investigations of public officials, and monitors criminal investigations and prosecutions, as well as other state agencies.

would take it away from him the next day because it was of public interest. They also told him that in order to leave the Chamber of Commerce, he had to sign a document. He signed the document, thinking that they would meet again. But it turns out that the company deceived him. They attached his signature to a document saying that he agreed to sell thirty-six hectares of land for 104 million pesos,[9] and that the compensation would be divided among him and another three claimants.

When we found out, we went back to talk with the company. We arrived at a verbal agreement that Fernando would sign away the deed to part of the land, but that they would return the part of the land where there was water, grass, and fruit trees.

THROW YOU IN THE RIVER

After Fernando signed the deed, the company didn't want to hear from us. They took away the viable part of the farm where the grass was, the improvements, and what was left of the water. They left us the bad part of the farm that didn't have water or fruit trees. In order to have water, we had to build some wood and plastic shacks on the part of the land where you could channel the water from—and that was supposedly the company's because of the signing of the deed.

In 2006, we had our second daughter, Mafe. Around that time, workers from the company would arrive every day, accompanied by the public security forces. Sometimes, squadrons of eight, ten, twelve policemen would arrive, angry from the start. One time, a policeman told me, "If you're not going to leave, let us know, because the river is really close to here." This means that they'll kill you and throw you in the river. People with uniforms exclusively used by public security forces would also arrive at the farm, but with their insignias covered. You couldn't tell if they were the police, guerrillas, or paramilitary groups. They said we were

---

[9] Approximately U.S.$40,000.

squatters, that they would put us in jail, and that our children would be handed over to Family Welfare.[10] Seeing so many people surrounding the house filled me with fear. On three occasions, they shot over our shacks at night so that we'd clear out. But I never thought about leaving the farm with the girls. Exactly the contrary: we were a family and as a family we stuck together in everything.

Unfortunately, with all the problems that Fernando had to live through, he became depressed. It was sad to see a man crying like a little boy. He began to act aggressively with me, hit me, mistreat me. I told him I couldn't take it anymore. I had to leave him. You have to accompany your friend to the cemetery, but you can't bury yourself with him. Our relationship as a couple ended in late 2009. Even though I continued checking in on him and accompanying him in the process with the farm, Fernando and I didn't have the life of a couple, and my daughters and I almost never went to the farm.

I DON'T HAVE ANY OTHER ENEMIES

One Sunday in October 2010 at 1:15 a.m. someone knocked at my door. I had been sleeping, and when I heard them knock a second time, I asked, "Who is it?" They didn't respond, but knocked a third time, and then a fourth time. After the fourth time, they started forcing the door, but couldn't open it. Then a male voice said, "Professor, Professor, open the door. Open the door, or it'll be worse because I'll knock it down." I became very afraid and went and sat down on my girls' bed, where they were sleeping. At the time, Esmeralda was seven and Mafe was four.

I was stunned. My mind had stopped. The man struggled at the door, pushing and pushing for about five minutes. When I heard him starting to go back down the front steps towards the street, I immediately left the bed. I looked through the peephole in my front door and saw him go about

---

[10] A government social services agency charged with protecting families and children.

halfway down the stairs, turn around and tuck a silver-plated gun in his waistband. He finished going down the stairs and crossed the street, where there was another man waiting for him. The two of them walked to the middle of the road, looked up and pointed at my balcony, and left.

I couldn't sleep that night; I was dead from panic. I stayed in my house all of Sunday, and at four in the morning on Monday I left for Medellín[11] with my brother. I thought that maybe the men would get me in the middle of the trip and kill the girls, so I went ahead with my brother and asked my sister to bring the girls on the first bus leaving Anorí that morning.

I can't be certain, but I think that the attempt to enter my house was related to the problem on the farm. By then, Fernando and I had denounced the army, the police, and the company. I don't have any other enemies in the community.

MY STORY DOES NOT END

When my daughters arrived in Medellín I went with them to my union, the Association of Educators of Antioquia (ADIDA). I told them what had happened to me and they took me to the union's human rights office. From there, I was sent to the Ombudsman's office,[12] which placed me and my girls in a shelter. We stayed there for three weeks, sharing a room with two other families. One of the families came from Turbo, Antioquia, and the other came from Mutatá, Antioquia. Everyone talked and shared the same pain.

Two of my sisters lived in Medellín in a very tiny house. After living in the shelter, I went to stay with them and slept in a small room with my girls. Then my younger brother came to live in Medellín, so we went to stay at his apartment on some small mattresses. During that time, I

---

[11] Medellín, the capital of Antioquia province, is about 170 kilometers from Anorí.

[12] The Ombudsman's office is a state entity charged with promoting and defending human rights and international humanitarian law.

was very afraid and I didn't sleep. Whenever I went out onto the street holding my daughters by the hand, I looked around, thinking that at any moment someone would shoot me.

In February 2011, my teaching post was relocated to Bogotá. Now I'm teaching biology and chemistry at a high school. My daughters and I have a little house here, but it lacks a lot of things, because everything stayed behind in Anorí. It would have been too expensive to move things to Bogotá. The girls sleep in a bed and I sleep on a mattress on the floor.

My question is, where can I be safe? I'm a defenseless person without any political role or anything—what part of the country can I go to where my daughters and I will feel safe?

My story does not end. My story is beginning now, because it's a new stage; the stage of forced displacement. I'm starting over from zero. I have the great treasures that are my daughters, but I don't know what their future is. What can I offer them now if I can't even give them safety?

The girls are very affected; their behavior completely changed. They used to be really relaxed and now they're very aggressive with each other. Esmeralda, who is now eight years old, recently peed on the living room furniture. Her performance at school has gotten worse, and even her handwriting has changed. Mafe, who is now five years old, has started stealing her classmates' things and taking them home with her.

The saddest shadow of all this story is that not only is Fernando alone, but he is also plunged into complete depression. He once said something very nice: that he's an Indian for the land. For the Indians, the land is the mother, and for him, the land is his mother. He doesn't cut down trees, because they feed the birds. And he plants crops so that the animals will eat them. He said that he would prefer to be poor in the countryside than rich in the city. To set up that farm, he worked from sun up to sun down without Saturdays, without Sundays, and without vacations, just for someone to come and take it from him.

I hope that better times will come. At least I have my work; there are people who have almost nothing. I met a man online a few years ago. His name is Diego, and I've told him my entire story. Around June

2011, he proposed to me. I told him that I officially wanted to be his girlfriend, and think about the possibility of sharing a life with him. He's Peruvian and lives in Utah, and he's talked to a lawyer about getting me a visa to go to the U.S. I love my homeland, and even though I never planned on leaving it I'd be open to living with him in the U.S. with my two girls. We recently celebrated his fiftieth birthday over the internet, with cake and everything. I've seen that he's a good, noble person, and, well, life goes on.

RODRIGO MEJÍA

AGE: *38*

OCCUPATION: *Former mule driver, lumberjack*

HOMETOWN: *Planeta Rica, Córdoba*

INTERVIEWED IN: *Montelíbano, Córdoba*

Rodrigo Mejía describes himself as a wanderer. Since the age of eight, he has dealt with adversity by "moving from one place to another, from here to there and there to here." As an adult, whenever armed groups threatened him, his family or his livelihood, Rodrigo picked up and left for another part of the violence-plagued Bajo Cauca region in Antioquia. In this region, armed groups fund themselves with coca profits and, increasingly, through informal gold mines.[1] Although he's been forced to flee five times over the last twenty years, Rodrigo never considered himself displaced by Colombia's conflict until 2010, when a battle of wills with the local FARC guerrilla commander led him to lose his right hand. Today, he struggles to survive with his wife and three children in a squatter settlement in Montelíbano, Córdoba.

Names in this narrative have been changed at the request of the narrator.

---

[1] Environmental authorities estimate that there are 2,000 bulldozers working in illegal mines in the Bajo Cauca region alone, operating in an area of 8,500 square kilometers.

I'LL GO WITH YOU

When the guerrillas were around, I fought for what was mine.[2] When the paras[3] came, I fought for what was mine. A guerrilla commander once said to me, "Brother, you have to pick sides." And I said, "No, I choose no side." I was neither a para nor a guerrilla.

I was born in Planeta Rica, Córdoba province, but I've spent most of my life in Antioquia province. My mom died when I was just a month old and my dad left me, my brother, and my sister with an aunt to raise us. She used to beat me a lot so I left home when I was about eight years old and was taken in by a man named Toño. He was like a father to me. He took me to work in a village called Santa Isabel in El Bagre, Antioquia, and taught me how to handle mules, tie them up, and give them medicine. I learned a lot from Toño, and soon I became a mule driver. We would load the mules up with fuel, cyanide, and supplies to take to the gold mines up in the mountains. By the time I was seventeen, I had eighteen mules and two horses of my own.

But that's when things started getting really complicated in El Bagre. The paras came in 1990 and they came to kill. They were killing all the mule drivers because they said that we took supplies to the guerrillas up in the mountains.

I told Toño I was going to leave to try my hand at felling lumber. He said, "I won't stand in your way, mi'jo.[4] If you want to leave, go. But always remember me."

---

[2] The Revolutionary Armed Forces of Colombia (FARC) and National Liberation Army (ELN) are the two largest guerrilla groups in Colombia. Founded in the 1960s and claiming to represent the country's rural poor in the fight against Colombia's wealthy classes and U.S. imperialism, both groups commit widespread abuses against civilians, including killings, threats, and recruitment of child soldiers.

[3] "Para" is conversational shorthand for paramilitary. The paramilitaries are right-wing groups that began to form in the early 1980s with the purported aim of fighting left-wing guerrillas. Backed by the military, landowners, drug traffickers, and political and economic elites, they murdered tens of thousands of civilians.

[4] A contraction of "mi hijo" (in English, "my son"), used affectionately for male friends or relatives.

My life has been moving from one place to another, from here to there and there to here. When work is slow, or one armed group or another starts bothering me, I pick up and leave. Even when I got together with my wife Edith in 2003, I didn't settle down. I told her, "I need a woman who'll come with me." When our daughter Darley was born in 2003 we were in a village called Versalles, in Antioquia. When Leidy was born in 2006 we were in El Bagre. And when Gustavo was born in 2009 we were living at a farm eight hours by mule from the nearest village, called Las Negritas, which is part of the municipality of El Bagre. That's pure mountain, pure jungle, with some farms in the middle.

We'd gone to live there in 2007. At that time, it was covered in wild brush and jungle. The first year I cleared twenty hectares. We lived in a makeshift house and planted corn, rice, plantain, yucca, and yams. The first year you always suffer in the countryside but by the second year you're harvesting food.

THE MOUNTAIN WENT TO HELL

Those two years were the most stable part of my life because things there were calm. The guerrillas weren't around, there were no paramilitaries. But around 2009, the whole mountain went to hell. That's when huge machines started coming up the mountain to extract gold.[5] And as the machines went up, the plague came down. Suddenly the guerrillas were everywhere. They would charge the miners 8 million pesos[6] to allow the backhoes onto the mountain. And then they'd have to pay a percentage of production to the guerrillas.

One day I ran into the local FARC commander Jimmy on a path when I was on my way home with my mules. He was tall, heavy-built and white with blue eyes. He was with two other guerrillas. He asked, "Are

---

[5] In 2009, world gold prices jumped 24 percent, sparking a gold rush in Colombia, which is considered to have one of the richest gold deposits in the Western Hemisphere.

[6] Approximately U.S.$4,000.

those your mules?" I said, "Thank God, yes, they're mine." He asked me if I was selling them. I said, "Why would I want to sell them?" He said, "Okay," and we each went on our way.

The following day two guerrillas showed up at the house and said, "Jimmy sent us to tell you we need a pig. You either sell it to us or we take it." I said, "Well if you're going to take it, take it. I'm not selling pigs." They grabbed one of my pigs that weighed about 120 kilos, tied him up and took him.

My wife Edith said to me, "Oh dear. It looks like things are going to get complicated around here." It came time to do a second clearing. I cut trees down with the chainsaw and cleared the brush. The guerrillas would come from time to time and say, "We need ten hens." I'd say, "Take them, but I won't take them to you."

One day in late January or February of 2010 Jimmy came to the farmhouse with about fifty of his men. He hung his hammock and told the other guerrillas to go off and relax. Things started off cordial but then he said, "Are you very brave or what? What's wrong with you? Every time I send for something at your farm you talk back." I said to him, "Let's talk man to man because I have the same equipment between my legs that you have. The only difference between you and me is that you have that rifle.

"I don't give away things willingly because what I make with the sweat of my brow and what that woman over there makes with her hands should be respected. Around here the laws are made by those who carry the rifle. You guys are the law around here and you say you protect the peasants. But what you do is the opposite because what you do is steal from us." He didn't like what I was saying but he just walked away.

A DOG IN THE MANGER

I ran into Jimmy again a few weeks later and he said, "Why don't you work with us?" I said, "What do you mean, work with you?" He said that since I had twelve mules, he would put up eight more and we would work two teams of mules and split the earnings. I told him no.

A new para group called the Paisas[7] had occupied the nearest village, Las Negritas. At any moment one of those guerrillas could switch sides and join the paras and then say, "Look, that guy used to give us guerrillas plantains and yucca. He would kill pigs for us and throw parties." So then the paras might come and kill me, *pa! pa!*

Jimmy called a meeting in early March 2010 in a village up in the mountains known as La Union. At the meeting, I made a complaint. The guerrillas would charge us mule drivers a toll of 5,000 pesos[8] per mule. They'd stop us at any point on the trails and if you didn't have the money they'd take your goods. But the trails were in horrible shape. Imagine riding a mule and the stirrup dragging through the mud. So I stood up and said, "Since you are the law in these parts, you should organize things because those trails are in bad shape and not every mule can go up them. And you charge all the backhoes that go up 8 million pesos. Where does that money go?" Jimmy answered that the money went to support their cause and for their food and supplies. I knew I'd pissed him off but I didn't think anything would happen.

YOUR BODY FEELS IT

A few weeks later, the Monday of Easter Week in 2010, a couple of guerrillas came to the house and told me that they needed four of my mules, saddled. I had ten mules then because I'd lost two. I said, "What do you mean you're going to take the mules? Those mules are mine. It's because of them that my children have something to eat."

One of the guerrillas said, "Jimmy told us to take them." So I said, "Well if you want, I'll sell them all so you can take them and I won't have

---

[7] Neo-paramilitary groups, such as the Paisas, emerged in 2006 in the wake of the demobilization process of the AUC national paramilitary coalition. Led largely by former paramilitaries and often employing the same criminal, political, and economic networks as their predecessors, neo-paramilitary groups have a powerful presence in many regions throughout the country.

[8] Approximately U.S.$2.50.

to see you anymore." I was fed up by then with the guerrillas. They left without the mules.

When something is about to happen, your body feels it. The night of Good Friday I didn't sleep. I'd get up, drink sugar water.[9] My wife Edith would say, "What is it?" I told her I didn't know. "My body itches all over." I would get up and scratch myself against the wooden posts of the house.

On Saturday around 5:30 a.m.: *toc, toc, toc.* I was lying awake in bed. I said, "Who is it?" From behind the door someone said, "Open up."

I opened the door and recognized two FARC milicianos[10] before I saw a machete coming down toward my head. I raised my right arm to protect myself and as soon as I lifted it, *chas!* My right hand fell to the floor. Then he swiped me with another machete chop to the legs. He got me in the left knee and I fell to the ground bleeding. Then the other miliciano shot at me three times with his revolver, but didn't hit me once. I didn't move and they thought I was dead. I heard them outside rounding up my mules.

I called to my wife who was hiding upstairs in the bedroom. I said, "Hurry, tie something on my arm to stop the blood!" She put a piece of cloth over the wound. My hand had been cut off about three inches below the elbow. The second machete blow cut my knee but it didn't slice through.

The kids woke up and saw me covered in blood. Darley, who was seven years old, ran around frightened yelling, "My dad is going to die! My dad is going to die!"

We all sat on the bed and cried together. We were all alone on the mountainside. The closest neighbor was three hours away by mule. But luckily my compadre Vicente had asked me the previous Sunday if he could come for some corn to plant on his farm. It's the custom to plant

---

[9] Sugar water is commonly used in the Colombian countryside to calm the nerves.

[10] A miliciano, roughly translated to "militiaman" in English, is a member of a guerrilla group that typically dresses in civillian clothes and doesn't participate directly in combat, but provides information and support to other guerrillas.

corn on the Saturday of Easter Week because the belief is if you plant it that day the harvest never fails.

We were huddled in the bedroom when Vicente arrived at about six in the morning. He knocked on the door and my wife opened and said, "Ay compadre! He's dying in my arms. The guerrillas came to kill him this morning and look how he is." She took him in to see me. He said, "Well we're not going to let him die." He tied a tourniquet tight above my elbow and put ground coffee on the wound to stop the bleeding.[11] He packed my severed hand in a jar with water.

Vicente went out and saddled up a mule. The guerrillas had taken seven and left me with three. I got on and headed for town by myself. But I didn't go on the main path, I went through the woods. I kept fainting on the mule and even fell off once. I crossed paths with some miners on their way up to the mine and asked if they'd seen any guerrillas. They told me they hadn't and I kept going until I got to Las Negritas. It took about eight hours.

RODRIGO EL MOCHO

As soon as the nurse saw me at the health clinic in Las Negritas, she ordered an express car service to take me to the town of Puerto López, where I met up with Edith, who brought the jar with my hand. She had left the kids with Vicente's wife.

In Puerto López, an inexperienced doctor killed my hand. He put it in alcohol with silicone and the tendons shriveled. He should have known to put it on ice but he didn't.

I was given a referral for Caucasia, a bigger town with a better hospital a couple of hours away. I wanted to buy a little coffin and bury my hand. But my hand stayed behind in Puerto López. I asked Edith, "Why didn't you bring it?"

---

[11] Ground coffee is a common home remedy in Colombia for minor cuts.

Edith and I arrived in Caucasia at about three in the afternoon. I kept fainting and the world would drop away. I felt like a chicken that had been beaten with a shovel. I spent two weeks at the hospital in Caucasia. My compadre Vicente went to visit me and brought the children.

I remember the doctor there was the first one to call me mocho.[12] He said, "From now on your name is no longer Rodrigo. It's Rodrigo El Mocho." I laughed but I wanted to die. I thought, *How am I going to work without my hand?*

When I got released from the hospital we went to the town of Barbosa, which is 240 kilometers from Caucasia, close to Medellín. We stayed there with the aunt who raised me. I refused to leave the house. I was embarrassed because of my hand. But I realized that I had to work to feed my family. In July we went back to Puerto López, and two weeks later we went up to our farm.

Our farm had been raided. Another mule had been lost and someone— I suspect it was the FARC—had taken all the cattle and three fat pigs that were ready for the knife. I had been planning to sell them on Easter Sunday. I lost everything. Six hectares of corn had been ready for harvest when we left, as well as three hectares of rice, and two hectares of yucca. All of that was lost to the weeds. I started trying to recover what I could.

About a month later, in August 2010, at around 9:30 p.m., there was another *toc, toc, toc* at the door. It was two guys wearing face masks. One of them said, "We don't want to see anyone around here. We give you twenty-four hours to get out." I said, "What are you? Guerrillas, paras, army?" One of them said, "We've delivered the message."

It was 9:40 p.m. Edith grabbed the two mules, saddled them, we loaded them with what we could, and grabbed the children. We got to Puerto López at eight in the morning.

I gave up. Apparently we're not meant to be on that land. I sold the two mules and we came to Montelíbano, Córdoba. We left everything back at the farm.

---

[12] Mocho is a colloquial term for someone who is missing a body part.

These days, we live in a squatter neighborhood on the outskirts of Montelíbano. I get up at about one in the morning to go collect wood for the fire. I've had to learn to use a hatchet with my left hand. Something like this, it traumatizes you. I'm always nervous, I don't sleep at night. I used to weigh ninety-seven kilos and now I weigh seventy-two.

I've had to start from scratch many times in my life but this is the hardest because of my hand. If I had my hand I wouldn't be here. I'd be on a mule, or up in the mountains felling lumber, doing anything. But like this, there's little I can do except wait for someone—the government, an NGO, a kind-hearted person—to give me something.

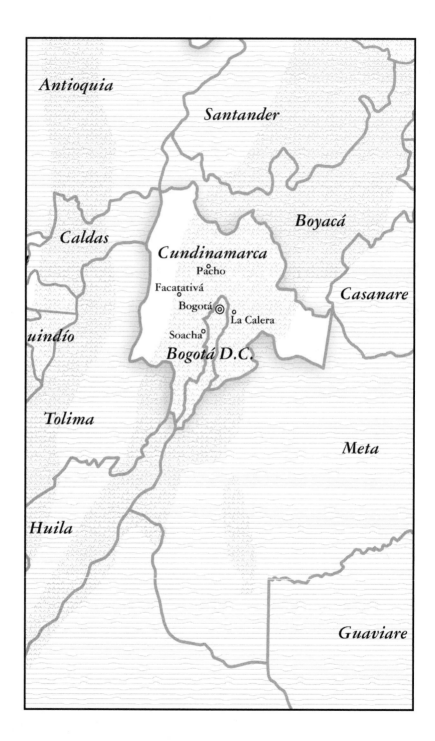

A BIG SPLENDID PARTY

Bogotá

Perched high in the Andean mountains in central Colombia, Bogotá is both insulated from the country's conflict, and at the heart of its maladies. Dubbed the "Athens of Latin America" because of its universities, museums and libraries, the capital city's inhabitants are renowned for speaking the purest Spanish in the world.

During the late 1980s and early 1990s, drive-by shootings, high-profile kidnappings by leftist guerrillas, and spectacular car bombs planted by top drugs lords kept Bogotanos on edge. Residents were on alert for any car that appeared to ride too low, fearing it could be carrying explosives.

Those days are largely a thing of the past. Bogotá's restaurants, art galleries and nightclubs have recently earned it glowing praise from travel writers, and placed it on the tourist map. One can easily sit at a café in Bogotá's swank Zona Rosa district and have no inkling of the country's conflict.

Yet the conflict is very much alive in Colombia's capital, starting downtown with the national Congress: in recent years, more than 120 Congress members have come under investigation for alleged paramilitary ties, and more than forty have been convicted. The consequences of a violent countryside are also felt in Bogotá, which is the primary recipient of displaced people in the nation. Each year, thousands seek refuge in the anonymity afforded by the city's seven million inhabitants. And Colombia's worst human rights scandal in recent history erupted in Bogotá's backyard. In 2008, several mothers from Soacha—a sprawling suburb of the capital—denounced the murder of their sons by the army, which had reported them as members of illegal armed groups killed in combat. These accusations triggered investigations that would uncover a widespread pattern of similar abuses throughout the country.

CATALINA HOYOS

AGE: 45
OCCUPATION: *Actress, model, businesswoman*
HOMETOWN: *Bogotá*
INTERVIEWED IN: *Bogotá*

The Colombian cocaine industry in the 1980s fueled a period of great excess and exploitation, in which drug traffickers like Pablo Escobar, Gonzalo Rodríguez Gacha, and the Rodríguez Orejuela brothers brazenly bought off politicians and police, and kept private zoos on their sprawling estates. Much of Colombian society turned a blind eye, but by the middle of the decade, some politicians began denouncing the negative impact of drug trafficking. In response, a group that called itself the "Extraditables," made up mostly of members of the Medellín Cartel led by Pablo Escobar, declared war on the government and demanded a ban on extradition to the U.S. for drug traffickers.[1] As part of its campaign, the "Extraditables" ordered the assassination of Liberal Party presidential candidate, Luis Carlos Galán, and placed car bombs at the headquarters of the domestic intelligence agency, DAS, and the main office of the El Espectador newspaper in Bogotá. The group is also believed to have been behind the November 27, 1989 bombing of the Cali-bound flight Avianca 203, which killed 110 people. Catalina Hoyos's father was on that

---

[1] The group's motto was "Better a tomb in Colombia than a jail cell in the United States." Extradition was banned by the 1991 Constitution, but it was reinstated in 1997.

plane. In her narrative, she describes life as a model in the 1980s and the devastating effect of cartel violence on her and her family.

Names in this narrative have been changed at the request of the narrator.

COWBOY BOOTS AND A BEAUTY PAGEANT

I was born in Tolima province but grew up in Bogotá. I come from a well-off family, but mine was never a normal family that sat down to meals together. My dad was always studying, traveling. He wanted to help make a better society, and his missions included helping children of the Indians of Vaupés province and the poor black communities in Chocó province. He was also a film buff, and he helped found the film school at the National University. He was never one of those fathers who plays with his children, but he was loving with me, my sisters Verónica and Angélica, and my brother Alberto. My mom, on the other hand, is a very tough woman. She was a criminal prosecutor.

My parents separated when I was fourteen years old, and it was around that time that I decided I wanted to be an actress. I'd go see a movie and for the whole week I'd pretend I was the leading lady.

When I was fifteen, a friend from school won a beauty pageant in a town called Pacho, about eighty kilometers from Bogotá. She invited all her friends to go to the party where she was going to receive her sash. Pacho was this small town, and I remember when we arrived at the town hall, the police chief was there with all the municipal authorities. This was a real backwater!

Then this fat, little, dark-skinned guy came up to me. With the big hat and the jewelry, he had all the look of a traqueto,[2] a drug trafficker. He looked at the cowboy boots I was wearing and asked me where I'd got them. I told him the name of the store in Bogotá, and right there he told one of his people to go to Bogotá and buy a pair for him. I thought

---

[2] Traqueto is Colombian slang for a drug trafficker. The word comes from the sound of a machine gun.

it was funny, but the whole scene was sort of sleazy. Those people were so arrogant, with all the money they had.

I phoned my mother after that, because she'd told me to call her once I'd arrived. She asked me who was at the party, so I asked some of the people for their names and I started telling her. Then she said, "Get in a taxi and tell them I'll pay the fare here," so I left the party right away. It turned out that the guy who'd asked me about the boots was a drug trafficker named Gonzalo Rodríguez Gacha.[3] The place was filled with traquetos. I didn't really know who they were at the time, but since my mom was a prosecutor who dealt with drug trafficking cases, she knew.

When my brother and sisters and I were growing up, my mom would tell us that when she took on cases against drug traffickers, plane tickets to Disney World would arrive at her office with the names of all us kids. It was a bribe, but at the same time it was a threat, showing that they knew our names. She'd also get envelopes stuffed with cash. But my mother never accepted a bribe in her life.

COCAINE WAS PASSED AROUND
LIKE HORS D'OEUVRES

I finished high school in 1982, when I was sixteen, and started studying at an acting academy. When I was seventeen I got my first modeling contract, which was for a local clothing store. After that I was on television and in magazines, and I could make maybe 400,000 pesos[4] in a single photo shoot. From one moment to the next I was suddenly part of the elite, the twenty or so professional models that were working in Colombia back then. I'd travel around the country to runway shows,

---

[3] Rodríguez Gacha, also known as El Mexicano, was a Colombian drug lord and, with Pablo Escobar, one of the leaders of the Medellín cartel. He was a native of Pacho, Cundinamarca.

[4] About U.S.$1,300 at the time. The minimum wage at the time was 25,000 pesos per month, or U.S.$83.

and at one point I was in about fifteen different television commercials at the same time. I would see myself on TV and say, "That's me!"

It was a life of parties. In Bogotá, cocaine was passed around like hors d'oeuvres. At any party in Colombia you'd go into the bathroom and there would be lines on the sink counter. I tried it once at the Keops discotheque, which was all the rage then. It was one of the most anxiety-producing experiences of my life. My heart started racing, and I thought I was going to die! I managed to get home, but I sat outside on the steps until the effect wore off because inside the house I felt like a caged animal.

There were always traquetos at the parties. I've sometimes thought that, if I hadn't had the education my parents gave me, I would have ended up the wife of one of those traquetos, like a lot of the other models did. Why would I be any different? But I saw these people differently. I mean, if I went to a party and it was filled with traquetos I didn't say, "Uy! I'm not going because I don't mix with those people." I went, but I kept them at a distance.

My father never really approved of my career choice. He was an intellectual, and he thought the telenovelas I acted in were trash. But we had a good relationship.

In 1989, when I was twenty, my dad was working in New York at a development organization. He came back to Bogotá one Sunday in November and we got together at my sister Verónica's house. My brother Alberto wasn't there at the time because he was studying at the Naval Academy in Cartagena. At the get-together, my dad, my sisters and I all started planning a vacation together. My dad was going to be lecturing at the Universidad del Valle in Cali for three or four days, and we were making plans to all go to the beach afterward to Cartagena or San Andrés. It was the first time in six months that we'd seen him. By that time, I had moved out of my mom's house and was living in a big house in La Calera, a wealthy suburb in the mountains above Bogotá.

During the meal my dad began to speak to each of us sisters about our lives. He also talked to me about each one of my sisters and my brother, telling me to take care of all of them. He said, "You have to take care of Alberto, he's still young. Take care of Vero." Vero is Verónica, my little sister who he thought had married too young. He told me to believe in myself and to believe in my instinct. I remember I got a cold shiver; I had the feeling my dad was saying goodbye. I remember thinking, *What's going to happen? Why is he telling me this now and not in Cartagena while we sunbathe and have a few drinks?*

WHAT DID YOUR DAD LOOK LIKE?

The next day, November 27, 1989, I went to the gym early like I always did. I always called my mom early in the morning but that day I called my godfather first. He asked me if I'd spoken to my mom and when I told him I hadn't he said, "Call your mother." I asked him, "What happened?" and he just insisted, "Call your mother." I called my mom and she told me the news. The plane my dad had taken to Cali had exploded over Soacha.[5] The plane had taken off at 7:10 a.m., and five minutes later it blew up, killing 110 people.[6]

I got in my car and rushed to my mom's house. In the car, I turned on the radio, and the announcer was reading out the passenger list. The presidential candidate César Gaviria was apparently supposed to be on that flight.[7] The radio announcer said a bomb had blown up the plane, and that Pablo Escobar and Rodríguez Gacha were suspected of ordering the attack. At that moment, I remembered that I'd met Rodríguez Gacha at the party in Pacho years before. I had met my dad's executioner.

I went to my mom's house and my two sisters were already there. It was chaotic. Everyone screaming, crying. I spoke again with my god-

---

[5] A poor, industrial suburb of Bogotá, seventeen kilometers from the city center.

[6] All 107 people on board the plane were killed, as were three people on the ground hit by falling debris.

[7] Gaviria had replaced Luis Carlos Galán as the Liberal Party candidate for the 1990 presidential elections after Galán was gunned down in August 1989 in Soacha, on orders from Pablo Escobar. He was elected, and served as the president of Colombia from 1990–1994.

father. He had an air transport company that chartered planes and helicopters for oil companies and he asked me if I wanted a helicopter to fly over the crash site. But I said no. I wanted to be on the ground to see what happened. I grabbed my two sisters and we set out in the car through Monday morning traffic toward Soacha. I told them, "Do you want to live with the doubt? Not me." We could have waited quietly at home to get the notification of my dad's death but I needed to see. When we got to Soacha, the residents there guided us to the crash site because the plane had fallen in a mountainous part of Soacha, not in the town center.

It was about nine in the morning when we got to the crash site, and we saw that it had been cordoned off by the army. They weren't supposed to let anyone into the site but I said to one of the soldiers, "What would you do if it were your dad on that plane?" He saw us three girls—I was twenty, Verónica was nineteen and Angélica was twenty-one—and he took pity on us. He asked me, "What did he look like?"

I told him, "My dad always wore a turtleneck and corduroy pants." The soldier said, "I know where he is." We walked uphill about a kilometer and saw pieces of clothing on the ground, a briefcase and body parts. There were body parts everywhere; we walked among heads, limbs, and guts. I have never forgotten the scent.

DISCONNECTED FROM THE PLANET

After a long while, the soldiers came up to us with a huge black bag and they shook a body out. I almost fainted. My dad was a handsome man; he looked like Jack Nicholson. But the face of the dead person was frozen in a scream that he must have let out from way up there. His mouth was completely open, and the expression of distress on his face was clear. His skull was open and his brains had exploded. I looked at my sister Angélica. She was a beautiful woman, like a Colombian Pocahontas, but when she saw the body fall out of the bag she became disconnected from the planet and she didn't speak.

I couldn't believe it. Eight or ten hours earlier we'd been with him. At three in the afternoon the day before it had been all about planning a vacation, the beach, laughter, delicious food, wine. At 7:45 a.m. the next day: death.

The soldiers asked us, "Is it your father?" It looked like him, but my sisters and I began to doubt it, especially my little sister Verónica. She said, "I don't think it's him." It was very difficult. I felt that it was him, but I wanted to be absolutely sure. Verónica said, "Look at his hands. They don't look like his hands." My dad's hands had been very pretty. He was a vain person, and his hands were spotless. This man who fell from three thousand meters, his skin was intact, but every inch of bone in his body must have been broken to pieces because his hand was like rubber; it bent this way and that.

I thought, *What do we remember about my dad that was unique?* And it was his feet. When he was little his mother made him lace up his boots really tight and it deformed his instep; it was really high. So in the end we recognized him from his feet.

The whole time Angélica was silent. She just looked at us and said nothing. She was completely gone. Through all of this process I was the one who stayed completely sane. My dad had always said that I was the crazy one—his nickname for me was "La Loquita." I was the one who drove really fast, I was the model, I did what I wanted. He thought the sane one was Angélica, but no. I realized then that I had to take the reins because no one else would.

Then a doctor came, and without saying a word, he knelt down and sliced my dad open. He looked at the organs and then he said, "Okay, let's close him up." He took a needle and thread and sewed four big stitches. Then he handed us a little piece of paper with a number, like the kind you pull at a butcher shop to wait your turn. The piece of paper had "438" written on it. The doctor said we could use that to claim our dad's body at the Forensic Medicine Institute in Bogotá.[8]

---

[8] The national coroner's office.

BODIES IN A DUMP TRUCK

My sisters and I stayed and watched as the rescuers threw the body bags into a muddy dump truck. The relatives of other passengers had also shown up at the site, and the rescuers were piecing bodies together to present to them. We were lucky to have a full body; others were content with just an arm or a leg. We stayed for five hours in the hot sun, watching, because I wanted to make sure that they put my dad in the dump truck, that they weren't going to leave him. We finally left at about two in the afternoon and went to my mom's house. She was hysterical, screaming. Even though my parents had separated, my mother was still in love with my dad. A fortune teller had once told her that my dad would come back to her, so she was waiting for him. We got to her house and we gave her medicine to calm her down.

It was raining when my sisters and I went to the Forensic Medicine Institute at about five in the afternoon. But when we got there we were told that the bodies hadn't arrived yet. We said we'd wait. We finally left at ten, after the officials at the Forensic Medicine Institute told us they wouldn't hand over the bodies that night. It was still raining.

I took my sisters home, and went to my house. It was something like two or three in the morning. I was crying as I drove up the hill because that's when I said to myself, *Now I can cry.* I got home, went into my bedroom and built a fire in the fireplace. I sat in front of it and I said to my dad, "I'm not going to sleep until you tell me what happened." I stayed up all night; I was struggling to understand what had happened.

My little brother Alberto arrived from Cartagena early the next morning, and I went with him and my sisters to the Forensic Medicine Institute at seven. I told the person in charge there, "I've come for my father," and he said, "Look, there's been a problem. The body bags broke, and all the bodies have been mixed up, so you'll have to go in and ID him." The little number I'd been given was useless.

My brother said, "I don't think I can do this." And I said, "You're the man of this family now. Grab onto my arm as tight as you can and we'll go together, but you can't live with the doubt of whether it really was Dad or not." So we went into a muddy, open-air courtyard filled with body bags. We had to walk among the dead, among the severed limbs, as an official from the Forensic Medicine Institute opened the bags and asked, "Is this him?" The decomposition process, after sitting out in the sun and then in the rain overnight, was incredible. When we finally found our dad, it was horrible, because his body was slimy; his skin had sort of melted.

We took his body and held a funeral a few days later. We couldn't have an open casket because of the state he was in. Lots of people sent flowers, and there were nice eulogies. I fell into a sort of limbo; I was there but I wasn't. I didn't eat. In that week, I lost something like eleven kilos from the anxiety, from not sleeping. Then, two weeks after my father was killed, my sister Angélica started doing heavy drugs. She's never gotten over it. She's been in and out of rehabilitation clinics seven times.

ONE DOWN

After the funeral, my family hired a well-respected lawyer to sue the state for the bombing, because the airport security controls had failed. In the days following the bombing, investigators determined that someone had walked onto the plane, left the bomb in a briefcase under a seat and walked off. The lawyer was also handling the cases of several of the other families from the plane. However, three days after we hired him, the lawyer was gunned down at the door to his building.

About a month after my dad was killed, I was riding in a taxi in Bogotá. I was chatting with the taxi driver because I like to do that. He was listening to the radio when the announcer said that the drug trafficker Rodríguez Gacha had just been killed.

I said, "Stop, please, please stop." The driver said, "Why, what happened?" I said, "Do you have a minute?" He stopped, and I got out, looked up to heaven and gave thanks to God. "One down," I said.

By that time I felt I couldn't live in this country any more. I was incensed by everything that was happening with the drug traffickers trying to take over the country, the war they had declared. So on February 11, 1990, I left Colombia for New York on a temporary visitor's visa. I lived in a tiny apartment on 58th Street between and Fifth and Sixth Avenues, but I wasn't exactly struggling. I started working at an art gallery, and I studied language and literature at Columbia University to improve my English. I then started studying film direction.

I met my husband Pedro on a trip back to Colombia in March 1990. I was there for an event in my dad's memory. Pedro is Spanish and he worked at a bank there. He would fly up to New York on the weekends to see me, and a year later we got married and moved to Spain. We had two children, Juan Carlos and Pilar. Now we live in southern Florida.

For many years I was embarrassed to admit that I was a victim of my country. And I was afraid to remember, to face all that again. I never spoke about how my dad died. You try to forget because that's your medicine. I only started facing it in 2011. I've lived outside of Colombia for more than twenty years and I go back for visits, but I wouldn't live there. Drug trafficking has been a cancer on this country. It's contaminated everything, it's penetrated everywhere. And I never want my kids to think that's normal.

CARMENZA GÓMEZ

AGE: 55
OCCUPATION: *Cook*
HOMETOWN: *Villavicencio, Meta*
INTERVIEWED IN: *Bogotá*

Members of Colombia's armed forces have come under investigation for the killing of thousands of civilians over the past decade. Many of the cases were "false positives," where soldiers executed civilians, dressed them up as guerrillas or members of other illegal armed groups, and reported them as combatants killed in action. Soldiers were offered incentives for enemy deaths, such as vacation time and promotions, according to a report by the U.N. Special Rapporteur on Extrajudicial Executions, who described the killings as the "cold-blooded, premeditated murder of innocent civilians for profit." In 2008 a media scandal over the killings of poor young men from Soacha, an industrial suburb of Bogotá, prompted the Colombian government to dismiss twenty-seven members of the military, including three generals. Colombia's Attorney General's office has opened investigations into more than 2,800 extrajudicial killings attributed to state agents, with the majority of the cases allegedly committed by the army between 2004 and 2008.

Carmenza Gómez's son was one of the more than a dozen young men from Soacha who were lured by false promises of work, then executed by the army and reported as members of guerrilla or neo-paramilitary groups killed in combat. Six months later, another of her sons was shot dead while investigating his brother's execution. Carmenza's public outcry and pursuit of justice as part of a group of "Soacha mothers" provoked a series of death threats against her and her family, which has forced her to repeatedly change homes within Soacha and Bogotá.

SCRAPINGS AT THE BOTTOM OF THE POT

I'm the daughter of Santanderean parents who left Santander province when they were displaced in the times of La Violencia.[1] Back then people fought over colors, because one was Liberal and red, and the other was godo[2]—Conservative—and blue. My parents were Liberals, so the godos kicked them out of Santander.

My parents moved to the Eastern Plains and bought a farm there. I was born in 1956, the youngest of fourteen brothers and sisters; I was practically the scrapings at the bottom of the pot of that marriage. My parents got separated when I was five years old, so I stayed with my mom and three other siblings, and I grew up working with her on the farm.

When I was thirteen years old, I got tired of studying and I told my mom I was going to work. She wouldn't let me, so I ran away to the city of Villavicencio, the capital of Meta province. I worked as a maid at a family's house until I was fifteen years old, which was when Luis Alfonso appeared in my life. Luis Alfonso was a twenty-year-old mechanic, and we made a home together on a farm in the Eastern Plains.

I had five children with him: Nydia, Yaneth, Norma, William, and John. Over the years, we went from farm to farm, working and struggling. In 1980, when I was twenty-four years old, I decided that we should go back to Villavicencio because the girls were growing up. At the time my

---

[1] La Violencia (The Violence) refers to a period of civil conflict fought between the Liberal and Conservative political parties from 1948–1958, during which an estimated 200,000 people were killed and as many as two million displaced. The province of Santander was one of the hardest hit by the partisan fighting.

[2] Godo is a pejorative name for a Conservative. The Liberal and Conservative parties were Colombia's two main political parties until the 2000s.

eldest daughter Nydia was nine years old, and my youngest son John was about to turn one. Since the girls were school age, it was a priority for me that they study. But I was afraid to send them from the farm to study in the village because the roads in the countryside are very dangerous. So we went to Villavicencio and put my daughters in school. During that time, I worked as a cook at a restaurant and Luis Alfonso drove a tractor-trailer. He was a very jealous man, and very chauvinistic. He'd come home pissed off, accusing me of having another man. He was very aggressive and he'd beat me. Once I went to see my mother and told her about it, and she said, "Hit him back with whatever you can find." And I thought, *She's right. I'm not going to let myself get hit without fighting back.* So I sharpened my claws, and when he fought with me, we'd go at it like cats and dogs. Once, when he punched my face, I grabbed his noble parts and left him unconscious. Our relationship became one of obligation, for my children.

Luis Alfonso always said that if I left him, he'd kill me and the kids. But I saved and saved my money, and stored it at my neighbor's house so that I could leave him one day.

In January 1982, I finally left Luis Alfonso. I took a four-hour bus ride with my kids to Bogotá, where I had a sister. But when I tried calling her from the bus station it was always her husband who answered. He and I didn't get along well so I'd hang up, but I kept calling, hoping my sister would eventually answer. I ended up sleeping at the bus terminal for three days, cuddling my kids in a corner of the station. Finally my sister answered and we went to stay at her place.

I started working as a cook at a grill and everything was going well until around March, when my brother-in-law started pursuing me. I told my sister about it and she didn't believe me. Instead, she complained to him about it, and he went into my room one night and slapped me. I had scissors in my hand and cut a piece of his jacket. That night, they kicked me and my kids out onto the street.

I PROVIDED FOR MY KIDS

I found a little room for us to live in, and after a while I started working at a brick factory. That's where I met José. I don't know whether it was good luck or bad luck, but I became pregnant again.

I stopped working at the brick factory when I was six months pregnant and went to work in a restaurant for a woman named Rosa. My son Víctor was born in my house on March 13, 1985, when I was twenty-nine years old. A neighbor helped deliver him, and became his godmother.

I would take Víctor with me to the restaurant. Rosa made him a little crib in the corner, and I'd put him there while I worked. After Víctor was born, José convinced me to live with him. But it was the same problem: he was a jealous man. He didn't hit me, though, because he knew that if he dared to, he'd have some serious problems.

When Víctor was two years old I got pregnant again, because José wouldn't let me use birth control. Jeison was born on January 30, 1987, and when he was about seven or eight months old, I got pregnant again. This time, José told me to have an abortion, and I told him, "If there's panela water[3] for the kids that we already have, there's panela water for the kid who's on his way. If you're bored with me, leave." He left the next day.

I had my son Alejandro in March 1988. He and José's other two sons don't have his last name. I never bothered either of the fathers of my children, asking them for money for my kids. Never. I worked, and I provided for them.

HE WENT TO WORK ON THE COAST

We're a very close family, and all my children are friends with each other. I love them all equally but my kids used to say I loved Víctor more. He was special with me, very loving. At one point, the only work I had was selling

---

[3] Panela is an unrefined food product made by boiling sugarcane juice into a hard, crusty block. It can then be dissolved in hot water to make a drink.

coffee on the street, and Víctor, who must have been around ten years old at the time, insisted on getting up at three in the morning so he could come with me. Sometimes when we were at home, he'd turn on the music and grab me to dance, or he'd just sit on my lap and hug me. And when he was older, whenever he came home or left the house he would ask for my blessing: "Cuchita,[4] give me your blessing."[5] If he was out having a drink with friends and there was trouble in the neighborhood, he would also call me and ask for my blessing.

Eventually I moved into a housing complex in the San Mateo neighborhood of Soacha, a suburb on the southern edge of Bogotá. I was living with my kids William, Víctor, Alejandro, and Yaneth. Norma lived in the same complex and was always at my house. Nydia and John lived in different neighborhoods.

My sons Víctor, William, and Jeison all served in the military. I was afraid they'd get killed in combat. I would ask my God, my little Virgin Mary and the Virgin of Santa Marta to protect them from everything bad and dangerous. But I felt proud that my kids had completed their military service because they served the nation. I also have five brothers who did their military service, as well as nephews who are professional soldiers. I used to see a soldier and be captivated.

On Friday, August 22, 2008, I was getting ready for work when Víctor came home from his job as the doorman at a bar. He went to my room and said, "Mami, have you bought the gas for the stove yet?" I said, "No, papi, I haven't." He said, "I'll bring 12,000 pesos,[6] which was my tip last night." I said, "Keep your money and this Sunday we'll go buy the gas." Víctor had a five-year-old daughter by then, and he didn't make enough at the bar to support her and also help me out with the rent. He hadn't been able to get

---

[4] Cuchita is a colloquial term that means old lady but is very commonly used as an endearing substitute for mami.

[5] It's common practice for mothers to give children their blessing by making the sign of the cross over their heads as protection.

[6] About U.S.$6.

a steady job because even though he had his military service card,[7] I had only been able to pay for his schooling up to eighth grade.

I went to work again on Saturday morning and left my kids sleeping in the apartment. When I got home that night the doorman at the housing complex told me that Víctor had gone out with his brother Alejandro at 6:30 p.m.

Alejandro came home at around 9:30 p.m. and I asked where Víctor was. He said, "Mami, he went to work on the coast." I said, "The coast?" Víctor had never been to the Caribbean coast. Alejandro said that two men and a woman had left with Víctor for the coast, and that he would return in a week or two. I asked, "Did he take any clothes?" and Alejandro said no, that he hadn't even taken his toothbrush. It seemed strange to me; whenever Víctor went to stay at his girlfriend's house, he would pack a toothbrush and a pair of underwear in a bag. And it seemed incredible to me that he had left without asking for my blessing like he always did.

Over the next few days, I waited for Víctor to call, and kept asking Alejandro, "Your brother hasn't called? He hasn't left a message?" He'd say, "No, Mami, nothing." I had no way to contact Víctor because he didn't have a cell phone. Then on September 1, at around ten at night, all of my kids were running in and out of my house. I thought, *What happened to these kids? Have they gone crazy?* I asked Yaneth what was going on and she said that Jeison and William were making calls looking for jobs. I believed them, because at that point I was practically the only one in the house who was working.

The next day I woke up, went into Yaneth's room, and found Norma, Jeison, Alejandro, and William in there. Yaneth looked drawn. I asked them, "What happened? What happened? Yaneth, you have a look on your face." They said, "Nothing Mami." But I had a feeling something was going on.

---

[7] An ID card that certifies that a man has completed his mandatory military service. Many employers require the card to hire someone.

That day I had a checkup at the Samaritana hospital for my varicose veins. When we were waiting for the surgeon to see me, Yaneth left the room and called Norma. After a while, she came back crying. I knew that something strange was going on, but I thought it was because Norma had just separated from her husband.

After the checkup, we were walking towards the hospital door when Yaneth told me, "Mami, I have to tell you something." A chill immediately ran down my body. I asked her, "What happened?" She said, "Mami, we have to go to the Forensic Medicine Institute."[8] I asked again, "What happened?" She said, "Mami, Víctor was killed."

I HAVE TO REVEAL THE ARMY'S DIRTY SECRET

I fainted when I heard about Víctor. When I came to, I was on a stretcher; Yaneth was by my side and a nurse was giving me oxygen. I immediately remembered why I had fainted and I felt an enormous loss and pain. I stood up and told Yaneth, "Let's get a taxi and go to the Forensic Medicine Institute." I passed that building every day on my way to work and I never thought I would have to go there to identify one of my children. Yaneth told me that Víctor's body wasn't there, that he had been killed in Ocaña, Norte de Santander province.[9]

She told me how she and her siblings had found out about Víctor's death. He had left Soacha with two other young men named Jader and Diego. Diego had a cousin who was doing an internship at the Forensic Medicine Institute in Bogotá at the time, and about five or six days after Víctor, Diego, and Jader disappeared, the cousin logged onto the institute's database and saw a photo of Diego, dead. He immediately called Diego's mother and let her know that her son had turned up dead with two others from Soacha. Diego's mother immediately spread the news in the neighborhood, and eventually someone told my son John.

---

[8] The national coroner's office.

[9] Ocaña is 680 kilometers north of Soacha.

When we got to the Forensic Medicine Institute, Nydia, Norma, Jeison, and José—Víctor's dad—were there. The Forensic Medicine officials showed me a photo of Víctor on a computer. The photo showed a bullet wound between his eyes. The officials told us we had to go get him quickly, because if we didn't he'd be buried in an unmarked grave.

After making arrangements for a funeral home, my kids and I left for Ocaña at four in the afternoon on September 2, 2008. A friend of John's drove us in his car and Norma and Yaneth went in the hearse with the empty casket. I cried in the car. The only thing John said during the journey was, "Don't cry, Mamita, don't cry." The ride seemed eternal to me. It rained and rained, and there was horrible thunder. I kept thinking, *Why my son? Why was my son killed?* We picked up one of my brothers who lived in Aguachica, Cesar, and arrived in Ocaña at nine in the morning.

When we got to the local morgue I said, "I came for my son Víctor Gómez's body." A morgue official said, "He died in combat." Imagine my surprise. I said, "Died in combat? My son wasn't any guerrilla."[10] He said, "Yes, the army killed him. They handed him over to the morgue on August 25 at 8:45am." I said, "But he disappeared on August 23. How was my son going to become a guerrilla in such little time?" Then the official said, "There are a lot of young men from Soacha here who were killed in combat and who are buried here in unmarked graves."[11]

When I heard that, I grabbed the man in charge of the morgue and said, "Why? Why my son?" He said, "Calm down, Ma'am." I said, "I'm not going to keep quiet about this, I'm going to speak out." So he asked me if I wanted to speak to the media. I said, "Yes, because maybe there

---

[10] The Revolutionary Armed Forces of Colombia (FARC) and National Liberation Army (ELN) are Colombia's two main guerrilla groups. Founded in the 1960s and claiming to represent the country's rural poor in the fight against Colombia's wealthy classes and U.S. imperialism, both groups commit widespread abuses against civilians, including killings, threats, and recruitment of child soldiers.

[11] According to press accounts, the army initially reported Víctor Gómez as a member of the Águilas Negras, a neo-paramilitary group, killed in combat.

are some other mothers who think that their sons are away working, but they're really dead and buried here in unmarked graves. And if I have to die here next to my son, I'll die here."

Various print and television journalists arrived to take down the facts about what had happened and how my son had been killed. I gave interviews while my daughters and brother filled out the paperwork for Víctor's body to be released. When my brother came back, he said, "No more. Let her be, she's not feeling well. Don't ask her any more questions." But I said, "No brother, I have to reveal the army's dirty secret."

My brother wouldn't let me go in and see Víctor's body—he didn't want me to faint again—but later he told me Víctor had been shot thirteen times.

After the morgue handed over my son's body at eleven in the morning, we immediately left for Soacha and arrived at the funeral home at one in the morning. At Víctor's wake, I was sitting on a couch hugging his daughter when I saw two women walk in. I heard one of them say, "I don't have any tears left, and my feet are covered with blisters." They looked at Víctor in the coffin and walked out. Then my daughter Yaneth came and asked me to go outside because one of the women needed to talk to me. Her name was Luz Edilia, and she was the mother of Jader, one of the two young men who had died with Víctor. She told me she had been asking for donations to bring her son from Ocaña. She told me that she'd also talked to the media; she and I were the first mothers to go on television to denounce the killings.

On September 5 we placed Víctor in a tomb in the Chapinero Cemetery. I didn't want a grave because I have a phobia of dirt, and I didn't want to leave my son anywhere where he'd be stepped on or where water would fall on him. My son John had been very close to Víctor, and he swore at Víctor's coffin that he would find out who had recruited him to leave for the coast.

Víctor left a five-year-old daughter behind. She lives with her mom, who doesn't let me see her. I think it's because I didn't approve of the relationship, and maybe she thinks that I want to get custody of their daughter. It makes me sad, because she's the only thing that remains of him. She's the spitting image of Víctor. To look at her is to see Víctor's face.

FALSE POSITIVES

There were other young men from Soacha who had been missing for six or eight months. I started going to the Forensic Medicine Institute with mothers who didn't know where their sons were, to see if there was any news there. I'd also be at the Personería's office[12] in Soacha when another mom arrived, and another, and another, with the same problem. That's how I got to know the other mothers from Soacha. In total, fourteen young men from Soacha had been taken away and killed by the army. The victims included a mentally disabled boy who was twenty-six years old but had the mental age of a nine-year-old. There were also two minors—one was sixteen and the other was seventeen. Víctor, Diego, and Jader were the last ones who were taken away in 2008.

Diego and Víctor were the only two in the morgue in Ocaña, so Diego's mom and I were the only ones who were able to have a wake for our sons. Most of the other sons had been in unmarked graves for six or eight months, and their bodies had decomposed. I went with one of the mothers when her son's remains were exhumed for a second time in order to confirm his identity with a DNA test. The hole was filled halfway with water.

The national media ran with the story that September. In October, President Uribe went on television and said that the young men from

---

[12] The Personería is a municipal entity charged with monitoring citizens' constitutional rights.

Soacha were criminals who had been killed in combat.[13] He also said that we mothers had gotten together to tarnish the reputation of the army. The current president, Juan Manuel Santos, who was then defense minister, said the same thing.[14] Our sons started to be called "false positives." My son Jeison, who had recently left the army, explained to me, "Mami, 'false positive' means that the army kills a peasant or someone, and they legalize them. They make them pass as a guerrilla in order to win a medal, days off, a higher rank, or a post in another country."

So what caused so many deaths of so many young people were the rewards that were offered to the army.[15] Soldiers would get a reward for each guerrilla that was killed. Our sons weren't combatants for illegal groups; they were good young men.

---

[13] In a speech on October 7, 2008, then-president Álvaro Uribe said, "The Attorney General maintained that the young men who disappeared from Soacha were killed in combat and they weren't there to pick coffee. They went with criminal purposes and didn't die the day after their disappearances but a month later." In October 2011, Uribe publicly stated, "I've talked on many occasions with mothers from Soacha. And many of them in very private meetings with me confessed that unfortunately some of their boys were involved in illegal activities."

[14] On May 4, 2009, then-president Uribe said, "There are many cases of false complaints... there are unscrupulous people who are eager to discredit the policy of Democratic Security." President Juan Manuel Santos, who was defense minister at the time, stated the same day, "We have discovered that there are many false complaints, a lot of people who want to make legitimate combat deaths—of terrorists and guerrillas who have been killed in combat—appear as extrajudicial executions, in order to spatter or stain the good name of our military institutions."

[15] In a 2010 report, the U.N. Special Rapporteur on Extrajudicial Executions said, "According to information provided by the Government, rewards cannot be paid to public servants (such as soldiers)... However, other sources of payment in the form of 'confidential expenses' and commanders' discretionary funds are of serious concern...Significantly, members of the military have also been provided various incentives to kill, including vacation time, medals, and promotions."

HIS FEET WERE STILL WARM

My son John, who worked at a brick factory, started investigating who had recruited Víctor. He never told me what he was finding out, but shortly after his brother's death he told me that he was getting threatened. He said he'd received telephone calls telling him not to stick his nose where it didn't belong. I told him, "No more, mi'jo. I'm going to file a complaint." He said, "No Mami, don't file a complaint, because the threats are also against you and my kids. I don't want them to do anything to you." I told him to leave the neighborhood, to leave town, to go somewhere else. He refused.

In the middle of October 2008, I got a call at about one in the afternoon from the hospital in Fusagasugá,[16] telling me that John had had an accident. Right there I knew it was no accident, that it had to do with Víctor's death. He was being transferred to Bogotá, and I was told to wait for him at the Samaritana Hospital there. John had been temporarily paralyzed from the waist down.

Two policemen had apparently been helping him investigate Víctor's killing, and they had gone to Fusa together. The three of them had been drinking at about eight at night, and then the two policemen took John to a bridge and pushed him over.

He said that as he was falling he reached out with his hands in the dark to try to break his fall, but he fell on some rocks and passed out. When he came to, he figured it was about one in the morning; there was a bright moon. He said he was very cold and when he tried to move, he couldn't. He passed his hand across his forehead and his hand came away bloody. John told me that he asked for God's forgiveness, and that if he was going to take him, to take him right away. He passed out again and when he woke up again it was already day. He dragged himself with his arms to a path, and saw a man carrying oranges walk by. The man stopped, squeezed an orange and gave my son some juice. Then he picked John up, threw him over his shoulder

---

[16] A town about sixty-five kilometers south of Bogotá, also referred to as Fusa.

and carried him to the side of the main road. The man left him there and walked away. Later, a police car passed by and took him to the hospital in Fusa.

I told John to tell me the names of the two policemen, but he refused. Time passed and the threats began again, but he still wouldn't let me file a complaint.

At the hospital, the doctors performed a surgery on John that allowed him to walk again. He had to wear a brace, but after a month he could walk. I remember that December 10 was my granddaughter's fifteenth birthday. John danced the whole night. He wore the brace, but he even danced reggaeton. That day he was so happy.

On February 4, 2009 a friend called at around 6:30 p.m. and said that she had to tell me something very urgent. I immediately sensed that something had happened. I said to my son William, "Uy William! Holy God, protect John and don't let anything have happened to him." A little while later my friend knocked at the door, and when I opened it she told me that John had been shot.

I ran out of the house like a crazy woman and went to the Soacha Hospital. The doorman wouldn't let me go in, so I grabbed him, threw him to the side and went in. I saw John on a stretcher inside the emergency room. Some police agents who I already knew from Víctor's case were there. They said, "Calm down Miss Carmenza, your son is fine. He's only been shot in his hand." I said, "If my son's fine, then I want to talk to him." A moment later the doctor came out and said, "Your son is in a very serious condition. He was shot in the face and he has an internal hemorrhage. The bullet is embedded in his neck. He has to be transferred to the Samaritana Hospital." I thought, *I have a lot of faith in the doctors at the Samaritana.*

My daughters and John's girlfriend were outside, and together we waited and waited for John to be transferred to the Samaritana. John's girlfriend told me that he'd received a phone call that evening. After the call, he told her he was going out but that he'd be right back. About fifteen minutes later she got the news that he had been killed at a store, where he'd been called to a meeting. He'd been sitting outside the store when two guys on a motorcycle came up and shot him three times with a pistol with a silencer. One of the bullets shattered a store window, and the storeowner went out to see what was going on. He found John on the ground, choking on his own blood.

It was after ten at night when John was transferred, but to the San Mateo Hospital because there weren't beds available at the Samaritana. I saw him being lifted into the ambulance; his face looked like a monster's. He was already in a coma, and the paramedics were giving him oxygen through his mouth. He stayed at San Mateo hospital the entire night, and we watched over him.

The next morning, at around 9:15 a.m., the doctor took me into a room. He said, "Sit down." When he said that, I said, "My son died." He looked at me but didn't say anything. I said, "Doctor, tell me the truth. Did my son die?" He said, "Yes. He had a heart attack ten minutes ago and died."

I went to see John in his room. His feet were still warm. I held his hand and spoke to him. I asked him why he hadn't let me report the threats and the attempt on his life—maybe we could have got some help so he could have left town. I asked him to forgive me for not having been able to give him everything he may have needed.

After I left him, I thought, *My God! I don't have any money. Where will I take his body?* My kids had a lot of friends from the neighborhood where they were raised, and some of them had been with me at the hospital from the moment they heard John had been wounded. One of the friends went to the neighborhood to collect money and brought me 380,000 pesos.[17] My sister, who I'd lived with when I first got to Bogotá, also gave me 60,000 pesos,[18] and the Personería in Soacha helped me too. I thank God, because people helped me with a lot of love, and I had money to give my son a funeral.

---

[17] About U.S.$190.

[18] About U.S.$30.

John was placed in a tomb on February 7. And from what was left over of the money that his friends had collected, I got a very nice tombstone for him.

I'D GO ALONE AND SIT DOWN
NEXT TO THEIR TOMBS

The threats started two weeks later. I remember the call so well. On February 17, I started working as a cleaning lady at the National Institute for Health, and on the twenty-fourth I got a call on my cell phone while I was at work. A woman who said her name was Clara told me she was from the SIJIN police.[19] She asked me, "Where did you file the complaint for the death of your son?" I said, "Which of the two?" She asked for my home address so she could come and ask me some questions, and I said, "No, I'm not going to give you my address. They've already killed my second son, and just the same they can come for me and my other kids. Please, I don't want any more dead people in my family." I had a strange feeling about the phone call, and I didn't believe that she was from the SIJIN. So when my daughter Norma called me, I told her about it.

She said, "Mami, the same person called Nydia and said the same thing." Norma told me that silly Nydia had given them our address. But Nydia was threatened openly. "Clara" asked her if she knew where the complaints about my sons' killings had been reported, and Nydia told her that she didn't know, but that we already knew it was the army who'd killed them. That's when Clara said to my daughter, "Bitch, watch out. We have your address, and you're going to turn up with your mouth full of flies, just like your brothers."

Soon after that call, Nydia moved out of her house and changed her cell phone number. I moved to Bogotá and sent Jeison and Alejandro to

---

[19] The Sectional Judicial Police (SIJIN) is a branch of the national police force.

live with their sisters. I'd stay a day at my daughter's house, a day at my sister's house, a day at my cousin's house, and a day at my niece's house.

A man I knew who worked for a human rights NGO suggested I apply for asylum in Canada. I sent the papers to the Canadian embassy, and my grandchildren got excited. But after two months I thought, *Why should I run away? I didn't kill anyone, I haven't robbed anyone. My two sons were taken from me.* I decided I didn't want asylum. I went back to Soacha, but I didn't go back to the same house as before. I had to continually move from house to house every two or three months.

I've been discriminated against when I've looked for places to live. It's because I'm under threat. People recognize me here because I'm the Soacha mother who goes on television most. The landlords tell me, "I can't rent to you, because if they come kill you, they'll kill all of us."

Six months after John was killed, my daughter-in-law sent me his two sons: Sebastian, who was eight, and Esteban, who was seven. She dropped them off on a holiday and I thought it was just for a day or two. But she didn't come back for them. She left them only with the clothes they had on their backs. I took the boys to live with my daughters Norma and Nydia, since they have sons the same age, and now they have legal custody of the kids. At first the boys suffered a lot after having lost their father and then their mother. But they're better now.

The people at the National Institute for Health held me in high esteem. Because of the threats against me, when I left work, the doorman would go with me to wait for the bus. And the director of the Institute had given the order that if someone went asking for me, for the doorman to say that I didn't work there.

I used to go to the cemetery a lot. On Sundays I'd spend half a day at the cemetery where John is and half a day at the cemetery where Víctor is. I'd go alone, sit down next to their tombs and cry a lot. I would talk to them. I asked John why he hadn't told me what he knew. I asked them to forgive me for not giving them more. Around that time, I was always sick, I'd have headaches and I didn't want to eat. I looked like a piece of wire, I was so skinny. My daughters would say, "Your clothes hang off of you." A doctor told me not to go to the cemetery so much, that it was killing me. So I started going only once a month.

A colleague at the Institute told me to write down everything I was feeling and thinking. I couldn't sleep at night so I got a notebook and wrote everything down. That helped some.

The group of Soacha mothers who had also lost their sons started getting support from psychologists that were provided to us by an NGO. I used to say that psychologists were for crazy people, but it's not true. The psychologist I saw helped me a ton. She would take us on little trips for two or three days, for group therapy sessions to help with our depression.

The Soacha mothers have all supported each other. We're practically a family, and I love them a lot. I'm the one who reaches out to them most to see how they're doing. The other mothers from Soacha have been sent leaflets with all of our names calling us the "crybabies of Soacha." The leaflets warn us not to be so public, and for us to watch out because we'll end up like our sons.

In May 2009 Sgt. Jáner Duque Marín, Cpl. Richard Armando Jojoa Bastidas, and soldiers Nilson Antonio Cubides Cuesta, Mauricio Cuniche Delgadillo, José Orlando González Ceballos, and José Adolfo Fernández Ramírez were charged with aggravated forced disappearance, criminal conspiracy and falsification of documents. Others were charged as accomplices. By May 2012, the trial had yet to begin. According to the prosecution's investigation, the "recruiter" handed three young men, including Víctor, over to the military in Ocaña at 6 p.m. on August 24, 2008, one day after Víctor left home in Soacha.

A BIG SPLENDID PARTY

Seventeen people have been arrested in Víctor's case, including corporals, sergeants, and professional soldiers. I would get angry when I saw the accused in court during the preliminary hearings. They'd sit on one side of the courtroom and us mothers would sit on the other side. I'd stare at them and they'd bow their heads. In order to delay the hearings so that the time limit on their preventive detention would expire, the defendants' lawyers would say that the defendants were sick, or that their mom died, or that they had a toothache. When the judge postponed the hearings, the defendants would laugh and start making fun of us. There have been threats against our lawyers, and one of the lawyers working on my case quit because of it.

On January 7, 2010 the defendants were released from custody because the time limit on their preventive detention had expired. When they were released, the military threw them a big splendid party at a military garrison.[20] But the case continues. There's also an investigation into John's murder, but no one has been arrested.

EVEN IF THEY ASKED FOR
FORGIVENESS ON THEIR KNEES

I've been living at my current apartment with William and Alejandro for a year, which is the longest I've stayed in a single place since I started receiving threats.

Alejandro is still recuperating from Víctor's death. He feels guilty, saying that maybe if he'd told his brother not to leave on that trip to the coast, he wouldn't have been killed.

Jeison lives with his sister Yaneth. He'd already moved out of the house when he was eighteen, but with his brother's death, he became afraid to live by himself and felt very alone. Now he has to be both a father and an uncle for John's kids.

---

[20] The Defense Ministry ordered the forty-six defendants in false positive cases who were released from preventive detention at the end of 2009 and beginning of 2010 to be confined to the Artillery School in southern Bogotá. On January 25, 2010, the human rights department of the Defense Ministry reportedly held an event for the defendants and their families in which they provided massages, clowns, and aromatherapy.

I've been asked if one day I'll be able to forgive the people who did this. I'll never forgive them. And the same for former President Uribe and President Santos,[21] because they were the principal heads of the military forces. What I want is for the despicable people who killed them and their superiors to be behind bars. But they have to be in regular prisons, not a military garrison where they're taken on vacation, to have a good time and eat well, like they were doing at Tolemeida.[22] We're asking the government to put those responsible for our sons' deaths into regular prisons, like any other criminal, any other murderer.

I have photos taken of me with Víctor at an army battalion. In the photos, I have an army hat on and I'm hugging him. When I look at that photo now it makes me angry. I'm angry that my son served the nation for eighteen months, and that he had to die at the hands of his ex-comrades. Maybe if he died when he was doing military service, I would have said, "Fine, he died defending the nation." But no.

It's very clear that the army is supposed to protect the population from terrible things like the guerrillas and the paramilitaries.[23] They're not supposed to do away with the population. I never thought that the army would do that to him. I trusted them.

---

[21] To date, no evidence has surfaced criminally implicating former President Uribe or President Santos in "false positives."

[22] In April 2011, *Semana* magazine, Colombia's leading newsweekly, revealed the extremely lax conditions at the Tolemeida military base, where many members of the military convicted for human rights violations, including false positives, were detained. *Semana* reported that many of the detainees left when they pleased, lived in cabins rather than cells, and ran their own businesses within the detention center.

[23] Right-wing paramilitary groups began to form in Colombia in the early 1980s with the purported aim of fighting left-wing guerrillas. Backed by the military, landowners, drug traffickers, and political and economic elites, they murdered tens of thousands of civilians. After many paramilitaries were demobilized in 2006, armed neo-paramilitary groups such as the Urabeños and Paisas began to emerge. Led largely by former paramilitaries and often employing the same criminal, political, and economic networks as their predecessors, neo-paramilitary groups have a powerful presence in many regions throughout the country.

JOHN AND VÍCTOR HAVEN'T LEFT MY ROOM

John and Víctor are still with me. I tell myself that they're on a long trip. I've kept all of Víctor's things. I've kept his stuffed animals: a frog, a bear, a dog, three dolls. I have his military cap, which he gave me. In Alejandro's room there's his bandana, a Santa cap, and containers that he used to fill with screws and things. I also have some of John's posters and photos. Alejandro won't let anyone touch them. Every time I've had to move, those are the first things I organize.

Víctor visits me in my dreams. Once I dreamed that he came up to me and patted my head and said, "Good going, Mom. Keep up the fight."

Another night, at around seven, I put some water on to boil to make panela water, and then I lay down on my bed. At around ten at night, I heard someone say, "Mami, the panela water is drying up." I said, "Shoot, the panela water!" I stood up and when I went to open the door to my room, *pum!* Someone opened it. There was still half a pitcher of panela water left. The next morning I asked Alejandro, "Did you tell me that the panela water was drying up last night?" and he said, "No Mami, I was sleeping."

Other times I turn off the TV and it turns on by itself. Or I'll be watching TV—and it will turn off. And I feel John and Víctor in my room. I know that they won't leave until there is a conviction.

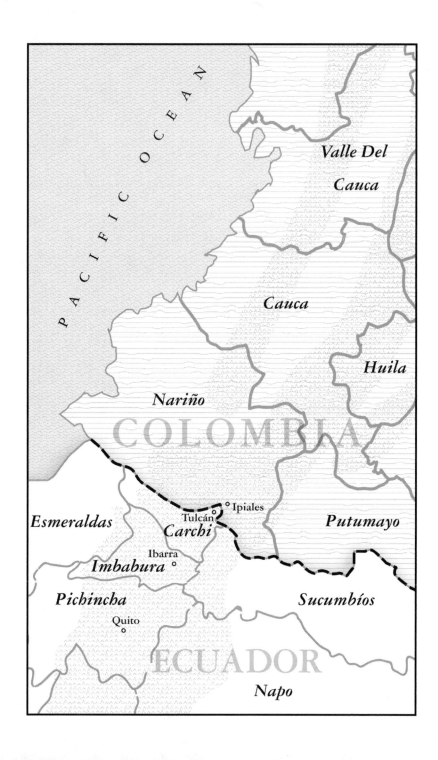

I'M NO ONE HERE

Ecuador

Some 500,000 Colombians have sought refuge outside the country, often after having been displaced at least once within Colombia, according to the Office of the United Nations High Commissioner for Refugees. Many slip quietly over the borders into Venezuela, Ecuador, or Panama and try to make a new life for themselves without ever registering as refugees.

Of the Colombians who do seek asylum, eight out of ten do so in Ecuador, which shares a 600 kilometer-long border with Colombia that is mostly covered in dense jungle or high-mountain woodlands. Colombians cross the San Miguel River from Putumayo province to Sucumbíos, they traverse highland passes near Ipiales or go by sea from Tumaco to San Lorenzo on the coast. They settle in border towns such as Lago Agrio or Tulcán or go deeper into Ecuador to Ibarra and the capital, Quito. More than 150,000 Colombians have requested refugee status in Ecuador since 2000 (with numbers rising daily), but only 55,000 had been granted asylum by December 2011. Today Ecuador hosts the largest population of refugees in Latin America, nearly all of them Colombians.

Colombians often find an uneasy peace in Ecuador. While in most cases they have escaped threats to their lives that they faced in their own country, in Ecuador they confront discrimination and scorn. Many Ecuadorans blame Colombian refugees for any uptick in crime, and complain that Colombians strain already weak educational, health, and social institutions. Colombian migrants find it hard to secure steady jobs, their children are often the object of ridicule at school, and Colombian women are frequently stereotyped as prostitutes. Many Colombians seek to be resettled in a third country.

DANNY CUERVO

AGE: *26*
OCCUPATION: *Handicrafts vendor*
HOMETOWN: *Bogotá, Colombia*
INTERVIEWED IN: *Ibarra, Ecuador*

We met Danny Cuervo in the Ecuadoran city of Ibarra. He arrived in the country in 2004 after fleeing from one of the right-wing paramilitaries' biggest training camps in the Eastern Plains of Colombia. He had gone there half-willingly when he was nineteen, lured by the promise of money to support his soon-to-be-born son. He immediately realized it was a mistake, and managed to escape. Fearing the paramilitaries would track him down and kill him, he fled to Ecuador. Today he struggles trying to raise two small boys as a single father, while fighting the discrimination and exclusion that many Colombian refugees suffer in Ecuador.

Names in this narrative have been changed at the request of the narrator.

THE RESPONSIBILITY OF HAVING A FAMILY

My mom tells me that when I was little I almost died of a fever. It was a really high fever, and I went into convulsions. She entrusted me to the Baby Jesus and I survived, so she's always told me that I am God's child. And I, too, am devoted to Baby Jesus. I always turn to him when I need help.

I was born in Bogotá in 1985. My mother and her family are from the Eastern Plains, but because of the economic situation at that time, many of them had to move to Bogotá. I lived in a neighborhood in downtown Bogotá, near the presidential palace and the Palace of Justice. There, my mother and I lived in a room with my grandmother and my two uncles. At that time, my dad was in prison in the United States for being a drug mule.

While my dad was in jail, my family moved to Villavicencio, Meta, about 115 kilometers east of Bogotá; it's considered the gateway to the Eastern Plains region. My mom's father lived there, and we rented a house five blocks away from him. I was about ten years old. My dad came back from prison about a year later and my mom went back to Bogotá to be with him. Not long after, my mom became pregnant with my brother, Jorge. I stayed in Villavicencio for a time with my grandfather. He had a buñuelo[1] factory so I'd sell buñuelos on the street after school.

Around that time, we heard that in my mom's hometown of Guamal, about forty kilometers from Villavicencio, a cousin of mine was killed because he'd wanted to work with the paramilitaries and apparently he talked too much.[2] He started bragging, telling everyone he was going to make a lot of money working for them. Then one day he disappeared, and a few days later the authorities found a headless body in a field outside of San Martín, near the town of Granada.[3] The body was already decomposing, but his mom identified him by his belt buckle.

After that, I went back to Bogotá to live with my mom and dad, but over the next few years we kept moving back and forth between there and Villavicencio. Through all this moving, I never finished my studies; I only studied up to the first year of high school.

---

[1] A typical Colombian donut-like fried bread, made in the shape of a ball.

[2] Right-wing paramilitary groups began to form in Colombia in the early 1980s with the purported aim of fighting left-wing guerrillas. Backed by the military, landowners, drug traffickers, and political and economic elites, they murdered tens of thousands of civilians.

[3] Twenty kilometers away.

In 2001, when I was about sixteen, I decided to leave home. My parents, who'd had my sister Tatiana the year before, were in Villavicencio at the time, and I went to live in Bogotá at a friend's house and started working as a kitchen assistant at a vegetarian restaurant. The following year, I met a sixteen-year-old girl named María. She's Ecuadoran, tall with long hair and dark skin. She has indigenous features. I fell in love really deeply. I had never felt the kind of support or affection that she gave me.

We'd been going out for about three months when she came to live with me in the little room I was renting. In 2005, she got pregnant. The truth is, it took me a while to get used to the idea. I didn't have any money, and my mom and dad had never talked to me about the responsibility of having a family.

María was about two months pregnant when I got fired from the vegetarian restaurant for arguing with the customers. So I started working independently. I bought some underwear that I'd sell on the streets, but it didn't go well. Then I tried to make and sell handicrafts, but that wasn't going well either. Then my mom called me and told me there was a job available at a chicken processing plant in Guamal. She'd heard about it from an aunt there. The aunt had said it was good work, it paid 40,000 pesos[4] per shift, and that she'd put me up while I worked there. So I went, but María stayed in Bogotá because she was still in high school.

At the plant, my job was to kill the chickens. They'd be hung up by the feet on a hook, and I'd grab the head and slit the throat. I didn't like it. It was ugly killing like that. But I thought of my girlfriend and my baby, and that I needed to do it to provide for them.

THE PARAMILITARIES MADE IT
ALL SOUND SO WONDERFUL

Guamal was filled with paramilitaries. I had always seen them when my family went there on visits. In fact, a lot of the paramilitaries there had

---

[4] About U.S.$16 at the time.

been friends of my mom from when she was little, and some of them would ask me about her. But my mom told me to stay away from them. She said, "If the paramilitaries talk to you, just tell them that you're studying, and that you're a good boy."

The paramilitaries would go around in a pickup truck collecting the vacuna[5] from every farm and business in town, according to its income. The chicken plant made a lot of money, so the paramilitaries would come by every weekend to charge.

One time, about four months after I arrived, the paramilitaries were making their rounds when one of my mom's old friends said to me, "Morocho,[6] what's up?" I said hello, and chatted a while with the group he was with. It seemed normal. The truth was, I knew the paramilitaries were bad—I'd heard that they killed people with chainsaws—but I was never afraid because my mom knew these guys.

The following Saturday, the pickup came again to collect the vacuna, and the paras[7] called out to me. They asked me if I wanted to work with them. "What would I have to do?" I said. Obviously I didn't want to kill anyone; I didn't want to do any of those things. I just wanted money for my family, so we could be more stable.

They told me the work would just be collecting the vacunas, that it was nothing. They said they'd give me a motorcycle and a bag to collect the money. They would tell me where I needed to collect, how much to collect, and then I'd have to bring the money to their office. They said that I'd earn much more money with them, and that after some time the motorcycle would be mine, and then later they'd give me a car. They made it all sound so wonderful, so I agreed.

The leader of the local group was called Commander Conejo.[8] He told me to get in the pickup, and that they'd take me to the office to talk

---

[5] Vacuna, literally "vaccine," is what Colombians call extortion payments demanded by different criminal and/or armed groups.

[6] Morocho is a generic nickname used for people with dark hair and skin.

[7] "Paras" is conversational shorthand for paramilitary.

[8] Conejo means "rabbit."

to the senior commander about what I was going to do. We went to the nearby town of San Martín, where they had their main office. When we arrived I realized it was a clandestine office, because in front it looked like a place you'd go to make phone calls, with telephone booths. But you went past the telephone booths through another door and there were about twenty paramilitaries there, dressed as civilians but armed to the teeth. I started to feel afraid.

I asked who I needed to speak to and they told me they'd take me to talk to the big man, the commander who was in charge of everything. They said he would tell me what I had to do. But the truth is, I was scared; I felt something weird, that something very ugly was going to happen.

I said, "I'm going to the store. I'll be right back!" and tried to leave, but they didn't let me. They told me, "No, no, no. You have to stay here. First you have to talk to the boss." As I waited, the paras talked among themselves about their business.

I was there for about two or three hours. It was already dark by the time I was taken back into the pickup. Some paras got on motorcycles and others got in cars. We drove around San Martín for a bit and then I was told I would be blindfolded. I was so scared, I thought, *Holy God*. My dream was to go home with money, see my child born in good conditions, and have money to raise him. But by that point, I was thinking I'd made a mistake going there.

I HAD SIMPLY BEEN RECRUITED

It felt like we were driving for about an hour or forty-five minutes on a dirt road. It was about seven at night when the car stopped and they took the blindfold off. I didn't know where we were; all I knew was that it was a jungle.

The paras took me to a camp in the middle of the jungle. There were around a hundred and fifty men there, and some women too. They were in uniform, some were all in green, others in camouflage. They wore boots, some had green hats; some had kerchiefs tied around their necks. They were between fifteen and forty years old; the older ones were the commanders.

Some of them were cooking in a tent, and smoke was pouring out of it. I was told to get in line for food but I wasn't hungry. One of the paramilitaries said, "Eat, because you'll be hungry later." So I got in line, and I met a boy there. He was friendly, and young—even younger than I was at that time. I asked him if they were going to kill me. He said that they wouldn't kill me, that I had simply been recruited, and that I'd be there for some time while they taught me things like how to shoot and other survival stuff. The boy told me he hadn't seen his family since he'd been recruited. He said, "My family are the people here. I can't call, I can't communicate with anyone else." That made me even more scared.

I was handed a cup to receive the food. It was rice soup. I ate it, and then I was told to go to sleep early because they would wake me up very early the next day. I wanted to sleep near the boy who had talked to me in line, so I lay down next to him on the ground, underneath a plastic tarp. The boy lent me a blanket.

I didn't think I would be able to sleep, and soon I started to cry. The boy told me not to cry. I told him I didn't want to be there, and he said, "There's nothing to be done now." He told me that the next day the commanders would explain everything: that once you're in, the only way you can leave is if you're dead. I cried even harder then, and the other men who were around us told me to shut up, to stop fucking around, that I was acting like a little girl. Someone said, "We'll teach you to be a man here."

I quietly said to the boy, "Please help me, I don't want to be here." And he said, "I can't do anything. I'm just like you here." I explained to him that I came from a poor family, and that I'd come to the Eastern Plains to work for my soon-to-be-born child. He said that even so, he couldn't do anything.

Somehow I fell asleep. It felt like I'd only slept about five minutes when the boy woke me up. Everything was silent and dark. He whispered to me to get up and not to make any noise. He told me I shouldn't put my shoes on but to carry them in my hand. Then he led me to a corner of the camp that was unguarded. Once we were outside the camp, he said, "You know what, brother? I'm helping you because I understand. That's how I wound up here too."

Then he said, "Well, let's walk," and we walked in silence for about forty-five minutes over sharp rocks, but I didn't mind the pain.

We reached a point and he told me to run. He said, "Start running in that direction until you find a road. I can't help you anymore because I have to get back." He told me that if I got caught, I couldn't say who'd helped me. I thanked him and put on my shoes and started running. He never told me his name.

DON'T HIDE HIM

I ran, ran, ran. I was really scared. The shadows of the trees looked like people, as if they were watching me. The boy had told me I'd find a road soon, but I couldn't find it, and I said to myself, *I must be getting lost*, but I didn't stop running. I ran and I cried, I slipped and I tripped. And sometimes I felt I couldn't keep going. I stood for a while to rest, to wipe away my tears, and blow my nose on my T-shirt. It was warm. I could hear the sound of the birds and the cicadas.

I tried not to blink or close my eyes because I thought, *If I close my eyes I may get lost*. I was very anxious. Just when the sky was starting to get a little lighter, I could hear a car every once in a while, so I knew I was close to the road. I kept running until I found it. I started walking along the road, but I didn't know which direction to go because I was totally disoriented. I started walking to my right for about fifteen minutes: then I jogged, stopped, jogged, stopped. It scared me that the paramilitaries might pass by me in their pickups or motorcycles, but not a single car went by.

Then I saw a bus coming. I waved it down and I got in, but the driver didn't want to take me because I was really dirty: I was soaking with sweat, my shoes were muddy, and my T-shirt was full of snot. And I only had something like 3,000 pesos,[9] all in coins.

I said, "Please, please, take me even if it's only one kilometer."

The driver said, "Get off." I had to stand in the aisle of the bus and ask the driver and the passengers to help me because I'd been robbed; I didn't say anything about what had really happened. And the passengers began to tell the driver, "What's the matter? Take him, don't be selfish. Help him." Most Colombians are like that.

The driver said, "Well, if you're going to pay his fare, fine." A woman passenger helped me. She asked me what I had and I gave the coins to her and she paid the difference.

I was lucky that the bus was going to Villavicencio. When I got there, I went to my mom's house, and she asked me what had happened to me. When I finished telling her what had happened, she told me I couldn't stay there. She said I was stupid for having gone with the paramilitaries. She said, "Remember I told you to stay away from them? I was trying to protect you. You have to go."

I said, "Well, I'm going to Bogotá." I didn't have a single peso for the bus fare, and my mom didn't have money either. My dad wasn't there. So I spent the night at her house and I left early the next day to beg on the streets of Villavicencio. By lunchtime I had managed to make some money.

As I was getting back to my mom's, I saw a motorcycle parked in front of her house. I didn't see a license plate on the motorcycle; I always looked for motorcycles without plates because everyone knew the paramilitaries never had them. I waited about twenty minutes around a corner, watching the house. Eventually, two men walked out of the house, got on the bike and left.

When I went in the house, my sister, who was three years old, my brother, and my mom were all crying. My mom said that the paramili-

---

[9] About U.S.$1.50 at the time.

taries had come looking for me, and one of them had put a gun to her head and to my brother's too. They had told her, "Don't hide him. Tell us where he is or we'll blow your head off." My mom told me to go to Bogotá. She borrowed money from a neighbor and gave me the fare.

ECUADOR

By that time, María was six months pregnant. I went to the room where I'd lived with her, but she wasn't there. I went to her mother's house and María wasn't there either. But my mom had called María's mom and asked her to help me.

I told María's mom everything. I asked her, "What do I do? My mom is all nervous. I don't know what to do." She told me I should go to Ecuador. I wanted to go there with María, but I couldn't find her, so I had to go alone. Her mother paid for my bus ticket to Ipiales, the city on the Colombian side of the border, and she also gave me 20,000 pesos.[10]

The whole way there, on the seventeen-hour-long bus ride, I kept telling myself I would return. I thought, *Maybe in a month, maybe in two months or a year. But I have to go back.* I left without saying goodbye. But I had to leave, damn it—I was thrown out by the violence in my country.

I cried a lot during that whole trip. I don't think anyone can imagine what it's like to leave like that, with nothing. I knew I had to face the world alone. I knew that I was leaving my whole life behind: my child, my girlfriend, my mom, my brother, and my sister.

When I got to the border, all I had to do was show my Colombian ID and I crossed the bridge that separates Colombia and Ecuador. I went into the border city of Tulcán and asked around if Quito, the capital, was far away. People told me that it was five or six hours.

I got on a bus to Quito, and when I arrived, night was beginning to fall and I had nowhere to sleep. I asked around on the streets where I

[10] About U.S.$10 at the time.

might be able to find shelter, and a Hare Krishna monk said that I could stay at their temple.

The monks gave me food and a place to sleep for two days. Then they gave me incense to sell on the streets. I'd work my way down one street block, then on a long avenue, and then down another block. I've always been a warrior, a good salesman. My mother always taught me that he who persists, perseveres. And that was what I thought about. I said to myself, *I have to persist. I can't let myself die.*

So I sold incense, and little by little, I started saving some money. I would collect the coins and change them for a dollar bill, and then I would take the dollar and put it between the pages of a book. Eventually I managed to save fifty one-dollar bills[11] in that book, and I told myself, *Yes I can!*

I moved to a hotel. I paid just $4 a night in a small room with a bed and nothing else. At the hotel there were other Colombians who lived and worked in Quito. Some of them were refugees. One of them worked on the buses, selling perfumes, and he asked me how much I made selling incense. I said I did all right but he said I could do better if I got on the buses. So one day I went with him. He taught me how it was done and after the first day I was on my own.

At first I wasn't very good at speaking on the buses. I was embarrassed by all the people looking at me, and I'd get confused—I would charge 50 Colombian pesos instead of 50 cents—or the bus would brake and I would fall down. But slowly I got used to it and people bought from me, maybe because of my positive attitude.

SEEKING REFUGE

Six months went by. During that time, my son was born. María called me to tell me, and we named him Alex. I asked her, "Does he look like me?" and she said, "His feet do." I was anxious to see them.

---

[11] Ecuador adopted the U.S. dollar as its currency in 2000.

I had entered Ecuador as a tourist and then applied for extensions to my permit to stay there. But I ran out of extensions, and I became illegal. One day, some immigration policemen grabbed me on the street. I guess they thought I looked suspicious or something. I cried, I told them what I had been through, but they didn't believe me. They said I was a thief, that I was a pot smoker. Well, I cried so much that they let me go. "Get out of here," they told me. "Don't let us see you again. You have to get your papers in order."

The same friend who taught me to work on the buses told me that in Ibarra, a city about 112 kilometers north of Quito, there are a lot of Colombians who've had problems like me who get help there. He said they're given relief packages and get help with sorting out papers and applying for refugee status. Right there, I said, "I'm going. I'm going right now."

In Ibarra, I met with the UNHCR[12] and they gave me a refugee claimant card. They asked me if I was alone and I said yes, but I told them I had a little boy in Colombia, that I didn't even know him. They told me to try to bring him here.

One day in 2005, I met María and my son Alex in the city of Cali in southwestern Colombia. It was just one day and one night. I was scared about going back into Colombia, but I wanted to meet my son. He was big; he was a year old when I met him. I saw him and right there I began to cry. Then I quickly took off his shoes to look at his feet. I didn't see the resemblance. María said, "Don't you think he's your child, silly?" And I said yes, but he didn't look anything like me.

Later, María would come to Ibarra to visit me in the small room I'd rented, but she would leave the baby with her mom. When María came, my mom would send her with used clothes from my cousins. I've always been a good poor person; I wear those clothes proudly.

María and I were still sweethearts. She'd stay two days, three days, even a week, but she always went back to Colombia. During those visits

---

[12] United Nations High Commissioner for Refugees, the U.N.'s refugee agency.

she became pregnant with my second little one. He was born in 2006 and we named him Gustavo.

When we spoke on the phone, María always said she would come and live with me. I told her that here in Ecuador we could get ahead because there are many opportunities here, and we could both get by with the little ones. She always told me, "Yes, yes, yes. I'll go, I'll go."

Then once, when I told her to come, that she was from Ecuador, she said, "But I'm not really from there. I was born there, but I live here, my mom is here, my stepfather is from here, my brothers are in Colombia. I am no longer from Ecuador. But I'll try to visit, I will try."

I started buying handicrafts in Otavalo—a town where Indians sell their crafts—and selling them on the buses. The lady who I always bought them from was fond of me. She told me that I'm very tough. I told her that I had two children and that they were coming, and she said, "That's great." Then she recommended I talk to a brother of hers who lives here in Ibarra, an Indian. I called him and he told me I could rent a room from him. He started renting me a bigger room for $20 a month. That man is an angel of God. He has helped me a lot.

Once I had the new room, María said yes, that she would move to Ecuador, but that I should go pick her and the boys up in Bogotá. That was in 2007—the eldest was two and the second was less than a year old. She said that I had to sign some sort of form to be able to take the kids out of the country. I said, "Oh no, I'm not going to Bogotá for anything in the world! Let's meet in Cali, let's meet in Popayán, or somewhere else, but not in Bogotá."

I thought I couldn't go back there because if there was a paramilitary roadblock and they found my refugee applicant card they would chop me up right there. But María said the condition for her to come was that I go there, because the children could only leave with the permission of both the mother and the father.

So I went to Bogotá. I asked a taxi driver friend in Tulcán, the Ecuadoran city on the border, to keep my refugee documents in Ecuador. I crossed over with my Colombian ID. My God, I was so nervous. I didn't want to talk to anyone in Colombia, no one. The guy who sat next to me on the bus to Bogotá kept asking me things. I didn't say that I lived in Ecuador, I said I lived in Ipiales. When he asked why I was going to Bogotá, I said, "I'm going to try to buy some merchandise to sell." I tried to cut off the conversation because I was really scared.

I got to Bogotá and María and I got the permits for the two children to come. I was only there for two days, and we left right away. I didn't see my mother because she'd always insisted that I shouldn't return to Colombia. If I'd gone to see her she may have got scared.

Two days after María and I arrived in Ibarra with our children, I took them to the UNHCR. There, they took their pictures and made them refugee claimant ID cards. HIAS[13] gave me flour, cooking oil, lentils, sugar, and sardines.

Soon after, my refugee request was granted. I'd been so scared that I'd be refused. I'd thought, *If I get denied I'll pick up, damn it, and go somewhere else, Peru or Chile.* I told myself, *I may have to continue suffering with my children, yes, but I won't go back to Colombia. How can I put my children at risk?*

Things were different with María because we had been apart for more than a year. Soon after she arrived with the boys, she wanted to go. She no longer wanted to fight for us. I told her that I felt very lonely. I begged and pleaded. I said, "Please stay. Who am I going to live for if you and the children go back? I fought so hard to get you here and now you want to go?" She said, "Let's do something. I do want to be here, but the thing is, I'm studying there in Bogotá, I have my work there. I'm going to bring some papers from school, recommendations to see if I can get a job here and I can help you. I'll leave the little ones so you don't get lonely until I come back."

I said, "Sure!" My children were my happiness. I said, "Don't take too long." She left, and I stayed with my little ones. But María had tricked

---

[13] HIAS, the Hebrew Immigrant Aid Society, is the international migration agency of the American Jewish community. They provide assistance to refugees across the world, including in Ecuador.

me. After that, she came back once in 2008 to spend Christmas with us. Then never again.

ARE YOU COLOMBIAN? SORRY

I've been raising my children alone here since María went back to Colombia. One is five years old and the other is three. It's hard.

Ecuadorans humiliate you here every day. I've tried to find steady work many times. I've looked in supermarkets, in a rotisserie chicken restaurant, in the market, but people say, "You're Colombian? No." Many times I've also tried to find another room to rent, something a little larger, and I get the response, "Are you Colombian? Sorry, sorry."

I've had a lot of problems with Ecuadorans. One day I was working on a bus from here to Otavalo. That morning, I had given the children breakfast, but there wasn't enough for me, so I'd left our room hungry. Then I'd gone out to make enough money to buy something for our lunch. I got on a bus and I started to go around selling some necklaces made of stone, and I gave my talk:

My name is Danny. I'm not from here, I'm from the neighboring country of Colombia. But thank God I've been a refugee for more than three years, naturalized in this beautiful country, which has given me beautiful opportunities.

I'm an artisan; I didn't come empty-handed. I've made this beautiful necklace. It's made out of nylon and stone. I won't be the one who puts a price on it. If you think that my creativity could be worth $1 or $1.50, I'll take it, whatever the necklace is worth for each person.

I'm also going to do something nice for those people who don't have money. I'm going to give one as a gift, but with a commitment. The commitment isn't with me, but with your conscience, your heart. If tomorrow you find a kid or an elderly person on the street, don't discriminate against him for the condition that he's in. Rather, give him something. Maybe it seems strange to you and you'll ask why I say that. I do it and say it because I believe in the law of compensation. That beautiful law that has taught me that if today we act correctly toward other liv-

ing beings, tomorrow we won't lack anything. I won't inconvenience you anymore.
Maybe you'll like this beautiful art and you'll want to buy it.

But I didn't sell anything. I got on another bus going to Atuntaqui,
but I didn't sell anything there, either. From Atuntaqui back to Otavalo
I sold nothing. On the bus from Otavalo back to Ibarra, I was desperate,
extremely desperate.

I began to hand out the necklaces to the passengers, saying, "Excuse
me, sorry. Look for just one minute, check out the craftsmanship." I got to
a gentleman in a suit, with glasses, apparently well educated, and I said,
"Excuse me please, check out the necklaces." I used the informal "tú" form
to address him. He said, "Don't use 'tú' with me. What balls! What am I
to you that you treat me that way?" Everyone stopped to look at me. I said,
"Okay, have some respect. I'm working here, I won't bother you again. If
you don't want to look at a necklace, that's fine." This time I used the formal "usted" form to address him. He called me "abusive and rude."

After handing out the rest of the necklaces I started giving my regular
speech about the law of compensation—that if we act correctly today, tomorrow things will go right for us. I kept talking, but in the back, almost
in the last seat, I could hear: "Colombians play the fools, but they get on the
bus to steal. Just let your guard down and see that he'll rob you."

It was hurtful and I thought, *I have to say something to let out my anger.*
I went toward the back of the bus, and I said, "You know what, shut your
mouth, unless you want me to hit you!" Just then all the passengers stood
up. At first I thought it was to defend me but then I saw that they were
against me. "Shut up and have some respect," they told me. "You're not
in your country. If you have work and eat it is thanks to our country. You
come here to take the jobs of Ecuadorans."

A man pushed me and said, "Have some respect brother." I couldn't
take it anymore. I took the necklaces and *pa!* I hit him in the face. And
because they were made of stone, they broke his nose.

The other passengers grabbed me and called the police. It was horrible; I had gone out to make enough money to buy food for lunch and I

ended up being locked up. I called home and asked the daughter of my landlord, who took care of my children when I went out, to watch over them. I spent five days in jail for making a public scandal.

From that, I learned that no matter how much I get humiliated, no matter what people say to me, no matter if I get beaten, I have to stay poker-faced. Maybe it's not what I want, but I have to do that. I have to take it, I have to swallow my pride, my anger, my pain, because if I say something, I may get locked up.

SO GOD WILL REMEMBER ME

There's a movie called "The Pursuit of Happyness," starring Will Smith. After I saw it I thought, *That's how I have to be.* It's about a dad who couldn't get ahead. He has debts, and so many problems that his wife leaves him with their little one. And he begins to walk with his little boy. He gets evicted. He has no job, he has to go hungry in order to give food to his little one. They have to sleep in homeless shelters. That movie really got to me. I feel like it's my movie. At the end of the film he becomes a billionaire, and he employs many people who struggle like he did. That's something I would like: to some day be well off so that I can give a hand to many people in need.

My children really love me; they have struggled with me. We have been through the good and bad. When I have a little bit of money I buy them a salchipapita.[14] Sometimes they say, "I want you to make the burgers the way you make them." And so I run out fast, I buy ground beef, I get spices, and make their burgers.

If they knew what I feel, if they knew how much I ask God to help us! I always turn to the Baby Jesus. On Sundays I go to church and say, "Baby Jesus, I'm here with my little ones." Every time I go, I leave something of mine there so God will remember me. I used to leave little photos I had

---

[14] A street food of chopped hot dogs and French fries.

of me but then I ran out, so once I left an expired refugee claimant card. Sometimes I leave a letter.

I met a girl here that I like a lot. She's my landlord's daughter, the one who always helps out with my kids. I like her because of the way she acts with my kids, but I haven't told her anything because I feel that maybe she doesn't have time for me, because maybe I don't have anything to offer her. I don't have money and I don't have anywhere to invite her to. So, it's embarrassing. But the truth is, I have a heart and I fall in love and I get excited. I think that some day I'll tell her that I like her.

My mom came to visit me in February 2011. I was very happy because I hadn't seen her since I left Villavicencio in 2004. I also saw my sister. The last time I'd seen her she was three and here was this big girl who was nearly nine. I say, *God, how quickly life goes by.*

My mom told me straight out that I couldn't return to Colombia. She said she was still getting anonymous calls. The caller would say, "We know where your son is," and hang up. I asked her, "Why didn't you tell me before?" She said, "I didn't tell you, because how could I bring you that anxiety?"

Supposedly there are paramilitaries here too. Around July 2011, I heard that a Colombian who owned a liquor store in the center of town was killed. The word is that it was the paramilitaries who did it. He was shot four or six times, and he died.

I got scared. I sold the only things I had—my television, my DVD player, and a bed—and I went with my boys to Quito, where we spent two months living in a hotel.

But I couldn't make it there selling necklaces on buses. We were going hungry, and I eventually decided to come back here to Ibarra. I rented the same room from my old landlord, and I had to buy a mattress on credit.

I don't want to go back to Colombia. I haven't told my children anything about what happened to me and I hope they never know. My children only know that Colombia is dangerous because they watch Colombian television shows. The farther away the better, so I can forget everything I've been through.

In mid-2011, I applied to be resettled to a third country but was rejected by the UNHCR.[15] They say no other country wants me because I supposedly went willingly with the paramilitaries. They said maybe Brazil would take me, but I looked on a map and Brazil has a border with Colombia too.

I cry a lot because I often get depressed. But I don't let my boys see me cry; I leave the house and go out onto the street. I say, *God, what is there for me?* Sometimes I call my mom crying and say, "Mom, what the hell happened to me? What have I done to have to be paying like this?" And she says, "Mi'jo,[16] relax. My God has assured each one of us a little piece, an opportunity. He hasn't given you yours yet, but my God has a piece for you, he's got it there for you." God willing, someday I'll get mine so I can be at peace.

---

[15] Resettlement involves the assisted movement of refugees to safe third countries. The UNHCR helps refugees resettle when they are unwilling or unable to return home because they would face persecution, and live in unsafe conditions or have specific needs that cannot be met in the nation where they initially sought refuge.

[16] A contraction of "mi hijo" (in English, "my son"), used affectionately for male friends or relatives.

RICARDO SIERRA

AGE: *31*
OCCUPATION: *Car painter*
HOMETOWN: *Tuluá, Valle del Cauca*[1]
INTERVIEWED IN: *Ibarra, Ecuador*

Ricardo Sierra was born in Tuluá, a small city in southwestern Colombia. By the age of twenty-one he had a wife and two daughters, and a stable job at a car-painting shop. In 2002, botched business dealings between Ricardo's brother and paramilitaries led to his nephew's murder, and turned their entire family into a potential target for the armed group. Fearing retaliation, Ricardo and his family fled to Facatativá, a small town outside of Bogotá. After living there for a year and a half, Ricardo and his family moved back to Tuluá in 2003 and had their third child. A series of threatening phone calls and attacks on Ricardo's family caused him and his family to flee again in 2008, this time to neighboring Ecuador. We met with Ricardo at his home in the city of Ibarra, a primary recipient of Colombian refugees. He recounted the abrupt intrusion of the war into his early life, and considered whether he regretted coming to Ecuador, where his family has faced constant discrimination for being Colombian.

Names in this narrative have been changed at the request of the narrator.

---

[1] Tuluá is a false location employed here to protect the narrator's identity.

RICARDO THIS, RICARDO THAT

I can tell the story as if I lived it yesterday—as if I had just arrived here in Ecuador. But I have a problem with the dates. The only date I remember is the day of my nephew's death; it can't be erased from my mind. It's very difficult because there are times when I remember him and the tears come.

I was born in 1980 in Tuluá, a city in Valle del Cauca province. My dad worked in construction and my mom was a seamstress. We're eleven brothers and sisters, and I'm number eleven. Since I was the youngest, everyone used me as the errand boy. My siblings would say, "Ricardo, get the cigarettes! Ricardo, go to the store! Ricardo, get the coffee!" It was tough. So when each sibling grew up and left home, I'd celebrate.

All of my siblings are partiers except for me. When there was a party at my house, I'd sit down and just watch my brothers and sisters dancing, until one day, when I was twelve years old, I decided to dance, and I knew how! I'd learned just from watching—it's in the blood.

My brothers were womanizers; they have kids scattered everywhere. Sometimes there were scandals at our house because a woman who lived with one of my brothers would arrive and he'd be with a different woman. I learned from them not to be like that. I said to myself, *No, no, no, that's not my way of living.* Living with them taught me to respect women, respect your household, and have a family.

I raised my brother Miguel's son Jairo ever since he was born in 1989, when I was nine years old. Miguel worked all day selling eggs and onions, so everyone in my house would tell me, "Ricardo, watch out for the boy! Ricardo, go check that the baby's bottle is okay!" Ricardo this, Ricardo that. But I became very attached to Jairo. I'd always carry him around, and when he was eight months old I taught him how to walk. I'd fall asleep with him and he'd touch my face to wake me up. A love was born. He was like my son, even though I was a kid too.

IT'S WHAT YOU CALL BEING IN LOVE

I graduated from high school when I was eighteen years old, and I went to work at a clothing store. During high season, the manager said she needed more workers, so each salesperson brought someone in to work at the store. One of my co-workers brought her nineteen-year-old sister Salud, and there began to be an attraction between us. We liked each other, and after a month we became a couple. I felt that she was right for me.

When I introduced my mom to Salud, she tried to prohibit me from seeing her because she knew that I looked at Salud with different eyes. My mom said to me, "My boy's gone. Salud's not the same as your other girlfriends; she's going to take you away from the house." The same thing happened when I went to Salud's house. When I showed up, her mom spurned me because Salud looked at me with different eyes. It's what you call being in love.

We'd been going out for six months when Salud became pregnant. It was a big scandal, and her sisters advised her to get rid of the baby. But Salud and I went to live together in a room at my sister's apartment, and our daughter Lina was born in March 2000. She is beautiful. A year and two months later, we had our second daughter, Andrea.

With the two girls, Salud and I found ourselves short on money, so I went to work at a car-painting shop. The cars would arrive from Korea in all different colors, and we'd convert them into taxis by painting them yellow. I started as a shop assistant, but my bosses saw my motivation, so they paid for me to go on a two-week-long car-painting course in Medellín. I got the best grades out of everyone at the course, and when I returned, my boss promoted me to painter's assistant. The car-painting shop sent me to some more trainings in the city of Cali, and after I got back from those, everyone at the shop said, "This guy is really fast, and he saves a lot of paint." So I was promoted to painter.

And that's where the good life started for me. I was making 1,600,000 pesos a month,[2] and I had bank accounts and credit cards. It was cool.

---

[2] About U.S.$550 in 2003.

JAIRO

Around 2002, urban factions of guerrilla and paramilitary groups began to appear in Tuluá. The city became dreadful. I'm a native of Tuluá, and I knew how to go around my city; I knew which neighborhoods had criminals, so I wasn't that worried about common crime. But when the urban guerrillas and paramilitaries were there, I didn't know where to go, because I didn't know where they were. There was more uncertainty then, because you didn't know if maybe your neighbor was a guerrilla. I was worried for my family, and I didn't want anything to happen to me, because if it did, they'd be left in the air.

One Sunday in early February, I came home at five in the afternoon after running some errands, and my wife told me that my brother Miguel had come by the house with his son Jairo. They were on their way to Miguel's sister-in-law's wedding party. Jairo was twelve years old at the time, and he was a very good kid. He'd told Salud that he wouldn't leave the house until he went to Lina's room and said bye. He hugged her, gave her a kiss, and left with his dad.

It was almost six in the evening when the phone rang. I answered, and the guy on the other end said, "You're Ricardo, right?" I said, "Yes, I'm Ricardo." He said, "Is your brother's name Miguel?" And I said, "Yes, what happened?" Then he said, "Look, there was a shootout and they hurt Miguel. And the boy's dead." I said, "Where are they?" He told me, "They're at the Central Hospital."

I calmed myself down and told myself that it wasn't Jairo. I thought, *It must be some little friend of Miguel's who's been identified as his son after the shootout.*

When I got to the hospital I saw Miguel and his wife Silvia. Miguel was sitting on a stretcher and he'd been shot in the leg. Silvia had been shot in the shoulder and a nurse was sewing stitches and cutting her shoulder. Silvia had her head lowered, and she didn't say anything. Her fourteen-year-old niece was also there—she'd been shot in her arm—and also her three-year-old niece, who'd been shot in the shin. They had all been at the wedding party.

Miguel looked up at me and started to cry. That's when the bad thoughts began to enter my mind. I hugged him and asked, "What happened?" Miguel said, "They killed my boy." Hearing that was like being stabbed. I stood there looking at my brother, but it was as if he were moving towards me and then away from me. My heart was pounding. I said, "Don't fuck around! You haven't let the boy get killed, have you?" Miguel just said, "They killed my boy," and lowered his head.

I punched him in the face. He didn't even notice when I hit him; it was as if he were dead as well. I asked him why he hadn't protected his son. I said, "You're the one who had to die, not the boy." Miguel asked me to forgive him, and he hugged me and started to cry.

I took off running and asked the hospital doorman where the morgue was. He told me where it was, but he said that I had to wait for the Attorney General's office to arrive to pick up the body. About an hour and a half later, two prosecutors and a policeman arrived. One of the prosecutors went into the morgue, saw Jairo's body and then she came out and said that they needed one of his relatives. Silvia's wound had been sown up by then and she was with me at the entrance to the hospital. She looked like a zombie. The prosecutor said that she couldn't go because she was in shock. So I said I'd go.

I went into the morgue with the prosecutor and I hugged Jairo strongly; at the time I thought it might be strong enough for him to come back to life. The prosecutor wanted me to help her flip Jairo over so that she could take photos of him. Jairo was very overweight, and they couldn't do it by themselves. I said, "I used to be the only one who carried him around. And if I could lift him when he was alive, I can also do it now that he's dead." I flipped him over and undressed him.

The boy had eleven gunshot wounds; he had been destroyed. One bullet had entered through his mouth and exited through the back of his head. There were shots to his heart, and all down his leg. The prosecutor was shocked. She said it looked like there'd been a burst of machine gun fire from his feet to his head. She told me, "The boy wasn't killed by stray bullets in a shootout. He was gunned down."

TODAY IT'S OUR TURN TO SUFFER

That night, my siblings and I slept on the sidewalk outside of the morgue, waiting for the coroner's office to finish the autopsy. We wanted to be with Jairo until the end. On Tuesday night, two days after the shooting, the funeral home took him to his house. He stayed there all night so that people could visit him and say goodbye.

The funeral was on Wednesday. My brother delayed surgery on his leg so that he could go. He and I were the only ones who didn't let go of the coffin as we carried it from the house to the church for mass, and from mass to the cemetery where he was buried. Miguel had grabbed one corner of the coffin and I'd grabbed another. My other two brothers took turns because Jairo weighed a lot. But the coffin didn't weigh anything to me; Jairo never weighed anything to me. I think that I could have carried and buried the coffin by myself.

All of my brothers and sisters went to the funeral. Everyone was bitter, and there was a deathly silence. Nobody had accepted the tragedy. I was inconsolable. I couldn't believe that the boy was dead. My brother Carlos hugged me and said, "Papi, this is the war that Colombia lives every day, and today it's our turn to suffer."

After the funeral, my family went back to Miguel's house and sat in his living room. My brother Víctor said that some guys had gone up to him at the funeral, acting weird and threatening him. They said that they were going to kill everyone.

All my siblings wanted an explanation from Miguel. We said, "What's going on, Miguel?" He lowered his head and said, "I ruined all of your lives." We all asked, "Why?" Then he said, "Let Alfonso explain." Alfonso was Miguel's brother-in-law, and he was a bodyguard for the mayor of Tuluá. He didn't want to say anything, so Miguel said, "Alfonso works for the guerrillas."

One of my brothers is a truck driver, and he immediately said to Miguel, "You told me that you needed me to drive some trucks in the jungle. So those trucks must have been for the guerrillas?" Miguel said, "Yes," and lowered his head.

So we all started saying, "Ah, you got involved with the guerrillas. You're a guerrilla," but Miguel said, "No." According to Miguel, the people who had attacked the wedding were paramilitaries because a business deal they had with Alfonso had gone down badly. He said, "What happened is that it looks like Alfonso wanted to work for both sides—get weapons and uniforms for both sides."

Miguel said that he went around with Alfonso when he did his business, but that he didn't know what the business was. He said that there'd been a meeting with some paramilitaries at an ice cream store on the Sunday of the wedding. Two guys had stepped away with Alfonso to talk with him, and two other guys had stayed with Miguel, watching him. Eventually, Alfonso came back and said that they could leave. He told Miguel that he had to meet with a paramilitary boss, but it was at the same time as the wedding, so he wasn't going to go to the meeting. Alfonso's cell phone rang and rang, but he turned it off. Later that day, the paramilitaries must have seen Jairo going around with Miguel on his motorbike when he went to visit our house.

Years later, a friend of my family's told me that, on the day of the shooting, he was sitting across the street from the house where the wedding party was. He told me that he saw a truck coming full speed, the wrong way down the one-way street, and stop outside of the house. Jairo was standing in the doorway of the house, and he ran inside when about six guys got out of the truck and started shooting. My friend says he threw himself on the ground and then lifted his head up to see who was shooting. He saw the guys go into the house and heard, *ta, ta, ta, ta, ta!* They lit up the house. The guys got back into the truck, continued down the street and disappeared. My friend went to see what had happened, and found Jairo in the house lying face up. He was still moving, like he was trying to live.

Miguel had escaped the shooting by running away to hide. Alfonso had also run away. Seven people were injured, and Jairo and one of Silvia's brothers had died.

I'M FLEEING FOR MY CHILDREN

My brother was never clear with us about what he owed or what he needed to hand over to the paramilitaries. He just told us, "I ruined your lives, forgive me," and left Tuluá with his wife and kids the day of the funeral. That was the last we saw of him.

On Thursday my brother Víctor showed up at my house, pale with fear. He was so scared that it terrified me. He said that he'd been riding on his bike and some guys approached him on a motorcycle and threatened him with a gun. It was the same guys who had talked to him after the funeral.

I immediately said to Salud, "Let's go." And that same Thursday, we left for Bogotá. I knew that armed groups are never satisfied when they don't get what they want. It's easy for them to begin killing people until the guilty person shows up. They'll just say to themselves, "Fine, Miguel hasn't shown up. Let's kill his people to see if maybe his heart is moved and he shows up." One of my sisters also left that week, for Costa Rica. Alfonso had ruined his family, and Miguel had ruined mine.

It was very hard for my wife's family. When we went to say goodbye to them, they said that we didn't have any reason to flee, but I told them, "I'm not fleeing because of me, I'm fleeing for my children." I didn't want to see one of my girls bleeding in the hospital.

After a twelve-hour bus ride, we arrived at my aunt's house in Facatativá, which is forty-five minutes northwest of Bogotá. We stayed there for a few nights, and then I went to see a childhood friend who lived there. He lived with four siblings in a three-story house, and he told me he would rent the third floor to me. He'd previously kept his dog on the third floor, and just as I arrived, the dog had disappeared.

There were fleas, dog hairs, and dog shit on the floor, but I fixed it up. We didn't have a refrigerator or any other furniture because we'd left everything locked up in a room at my parents' house in Tuluá. We paid about 100,000 pesos[3] a month in rent.

---

[3] About U.S.$35 in 2003.

I started to look for work because my savings were running out. I didn't find any work as a car painter, but one day I saw a notice for work on a flower farm. So at four the next morning, I showed up at the bus stop to wait for the company to pick me up and take me to the savanna forty minutes away, where the farm was. When I got there, I was given work as a transporter. The flower cutters would collect the flowers and hook them to a cable that ran across the entire farm, and I'd walk the flowers along the cable. I'd walk about seventeen kilometers each day. I'd even have fun, because I'd jog along the cable to keep in shape. I made the minimum wage on that job, which was around 430,000 pesos[4] a month, compared to the 1,600,000 pesos[5] a month I'd made in Tuluá.

After a while, my sister Alicia came to visit us. She got mad and asked us why we lived like that after we'd had such a nice house before. She told me and my wife, "Get a nicer apartment, pay 100,000 pesos[6] a month, and I'll pay the rest." So we moved to a better house in Facatativá, paid 100,000 pesos and had the other 100,000 pesos of rent subsidized by my sister and my parents.

Then my mother-in-law came to visit to see how we were living. She really brought my spirits down. She asked me how I was going to take her little queen away from her house and then have her living like that. And how were the kids going to grow up in those conditions? She scolded me, and it worked. After living in Facatativá for about a year and a half, Salud and I returned to Tuluá in the middle of 2003.

EVERYTHING SEEMED NORMAL

When we got back to Tuluá, we found that my siblings had broken into the room where we'd stored our things at my parents' house. They had

---

[4] About U.S.$155 in 2003.

[5] About U.S.$555 in 2003.

[6] About U.S.$35 in 2003.

looted everything: they'd taken all the clothes, my tape recorder, and a Nintendo 64 that I'd had. The only things left were our refrigerator and bed.

Salud and I rented a house and set up a video-game parlor in the living room, where we'd rent out Playstation 2 and Xbox to play by the hour. We had our son Gustavo in December 2003. I eventually went back to working at the car-painting shop, and Salud would stay at the house, running the video-game parlor. After a few years, we were living very well. We had a washing machine, a refrigerator, and all the things that a person with a good job has in their house. Everything seemed normal.

The trouble began around 2007, when some guy started calling my house asking for Miguel. He sounded aggressive, and he called the house about three times. Each time he'd say, "We need your brother Miguel!" I'd say, "He doesn't live here," and he'd say, "But you're his brother." And right then I'd hang up. Salud would ask me who'd called, and since she's very emotional, I'd always tell her, "Wrong number."

Around that time my wife started to get scared. She said that, on two occasions, a car followed her when she was taking our daughters to school. I told her that she was imagining things. But then one afternoon, Salud was taking our youngest daughter Andrea to school on the back of a motorcycle taxi when all of a sudden a car hit them from behind. The motorcycle driver was agile and managed to straighten out the bike, but the car came back and hit the motorcycle again. It wasn't a normal accident; the car had made an attempt on Salud's and Andrea's lives.

Later that year, three men broke into my sister Alba Luz's house and hit her on the head with some sort of bar. She was left unconscious. When her kids found her at the house, she was bleeding from her nose and mouth and had begun to choke on her own blood.

I took my sister Alba Luz to live in my house for a few days while she recuperated, because I had the quietest house out of the siblings. It was sad, because she'd had long hair, and the doctors had to shave it all off. There were some horrifying stitches; it was like a zipper around her head.

This was the straw that broke the camel's back. I told Salud, "It looks like it's the same problem with Miguel again." I told her about the phone calls, and said that we had the option to emigrate to Ecuador. We had been there once on vacation, and I knew that it was cheaper to live there. I said, "At least we'll live in peace there." We waited a few months before we decided to leave, because at that time I still didn't have the strength to go. I knew it was going to be a hard change.

GOD, OPEN HEARTS FOR ME

In May 2008, I packed three enormous bags. One of the bags was only filled with toys for the kids because I said to Salud, "Let's take something for them, so that they can at least have fun as we settle in." We took a sixteen-hour bus ride to the city of Ibarra, Ecuador. We began a new life, but it started off ugly.

A brother of mine had gone to live in Ibarra a year or two before. The day after I arrived, he connected me with some people who showed us a place to live. The building they showed us used to be a brothel. There was a guy living there who told us that he'd rent us a unit for really cheap. It was a dump, but we didn't have anywhere else to go, so we accepted.

A couple of days later, Salud and I went to the UNHCR[7] to request refugee status, and we were attended to very well there. The HIAS[8] gave us $25,[9] and some mattresses and blankets. They helped us a lot economically.

My brother lent me an old motorcycle of his, and I packed a bag with my painting guns, sanding machine, mask, and all the rest of my professional gear, and went to look for work. When I look for work I always say a blessing, "God, open hearts for me." Because that's what's most impor-

---

[7] Office of the United Nations High Commissioner for Refugees, the U.N.'s refugee agency.

[8] HIAS, the Hebrew Immigrant Aid Society, is the international migration agency of the American Jewish community. They provide assistance to refugees across the world, including in Ecuador.

[9] Ecuador adopted the U.S. dollar as its currency in 2000.

tant—that people listen to you and then decide if they want to give you the work or not.

In my first days in Ecuador, a Colombian told me that if I wanted to be accepted there, I should distance myself from Colombians and get closer to Ecuadorans. I understood what he meant when I started looking for work. When I showed up at the car shops, I'd say, "I'm a professional painter, I have years of experience," and show them proof of the courses I had taken. A lot of people felt bad for me and told me that there weren't any openings. But one guy looked me in the eyes and said, without any embarrassment, "No, I don't give work to Colombians because Colombians hurt me." I said, "What do you mean?" And he said, "Look, I've given work to Colombians. Some ask for money up-front and then don't come back. Others steal things from the cars. Others are problematic and charge more than they're owed. And if you don't pay them they become aggressive."

When he said that my eyes watered up. But I got back on the motorcycle and went around to all the other car shops in Ibarra. I went to ten shops until someone pointed me to a car shop that urgently needed a painter. It was an awful place. There were cans scattered on the floor and there was dust everywhere.

A guy there named Israel asked me what I needed. I told him, "I'm a master painter, I'm a professional," because in Ecuador everyone is called a "master." I showed him my résumé and he asked me, "Do you know how to paint?" I told him, "Yes," and he said, "How will you show me that you know how to paint?" I told him, "Have me paint whatever you want me to paint." He told me to come back the next morning.

The next day I got up early and showed up at the shop at seven in the morning. I stood there at the front door until the shop opened at eight. The other painter arrived at nine; he was a young guy with a disabled right hand. He'd had polio or something. He started to paint a new car, and I saw that he wasn't painting well.

Israel looked at the car and then he looked at me. He asked, "Is it well painted, master?" I felt bad, but I said, "No, it's not." He asked why, and I said, "Because it's grainy and has black dots." I repainted the car, and it turned out clean and shiny. Israel looked at me and said, "Master, you're hired."

I'm grateful to that man, because he gave me a hand. He opened doors for me here in Ibarra.

WE HAVE SOMETHING CALLED DIGNITY

In August 2008 a strong wind lifted the roof of our house twenty or thirty centimeters off of the wall, and then it crashed down. After that, we moved to an apartment that was a little nicer, but still really small.

The Ecuadoran government granted my family refugee visas in November 2008, just six months after we arrived. When they gave us the visas, they gave us all the rights of an Ecuadoran, except to vote.[10] Voting is mandatory in Ecuador, so everyone has a voting card. It's the first thing that's asked of you when you want to work at a company or ask for a loan. Banks don't accept my Colombian ID card when I go to cash a check. I'm no one here. The government accepts you as a refugee, but they know that you'll always have to work hiding, under the table.

I worked at the car shop for six months and I put in a lot of effort; almost every day I worked from seven in the morning until eleven at night. But in November I started to work at another car shop because I was going to get paid more there. But I didn't make more than $220 a month, and with that I had to pay $80 a month in rent as well as pay for food, utilities, and for my three kids to go to school. Sometimes work would be scarce at the car shop and I could only work three times a week.

I got frustrated and told Salud to look for work and help me out. One of the social workers from HIAS told Salud there was a shoe store that was looking for salespeople. Since she'd sold clothes when we met each other, I told her, "Sweetie, it's your kind of work." But when Salud showed up at

---

[10] In Ecuador, refugees are entitled to fundamental rights, including the right to free movement, the right to work, and the right to access the national justice and healthcare system.

the store, the owner looked at her and said, "I don't give work to Colombians. Sorry." Salud cried. She was sad, because as an adult in the country where you're from, you belong to your country. And you arrive in another country and it's different, and you have to lower your head. We human beings have something called dignity and pride.

At the end of 2009, my wife found work cleaning rooms in one of the "love motels" in the area. The employer gave us two rooms at the motel to live in. Salud's friends criticized us for living there, and said that it was a motel where couples would go to sin. It was a very heavy environment. The first thing the owner told us was, "I don't want to hear the kids because it has to be silent here. And if the kids see the couples go into the motel, the couples don't like it." So the kids were often shut inside the room while Salud worked from eight in the morning until eight at night.

At the time, Lina was nine, Andrea was eight, and Gustavo was six. Their performance at school had started to decline, so in January 2010, we moved out of the motel and into a house in the same neighborhood.

SWEAT, RUN, AND FORGET

People think that all of the Colombian women who live in my neighborhood are prostitutes because there are four brothels there, and all the women who work there are Colombians. At school, Lina's classmates ask her what brothel her mom works in. One time when Salud was at mass, a priest said that the prostitutes who worked at the neighborhood brothels were the parasites of humanity, and right then everyone in the church turned to look at her. She had to leave the church.

One time one of my Colombian co-workers went to buy some paint, and when he came back to the car shop, he told me, "Everyone is going crazy over the death of that guy whose throat was slit." Two Colombians had slit an Ecuadoran's throat at a motel, and just when he arrived at the paint store, people were talking about the news. The people there were saying, "Those disgusting Colombians, they only come here to do harm, to kill." My friend told me that he changed his accent to speak like a

Peruvian. I responded, "A lot of times, God puts you in a place so that you change people's perception. And maybe your job here in Ecuador isn't to work, but to change the image that people have of Colombians." My friend lowered his head and kept looking at me. I said, "Don't deny your homeland. You were born in Colombia and you're here because of problems."

I think it's my duty to change the image of Colombians. I want to say to the world, "There are millions of Colombians just like me. Maybe they live here in Ecuador, but you just haven't seen them. Or maybe you don't allow them to get close to you, so you don't know them."

I'm on a soccer team here in Ibarra, and when I play, I represent my country. The head of the team calls me "Colombia." When I play on Sundays, it goes beyond just playing. I get out all of my stress and blow off steam. I don't play to hurt anyone, but rather to sweat, run, and forget. My ninety minutes are perfect.

I've been ejected from two games. One time when I was playing, some guy slapped me in the face, so I went up to him and said, "Calm down, dude." He said, "I can't stand Colombians." So I took him out with a slide tackle. I knocked him down so that he'd respect me. And then I took his hand and said, "Now we're at peace." I stopped the quarrel right there. I was ejected from the game and I sat down to watch the rest of the match. My wife asks me, "Why do you get yourself ejected from the games?" And I tell her, "Because above all else you have to be a person, and make yourself valued as a person."

I HAVE KIDS WHO NEED TO SEE HAPPINESS

In October 2011 I had an interview with a U.S. official to see if we could get relocated there. I thought that my kids would have a better education there.

In the interview I was asked whether my brother Miguel was guilty of working with armed groups. I said yes. I consider him to be guilty because when you're an adult, you know what's good and what's bad. I think that my brother was working with Alfonso and that he knew who he was working with.

When I left the interview I kept thinking that I was judging my brother, and that it was a sin. So that night I went to the priest and confessed. I asked God for forgiveness for judging my brother. I told him that I didn't know if I had forgiven my brother or not and that I felt bad about it. I said that I wanted to forgive him and not judge him anymore.

I was later told that our application to go to the U.S. had been rejected. The news was hard to take.

My dad insists that I return to Colombia, but I can't turn back. I don't go back because of how it would be to raise my kids there. I don't go back because of violence and the economic situation there. My homeland is expensive; my homeland is dangerous. One time Lina told me, "Dad, I think that if we returned to Colombia we'd be regressing." And she's the one who suffers most from the contempt of the other kids. It's been awful for Lina in school. One of her classmates threw her down the stairs, and she was left unconscious. Another time, a boy gave her a razor in P.E. class and told her to cut another girl with it. When Lina said that she wasn't a murderer and threw the razor on the floor, all her classmates started to say her dad raped her.

We've lived through a lot of ugly things and humiliations, and maybe we're a little poor here, but I've lived in peace. I live in peace here because I know that my kids will go to school and nothing will happen to them. I've already lived the war; I already know what it is to feel the pain of losing a close family member.

But still, I regret having come to Ecuador. I had a really good life in Colombia, really good. It makes me angry when I open the refrigerator and there's nothing, when the pantry should be full and there's nothing. But I can't show my rage because I have kids who need to see happiness. I can't fail them, because I wouldn't be able to forgive myself the day that they told me, "It's your fault for who I am." When I go to sleep exhausted and wake up exhausted, I throw some cold water on my face to keep going.

THROWING STONES
AT THE MOON

The Southwest

Over the past two decades, Colombia's southwest has been among the most violent and volatile areas of the country, hosting an explosive mix of coca crops, gold mining, paramilitary groups, leftist guerrillas, drug lords, and security forces—with large Afro-Colombian and indigenous communities caught in the crossfire.

Putumayo province lies on Colombia's jungle-covered border with Ecuador, and was an outlaw frontier region where coca crops took a strong and early hold. Farms of hundreds of hectares of coca were common in the 1980s and 1990s, when the province came to have the highest concentration of coca in the world. The Revolutionary Armed Forces of Colombia (FARC) held nearly unrivaled control over the region, taxing cocaine smugglers. By 1999, right-wing paramilitaries had established a foothold in the province through a campaign of terror that included massacres, forced disappearances and displacement. When the U.S.-backed Plan Colombia was launched in 2000 to fight the drug trade with aerial fumigation of coca crops, U.S. and Colombian authorities considered the province ground zero in the war on drugs.

As fumigation and violence pushed coca farmers from the province, many moved westward to Nariño, and the conflict followed. With a long, secluded Pacific coastline, remote navigable rivers, deep mountain valleys, and a jungle-covered border with Ecuador, by the late 2000s Nariño became the new battleground. The FARC, ELN, and various factions of the Rastrojos and Águilas Negras—neo-paramilitaries that emerged after the demobilization of the Libertadores del Sur bloc of the AUC—battled it out for command of coca crops, trafficking routes, and land. By 2010, the coastal municipality of Tumaco had a homicide rate nearly five times the national average. The following year, local authorities reported that four out of five killings there were attributed to the Águilas Negras or Rastrojos. Bombings, massacres and public executions grabbed national headlines.

North of Nariño lies Cauca province, which has a similar mix of mangrove-covered coastline and high Andean mountains. The province has become a key drug trafficking corridor, connecting coca, poppy, and marijuana crops to the Pacific coast trafficking routes. After recovering somewhat from heavy losses between 2003 and 2008, the FARC have made Cauca one of the most active fronts in the conflict. In 2011 alone, thirty-seven separate FARC attacks were reported in the province. It was there that the Colombian military killed top FARC commander Guillermo León Sáenz, alias Alfonso Cano, during a military operation in November 2011. Cauca is also home to the well-organized Nasa Indians, who have declared themselves and their territory neutral in the war, but cannot escape conflict between the army and guerrillas: forty-seven Nasa were killed in 2011.

FELIPE AGUILAR

AGE: 46

OCCUPATION: *Farmer*

HOMETOWN: *San Joaquín, Cauca*[1]

INTERVIEWED IN: *Pasto, Nariño*

Felipe Aguilar has farmed all his life, growing both legal and illegal crops, including coca, plantains, and yucca. The FARC, Colombia's largest guerrilla group, has forced him to flee his farms in Putumayo and Nariño provinces three times. We first interviewed Felipe in February 2011, three months after members of a neo-paramilitary group called the Rastrojos gunned down his ex-wife and three children in a massacre in Nariño. As he tells his story, he pulls out photos of the children who died. Óscar, his surviving ten-year-old son, sits by his side, tracing the outline of his dead sister's ID card photo and decorating it with hearts.

Names in this narrative have been changed at the request of the narrator.

I CAN'T CRY

I try to cry and I can't. A psychologist told me, "Mr. Felipe, you have to cry. You have to let out what's inside of you, because it's dangerous."

---

[1] San Joaquín, La Guayacana, Iscuandé, Medellín, and Cali are all false locations employed to protect the narrator's identity.

The pain is here in my chest, but I can't cry. Except when someone tells a funny story, then I cry with laughter.

I was born in San Joaquín, Cauca province, in 1965. My dad was black, and my mom was white. I'm the oldest of ten brothers and sisters. Including my dad's side, we were thirty-six kids in total, because when my dad met my mom he'd already had twenty-six children with other women. I know some of them, but not others.

My siblings and I worked in the countryside and studied in town. Some years we went to school in the countryside because we had to help my dad on the farm. We'd get up at three in the morning, round up the cattle and milk them. At six in the morning we'd give the milk to the milkman and bathe before going to school. It was a one-hour walk to school, and we'd always arrive late. I didn't like studying, and I only went up to the fifth grade. What I liked was to work; I've always liked agriculture.

My dad was good to us, and I was very close to him. When he saddled up his horse to go to work on the farm, I'd watch to see what time he left so that he'd take me with him. He'd tell me to stay at home, but I'd walk a little farther behind him so that he couldn't see me. He'd stop and say, "Felipe, are you there?" I'd stay quiet. He'd say, "Go back to the house." In the end, he'd see me and tell me, "Well, come along." He'd sit me on an extra mule and I'd go around with him happily.

My dad treated us well, but my mom had an acidic character; she was a fierce, angry woman who punished us hard. No one liked her. She fought with the neighbors and with our farmworkers.

When I was fourteen, my dad was killed in town, and my mom didn't come back to the farm after that. The rumor was that my mom had a lover, and that the two of them had killed my dad. A neighbor told me that my mom had even bought a house in Pasto and gone to live there. I had nine brothers and sisters to look after. I thought, *But how is this woman going to take off and leave me here saddled with all these kids?*

Anyhow, I continued on with the kids, struggling and struggling for years. As each sibling got to be around ten, twelve years old, he'd leave to go seek his own destiny.

MY GOD, THIS IS MY LAND

In the end I was left with one sister, Victoria. It was 1985; I was twenty and she was sixteen. I asked her, "Well, now what are we going to do? We're alone now, like an old couple that's raised all of its children."

I had a friend I'd gone to school with named Román who told me there was good work in Putumayo province.[2] He said that you could pick coca leaves there and get paid well. He told me, "Let's go, Negro![3] You're such a good worker, you'll make some serious money." But I was afraid to go. I heard that in Putumayo you had to cross huge rivers in motorboats, and where I grew up there isn't any water. I couldn't even imagine what a motorboat was.

By the end of 1987, it hadn't rained for the entire year and Victoria and I had lost two harvests. I thought, *Román's going to come one of these days and I'll tell him that I'll go.* And coincidentally he arrived a few days later and said, "Man, Negro, don't struggle anymore here. Let's go. We'll all find work there."

I said, "I heard that it's dangerous to pick coca,[4] that the police will grab you and take you to jail." But Román said, "In Putumayo it's all jungle, there's no one there." So I said, "Fine," left Victoria behind on the farm, and departed.

My idea was to get a little piece of land in Putumayo and harvest my own plants, not just be someone else's worker. And that's how things went. I worked on a woman's farm for three months until she told me, "Negro, out there in the bush there are baldíos." I didn't know what a baldío was. She told me, "A baldío is land that doesn't have an owner. You go and mark off what you think you can work, trace a path and say, 'This is mine.' And that's it, it's respected."

---

[2] Puerto Asís, the capital of Putumayo province, is 232 kilometers southeast of San Joaquín.

[3] In Colombia and Latin America, people often colloquially call Afro-descendent or dark-skinned people "negro."

[4] The leaves of the coca plant are the raw material used in making cocaine.

She took me to the baldíos. It was jungle. I knocked down huge trees with a hatchet and planted plantains and yucca. About three months later I went back to San Joaquín and told Victoria to come with me to Putumayo, and she did. Working and working, I made a good farm. The soil in Putumayo is incredible, you plant a yucca crop and seven months later you pull out at least thirty kilos of yucca per plant. Where I was from in Cauca, a yucca plant didn't produce more than a kilo. I said to myself, *My God, this is my land!* I built a house, and I also got seeds to plant coca. I didn't think I'd ever want to leave. But my sister Victoria didn't like the mud there, and she soon left Putumayo to live with a sister in Cauca.

I'LL TAKE HER AS IF SHE WERE MY OWN

In 1989 the FARC[5] took away my farm because I wouldn't pay them the vacuna.[6] Ever since I was little my father had taught me to work, and so when I started to have things, it made me angry that those slackers would come to take away what I'd earned through sacrifice. The guerrillas made me rent my farm to another guy so that he'd pay them the rent he owed me. I became afraid and didn't go back to the farm. Instead, I got organized again and set up another farm in a different village.

There was a man named Mido who lived in my village. He was the richest man in the region. We both bred fighting cocks, and I had a cock pit on my farm where he'd go for fights. We became very good friends. Around August 1990, he told me, drunk, "Some relatives of my wife are coming to stay. They're going to be two bangin' monas,[7] just like you like 'em." I loved women and he knew it. He said, "They're really fine. I'm going to give you one so that you get married right away." I told him, "Alright, but I have to see her first."

---

[5] The Revolutionary Armed Forces of Colombia (FARC) is the largest left-wing guerrilla group in Colombia.

[6] A vacuna is an extortion payment.

[7] In Colombia, mona is a term used to refer to a blonde or light-skinned person.

His wife's relatives arrived in September. I went up to Mido's farm and he introduced me to them. First I was with the girl named Rosa; that was the one I liked. But it didn't work out with her, so I turned to her sister, Carolina. She said she'd come live with me on my farm.

At that time, Carolina had a month-old girl named Clara. I told her, "I'll help you raise the girl. I'll take her as if she were my own." I became attached to that little girl and she became attached to me. I would always walk around carrying her. I'd take her with me when I went to work, hang a hammock from a tree and put her there. She called me "Dad." I loved that girl. Two years later Carolina and I had our first child together, a girl named Stefani.

The countryside was hard for Carolina: the mud, flies, mosquitoes, and insects. I had to be like a doctor, massaging one thing, treating another, rubbing her with lime, butter or oil. She'd see the workers with malaria and say, "I'm afraid that these animals will kill me, they'll give me malaria." But she never got it. In 1994, Carolina and I had our second daughter, Luisa.

I DREAMED ABOUT THE GUERRILLAS

We processed the coca on the farm. I learned how to process it by watching my neighbors. I would mix cement with gasoline and water. People said that the guerrillas were buying the coca paste,[8] but it was a long chain. They didn't buy it directly, but rather gave money to other people in the village to buy it on their behalf. Some months, no one in the village had money to buy the paste. So I had to sell it in the city of Puerto Asís, which was seven hours away by motorboat, and give the guerrillas 30,000 pesos[9] per kilo, which was the tax they imposed in the area.

Román worked as the administrator of my farm. He was my best friend. He didn't like to drink, but he'd drink with me because he knew I

---

[8] Coca paste is a substance produced at an intermediary stage of the cocaine-making process.

[9] About U.S.$36 in 1994.

was happy with him by my side. When he was drunk he'd tell me, "Negro, you're a big drinker. Stop drinking, stop walking by the river drunk at night, you're going to drown or get yourself killed." He was afraid of death; whenever he saw a gun his legs would shake. He thought that I'd die before him, and whenever he was drunk, he'd say, "I'm going to give you a good burial in San Joaquín."

Around that time bad people started showing up in the villages and everything got more complicated. Out on the paths we took to sell the coca paste, there were a lot of thieves. They'd grab you and rob you and kill you. So we'd go as a group of four with workers and shotguns and revolvers, all looking out for each other.

One day in 1997 my brother Antonio, who had also moved to Putumayo, asked me to lend him my revolver. He said he was going to take some product into town, so I agreed. Antonio killed a FARC miliciano[10] with that gun. The miliciano had wanted to kill my brother, so my brother killed him first. When the FARC found out that Antonio had used my gun, they turned against me, too.

Antonio left for the city of Pereira, and my family and I also had to leave our farm behind. We went to Puerto Asís and tried to sell the farm from there, but everyone would tell me, "No, those people won't allow anyone to buy that farm." After the guerrillas took my farm away, I was traumatized. I dreamed about the guerrillas, that they were chasing me, that they killed me.

In October 1997 I left Puerto Asís for the city of Pradera, in Valle del Cauca province. I was with Stefani, Luisa, and Carolina, who was six months pregnant at the time. We took two motorbikes and a pickup truck with us and left Clara to live with her grandmother.

Román stayed behind in Putumayo taking care of some horses that I'd left him. The guerrillas killed him about five months later. They de-

---

[10] A miliciano, roughly translated to "militiaman" in English, is a member of a guerrilla group that typically dresses in civilian clothes and doesn't participate directly in combat, but provides information and support to other guerrillas.

stroyed his head with three rifle shots. The only thing left was his neck. My poor friend, he'd been with me for ten years there in the bush. He never thought that he'd die before me.

A PRETEXT TO THROW ME IN THE RIVER

We arrived in Pradera without anything. We were poor, testing our luck. In January 1998, about three months after arriving, my son Manuel was born. I sold the pickup truck and bought a little house there with the money. I also started a bakery.

I'd get up at three in the morning to let the baker into the shop and close between ten and 11:30 p.m. Once Carolina and I got home, we'd count the money we'd made that day. We'd make little piles of coins worth 1,000 pesos each.[11] We'd count 50,000, 65,000, 70,000 pesos every night.[12] And with that we had to pay the waitress, the baker, the electricity bill, and the water bill. I became heartbroken. My wife and I would say, "I don't even feel like getting up each day."

Then, around 2000, a friend of mine called me. He was living in a village called La Guayacana in Tumaco, Nariño province, and he told me to go there, that there was good work there. I said to Carolina, "Quite frankly, I don't want to go back to the countryside anymore. What if we get there and I come across the people who kicked us off the farm? What if they kill me?"

But Carolina said we should go, so we left Pradera. When we got to La Guayacana, my friend helped us buy a 120-hectare farm about an hour outside of the village. I didn't have money, and the farm was worth 35 million pesos. So that we could give the owner 10 million pesos, my friend lent me 6 million and I sold two motorbikes that I'd brought from

---

[11] About 70 U.S. cents in 1998.

[12] About U.S.$35, $45, and $54 in 1998.

Putumayo for 4 million. I had to pay the owner the other 25 million[13] over a one-year period.

My son Óscar was born three months after we arrived in La Guayacana. We planted coca, yucca, and plantains on the farm. I have a cousin who flies fumigation airplanes for the government.[14] He would be in Caquetá province fumigating and call me and joke, "This week I'm coming to Nariño. Cousin, I'm coming to fumigate you." I would tell him, "I'll take out a white flag so you can tell where I am!"

In 2003, I built a little boarding house in town in La Guayacana, which was an hour away from our farm by land and water.[15] It had two floors and we usually rented apartments by the month to working people, mostly professors. They were apartments with a bedroom, a living room, and a kitchen. The business was going well. I had my third daughter Isabela in 2003, and in 2005, I had my third son, Pedro.

The next year, in 2006, my sister Victoria died in an attempt on my cousin Ramiro's life. She was riding along in the passenger's seat of Ramiro's truck in Argelia, Cauca, when hitmen fired two hundred shots at him and didn't even hit him. But they hit Victoria, with one shot right in her heart. I think members of my own family had paid the hitmen to kill Ramiro, because he had killed another cousin the year before.

Some time after my sister died, two guys arrived at our boarding house in La Guayacana and asked for a room for five months. After they had been staying with us for three months, people began to spread the rumor that some guys who seemed like paramilitaries were staying at my boarding house. Around that time, a friend of mine from the Community

---

[13] About U.S.$17,000, $5,000, $3,000, $2,000, and $12,500 in 2002.

[14] The fumigation program sprays herbicides from small aircraft, attempting to kill coca crops.

[15] Felipe's farm was located in the rural area of the subdivision of La Guayacana, and the boarding house was located in La Guayacana's town center.

Action Board[16] told me the guerrillas had called a meeting to ask for my references. When my friend asked them what the meeting was all about, a guerrilla told him that I worked with the paramilitaries, and that I had some of them living at my house.

Later, my friend asked me, "Why don't you avoid problems and ask the guys at the boarding house to leave their rooms?" I said, "If it's true that they're paramilitaries, how can I ask them to leave? They won't leave. And if they suspect that the guerrillas are pressuring me, they'll kill me." My friend just said, "Do whatever you can to have those people leave."

In the end Carolina and I decided to invent a story that we were going to sell the boarding house. We began to ask people to leave because we had to hand it over by a certain date. The guys left their rooms and I thought, *I got myself out of this one.* But that wasn't the case, because the guerrillas were still fuming. They called me to a meeting in the village and three uniformed guerrillas told me that I owed them a 7,500,000-peso[17] vacuna.[18]

I became afraid to even go to my farm. I thought, *I'm going to leave, because these people want to kill me. It's clear. They're doing this to me so that I get pissed off and say something bad so that they'll have a pretext to throw me in the river.* I put my farm up for sale. When the guerrillas realized that I was selling it, things got worse. I heard that they'd held a meeting with people from the area and told them that I couldn't sell the farm. They said that they'd be watching to make sure that no one would buy it.

Then one morning, the administrator of my farm came to the boarding house in town. He told me that the guerrillas had gone to look for me on the farm at 2 a.m. the previous night. He said that they'd looked for me in the shed and under the bed, and that they'd threatened the workers not to say that they'd gone looking for me. The administrator told me,

---

[16] Community Action Boards are small civil organizations that represent communities, communities and neighborhoods. Each board has a president who is elected to a three-year term.

[17] About U.S.$3,300 in 2006.

[18] Vacunas, literally "vaccines," are extortion payments.

"Don't go to the farm because those guys are furious. They're looking for you and they're going to kill you." After he told me that, I said to myself, *I'm never going back to the farm.*

I called my friend Enrique in Pasto[19] and told him what had happened. He said, "Come here. Don't stay there, because those people will kill you." I said, "What about my farm? I want to sell my things." He said, "My friend, you have only one life. Stop messing around and come here." We left La Guayacana for Pasto in 2007.

We lost twenty-five pigs, a big shed with about 250 chickens, and a little pond with red tilapia. The guerrillas plundered all of it. Thieves also entered our house in town and robbed our refrigerator and television.

NOW THAT YOU'VE LOST
EVERYTHING YOU HAD

When we arrived in Pasto I went to talk with Enrique. He said, "Why don't you register as a displaced person with Social Action?"[20] I didn't even know what a displaced person was, or what Social Action was. He said, "I've gone. You go and say what happened, that the guerrillas took your farm and they were going to kill you, and ask what you should do now that you've lost everything you had." A week later I went to Social Action to give a statement, and my family was registered as displaced.

Enrique had a sister who lived alone in Pasto and paid 300,000 pesos[21] a month in rent. He told us to go live with her and pay half of the rent. And we did. I looked for work but there's none in Pasto. I couldn't find myself. It's sad to see yourself standing in line at Social Action for

---

[19] Pasto is the capital of Nariño province.

[20] The government entity entrusted with coordinating assistance to the displaced population, to the poor, and to victims of violence. Social Action was replaced by the Department for Social Prosperity in 2012.

[21] About U.S.$150.

hand-outs—things that I'd never had to do before but that I had to do for my kids, who were between four and fifteen years old when I arrived in Pasto. If it had just been me, I would have gotten on a bus and gone to work on a farm. I was taught to work. But I thought, *Where can I go with these kids and my wife? Who'll give me work if I'm with all these people?* I felt a tremendous bitterness.

My wife's respect for me started to change. She loved money, and by that time we were completely broke. We only had the little sleeping pads that the Red Cross had given us. She didn't tell me directly that she wanted to leave, but I could see it. I would tell her, "We have a commitment to this family, we have to work hard and get ahead with these kids." I was very anxious and couldn't sleep. I fell ill. I told her, "You can't leave me alone saddled with these kids now that I'm sick."

I sent my eldest girl Stefani to La Guayacana to collect money from a guy who owed me. She was about sixteen years old at the time, and I told her to leave for La Guayacana at eight in the morning. I went on an errand downtown and when I got back at four in the afternoon she was still there. I asked her why she hadn't left yet and she said, "I'm waiting for Mom because she's going to come with me to the bus station." Stefani and Carolina left with Pedro at five in the afternoon. Carolina said, "I'll be right back to serve the kids dinner." I stayed at the house with Óscar, Manuel, Isabela, and Luisa.

It got to be almost seven at night and Carolina hadn't returned yet. I went to call her from a store across the street. I said, "Where are you? The kids are hungry, come back quickly to make dinner." She said, "Don't even wait for me because I'm not coming back. I'm traveling." I said, "Traveling where?" She said, "I'm going to La Guayacana with Stefani. I'm not going to live with you all anymore." The woman left.

It was a tremendous blow for me. I went back to the house and said to the kids, "I called your mom. She left, she's not coming back." Isabela was a sharp one. She said, "Let her leave. I'm growing up and I'll cook for you and wash your clothes."

Isabela was four-and-a-half years old at the time. She would pull a chair next to the stove, stand up on it, light the stove, and prepare panela water[22] and fry plantains. The girl lifted my spirits; she was attached to me. When I got sad, she would say, "What's wrong Dad? Are you thinking about Mom? Don't think about her. She left because she doesn't love us." She gave me strength. I sent Luisa, who was fourteen at the time, to live with a friend of mine in Pasto, and she later went to live with Carolina in La Guayacana.

WHEN I REALLY GOT SICK

Waiting for my wife to come back is when I really got sick. I went to the doctor, who diagnosed me with pneumonia. Isabela would wake me up at five in the morning, asking for breakfast. I'd make her breakfast and half an hour later she wanted more food. We had food but it was hard for me to wake up to cook and the cold water from the sink made me shiver.

One day a friend came to my house and told me I should send Isabela to live with her mom. Then another friend came by and said the same thing. Finally I decided. I took Isabela and Manuel to the bus station and sent them off to live with their mom in La Guayacana. Isabela was sweating and grabbed my hand tightly. She asked me not to send her away.

I was left with just my son Óscar, who was nine. I went with him to work in Tolima province and got a case of thrombosis. I was in a wheelchair for twenty days, and I couldn't open my left hand for a month and a half. Óscar flunked the fifth grade because he'd go with me to the hospital, and altogether he missed more than a month of school.

I couldn't stop thinking about my other kids. Not being with them was a prison. Without them, I was suffering, thinking, nervous, dreaming one thing, dreaming another. Eventually, I bought a little piece of land in Putumayo where I thought I could settle with them. I asked my wife to send them and she said that I'd have to wait until the end of 2010 when

---

[22] Panela is an unrefined food product made by boiling sugarcane juice into a hard, crusty block. It can then be dissolved in hot water to make a drink.

they got out of school. I said, "Don't lie to me, send them to me in Pasto. Otherwise, on December 10 I'm going to come to La Guayacana to get them, even if the guerrillas kill me there. I won't take it any longer."

At the time, Stefani and Manuel weren't living in La Guayacana. Stefani had met a boyfriend there and gone to live with him in Iscuandé, Nariño, and she took Manuel to live with her there.

I often talked to my kids on the phone. Isabela was seven years old and she would say, "I'm big now, now I'm a little lady." My little five-year-old son Pedro was even sharper than Isabela. He'd tell me, "My teacher told me that I'm a very special kid, that I'm going to be a doctor. I'm little Doctor Pedro." He'd tell me what they'd eaten for lunch, everything. When I told him I was going to hang up, he would ask to talk a little longer. But I'd have to hang up on him, because I didn't have any more money. I still have his words with me. He'd say, "Dad, take me with you, I want to go with you. I love my mom, but I don't like her. I'll help you work, I'll help you swing the machete."

When I talked to them on November 8, 2010 I told Isabela that I'd bought a little piece of land. I told her that I'd build them a nicer house, that each one of them would be able to go to a school near the farm, and that I'd raise chickens and have a shed of pigs and a fishpond. That's what I thought: *I've moved around so much. I want to get that land to settle down, bring the kids, and that's where I'll die. Or maybe when I get old my kids will come get me from there.*

THE TRAIL OF COFFINS

On Wednesday, November 10, my cell phone rang at ten at night. It was a friend of mine from Pasto. She told me that she had just received a call from La Guayacana, and that Carolina and Luisa had been killed. At first I didn't believe her.

I said, "And the other kids? Where are they? Who has them?" She said, "I don't know." I said, "Do you have a friend there who could go to the house and look for the kids, or go to the police station and look for the kids with the police? Is there someone to take care of the kids before I arrive tomorrow?" She said, "Sure, I'll see who I can send."

I thought, *Maybe my wife and the eldest girl are dead, but not the other kids.* Since La Guayacana is such a dangerous town I thought that maybe Carolina or Luisa had done something or seen something, and they killed them for it. I was lying down in bed next to Óscar and didn't tell him anything.

I received a call a little while later from another friend from La Guayacana telling me that my other kids had also been killed. By that time I was already crying. I didn't understand anything. I said to myself, *But why, God? I handed my kids over to you. What have you done to my family?* That night I sat on my bed and smoked two packs of cigarettes, lighting each one from the butt of the other.

The next morning I left Putumayo hoping to arrive in Pasto and then go to Tumaco, where my wife and kids' bodies had been taken. My friend from Pasto called me when I was on the road to say that little Pedro had been shot a few times, but that he was just wounded. I thought, *It's a lie that he's wounded. They've killed him as well.*

I arrived in Pasto on Thursday and early Friday morning my friend there told me that Pedro had died. All of my kids were N.N.s[23] in the hospital in Tumaco, without family or even a friend. I imagined how they might have been just lying there, discarded, poor little things. I was told that they had a freezer in the hospital and I imagined what color they'd be—purple. How could the little poor things be? Frozen, with ice on their mouth, I thought. I cried. I wanted to see them right away.

The Red Cross helped me with 700,000 pesos[24] per body for the funeral. A funeral home charged me 4,500,000 pesos[25] to bring them from Tumaco to Pasto, bury them, and buy the tombs. The funeral home took care of everything because I was too sick to do anything. A psychologist from the

---

[23] N.N., or "no name," from the Latin *Nomen Nescio*, is the morgue registration of a corpse that lacks identifying documents, and is likely to go unclaimed.

[24] About U.S.$350.

[25] About U.S.$2,250.

Red Cross kept calling me. She'd say, "You have to prepare yourself, Felipe." She thought that I was going to break down when I saw the coffins.

The coffins arrived in Pasto four days after the massacre. A man from the funeral home opened the trail of coffins, box by box. My family. We were all alive, and now look. *Half is gone*, I thought. We were eight and there were four in the coffins.

The day of the burial, a lot of people were amazed, saying, "Who's the father of the children?" Someone would answer, "It's the black man over there." I heard what they said: "He's not affected, he doesn't cry, he doesn't saying anything." I listened and nothing more. The pain is still here in my chest.

SINCE KIDS DON'T LIKE THE DARK

A prosecutor showed me photos of my wife and children on a computer in the Attorney General's office. They were left looking ugly. They had all been in the house when two guys with their faces covered arrived shooting. Luisa had tried to run. The police found her face down on the bed with bullets in her back. She was sixteen years old.

Isabela was sleeping in her little bed. You can tell that they put the barrel up to her eye because she was shot in her eye and her face was burned with gunpowder. There was a huge hole where her eye was; her little face was destroyed inside. One cheekbone was up by her brow. I believe that she didn't wake up, that she stayed there in a dream. She had the best death.

My wife died in the bathroom, on her knees. I don't know if she was trying to stand up, supporting herself against the wall. Or maybe she was repenting and was able to speak with God.

There was another man who had been there watching television. He was wounded but ended up dying a month later.

The boy was intelligent, sharp. Of all of them, Pedro was the only one who was able to flee from the house. He had run far away; he had escaped. But on the corner near the house there's a lamppost. It was about eight at night and since kids don't like the dark, he must have said, *No, the dark, how scary!* If he had run to the right where it was dark they wouldn't have seen him, but he went to where there was light and they saw him.

A member of the Rastrojos, a paramilitary group, was arrested five days after the massacre.[26] The Ombudsman's office[27] assigned me a lawyer, and I would talk with him. I'd tell him, "I want to know about the man who's in jail. I want to know what he said, to see why he did this, and what happened." Because I'm here thinking, *Why could it be? Why could it be that my wife died, that my daughter died? Why did they kill the children?* Sometimes I blame myself, could it be my fault that we separated, or was it her fault?

In the beginning I thought it was the guerrillas that had killed them. But I started to talk with people in La Guayacana and it doesn't add up. The people in La Guayacana say that my daughter Luisa had had a boyfriend in La Guayacana who was a SIJIN[28] police agent that had infiltrated the Rastrojos. But she didn't know that he was a paramilitary or from the SIJIN. They say that based on what her boyfriend knew about the Rastrojos, the authorities were able to capture a commander of the group there.

The boyfriend left the Rastrojos and went back to his work at the SIJIN. My girl Luisa stayed in the town. The Rastrojos were pissed off that the boyfriend had gotten their boss captured, and since Luisa used to go around with the guy, they were so upset that they killed her. That's the story that's out there.

The account coincides with a letter Luisa had written and placed in a Bible. In the letter she says that God has been bad to her; that God hasn't

---

[26] Neo-paramilitary groups such as the Urabeños, Rastrojos, and Paisas are armed groups that emerged in 2006 in the wake of the demobilization process of the AUC national paramilitary coalition. Led largely by former paramilitaries and often employing the same criminal, political, and economic networks as their predecessors, neo-paramilitary groups have a powerful presence in many regions throughout the country.

[27] The Ombudsman's office is a Colombian state entity charged with promoting and defending human rights and international humanitarian law.

[28] The Sectional Judicial Police (SIJIN) is a branch of the national police force.

helped her with anything she's asked for. But that now she asked him to help her because she was grateful that she'd been given her six siblings and a nice family, and she needed help. The letter said that she preferred that "they"—she didn't say who—take her away, but that they wouldn't take away her little siblings or do anything to her mom.

Still, I don't know what to believe. The only thing I know is that it was the Rastrojos who killed my family.

THROWING STONES AT THE MOON

After the massacre, I moved back to Pasto with Óscar, who's now ten years old, and Manuel, who's thirteen. Sometimes Óscar would think about his brother and sisters. He was very close to Pedro. "Yes, I remember Pedro," he would say, and start to cry. Before the massacre Óscar was happy because we were going to take Pedro to live with us. Pedro and Óscar would talk on the cell phone. Pedro told him, "Brother, I have a nice little toy car for you that we can play with." After the massacre some of their things from La Guayacana arrived in Pasto, and sure enough the little car arrived as well. Óscar and I say that it's the car that Pedro was talking about on the phone. And you can tell that Pedro hadn't played with it a lot because it looked new, intact.

In December 2010 I left Manuel with my cousin in a town in Cauca. I couldn't have him near Óscar because Manuel would hit him. After the massacre Manuel started saying that he's tough and would kill. He was looking for revenge. He liked weapons and said he'd be a soldier, policeman, guerrilla, or paramilitary. My cousin told me that he started behaving much better once he started working on her farm milking cows. Around April 2011, he went back to live with Stefani in a village in Iscuandé.

Manuel likes soccer a lot, and there was a small field close to Stefani's farm where people would go to play in the afternoons. Manuel would play every afternoon and started becoming friends with the guys who would go there. One day some guys went up to him and asked him if he wanted to go with them to play a soccer match in another town. They said that they would take him there on a boat for free and that there'd also be dancing. Since he loves soccer, he said, "Of course! I'm going to ask for my sister's permission."

A few days passed, and on June 16, 2011, four guys went to Stefani's house at six in the morning and knocked at the door. Manuel opened it. They said that it was the day of the soccer match and asked if he was going to go. Manuel woke Stefani up and let her know that he was going, but she wouldn't let him. So Manuel told the guys he couldn't go. They told him to at least go and see the boat that they were going to go in.

So Manuel walked with them to the river, which is about 650 meters from the house. When they got close to the boat, the guys told him, "You're coming with us." Manuel said that he couldn't because his sister wouldn't let him. Then two of the guys grabbed him, and Manuel fought back until they threw him in the boat.

One of the guys went towards Manuel with a knife and a piece of rope, and told another guy to start the motor. The motor wouldn't start. Manuel was scared and kicking and screaming, "Stefani! Stefani! Stefani!" The guy with the knife told him to stop making noise, and he chopped him in the hand and shoulder with the knife. Manuel's hand went limp; they'd cut all the tendons in his hand and his fingers. Manuel screamed louder, kicked the guy in the crotch, and dove into the river. He swam underwater until he got to the bank and peeked his head up. He was about fifty meters away from the boat, and they still couldn't start the motor. So he got out of the water and went through the bush back to the house.

When he got to the house, Stefani asked what had happened. He was crying and scared, and said that the guys had almost killed him. A neighbor lent Stefani and him a boat and they went up river to the town of Iscuandé. When they got to town they called me in Pasto. I said, "What happened, mi'jo?"[29] He said, "Some people almost killed me; they were going to take me away in a boat." I talked with Stefani and asked how he was. She said, "I'm worried. Manuel bled a lot, and he fainted. He's so

---

[29] A contraction of "mi hijo" (in English, "my son"), used affectionately for male friends or relatives.

pale." I told her to take him out of Iscuandé and to a hospital where he could get surgery.

A local government office in Iscuandé provided Manuel transportation and he arrived in Pasto the next day at seven at night. We went directly to the children's hospital. They operated on him and I stayed there with him for seven days. I don't know who had tried to take him away, but guerrillas and paramilitaries both operate where Stefani lives.

Manuel got physical therapy in Pasto, and then an NGO paid to send him to an institution in Medellín where he could study and live. They also paid for my transportation and three months of rent for me to move to Cali, where I'm living now with Óscar.

I haven't found any work. I'm not receiving anything from Social Action. They assigned me a number to receive humanitarian aid. It's number 122,500 and this week they were only at 88,000. By the time I get the aid, a year will have passed since I last received it. The government promises things sometimes, but it doesn't follow through. Sometimes things work out, sometimes they don't. It's like throwing stones at the moon.

In October 2011, the lawyer I had been assigned by the Ombudsman's office called me to tell me that the guy from the Rastrojos who was arrested for the death of my children had been convicted and given a forty-six-year sentence. I didn't care, because he killed them and you can't bring them back to life.

About two weeks ago I talked with the director of the institution where Manuel is staying. He said that maybe he's going to need another surgery because his fingers are dead. He can only move his thumb.

EVERYTHING I'VE LOVED,
MY GOD HAS TAKEN AWAY

Sometimes I say to myself, *Could it be that my God is punishing me for not having helped my mom?* Around 1984, before coming to Putumayo, I had found her on the streets of Popayán and she smelled horrible, a desechable,[30] pitiful. She had become a drug addict. When my brothers and I went to live in Putumayo, she came to live with us. Whenever I got drunk, I'd say, "Mom, tell me the truth, what happened with Dad? People say that you had him killed." She always denied it. Around 1997 she went back to Popayán and eventually disappeared. Sometimes I start to think, *Could it be that I'm paying the price for having spurned my mother?* But how could I have done more for her, with everything she had done to us? Now that I'm old, though, I also think, *Maybe my mom was telling the truth, and she didn't have anything to do with my father's murder.*

This is the end of my life; I can't take any more of this. I feel very bad now. I've worked so much, but working has been in vain. Everything's been in vain. I struggled so hard to raise those kids and they killed them. I start to think: *I have friends in Putumayo—bad, rough men who I've watched kill people, making trouble. And nothing happens to them.* I've seen them going around in their nice cars, they have their nice houses, nice family, well-raised kids, granddaughters and grandsons. I wanted to see all my children grown up, to see them marry. It's nice to raise a family and see the youngest son with a beard, the daughter with a husband, with kids. That's been my wish, but I won't be able to achieve it. I've become incredulous in life. Now I don't even know what to think. Everything I've loved, my God has taken away.

---

[30] Desechable is a derogatory term in Colombia that is usually used to refer to a homeless person. It translates to a "disposable" person.

ALFREDO ROMERO

AGE: *41*
OCCUPATION: *Street vendor*
HOMETOWN: *Ipiales, Nariño*
INTERVIEWED IN: *Pasto, Nariño*[1]

Alfredo Romero has no memory of his parents. When he was two years old his mother went missing, and his grief-stricken father drowned himself in a river. His uncle raised him in Ipiales, a small city close to Colombia's border with Ecuador. Alfredo started working at a mechanic's shop when he was eight years old, and in 1988, when he was eighteen, he left Ipiales to seek his fortune in the coca-growing boom in the neighboring province of Putumayo. He bought a farm there, met his wife, and started a family. In 2002, FARC guerrillas falsely accused him of being a paramilitary[2] informant, and gave him twenty-four hours to leave his farm. Alfredo moved with his wife and children to a farm in Patía, Nariño province, where he continued to plant coca. In 2005, paramilitaries discovered that he had sold a batch of coca paste, an intermediate substance made during the cocaine-

---

[1] Pasto, Patía, and La Guayacana are all false locations that were employed to protect the narrator's identity.

[2] Right-wing paramilitary groups began to form in Colombia in the early 1980s with the purported aim of fighting left-wing guerrillas. Backed by the military, landowners, drug traffickers, and political and economic elites, they murdered tens of thousands of civilians.

production process, to rival buyers. They tied him to a tree and attempted to force him to work for them. Alfredo fled his farm and tried his luck planting coca in a jungle-covered hamlet near the village of La Guayacana, in Tumaco, Nariño. In this narrative, Alfredo describes his third displacement, this time at the hands of the National Liberation Army (ELN) guerrillas, which maintained a presence in the area along with the FARC and the Águilas Negras neo-paramilitary group.

Names in this narrative have been changed at the request of the narrator.

THESE AREN'T GUNSHOTS OF DEATH

On May 7, 2007 the ELN[3] guerrillas called everyone in the hamlet to a meeting. They told us that they were going to be in combat with the army, and that we had to abandon our farms until they gave us the order to return. When there's combat, the guerrillas make people in the area vacate their farms so that if the army starts winning, the guerrillas can take off their camouflage, hide their weapons, put on civilian clothes, and act as if they were the owners of the homes.

That day, I took off for the highway and left my farm behind, which was planted with six or seven hectares of coca.[4] My wife and four children were living in Pasto at the time, because I didn't like to have them on the farm around armed conflict and coca crops. So my dogs and the chickens were my only friends on the farm. When the guerrillas made me leave, I poured out half a sack of feed for them to nibble on.

I'd been sleeping at a friend's house by the highway for five days, when I said to myself, *The chickens must have finished the food by now.* I told my friend, "I'm leaving." He said, "Don't go until the guerrillas give us the order to return." But I said, "No, the chickens are going to die on me."

I was going down the path toward my farm at five in the afternoon when I heard, "Hey, son of a bitch! Snitch bastard, didn't we tell you not to come

---

[3] Founded in 1964, the National Liberation Army (ELN) is Colombia's second-largest guerrilla group.

[4] The leaves of the coca plant are the raw material used in making cocaine.

here?" The guerrillas had been on a hill about six meters above me from the path. Two of them shot at me, *ra, ra, pum*. I flew back about six meters into a gully as little bullets entered my leg, stomach and shoulder. I thought, *These aren't gunshots of death*. I didn't think the bullets were going to kill me.

As a guerrilla fighter came over to finish me off, I acted like I was dead. Then another guerrilla came and told him, "Don't shoot anymore—the army will hear us. We have to retreat from here." Then they left.

My entire right leg felt warm. I looked down and saw that my pantleg was ground up. I felt high. I couldn't feel my body and I heard a *weeeeee* sound in my ears. I told myself, *Hang on, hang on*. When I took off my shirt, my belly was full of bullet holes. My left arm was dead; I didn't feel anything when I grabbed it. I couldn't walk or defend myself, and I thought, *God, don't take me away yet. My children are really young. Don't take me yet, don't take me yet.*

I was afraid that the guerrillas were going to come by and shoot me again, so I stayed there and didn't make a lot of noise. They knew I was from the hamlet and must have thought I was spying for the army when they shot me. When they prohibit you from going to your farm, you shouldn't go—and I'd disobeyed.

There, in the middle of the jungle, the mist falls when it gets dark, and the mosquitoes start to arrive. They went *huyyyy* in my ears and bit me. I could hear the frogs going *ruak, ruak, ruak* and the owl starting to yell *buaaaaa*.

What I was afraid of were the snakes, which really would have killed me. I said to myself, *If a snake comes here, how am I going to defend myself if I can't see anything?* It was dark and I only had a machete, which is your companion in the countryside—you don't go anywhere without it. If a snake arrived it would attack and retreat, attack and retreat, and finally leave me dead.

I took off my boot and there was a pool of blood in it. The jungle ants started arriving, to take it away. They wanted to climb up my legs.

I was terribly thirsty, and I saw that a water hose from a farm passed close by. But doctors say that when you have bullet wounds, you can't drink water because you have holes inside of you and the water filters through your body. By around one in the morning I thought, *How can I take it any longer?* I said, *Whatever God wants*, took out my machete and chopped the hose. The water came and I drank until I was about to burst and then I vomited. I felt even thirstier, and I drank more.

I was in awful pain. My leg felt as if it were about to explode. I would try to sit up and my head would fall back down. But I kept my courage.

I thought about my children, and in the end I thought, *God, forgive me for what I've done. If you're going to take me, take me. If not, don't make me suffer so much like this.* I begged God and prayed "Our Father" and prayed the Creed: "I believe in almighty God, creator of heaven and Earth. I believe in Jesus Christ, our Lord, who was conceived by the work and grace of the Holy Spirit and born of the Virgin Mary. He suffered under the power of Pontius Pilate, was crucified, died and buried. He rose from among the dead, ascended to heaven, and is seated next to God the Father. He will come to judge the living and the dead. I believe in the Holy Catholic Church, the communion of saints, the forgiveness of sins, the resurrection of the dead, and life everlasting. Amen."

Then I thought, *I want to sleep for a little while.* I fell asleep at three or four in the morning and woke up close to seven in the morning.

What a scare when I woke up! My feet and legs were covered in big-bottomed black ants! They tickled. I slid them off with my hand and thought, *If no one comes by the afternoon, I'll die here.*

At nine in the morning I heard a little noise and lifted my head up. I saw a neighbor from the hamlet and I said, "Hey, cousin"—because there in the Pacific coast you call black people 'cousin'—"Cousin, help me out!" When he saw me, he came up to me and said, "What happened?" I said, "Quiet! I'll tell you outside of the jungle."

He went to find help and came back about fifteen minutes later with some forty people from the hamlet. They tied a blanket to a piece of wood to make a sort of hammock, hung me in the middle, and raced me eight kilometers to the highway without stopping. They would touch my feet to see if I was going to make it, because death enters through your feet—they go cold first. It took about an hour to get to the highway. The army was on the highway, and at first they didn't know if I was a guerrilla. The people carrying me said I was just a farm owner, and so the army took me to a medical post, where I was given fluids. My wife arrived at the post from Pasto. After about an hour, I was transferred to a hospital in the city of Tumaco, where I was given seven pints of blood. Twenty-five little bullets had entered my body. I was in surgery from eleven at night until three in the morning. The surgeon had cut out about a kilo of my guts, and replaced them with artificial guts.

The nerves in my left arm were damaged, so my fingers don't work. My left arm is now 50 percent disabled, for life.

I was hospitalized in Tumaco for about three weeks. After I recovered, I called a friend of mine from La Guayacana and asked him to tell everyone who'd carried me out that I was going to go there on a certain day. I had them wait for me at an exit off the highway, and I went and gave each one of them a package of bread and cheese. I said to them, "Thank you very much, see you later." I couldn't stay there because the ELN has informants there and they would have killed me right away.

I went to live with my wife and kids in Pasto and never went back to that farm. I've requested reparations from the government for my arm since 2007, but I haven't received anything yet. I've been thinking about going to Ecuador next year, because I see that here in Colombia there won't be a solution for displaced people.

With just one arm, no one gives you work, so I started to work as a street vendor. When there are patron saint festivals in towns nearby, I go there to sell chips, lollipops, peanuts, cigarettes, cookies, and other little things. I have to always listen to the radio to see if there's going to be a festival somewhere, and when there is, I take off for that town with my nine-year-old son. I stay for two or three days at the festival, sleeping at a house in town or in a tent on the sidewalk, and I make a little bit of money. For example, I buy little packs of peanuts for 350 pesos each and sell them for 500 pesos.[5]

When I sell things I'm happy. But when I don't, I remember what I had on my three farms, what I left behind. To go around like I do after having had things before—there are times when I'm tempted to kill myself, drink poison. Then I'll remember my kids and reconsider: have a bad hour, and let it pass. Throw some water on my face and look for something new.

---

[5] About 20 U.S. cents and 28 cents, respectively.

ALICIA ZABALA

AGE: 37
OCCUPATION: *Victims' rights defender, street vendor*
HOMETOWN: *Almaguer, Cauca*
INTERVIEWED IN: *Ciudad Bolívar, Bogotá*

Despite a childhood marked by abuse and a self-professed fascination with weapons, Alicia Zabala resisted the urge to join the FARC guerrillas, which was the dominant armed group in her town of Almaguer, Cauca province. She left her hometown three times: twice by choice and once, in 2004, fleeing death threats from the very same guerrillas she'd thought of joining. Her displacement to Cartago, Valle del Cauca province, and her involvement in a victims' rights group, brought new threats against her and her family. In 2009 she was relocated to Bogotá by the government's rights defenders protection program. Only three months after arriving in Bogotá, Alicia began receiving new threats.

Names in this narrative have been changed at the request of the narrator.

I THOUGHT ABOUT JOINING THE GUERRILLAS

I was born and raised in Almaguer, Cauca, with my three older brothers, Jairo, Pablo, and Tomás, and a younger sister, Marion. Almaguer is an old colonial town with historic buildings. My family had a coffee farm and two coca[1] farms there, about an hour's walk from the main town. We lived on the coffee farm, but from the time I can remember, when I was about eight years old, my parents had me working on their coca farms. My mom would hang a bag on my shoulder and I had to fill it with coca leaves. That's how we were raised; it was the most normal thing. The leaves were sold by the kilo, so my mom would pay us a little something for the leaves we picked. We'd get 2,000 or 3,000 pesos[2] each, which I used for buying snacks at school. I liked to buy Amor cookies, they were my favorites. When you're little you get excited over anything.

That region is a pure guerrilla area.[3] From the age of thirteen or fourteen, boys and girls from the countryside would join the FARC. They either liked the thrill of weapons, or they bought the story they were sold about fighting for the peasants and leading a revolution to help the poor. A lot of times boys and girls would leave their village and go off with the guerrillas for three months of training. After three months, the guerrillas would ask if they liked it or not. They'd say, "Do you want to stay or to go back to your family?" So it was the boys and girls who made the decision. They were never forced to join.

When I was twelve, I thought about joining the guerrillas. My mom and dad fought a lot, and when they fought, my dad vented his anger on me and my brothers and sister. The few days that he didn't hit us it was a miracle. If we cried, he hit us; if we didn't cry, he hit us. He'd hit us with a strap, like the kind you use to beat horses and cows. Once my dad punched my brother Juan in the nose and there was blood everywhere. We had a terrible childhood, just terrible.

---

[1] The leaves of the coca plant are the raw material used in making cocaine.

[2] About 40 or 50 U.S. cents at the time.

[3] The Revolutionary Armed Forces of Colombia (FARC) and National Liberation Army (ELN) are Colombia's two main guerilla groups. Founded in the 1960s and claiming to represent the country's rural poor in the fight against Colombia's wealthy classes and U.S. imperialism, both groups commit widespread abuses against civilians, including killings, threats, and recruitment of child soldiers.

One day, when I was twelve, I finally stood up to my dad. He came at me to hit me, I don't remember why. As he was taking off his belt to hit me I grabbed his machete and raised it. I said, "Dad, if you hit me I'll kill you right here. I'm not a little girl anymore who you can hit whenever you want. I've grown up, and if you hit me, I'll bring down this machete on you and we'll kill each other." He backed off.

A week later, I left home. I was so sick of being hit that I thought about joining the guerrillas to get away from all that. But then an angel crossed my path. Doña Elsa was a woman in her forties who was from Almaguer but who now lived in Cali.[4] She was back in Almaguer, visiting her family, and I told her how bad things were in my house and that I was going with the guerrillas. She said to me, "Don't go with those people. Why don't you come with me to Cali and you can get work there and have a different life?"

Doña Elsa took me to Cali without telling my parents. There, she helped me get a job cleaning people's houses. I never communicated with my parents and it gave me pleasure, because I felt it was a sort of revenge.

AFTER I BECAME A MOTHER

After I'd been living in Cali for about three years, I met a man named Kevin at a party. I was fifteen and he was twenty-two, and we started dating. I liked him because he was hardworking and very sweet. He would remember that we'd been dating for so many months and bring me a little gift, like a stuffed toy animal. That made me fall in love with him. I went to live with him in a rented room, and when I was sixteen years old, I had my first daughter, Leila. Six months later I got pregnant again. Kevin and I started having problems, because I had only wanted one child. When I had my first daughter I told the doctors in the hospital that I wanted to be operated on so I wouldn't have any more, but

---

[4] Cali is Colombia's third largest city and is the capital of Valle del Cauca province. It is about 180 kilometers north of Almaguer.

they refused. They said that until I had two or three they wouldn't do it. So when I was seventeen I had my second daughter, Carola.

After I became a mother, I thought a lot about my parents. When Leila was two years old I sent them a letter. It was the first time I'd communicated with them since I'd left home. I told them about my life, about everything I'd lived since I left them. I sent them photos of the girls. My mom wrote back. She told me that when she and my dad found out I'd gone to Cali with Doña Elsa, they were going to report me as kidnapped, but in the end they didn't. She told me that eventually my family had given me up for dead.

In 1993, when I was almost twenty years old, I separated from Kevin and decided to return to Almaguer. We never recovered after I got pregnant with Carola. I went home to my town, far from him, because I didn't want him to be able to find me and maybe try to take my daughters from me. Leila was four when we went back and Carola was two and a half. I went back to my parents' house, and my mom was so glad to see me and my two little girls. My dad just said, "So that's what you went looking for—two daughters." But his attitude had changed. He never tried to hit me again.

IT SEEMED NORMAL

After returning to Almaguer, I set to work picking coca again, because that's what there is in those parts. We had the coca farms and my brothers, cousins, and uncles all worked the coca. They had crystallizing laboratories.[5] Sometimes I worked in the labs, sometimes in the kitchens,[6] sometimes picking leaves. Back then a kilo of crystallized cocaine went for about 1 million pesos.[7] The guerrillas were the ones who bought it from us because they wouldn't let in outside buyers. But sometimes one of my cousins

---

[5] Crystallization is the process by which coca paste is turned into cocaine.

[6] Kitchens are where the coca leaves are macerated into coca paste, an intermediary product in the cocaine-making process.

[7] About U.S.$1,250 at the time.

would take the cocaine to sell in the city of Pereira or to Cali. They did it with the guerrillas' permission, but my cousins had to pay them a cut.

The guerrillas had a camp in the hills above the main town. They'd come down and wander around the town. Sometimes they'd call a meeting in the schools or the community center, and they'd come by the houses saying, "The children can stay, with one woman to care for them. Everyone else, go to the meeting." At the meetings they'd warn us that, if we saw the military, we shouldn't leave our houses after six in the evening. They said that during a clash, if there was some sort of emergency and people had to leave their house, they should walk out naked so the guerrillas would know not to kill them.

The guerrillas had their informants, people telling them, "The army's coming this way." The army would come to fumigate the coca crops or to put pressure on the guerrillas. When the army came, the guerrillas would usually retreat. But when they did clash they'd shoot at each other from one hilltop to another. The bullets passed over the roofs of our houses. When the ghost plane[8] fired down on the guerrillas at night you could see a red tracer fire. People lived in a lot of fear. Every time there was a guerrilla attack or clashes with the army, I would hide under the bed with my daughters. They didn't say anything; it seemed normal to them. When you live a situation like that and it's all you know, it seems normal.

Even so, over the next few years I still thought about going off with the guerrillas. What stopped me were my two girls and my mom. My mom would say, "No, mi'ja![9] You're not going to go with these people!" But I did want to. I was very fond of guns; that's what attracted me the most. I liked the idea of training, of having a command, a rank. That excited me. I thought that I could vent all that anger that my parents had planted in me. But thank God I didn't join the guerrillas. I may not have

---

[8] Avión fantasma is the name given by civilians to the Douglas AC-47 "Spooky," a U.S.-made Vietnam-era airplane retrofitted for use in the Colombian Air Force.

[9] A contraction of "mi hija," (in English, "my daughter"), which is used affectionately for female friends and relatives.

survived to tell my story. Maybe I'd be in hiding, or in jail, or wounded or dead.

I REALLY LOVED THAT MAN

In about 1999, when I was twenty-five, I got work cleaning a house in Popayán, which is the capital of Cauca province and about 170 kilometers from Almaguer. I left because I didn't want to live in the countryside any more. I had gotten used to the city life in Cali. I took my oldest daughter, Leila, who was nine years old, and left Carola, who was seven, with my parents. I worked for about eight months at the house, and then I got a job working at a chicken restaurant. After that, I rented a small room and brought Carola to Popayán. Around that time, I met a man named Carlos at an Evangelical church I'd started going to. He was a taxi driver. After dating for about two years, we got married and I had my son Roberto in September 2001.

Roberto was born just after one of the worst guerrilla attacks on Almaguer. Every time the local police commander was changed, the FARC would attack. When I saw the news on television I called my family. They said that about two hundred guerrillas had attacked and they'd killed all the policemen except three, who'd hidden out in a tunnel under the church.

Just after Roberto was born, Carlos and I moved our family to his hometown of Cartago, in Valle del Cauca province. But before Roberto was a year old, Carlos and I separated because he had another woman. I went back to Almaguer with my kids and started picking coca again. I was crushed, because I really loved that man. It took me about two years to get over it.

Then, in mid-2003, I struck up a relationship with a miliciano[10] named Wilton. He was someone I'd known as a kid, and we began seeing each other casually.

---

[10] A miliciano, roughly translated to "militiaman" in English, is a member of a guerrilla group that typically dresses in civillian clothes. A miliciano doesn't participate directly in combat, but provides information and support to other guerrillas.

OMAR

I had a cousin, Omar, who was like a little brother to me. His parents lived just down the road from us, and when we were little we always hung out together—me, Omar, his sister Sandra, and my little sister Marion. He was always playful and fun to be around.

Back in 2001, Omar had left town without telling anyone where he was going. The family thought he'd gone to look for work. At the end of 2003 he returned to spend Christmas with the family, and it was such a joy for me to see him.

Three or four days after he arrived, Omar was killed. A miliciano friend of mine named Jaime told me what happened. The night before, Jaime, Wilton, and Omar had gone to a village in Almaguer and were drinking beer at a roadside bar. Jaime said Omar let the drinks go to his head and started talking about how he'd been in Huila province doing his military service in the army, and that he'd been in a counter-guerrilla unit. When Omar mentioned his military service, some milicianos pulled him outside and yanked his wallet out of his pants. There, they found his military service card.[11] They shot him dead right there. Jaime told me that Wilton was one of the milicianos involved in Omar's death. Right there, my relationship with Wilton was over.

No one knew that Omar had gone into the military, not even his closest family. I don't understand why he'd started talking about his military service or why he'd brought his military ID, knowing that the guerrillas there wouldn't allow that. He must have thought that, because he was a local, the guerrillas wouldn't search him.

IN THOSE PARTS, TRAITORS GET KILLED

Omar was killed on a Monday, and he was buried on Wednesday. At the funeral it was only Omar's parents, me, my dad, and Wilton. Wilton had

---

[11] An ID card that certifies that men have fulfilled their obligatory military service.

accompanied me at the vigil all night before the funeral, maybe just to see if we knew who'd killed Omar. He didn't know that Jaime had told me he was involved.

At the funeral, out of anger and pain, I told Wilton, "I'm going to avenge my cousin's death. This isn't over." Wilton just looked at me and asked, "And what are you going to do?" I told him I didn't know, but that I couldn't leave things like that, that those milicianos shouldn't have killed Omar. Wilton just looked at me, trying to read me. Then he told me that if I wanted to do something, he could get me a weapon. But I said, "If I need one I know where to get it." After the funeral, we stopped seeing each other.

That's when the war against my family started. The FARC commanders said that my family had known Omar was a soldier who was there to infiltrate the guerrillas and milicianos, and that we deliberately hadn't alerted them. We were being labeled traitors, and in those parts, traitors get killed.

Just after New Year's Day 2004, about a week after Omar was killed, there was a knock on our door. It was about eight at night, and my parents were in the kitchen with my uncle, Omar's dad. I opened the door; it was Jaime and two other guerrillas. Jaime said to me, "You have to leave. The commander has ordered you all to be killed because you're all traitors—you all knew that Omar had been in the army. So go, because I don't want you to be killed."

After they left, I closed the door and started crying and shaking. I told my parents and uncle what they'd said, and that we had to leave immediately. We started packing and getting things ready, and at four in the morning I set out with my parents, my kids and my uncle. My brother Tomás had left a few days before with my aunt, Omar's mother. We went over the mountains toward the road to catch the bus to Popayán. We hid in the bushes on the side of the road, and when we heard the bus coming we walked onto the road to flag it down. The day dawned and we were gone.

BE GRATEFUL THAT WE GAVE
YOU A CHANCE TO LEAVE

After we arrived in Popayán, my parents, my brother Tomás and my uncle and aunt went on to Huila province, just east of Cauca. My parents had bought a farm there a few years before. I didn't want to live in the country, so I stayed in Popayán with my kids. At that time, my daughters were twelve and ten, and my son was two. Popayán is a small city, and a lot of people from Almaguer would go there. I didn't feel safe because the guerrillas could go there dressed as civilians, looking like any other citizen. But it was a place I knew.

I started getting threats on my cell phone. I recognized the voice; it was one of the guerrillas from Almaguer who went by the name of El Águila. He would say, "Be grateful that we gave you a chance to leave. We expect you to keep your mouth shut, and if not, we'll find you wherever you are and kill you." I was so nervous that I didn't like to go out on the streets. Every time I heard a motorcycle backfire I thought I'd been shot. I had another cell phone and I'd get calls on that one, too.

I felt like a ship without a sail. I spent all my time crying and crying. I stayed in Popayán for three months and then I decided to go to Cartago, Valle. Carlos, my ex-husband, was still there and I thought he could help me. When I got to Cartago, Carlos didn't want to have anything to do with me because he had another woman. But he let me and the kids stay at his place for the time being.

A few days after we arrived, I was on my way to the local school to sign the kids up. I was walking and crying, and a woman named Julia came up to me and asked what was wrong. I started telling her about my situation, that we had just arrived, that we had nowhere to stay. She said, "I don't know you, but come to my house. I know my husband won't mind. I live in a shack but we can accommodate you." I told her I had no money to pay and she said not to worry, that she would help me find a job.

That night, she set me and my kids up with a bed in her living room. The next morning we sent the girls to school and Doña Julia and I went looking for a job for me. That same day I got a job as a dishwasher in a restaurant. We lived with Doña Julia but it was uncomfortable because she and her husband sold marijuana from their house. People would come over looking to buy, and I didn't like my kids seeing that.

About three months later, I went to talk to the director of the school because they were charging me for some supplies and I couldn't pay. I explained my situation. I started crying; at that time I'd cry over anything. So the school director told me he would help me. He told me that there was a small apartment on the school grounds and that if I liked it I could stay there with my kids, and that I could work in the school cafeteria. That same evening my kids and I took our clothes over to the apartment. And since we had nothing to sleep on, Doña Julia gave us the bed, and the school director gave us a set of plastic dishes, some pots and pans and lent us a gas stove. He even bought us groceries.

During that time, the threats kept coming from the guerrillas. The man on the phone would say, "You bitch, we're going to kill you." I said, "I haven't reported anything to anyone." But the guy just said, "Where are you, you bitch?"

I WANTED PEOPLE TO KNOW THEIR RIGHTS

After I moved into the apartment, the school director took me to the Personería[12] to register as a displaced person. I didn't even know there was a law that protected displaced people. You leave the countryside just like that and you don't know about laws, about justice. I knew nothing. But I was worried about telling my story, that it would get back to the guerrillas. So when I told my story I didn't give names or any specifics. The government started helping me pay for groceries and then they gave me 1.5 million pesos[13] to set up a cart to fry and sell empanadas.[14] During the day I

---

[12] A municipal supervisory entity charged with monitoring citizens' rights.

[13] About U.S.$600 at the time.

[14] Fried meat pastries in a cornmeal crust.

worked in the school cafeteria and in the evenings I'd bring out my cart and sell empanadas.

I became friendly with other displaced people who I'd met at the Personería, and eventually I joined a group that was supposed to advocate for our rights. But the leader there, all he did was charge people money for filling out forms or for giving them advice. So together with four other displaced people, I formed a foundation in 2006. I wanted to help people to not suffer like I had when I arrived displaced. I wanted people to know their rights. There were people going hungry; an elderly woman fainted during a foundation meeting and was taken to the hospital. The doctors there told us she'd died of hunger. But you never see that on TV.

MY BROTHER WILL BE KILLED IF HE STAYS

In April or May of 2006 my brother Tomás and my parents left the farm in Huila and went back to Almaguer. Tomás had previously left behind four children and his ex-wife in Almaguer, who he'd been supporting while he was in Huila. He went back to be with his kids and his ex-wife and my parents went with him. He figured that enough time had passed since we'd been forced to leave, and that nothing would happen to him, so he was planning to move back permanently. When I learned that, I decided to go to Almaguer to try to convince him to leave. I thought he could be in danger because the milicianos could think he'd come to take revenge for Omar. I couldn't call him because he didn't have a phone. I was scared of going there, but I needed to talk to him. I planned to go and leave the same day.

I was on the bus heading toward the village where Tomás lived with his ex-wife, and I heard a woman comment that a miliciano called Murillo had just been killed in the market in Almaguer. I thought, *Things are going to get complicated again*. I was so frozen with fear that I missed my stop. I jumped off the bus and ran to Tomás's house. There, I told him what I'd heard on the bus. He said, "Yes, Murillo was killed." I asked him, "Did you have anything to do with that?" He said, "No, but I was there and Murillo fell dead at my feet. He was shot next to me."

The rumor was that the guerrillas thought Tomás had killed Murillo. I asked him if he planned to leave and he said, "But I didn't do it. They must have seen that I didn't kill him. I have no reason to leave." I said, "Brother, I love you. Why didn't you stay away?" He said that it was hard to find work where he was living in Huila and he missed his children. I said to his ex-wife, "My brother is going to be killed if he stays here." I told her to leave with him, but she wouldn't listen to me.

I left the next morning. Tomás stayed. It was the last time I saw him alive. About a month later, at around midnight on June 20, 2006, my mom called. She told me that Tomás had been gunned down and killed in one of the villages of Almaguer. I was filled with an immense sadness and anger. I wanted to go to my brother's funeral on the twenty-third, but I was afraid that the guerrillas would come after me too. So I phoned the local prosecutor in Almaguer, who was a friend of mine. He said, "Come to Popayán and my bodyguards will meet you there and bring you to Almaguer. You can wear a disguise. No one will imagine that you're coming." I put on a black wig and a coat, and old lady clothes. I was going into the thick of it. The fear I felt was terrible. I got there the day of the funeral and watched him being buried—that was all I saw. I wasn't there for the wake, I didn't speak to anyone, and no one recognized me.

That same day I reported everything to the prosecutor's office in Almaguer: the deaths of my brother and my cousin, and the death threats against me. I said to myself, *If the enemy is stronger than you, the only way to get revenge is to denounce him.* So, despite my terrible fear, I filed complaints with the prosecutor. He took down everything but didn't give me a copy of the complaint. He said that if the guerrillas stopped me on the road and saw me with it, it would be the end of me.

About a month later, the prosecutor in Almaguer called me and told me that the police had raided some milicianos' houses and several of them had been killed, including one of the ones who'd killed Omar. Others, including Wilton, had managed to flee. I felt happy, but at the same time I felt remorse. Those milicianos were killed because of me. I don't know if I did the right thing by denouncing them.

After Tomás's death, I took my parents to live with me in Cartago, where I continued my work with the school and the foundation. I was the secretary of the foundation, and I learned to file tutelas[15] and other legal papers. We started helping people denounce crimes committed by the demobilized paramilitaries who were in the Justice and Peace process.[16]

By 2008, the foundation started getting death threats. Leaflets would show up under the door of the foundation's offices threatening all the group's officers. The leaflets were signed by the Águilas Negras, which is a paramilitary group that was created after the demobilization.[17] We would also get calls on our cell phones.

One day in May 2008 at about three in the afternoon, I was walking down the street when a motorcycle with two riders cut me off. One of them said to the other, "Is that her?" and the other said, "No, that's not her." I took off running and ducked into a store. When I turned to look I saw that the motorcycle didn't have a license plate. I think those men were looking to kill me but didn't recognize me. I shook all over and cried. Even my tongue trembled. I wanted to leave Cartago and go somewhere else but we had no money to pick up and leave and we had nowhere to go.

Then, one day in March 2009 my younger daughter Carolina, who was fourteen, answered my cell phone and burst into tears. She came running to me and said, "Mami, we're being threatened. A man just told me that we have twenty-four hours to get out of town or we will all be killed." I called

---

[15] A tutela is a widely used legal tool allowing citizens to file for judicial injunction against public authorities and private parties who they claim have violated their constitutional rights.

[16] In a deal struck with the government of Álvaro Uribe, paramilitary militias began gradually demobilizing by blocs between 2003 and 2006. Many mid-level and top commanders applied for benefits under the Justice and Peace Law, which obligates demobilized paramilitaries to confess to their crimes and offer reparations to their victims in exchange for reduced sentences.

[17] Neo-paramilitary groups such as the Águilas Negras, Urabeños and Paisas are armed groups that emerged in 2006 in the wake of the demobilization process of the AUC national paramilitary coalition. Led largely by former paramilitaries and often employing the same criminal, political, and economic networks as their predecessors, neo-paramilitary groups have a powerful presence in many regions throughout the country.

the police because the leaders of the foundation supposedly had police protection because of the threats. So I called and they put me in the Interior Ministry's human rights defenders protection program. Two days later the program sent me and my family, including my parents, to Bogotá.

MORE TANGLED THAN A SACK OF FISHHOOKS

We arrived in Bogotá on March 14, 2009, to a large section of the city called Ciudad Bolívar. It has winding streets and the houses and the shacks are built on the hills. First we shared a house with a woman named Jeimi, who was from Cartago. I knew her but I didn't know her well. She had just moved to Bogotá about two or three months before me.

On TV Bogotá looks shiny and clean, but they don't show the crazy people, the drug addicts, and the prostitution everywhere. My daughters were shocked by the city. But I thought, *It's so big, my enemies won't ever be able to find me here.*

Jeimi turned out to be more tangled than a sack of fishhooks. Soon after arriving in Bogotá, I had got a job selling BonIce popsicles on the street. Jeimi asked me if I wanted better work, and I said sure. So one afternoon she took me to meet two guys—her business partners. Jeimi introduced me, telling them that I needed work, and one of them said, "Okay, explain to her how it works." Jeimi told me that all I had to do was open a bank account, that they would put up the money to open the account and that I had to hand over the ATM card. She said that some money was going to be deposited in the account. They would take out money through the ATM, but if they needed to withdraw a large sum of money, they'd take me to the bank so I could do it personally. She told me that at some point I would have to withdraw 30 million pesos,[18] and for that they'd pay me 1,600,000 pesos.[19] I said okay, and the next day we went and opened the account.

---

[18] About U.S.$15,000 at the time.

[19] About U.S.$800 at the time.

A month later I got a call from Jeimi and was told that I needed to go to the bank to make a withdrawal. Jeimi picked me up in a taxi and we picked up another person on the way. At about ten in the morning we got to a plaza in Chapinero, a central neighborhood in Bogotá, and were told to sit on a park bench and wait. There were other people around, and when I saw them getting up and going into the bank in groups, I realized that nearly everyone in the plaza was there for the same reason. Jeimi said that there were people coordinating everything, so that five minutes after the wire transfers went through to the accounts, the account holders would be there making the withdrawal. She told me that when it was my turn, I shouldn't be nervous and I should act calmly. She said that if anyone asked where the money came from, to say that it was from the sale of a house. It dawned on me then that I was doing something that was against the law. They were laundering drug-trafficking money. I got really nervous. They had us sitting there all day until four in the afternoon. I thank my dear God that I didn't get called.

Jeimi said not to worry, that I would be called another day. But I said, "Jeimi, I'm too scared to do this. Tomorrow I'm coming to close the account." She said, "How are you going to do that? These guys are going to get really pissed off at you." I said, "I'd rather go hungry than do something like this. What if I go to jail? I'd risk leaving my kids and my parents on their own." I closed the account at the end of April.

Soon after, Jeimi left the house we shared. Then, one day in May, my daughter Leila came home a wreck. She was seventeen at that time, and had stayed late at school working on some project. By the time she left, all the other children had gone. As she left the school, two guys grabbed her and put her in a car and raped her. One of the men told her that if I didn't keep my mouth shut about the bank account scheme, the next time they wouldn't just rape her, they'd kill her and kill me. It was a horrible trauma for her. She said, "Mami, don't denounce it to the prosecutors or they'll kill us. Mami, don't get into more trouble." After that, we kept moving houses, from one neighborhood to the next.

A couple of months later, on July 19, Jeimi came to my house with two guys. When I opened the door they pushed me inside. One of the guys pulled out a pistol and threatened me in front of my children and parents. He said, "If you open your mouth about our business, you and your family are going to die. I'll make you swallow these bullets."

I said, "But why would you think I'd denounce you if you haven't done anything to me? You don't have to worry." I talked tough but inside I was shaking. One of the guys came back the next day, and said, "I hope you keep your word." Again I told him he didn't have to worry about me. I said, "I don't know anything, I don't know who you are, I know nothing about you."

By dawn on the twenty-first I was gone. I went to Pereira, where I had friends.[20] I didn't have anyone in Bogotá to lean on, and I was a wreck. I needed to calm my nerves. I was so scared. When I came back a week later I confronted Jeimi's business partners. I knew where one of those guys lived. I told him, "I'm not afraid of you. If you want to kill me, kill me. But you have to kill me and all of my family. Because if I die, they'll die of hunger."

But a few days later I did go and denounce all the threats, my daughter's rape, and the laundering scheme. I wanted justice. I wanted those bastards to pay for what they did to my daughter. I filed the criminal complaint but nothing's happened.

The last threat I got was on August 4, 2010. That threat was made to my daughters. I had sent them to buy rice, and two guys approached them and told them that their boss was in jail and that they were investigating to see who had been the snitch. The guys told my daughters to tell their "snitch of a mother." They don't know I've reported everything. They may not kill me on a suspicion, but if they knew, they would have killed me by now.

WHO'LL GIVE US BACK THE JOY?

Since then, things have been calm. Perhaps we can say we're safe from the bullets now, but we're not safe from starving. Many times we've

---

[20] Pereira is the capital of Risaralda province.

had to go to sleep with just a glass of panela water[21] for dinner. My son, who's ten years old now, often complains, "Mami, I'm hungry." My daughters, who are older, understand. I can't afford anything more. When there's money we have rice with egg or offal soup because that's cheap.

When things were really bad I'd sell BonIce popsicles on buses. Some days I made 3,000, 4,000, 5,000 pesos.[22] Once when I was selling BonIce it rained all day. I hadn't even been able to have a coffee and I hadn't made enough for the return trip home. It was already four in the afternoon, and I had to go turn in the cart and I didn't have a single peso. A man pulled up in a car and said, "I'm sure that, on such a cold day, you haven't sold much." I didn't answer. He said, "Here's 7,000 pesos[23] to go have a coffee," and I said, "Thank you sir. God bless you," and broke into tears.

Sometimes I stop eating to be able to pay the rent. At the shack where we live, the roof leaks every time it rains. But that was the cheapest I got. Right now I'm paying 120,000 pesos[24] a month. My mom still cries, and asks, "Mi'ja, when are we going back to the farm?"

The government of President Santos said that it wants the displaced to go back to their farms, to go back to their villages.[25] But if you leave as a displaced person, why would you go back? I can't go back. I run the risk of the guerrillas killing me, and if not the guerrillas, the villagers, because they are relatives of the milicianos who were killed because of me.

---

[21] Panela is an unrefined food product made by boiling sugarcane juice into a hard, crusty block. It can then be dissolved in hot water to make a drink.

[22] Between U.S.$1.50 and U.S.$2.50.

[23] About U.S.$3.50.

[24] About U.S.$63.

[25] The 2011 Victims and Land Restitution Law provides for financial compensation for victims of the conflict and aims to restore millions of hectares of land to Colombians who have been driven from their homes by violence.

Even if we could go back, who's going to give us back the few things that we'd managed to have? Who's going to give us back our farms? Who will give us back the animals? Who'll give us back the loved ones we lost? Who'll give us back the joy?

MÓNICA QUIÑONES

AGE: *38*

OCCUPATION: *Midwife, healer*

HOMETOWN: *Mosquera, Nariño*

INTERVIEWED IN: *Guapi, Cauca*[1]

Mónica Quiñones was born in a small Afro-Colombian community in the south-western province of Nariño. She lived there with her grandparents, parents, and nine siblings on a piece of land that had been passed down within her family over four generations. Around 1994, when Mónica was married with two young children, guerrillas tried to make her family grow coca, the plant that is processed to make cocaine, on their farm. When they refused, the guerrillas executed her two younger brothers and forced her entire family to abandon their home the same night. Mónica's family fled by boat to the town of Guapi, where they built a squatter settlement. Since then, Mónica has eked out a living as a neighborhood midwife and healer. In her narrative, she describes the devastating effect of a neo-paramilitary group[2] called the

---

[1] Mosquera, Guapi, and El Charco are false locations employed to protect the narrator's identity.

[2] Neo-paramilitary groups such as the Águilas Negras and Rastrojos are armed groups that emerged in 2006 in the wake of the demobilization process of the AUC national paramilitary coalition. Led largely by former paramilitaries and often employing the same criminal, political, and economic networks as their predecessors, neo-paramilitary groups have a powerful presence in many regions throughout the country.

Rastrojos on her family, including her brother's forced recruitment and the rape of her sixteen-year-old daughter.

The rape of Mónica's daughter forms part of a broader pattern of sexual violence against women in Colombia, which both triggers displacement and afflicts displaced women once they have relocated. In 2008, Colombia's Constitutional Court found that sexual violence against women is "a habitual, extended, systematic and invisible practice in the context of the Colombian armed conflict... (perpetrated) by all illegal armed groups, and in some isolated cases, by individual agents of the public security forces."

Names in this narrative have been changed at the request of the narrator.

HUMANITY HAS GONE BAD

Here in Guapi there are three groups: the guerrillas,[3] the Águilas Negras, and the Rastrojos, which are the paramilitaries. Displacement here and in all of Colombia is really, really tough. The war will always continue because the more people they kill, the more they come and take our kids to make their groups stronger and multiply. They kill twenty people and then they're in another community with their eyes on all the young people so they can recruit them. Somehow humanity has gone bad.

Around 2008 a neighbor lent my brother Juan a motorbike and he started driving it as a taxi. He was twenty-one years old at the time, had two kids, and lived in a house near me in the same neighborhood. He started coming home late at night, so I asked him, "Juan, why are you getting home so late?" He said, "Sometimes my friends ask me to give them a ride down to the bridge, to other neighborhoods." I said, "Be careful getting home late because the neighborhood is getting very

---

[3] The Revolutionary Armed Forces of Colombia (FARC) and National Liberation Army (ELN) are Colombia's two main guerrilla groups. Founded in the 1960s and claiming to represent the country's rural poor in the fight against Colombia's wealthy classes and U.S. imperialism, both groups commit widespread abuses against civilians, including killings, threats, and recruitment of child soldiers.

dangerous." He told me that his friends paid him well for giving them the rides, and that they'd started going to his house. I said, "Juan, these people want something from you."

One day he came to my house, sad. I asked him, "What happened, Juan?" He said, "Do you remember the people that came to my house? They're telling me to join." I said, "Join what?" He said, "Join their group, the Rastrojos." I told him he had to leave Guapi and he said, "I want to leave but I don't know how to or where to go. I don't have a job and I have two kids." I told him that our siblings could get some money together so he could leave, but he said, "They already threatened me. They said that if I leave they'll kill one of you. They told me that I'm their friend now, that they like me, and that they'd pay me to go with them to Los Andes."[4] I said, "What would you do in Los Andes?" And he said, "Be in the group, kill." I told him not to go.

Juan spoke with the Rastrojos and told them that he was going to stay in Guapi and continue driving his motorbike taxi. So they stole his motorbike in order to leave him without work. Four days later they showed up at his house and said that they'd already told him a lot of things, that he knew a lot and couldn't get out now. They told him that he had to join and that if he didn't, he'd have to hold a wake for one of his family members.

My brother entered into despair. He stayed shut up in his house, living in fear until a Rastrojos leader showed up one day and told him, "You have the green light today." The green light meant that the order had been given to kill him. "If you don't decide, we'll kill you."

So in 2009 he left with the Rastrojos for a village in Nariño. He called me to tell me where he was and said that he was sleeping in the cold, didn't have a blanket, and was starving. He said, "I can't run away because they'll kill you all." The only way he'll leave the group is if he's dead.

---

[4] Los Andes is a false location, and is employed here to protect the narrator's identity.

IT'S MADE A MARK ON THEM

In late 2009 the Rastrojos started to go after my son Jimmy, who was seventeen years old at the time. I saw him crying one day so I asked him, "What happened, mi'jo?[5] Tell me." He said, "Mami, I don't want to be friends with those people. I don't want to fall like my uncle Juan did."

The Rastrojos had been trying to get him to join the group. They talked to him about money, clothes, nice cell phones, and luxury things. They said that they'd even give him a motorbike so he could drive them around. They wanted to take him to Mosquera, where they're trained like soldiers. The Rastrojos pay their members about 700,000 pesos[6] a month to kidnap, kill, rob, extort, everything.

I told Jimmy, "No, you're my only son. It's true that we're hungry and don't have work, but there's no reason for you to join and maybe take someone's life away. I'll make sure you never lack food and a roof to sleep under. But you're not going to leave here."

On a Friday at the end of 2010, my partner at the time called me at nine in the evening, when I was at night school. I was finishing up high school. He said, "Your daughter came home sick. She looks like a wreck, like she was knocked around or something." My teacher let me leave class and when I got home I found my daughter Lucía, who was sixteen years old then, shaking and screaming. She'd been hit in the face and her cheeks were bruised. Her clothes were torn up and covered in mud, and there was a lot of blood on her skirt. I hugged her and asked what had happened, and she squeezed me with fear. She said that she'd been raped by the Rastrojos.

She'd recently become friends with a twenty-five-year-old guy, and he'd invited her to meet him that night at a soccer field. When she got there, three other guys appeared. The four of them raped her. When they

---

[5] A contraction of "mi hijo" (in English, "my son"), used affectionately for male friends or relatives.

[6] About U.S.$350. The minimum monthly salary at the time was roughly $250.

were raping her, they told her that she and Jimmy had to join the group. She told me, "They put a gun to my head and told me that if I said anything they'd kill you and me." She told me not to say anything. When I heard all of this, I started crying and screaming.

I bathed my daughter and cleaned her well. I'm a midwife; I learned from my mom and the tradition comes from my great-great-grandparents. Then I took her to the hospital in a taxi. We didn't say anything during the ride. I just stayed silent, shaking and crying. The police were at the entrance to the hospital when we got there. Nowadays the law is always at the hospital, watching out. Lucía was hysterical and the police asked what had happened. She said, "Nothing, nothing." They asked me, "What happened to the girl?" I said, "She has abdominal pains." The policeman said, "Tell me the truth. Something happened to her, look at her face, she's been hit. Did you hit her? We're going to call Family Welfare."[7] I just said, "Call them. I haven't done anything bad."

The nurses sewed four stitches in Lucía's vagina and took all kinds of tests.

The next day Jimmy was at the hospital, crying. He said, "Mami, I want to leave here." He told me that the previous night he'd gone to complain to the guys from the Rastrojos about Lucía's rape. He asked them why they had raped her. They said that for a while they'd been telling him and Lucía to join them, and that they'd meant it. They told him not to mess around, because they could kill him at any moment. They also said that I shouldn't open my mouth because they'd kill me too.

I took Lucía home from the hospital that Sunday. She cried and cried and didn't want to eat or even bathe. She didn't want to live.

On Monday two people from Family Welfare came to my house. They asked me, "What happened to your daughter, Mónica?" I said, "I can tell you, but our names have to be confidential. My daughter was

---

[7] Family Welfare is the government agency in charge of child services.

raped by the Rastrojos, and we're under threat. We can't do anything."
They said, "We have to get the girl out of here so that she can get better.
We can take her to a boarding school in Pasto."

Jimmy said, "I want to go too because I don't want them to kill me.
Or maybe I could join the group and then kill them." I also wanted to
kill them, but I said, "No, it's better for you to leave." Lucía and Jimmy
left with Family Welfare the next day. I said goodbye, crying with my
daughter. She said, "Mami, I don't want to go to Pasto, it's cold there. I
don't know where I'll go when I get there."

They returned about four months later, around April 2011. After
they got back there was a party in the neighborhood one night. I let Lucía
go with Jimmy. Three hours later, she came home crying with Jimmy.
She said she'd run into the guys who raped her and that they started making fun of her, saying they were going to do the same thing to her again.
Jimmy told me very clearly, "Mami, we can't live here. Wherever we go
in Guapi those people will be there." Lucía also said she wanted to leave. I
wanted to sell my house so I could leave, but no one wanted to buy it. I've
put up with so many things because I'm afraid to leave for a city where I
don't know what awaits me, or who can help me there. If I at least had a
person or entity that would help me, I would leave.

So I told her, "Relax, mi'ja,[8] you can start studying here in Guapi."
She said, "I'm not going to study anymore. I'm not going to finish
school; I'm not going to do anything." And since then she hasn't gone
back to studying. She's now seventeen years old and has only studied
up to the fifth grade. Jimmy is eighteen years old and has also studied
up until the fifth grade. Their education has stopped because of the
problem of recruitment, harassment, and her rape. It's made a mark on
them.

Lucía says, "I want to kill myself." In April, she drank Clorox, and
she's said that she's going to hang herself with some bed sheets. She can't

---

[8] A contraction of "mi hija," (in English, "my daughter"), which is used affectionately for
female friends and relatives.

be left alone. She says to me, "Mami, I want to die, I want to leave. Why don't you leave with me? Why don't you help us?"

So in October 2011 I sent Jimmy and Lucía to live in El Charco, Nariño province, with my cousin. But they called me in November and told me, "Mami, we want to come back because there's no work here. We don't have food. We miss you and the house a lot."

HALF OF MÓNICA REMAINS

There are people who dance and enjoy life. When I see those people, the happy families laughing with their kids, I feel that I don't have that. There was a time when I had that: when I was there at the river where I'm from, at weddings, making food, laughing, swimming until we got tired and cold.

Sometimes I dream about that land. When I don't have work, or money, or anything to cook, I remember all the things that my dad had us grow: yucca, plantains, sugar cane, pumpkin, avocado, guava, bananas, papaya, and cacao. We didn't have to buy it. When we saw that there was a lot we'd invite our neighbors to come pick it in a minga. A minga is when neighbors help you on your farm, and then you help them later. Groups of farmers get together to work on farms.

One neighbor would have fish and the other would have plantains, and one would say to the other, "Neighbor, I'll give you the fish for the plantains." But that doesn't happen here in Guapi. They can see you dying of hunger and they don't give you anything. Sometimes you have to go to sleep the same way you woke up—with an empty stomach.

Sometimes I feel as if I were living a borrowed life. Half of Mónica remains, because the other half is already dead. It died when my two brothers were killed, when my father died, when my brother joined the Rastrojos. And now, with my kids moving from one place to another. When you live a life like this, you live like the dead.

MARIANA CAMACHO

AGE: *57*
OCCUPATION: *Cook, house cleaner*
HOMETOWN: *Córdoba, Nariño*
INTERVIEWED IN: *Pasto, Nariño*

Though born in the highlands of Nariño province, Mariana Camacho considers Putumayo home. She and her family were part of the coca boom that swept the region, during which they witnessed and suffered the violent advance of right-wing paramilitary groups. Two of Mariana's sons were murdered and her husband was disappeared. The last time she saw her husband he was being held in the headquarters of the local paramilitary group. Between 16,000 and 35,000 Colombians have been disappeared, according to different official estimates. Many were buried in unmarked graves, while others were thrown into rivers or the ocean. Through the Justice and Peace process, by which many demobilized paramilitary fighters are confessing their crimes, investigators have uncovered 3,649 graves containing 4,503 bodies as of February 2012. Almost 1,700 remains have been identified and returned to their families. But Mariana continues to wait for the paramilitary who has confessed to killing her husband to reveal the site of his grave.

Names in this narrative have been changed at the request of the narrator.

PLUMP AND PRETTY

I'm from Córdoba, Nariño. That's a cold-weather town up in the mountains. I'm the oldest child—I have two sisters and two brothers—and I had to take care of them and also help my dad and my mom work on the farm.

I went to school for just six months and then I dropped out. I never wanted to study; I liked to work, to trade. So in 1964, when I was about ten years old, my mom borrowed some money, and she set up a vegetable trading business for me. On Sundays we'd load the chiva[1] with vegetables and on Mondays I'd go to the market in the town of Pasto, which was ninety kilometers away. I'd leave at two in the morning and arrive in Pasto at around 5:30 a.m. Then I'd unload in the marketplace and sell right there: onions, carrots, cabbage, potatoes, and other vegetables.

I'm not one to brag, but I beat out the other vendors. I was new but I had more clients than they did. I was plump, pretty; I wasn't so bad looking. And I had a way of treating people that was quite excellent. My mother always said that white people[2] should be respected. So I would remember that and treated my customers well. I was happy to be able to go back to my mother and say, "Here's what I earned." We started saving so we could pay back the money she'd borrowed for the business. And that's how I worked for a few years.

MOSQUITO BITES AND TIGERS

Around the same time that I started working, an uncle of mine said he was bored in Córdoba, that the farming was bad. He'd been told that in Putumayo you could just grab land and that it was free. Putumayo province was very far away, down the mountains in the jungle to the west. Eventually he went

---

[1] Chivas are wide, open-air buses used as transport in remote rural areas of Colombia.

[2] Most peasants from the highlands have distinct indigenous features while residents of Pasto have a more visibly European mix.

to La Hormiga in Putumayo and staked out five hundred hectares of land. When I was fifteen, in 1969, my uncle came back to Córdoba to visit. He said that it was nice in Putumayo, that it was warm and that he'd made lots of money. Then he said to me, "If you want to come, I'll pay you." My mom didn't want to send me, but I wanted to see what it was like, so I told him yes.

It took a full day on the bus from Córdoba to Puerto Asís. It was hot and there were mosquitoes. But as the bus drove down the mountains, the vegetation was so green. In Puerto Asís, I caught a motorboat that went upriver to a little village, where my uncle was waiting for me to take me to his farm.

My uncle's farm was one hundred hectares. He already had fruit trees, corn, yucca, plantains, and bananas. And he had cattle; I helped him milk the cows. It was very hot there. I was chubby and sweated a lot, so I had to buy some light blouses. Mosquitoes bit me on the legs. You'd just be sitting around and *tas*—these mosquitoes would bite! I was getting sick of it, and after a few months I told my uncle I was going to go back home. But then a friend of his, who was also from Córdoba, came by one day. She said, "Oh, don't go back. I'll pay you 1,500 pesos[3] to come work for me." I went with her because that was a lot of money back then. I thought, *I can send it all to my mom.* My job was to cook for the workers on her farm. I made huge pots of food for them, and on the weekends I'd pluck chickens for stews.

After the first month I sent all 1,500 pesos to my mom. My brothers and sisters told me that when my mom got the money she started to cry. She wanted to know how I was going to stay working there, that it was so far and that there were tigers.[4] She wrote to me, telling me to come back home. Instead I asked my boss to give me an advance and I sent another 1,500 pesos.

---

[3] Approximately U.S.$88 at the time.

[4] South America has no tigers but the jungles are home to a small spotted feline known as tigrillo, or tiger ocelot.

Over the next few years, my employer was very good to me. She gave me clothes, and I had my own room in her house. She said, "Here, mi'ja,[5] you eat what you want." There were crates and crates of eggs, cheese, milk, everything. With the heat, though, I only wanted to eat fruit and drink water and more water.

When I was nineteen I met a boy named Óscar. He worked at the farm next door. I was in the kitchen one day, and he came in with another boy and asked me to sell him some eggs. Then he started chatting me up, asking where I was from, because he said he could tell I wasn't from around there. I offered him and the other boy some chicha,[6] since we always had some there. "Sure," he said, "but make sure it's strong so we can get drunk!" I didn't like that he said that. But he kept coming back to flirt with me.

After a while he asked me to live with him. He said he would give me everything, that I worked too hard and I should leave my boss. Óscar said he would make me a house, that I wouldn't have to work anymore.

We married in La Hormiga in 1973. We spent the night with lots of people, drinking and dancing until morning. We stripped a cow and roasted the meat in the village.

First we went to live on my mother-in-law's farm. Then Óscar bought five hectares of jungle-covered land in the village of El Placer, which was on the road down to La Hormiga. The farm bordered the Guamuez River. He started cutting down jungle and then he planted corn, yucca, and bananas. He made me a two-room bamboo house; the kitchen was outside, but it was nice.

Óscar worked hard. And he drank. When there was a big corn or yucca harvest he'd drink with the neighbors. Or when the cattle sold well, he'd go and drink. It made me mad. I'd fight with him the next

---

[5] A contraction of "mi hija," (in English, "my daughter"), which is used affectionately for female friends and relatives.

[6] A homemade fermented corn drink.

day because I never liked to drink. But he worked hard, he never made me suffer, and he never hit me.

We had seven children over the next years. When the first baby, Liliana, arrived in 1975, I took her to visit my mom, who cried. I had another girl, Cristina, then three boys, Jaime, Jorge and Sergio. Then another girl Sara was born in 1990 and Camilo in 1991. Óscar loved the kids so much, and he was always responsible with them. For Christmas he'd give them four or five new outfits: shoes, clothes, everything.[7]

The farm was productive, and Óscar bought more land. I set up a store on the road and brought in supplies to sell to the farms and the workers there. Things were calm, and we lived well.

THEN THE COCA APPEARED

Then the coca appeared. It had to have been around 1985, because my fifth child Sergio had just been born. Our neighbors started talking about the coca;[8] it had already been planted all around the town of La Hormiga. Óscar and I went to a few farms out of curiosity, to see what it was all about. Around those parts, wherever you looked it was coca— you didn't see a banana tree or a stalk of corn anywhere! Coca is this little plant with round leaves, and the seed is tiny, like a lime seed but a little bigger. And it was expensive! People said that they'd buy the seed for 150,000 pesos[9] for an arroba,[10] and use it to plant seedbeds.

At first we didn't plant the coca. We were scared that the law would come after us. So everyone else was planting coca and there we were

---

[7] In Colombia, especially among peasant families, it's traditional to give children a new set of clothes as Christmas presents.

[8] The leaves of the coca plant are the raw material used in making cocaine.

[9] About U.S.$1,300 at the time.

[10] An arroba is a unit of weight used in some Spanish-speaking countries, whose exact measurement can vary depending on region.

with our corn and bananas that we'd sell in Pasto. We had enough money to live off, but we saw other people buying farms and cars.

Finally, after seeing everyone else do it, Óscar and I started to plant coca. We traded the cattle for coca plants and filled almost the whole farm with it. At first we just sold the leaves, but after a few years we learned how to make the coca paste[11] ourselves and sold that to buyers who came to the village. It was easy money and we started living well.

As my children started to grow I got involved with the village Community Action Board.[12] Óscar and I donated two hectares for a village school, and I think because of that and because I had a lot of friends, I got elected to the board. Óscar didn't like me being involved in that because I was hardly ever at the house, but I liked doing the community work.

Then, in 1996, we coca growers staged massive protests in Putumayo. The word was that the government was going to step up eradication of the coca, that they were going to bomb the fields with herbicide. The coca growers in the region said that we wouldn't let that happen because that's what we all lived off. If the government was going to do that, they'd have to give us something else that was worthwhile for us to plant. So each community organized protest groups to blockade the roads and take over oil fields.[13] I spent a month and a half occupying an oil field with about sixty other people from our village. I was on the organizing committee for my community and we took turns cooking huge pots of food for all the protesters. We did that three times.

---

[11] Coca paste is an intermediary product in the production of coca into cocaine, extracted when the coca leaf is crushed and mixed with kerosene and other chemicals.

[12] Community Action Boards are small civil organizations that represent villages, communities, and neighborhoods.

[13] Putumayo is an oil-producing province in Colombia where, until recently, only the state oil firm Ecopetrol operated oil fields.

Some people said that the guerrillas were behind the marches, but the guerrillas never made us march.[14] In our village, it was us from the Community Action Board who had organized the protests.[15] It's true that there were guerrillas in Putumayo, but they were always along the edge of the hills, in the jungle. They never came to force us to leave, or to ask for money, or to massacre people. The guerrillas never charged us anything. And the guerrillas did kill people, but only if they'd done something bad like steal money or kill someone. If a person stole money and didn't return it, they killed that one person. But they never displaced people. And never did they kill an entire family.

Then, after the protests ended, the killings started. People talked about a group called Mano Negra[16] that was killing people involved in the marches because they thought the protestors were guerrillas.

IT'S HIM. IT'S MY SON

One Sunday in 1996, shortly after the protests ended, I went with Óscar and my eighteen-year-old son Jaime to buy a car in El Placer. It wasn't new, but it was more or less in good shape. We said that the next day we'd

---

[14] The Revolutionary Armed Forces (FARC) and National Liberation Army (ELN) are Colombia's two main guerilla groups. Founded in the 1960s and claiming to represent the country's rural poor in the fight against Colombia's wealthy classes and U.S. imperialism, both groups commit widespread abuses against civilians, including killings, threats, and recruitment of child soldiers.

[15] In July, August, and September of 1996, more than 200,000 peasants marched from their farms to the nearest towns to protest the threat of eradication of the coca crops in the region. The government had begun fumigating large coca crops by air in reaction to the United States' decision to de-certify Colombia for what the U.S. judged as failure to cooperate in the war on drugs. The FARC, a guerrilla group that had a strong presence in the area, supported the protests. For three months the protesters paralyzed Putumayo province. Leaders managed to negotiate with the government, agreeing to self-eradicate coca in exchange for government investment in social programs and infrastructure. Neither side complied, resulting in intensified fumigation efforts and a dispersal of coca crops.

[16] Mano Negra is a generic term used in Colombia to indicate unidentified forces involved in killings and "social cleansing."

sell our other car and come back to buy this one. Óscar and I went back home, but since Jaime had a girlfriend in El Placer, he stayed there and said, "I'll go home later."

The next day I got up in the morning to cook breakfast. I usually got up at four in the morning so that by six the workers' breakfasts would already be packed. But that morning Jaime hadn't come home. Then it was eight, nine in the morning, and he still hadn't come. I got worried. *What could have happened?* I wondered. *Why didn't he come?* There were some clubs in town that he sometimes went to, but he never stayed out all night. He always came home.

I went to El Placer and asked some friends if they'd seen him. I also went to see his girlfriend's mother, but she said, "I haven't seen him since yesterday." All day I was thinking, *Where did my little one go?* I went home and told Óscar, who'd been in the fields all day. He said, "Jaime must have gone off with some woman." "No," I said, "because he never stays in town and he knows he has work to do."

Later that day, I went to see the police inspector about my missing son. He said he'd been called that morning to pick up a body of a boy in a nearby village called San Isidro. He said that the boy was listed as an N.N. because he was found with no ID on him.[17] The inspector described the clothing the boy was wearing. Then he said, "Here, he had this watch." I got dizzy when I recognized it. I had bought that watch for Jaime in Pasto. I said, "It's him. It's my son."

When the inspector told me that he'd sent the body to the morgue in La Hormiga, I realized that my son must have been driven right past our house on the road to the town.

When I got to La Hormiga, they had Jaime in the morgue. He'd been shot in the head. I thought, *Why did they do this to my son? He didn't owe anybody anything.* I hired a car and brought him home, and buried him in a nearby cemetery. Óscar couldn't cry. He just got all red.

---

[17] N.N., or "no name," from the Latin *Nomen Nescio*, is the morgue registration of a corpse that lacks identifying documents, and is likely to go unclaimed.

Once I'd buried Jaime, I got angry. I wanted to know why my son had been killed. I started asking around, and some ladies in El Placer told me, "Look, don't go asking so many questions because something could happen to you." After they told me that I left it alone.

Over the next few years a lot of people were killed. There was a soccer field down the road from my house in a place called Las Vegas. Bodies would turn up there all the time. People who lived around there said they'd hear a car at eleven in the evening and then *pin, pin, pin*, gunshots. The next morning they would go and see, and there'd be three or four people. Along the road where our farm was there was a bridge, and near there, there was a big guadua;[18] bodies would turn up behind that tree too. A lot of times they would be unrecognizable and had no ID on them, so they would be buried as N.N.s in the cemetery at El Placer.

THE FIRST BIG MASSACRE

The first big paramilitary massacre in Putumayo was in El Tigre on January 9, 1999.[19] Óscar and I heard about the killings the very next morning from some townspeople who stopped by the store. We got in the car and drove forty minutes to El Tigre to see what had happened. When we got there it was horrible. There were still about ten bodies on the bridge that crosses the Guamuez River; their throats were cut. We saw other bodies on the sandy banks of the river below. People were screaming and crying. I cried too; I felt like my head would explode. It was awful to see.

From El Tigre, the paramilitaries continued with massacres. Over the next year, they went village to village, massacring people in San Miguel, El Cairo, Los Angeles, La Esmeralda, Las Brisas, and El Em-

---

[18] Guadua is a type of bamboo tree common in Colombia and Ecuador.

[19] On the night of January 9, 1999, approximately 150 paramilitaries stormed the village of El Tigre, killing and torturing dozens of villagers. Official figures say twenty-six people were killed and fourteen were disappeared. Witnesses say many bodies wound up in the Guamuez River.

palme. In November 1999 they did a massacre in La Dorada, and El Placer.[20]

It was 2000 when one day my husband and I went to run some errands in La Hormiga, and we heard a rumor that there was some big meeting in town. We went with some of the townspeople to see what it was about. There was Carlos Castaño[21] and another paramilitary commander called Tomate. I recognized Carlos Castaño from the television. He had this crazed look on his face; it made me nervous. The paramilitaries wore uniforms just like the army, an armband that said AUC,[22] and they wore blue scarves around their necks. Castaño said they'd come to finish off the guerrillas and that everyone who planted coca worked with the guerrillas. One of the townspeople stood up and said it wasn't true, and that if they did that, a lot of innocent people were going to die. I told Óscar I wanted to leave, but the paramilitaries said no one could leave until the meeting was over.

On our way home, I told Óscar I was scared. I said, "Maybe we should leave town." But Óscar said, "Why should we leave if we don't owe anyone anything?"

After that, the paramilitaries established themselves in El Placer; they seized houses, took over everything. The commander there was a guy named Wilson. He was a fat man with a big mole on his face. He was mean and barked out commands. With his attitude he let everyone know that he was the one in charge.

---

[20] On November 7, 1999, paramilitaries of the Sur del Putumayo bloc murdered eleven people in El Placer and another six in La Dorada.

[21] Carlos Castaño was the founder and leader of the United Self-Defense Forces of Colombia, or AUC, an umbrella organization that grouped most of the regional paramilitary militias in the country under one national command. The Sur del Putumayo bloc was originally under his direct command.

[22] The acronym for the Autodefensas Unidas de Colombia, or United Self-Defense Forces of Colombia, the umbrella organization created in 1997 that grouped regional paramilitary armies across Colombia. It demobilized between 2003 and 2006.

WATCH THESE GUERRILLAS DIE

Because our farm was on the road down to La Hormiga, Wilson and the paramilitaries would sometimes come and hang out at our store. We had some hammocks under trees in the yard and sometimes they'd be there, just like that. They'd come with women and tell me to make them a sancocho.[23] They would chat with me and my children about the coca and about their work. Some of them were friendly, but others were always mean. I had brought four little French poodles from Pasto for my kids. One time one of the dogs was lying in the middle of the road and one of the paras[24] walked up to him and shot him dead.

The paras started setting up roadblocks nearby. They'd grab someone and take him away, saying he was a guerrilla. And I'd watch that and think, *I hope this never happens to me.*

One day, my husband and I were driving back home after delivering supplies in El Placer when we saw some paramilitaries at a roadblock. They were holding three guys on the road. Wilson, the paramilitary commander, was there. He came over to our car and said, "Just stay right there and watch. Don't move."

I said, "Let us pass," but he said no. Then he asked us, "Do you know those three sons of bitches?" We said we didn't. Then he said, "These here are guerrillas. We're going to kill them now." He brought out a small chainsaw, and made the three guys stand there in front of us. He said, "Watch these guerrillas die. This is what we do to all guerrillas."

He had that chainsaw and *blin*! he cut the head off one of the guys. *Blin*! Another one went down. They cut them up alive on the ground. The heads kept jumping. I don't know how, but they were jumping. I had my head bowed but I was watching sideways. I saw the pieces twitching. They looked like fish flopping, dripping on the ground there.

---

[23] A Colombian soup or stew with large pieces of meat, which can include beef, chicken, fish, and pork.

[24] "Para" is conversational shorthand for paramilitary.

I kept telling Óscar we should leave, and he still insisted that we didn't owe anyone anything. "They have no reason to kill us," he said. It was true but I was afraid for us, I was afraid for my children. By then Liliana was twenty-five and had two small children. Cristina was living with her partner in the town of El Placer. Jorge was working the coca on the farm and I had the three young ones, Sergio, Sara, and Camilo.

THEY TOOK EVERYTHING FROM ME

One day in February 2001, I got talking to Wilson, the commander. His men had just pulled a guy from a bus at a roadblock in front of my store. I asked him, "Why do you take people like that? Tell me, give me an explanation."

He said, "It's because the guerrillas have always lived here. And we have a list that we got from townspeople. That's why we're taking that boy," he said. "He's a guerrilla." I said, "I know that boy; he's a farmworker and I've never seen him with guerrillas."

Wilson looked at me and I saw something different in his expression. He didn't like what I'd said. He said, "You must be with them too." Then he called the others, got in their truck and left.

The next morning, at five, I stepped out into the yard and I saw a group of paramilitaries. They were about fifteen of them there with Wilson. Wilson said to me, "Doña, sell us some coffee." So I picked up a pitcher, filled it with coffee and passed it to him. Then he said, "Do me a favor and give me two packages of cookies." I passed them to him. "We'll pay you later," he said.

The paramilitaries asked me where Óscar was and I told them that he'd gone to a stream on the farm to fill a tank with water. They went to look for him and I stayed at the house, worried about what they might do to him. It was eight when Wilson returned to the house with the other paramilitaries. They asked me for some more coffee and while I was getting it for them, Wilson walked into the rooms of the house, which was attached to the store. He walked through all the rooms, looking around. I thought it was strange. I wondered what he was looking for, so I followed him.

He said, "Oh, look how nice all this is." He saw a shotgun in one of the rooms and he picked it up, looked it over and asked me why we had it. I told him it was to protect the farm.

Later that day when my husband came back to the house, he told me that Wilson had asked him about the trails on our farm that, according to Wilson, were used by the guerrillas. Wilson had asked him why he didn't inform the paramilitaries that the guerrillas walked across the farm. Óscar said he'd told Wilson he didn't have time to see who was walking through or not, and that he was just dedicated to work.

The next day Wilson came in the morning and said he knew that the guerrillas had been at the store the night before. He accused me of giving them supplies. At night, farmworkers would come to my store to play pool and watch movies on the VCR. And yes, we did have a large amount of supplies—sacks of sugar, packages of tuna, boxes of rice—which we sold to our neighbors.

I said to Wilson, "I give supplies to no one. I have names recorded in the notebooks of those who owe me." I passed him the book and said, "Look, here are the supplies I sell. I sell to all the farms because they need a lot of supplies. Here it says who buys on credit, and that when they harvest they pay me." Wilson looked at the book and then said, "Okay, we're going. So long."

A week later, on Friday I was in El Placer running errands and while I was in town one of the workers on our farm found me and told me the paramilitaries had taken my son Jorge from the farm in a pickup truck.

I went directly to the house the paras used as their headquarters in El Placer. It was a concrete three-story house that they'd seized. They had meetings there, and they even had a cock-fighting pit. I asked the paras there, "Why have you taken my son?" One of the paramilitaries said Jorge was a guerrilla, but I told them, "He is in no way a guerrilla!" But they told me that Jorge hadn't been taken to that house. I thought, *That means they must have killed him!* I went home and sent Sergio, who was fourteen years old then, to La Hormiga because I thought they might come for him too. I cried all night, thinking Jorge was dead.

The next morning, I went to El Placer to see if I could find out anything about Jorge and one of the paras told me that they had released him by the Guamuez River and ordered him to leave the area. I could hardly believe it! I went to the riverbanks on our farm to try to find him and when I saw a red checkered shirt that he had coming through the bush, I rushed to him and hugged him. He told me the paramilitaries had taken him to El Placer, that he thought they were going to kill him, but that some friends of his had convinced the paras to let him go. "The paras told me that I have to leave here." I took him directly to La Hormiga, gave him money and sent him to Pasto, the capital of Nariño province, where my mom and brother and sister had moved to.

GET OUT OF HERE

When I got back to the house at about four in the afternoon, I found my twelve-year-old daughter Sara and eleven-year-old son Camilo crying. Sara told me that the paramilitaries had come about a half-hour earlier firing shots in the air. They'd grabbed Óscar, tied his wrists with wire and taken him off in a truck.

I immediately went to El Placer. A neighbor took me and my son Camilo by car to the para headquarters. I walked right in the house and I was able to see Óscar in a back room. I couldn't see if they had him tied up because I just saw him from the shoulders up. We looked at each other but before we could say anything Wilson pushed me out and told me that I couldn't be there. He told me that they were just going to ask Óscar some questions and to go home and get my other children. "We need you all to come here," he said. I asked him if they were going to kill Óscar and he said no. By the time I went for the children—it was just Liliana, Camilo and Sara—and tried to go back to the village, the paras at the roadblocks wouldn't let us through. They ordered us to go home, but they held Liliana at one of the roadblocks and wouldn't let her come with us.

At about seven that evening, Wilson came to the house again with some paramilitaries. They pulled me and my two youngest children out into the courtyard and made us kneel there. Then one of the paras put a machine gun to my temple. Wilson said my husband had told them we had 50 million pesos[25] and fifty kilos of coca paste belonging to the guerrillas stored in the house.

He said, "If you give us that money and those kilos of goods, we won't kill your husband." That gun on my temple felt freezing. The other paramilitaries took my son and daughter to another part of the yard and kept asking them where their father kept the money, if their dad worked for the guerrillas. I was so angry that I told them to bring me my two children and kill them and then kill me.

"I have nothing!" I said. "Look for yourselves." And they did. They looked in all the rooms and found nothing. They even looked in the wells. Another group of paramilitaries showed up with my daughter Liliana and when they had us all together, Wilson said, "Get out of here."

Liliana went in and grabbed her three-month-old daughter and her son, who was two. We left and the paras stayed there in the house. The paras didn't let me take anything. I had photo albums filled with pictures; all that was lost. As we were leaving, Wilson said, "We don't want to see you here again. And if your husband doesn't deliver, we'll kill him." He said that wherever he found us, he would kill us.

The children asked why we were leaving; they asked where their dad was. I cried from the anger I felt, asking myself, *Why?* By that time, it was dark and we ran down the road, but it felt like the paras had come after us so we got off the road and ran through some fields until we got to La Hormiga.

We got there without a penny. I told some close friends there and the priest what had happened.

The next morning a group of my friends and I drove to El Placer to talk to the paramilitaries. When we got there I stayed in the truck, hiding. I didn't want Wilson to see me. The priest questioned Wilson and

---

[25] About U.S.$20,000 at the time.

asked for Óscar and said that if it was a question of money how much did they want. Wilson told the priest that Óscar had been brought in but that he'd been released the previous night. He said that if we hadn't heard from him it was because he was probably with the guerrillas.

We went back to La Hormiga and I decided to go to my mom's place in Pasto. I said that if Óscar really had been released, he'd go there—he had to have someone let us know, send some message. The friend gave me 200,000 pesos,[26] and I caught a bus to Pasto with my children. When I told the bus driver what had happened he didn't charge us anything for the fare. Someone tried to give me food on the bus but I couldn't eat. I just kept wondering, *Is Óscar still alive? Are they still holding him? Did they really let him go?*

I came to my mother's with my sons Sergio and Camilo, my daughters Sara and Liliana and her two children. My other son Jorge was already in Pasto. I stayed at my mom's for a few days, then at my sister's for a few months, and then I moved in with my brother. During that time I was so nervous, I didn't want to be left alone. I got sick and I had to have my spleen removed. The doctors said it was because of my nerves. I was traumatized by everything, to see how the paras had massacred people, to see everything they'd done. The children missed two months of school and they had to see psychologists because they didn't want to study. I worried about them at school, and I told the teachers to let me know if anyone came asking about our family.

My son Jorge never got used to Pasto. Shortly after we arrived there he picked up and went to Taminango, a town in the highlands, to harvest coffee. I told him not to go out too much there, that maybe the paramilitaries were going around killing people there too. He said, "Don't worry. They took me, but then they let me go because I don't owe them anything." He was a good boy; he helped me pay the utilities with what he earned there. I couldn't buy tons of food, but we didn't go hungry. He'd bring us yucca, plantains, and bananas, and he bought things for his little brother and sister.

---

[26] About U.S.$90 at the time.

On December 25, 2001, his girlfriend called me from Taminango. She said that Jorge was sick and that he needed me. I went immediately, but when I got there he was already laid out in the morgue. He'd been shot. That's when his girlfriend told me that the two of them had gone to a nearby village the night before, and that they'd spent the night dancing in an open-air bar. When it was getting light, at about five in the morning, two men pulled up on a motorcycle and shot Jorge. I'm sure it was the same guys who came from La Hormiga looking for him. They themselves told me that they wouldn't leave things be, that they would kill him. I buried him here in Pasto.

THEY GIVE THEM EVERYTHING

I've been in Pasto ten years, going on eleven. NGOs have helped me, supported me. But people here often say things like, "Those displaced bastards, they give them everything. And we who are from Pasto, poor people, we don't get any help." I always shut them up, but not in a rude way, no. For example, once I was at the hospital, waiting to be seen by a doctor, and a woman there said, "See, those displaced people come here and the doctors always see them first. And here *we* are, waiting like fools." I said to her, "Ma'am, don't say that. It hurts our feelings, because we've had to suffer and knock on a lot of doors to have come this far." When my children were in school, my daughter Sara would come home crying, saying she didn't want to go back. She said the other kids would say, "Here comes that displaced girl, trying to fit in."

All that makes me angry. We left our home after I'd lived there for twenty-eight years. We lived well there, we had things. Back then, I used to pay a woman 500,000 pesos[27] to help me cook. But here, I make just 200,000 pesos[28] a month to support my children. My children would

---

[27] About U.S.$225 at the time.

[28] About U.S.$100.

remember our life in Putumayo, especially around Christmas, and they'd say, "If my dad were here he'd buy us clothes." I borrowed from loan sharks at 120 percent so I could buy them things. I didn't let them suffer.

Between 2003 and 2006, some 30,000 supposed paramilitary fighters lay down their arms as part of a demobilization deal with the government of President Álvaro Uribe. The vast majority of demobilized fighters received pardons, but many top paramilitary leaders and mid-level commanders responsible for atrocities were jailed. Under the 2005 Justice and Peace Law, these leaders faced a maximum sentence of eight years in exchange for confessing to their crimes and offering reparations to their victims.

THREE PIECES

When the paramilitaries started to demobilize, my children and I thought that maybe Óscar was with them. We thought that they'd let him go and he'd come back. The paramilitary front in Putumayo demobilized in 2006, and some members started giving testimony as part of the Justice and Peace Law. I signed up to be recognized as a victim, but no one admitted what they had done to me.

Then, in 2010, someone in the Attorney General's office gave me a phone number for the demobilized paras in jail.[29] I wanted to see if I could contact the paras who disappeared my husband. Wilson, I'd been told, had been killed in El Tigre with his bodyguards years before.

The first time I called, I was polite. I spoke to a para they called El

---

[29] Initially, prisoners who were part of the Justice and Peace process were allowed unrestricted use of cell phones. Though that benefit was rescinded, smuggled cell phones are common in Colombian prisons. Personal conversations with paramilitaries do not qualify as official confessions under the Justice and Peace Law, but prosecutors may encourage victims of paramilitary violence to talk with the fighters informally in the hope of learning the location of clandestine graves. If these conversations turn up enough information, prosecutors may send a forensic team to the location, often accompanied by the paramilitary and the victim.

Médico. I remembered him. He was one of the ones who used to hang out at the store. It was painful talking to him, and I was shivering with rage. I said, *Give me strength and courage, Lord.* I said, "Look, I need to know about my husband." He said, "From where?" I said, "From 2001 near the dock, close to El Placer." Then he said, "Oh yeah, I know who he is. Call me again in two weeks. I'm going to investigate the case."

Two weeks later, my daughter Sara called him. He told her, "It was me who killed your father. We cut your dad into three pieces—that's what I was ordered to do, and that's what I did. If I didn't do it, Wilson would have killed me."

Until that day I'd still wondered if Óscar could still be alive. But after what that para told us, I thought, *Now I know.* I cried all afternoon and couldn't eat. My daughter cried and said, "Why'd they do that to my father?" Because she knew how the paras killed people by cutting them in three with a chainsaw—they'd grab them alive, and *tas tas* like they were splitting a tree. And that's what they did to him.

El Médico said my husband is in an unmarked grave. I knew of many graves there where massacred people were buried. He said he was going to lead prosecutors to the grave, but that was months ago, and he hasn't delivered anything.

We've spoken quite a few times. One time he called me to ask me to forgive him. I told him that the Lord will see what he does with him. The paramilitaries took three from me—two sons and my husband. So how do I forgive him? I don't forgive. I wish he could see how I suffer. I hope he dies there in jail.

I need to see my husband. My children also need that. Because they disappeared him, we never saw what happened to him. All I ask is to have him so we can cremate him and have him in the house. It's not right that he be out there in the jungle somewhere. He wasn't an animal, he was a person. He was a person who had done no wrong to anyone. We as a family need to have him.

IF YOU WEREN'T BRAVE, YOU HAD TO PRETEND TO BE

Eastern Plains

A sparsely populated flatlands region stretching east of the Andean mountains towards Venezuela, the Eastern Plains of Colombia figures as the Wild West of the national imagination. The plains' rugged cowboys attained mythical status for their battlefield feats during the nineteenth-century wars of independence. Liberal guerrillas from the civil war known as La Violencia spurned the central government and issued their own legal code in the region with the 1952 and 1953 Laws of the Eastern Plains. And the province of Meta—the closest to Bogotá of all plains provinces—has been a bastion of FARC guerrillas since their founding in the mid-1960s. In the 1980s, emerald czars and powerful drug traffickers joined the mix, buying up land, establishing private armies, and executing an extermination campaign against members of the Unión Patriótica (Patriotic Union), a legal political party founded by the FARC and supported by other leftist movements.

In 1997, the right-wing paramilitary umbrella group known as the United Self-Defense Forces of Colombia (AUC) made its first incursion into the region with the Mapiripán massacre, during which some 200 paramilitary troops tortured, mutilated, and executed dozens of residents. The AUC consolidated its control of the plains, extorting cattle ranchers, pillaging oil-funded municipal coffers, and managing cocaine labs and export routes to Venezuela. Their enormous wealth spawned infighting: in 2003 and 2004, rival paramilitary factions waged a war against each other, costing up to 3,000 lives. Meanwhile, the Colombian military focused its U.S.-backed counter-insurgency efforts against the FARC in Meta, Guaviare, and Caquetá provinces. The Eastern Plains became a strategic drug trafficking corridor, as Venezuela became a major transit point for Colombian cocaine.

The plains remain central to the conflict's story, with the deaths in 2010 of two of its most significant actors. In Meta, Colombian security forces killed the top military commander of the FARC known as Mono Jojoy and "Cuchillo," the leader of the Popular Anti-Communist Revolutionary Army of Colombia (ERPAC), the main neo-paramilitary group in the region. Though weakened, both groups continue to operate, manage the drug trade, and displace civilians: 4,230 people fled their homes in Meta in 2010 alone, according to government figures.

JESÚS CABRALES

AGE: *39*

OCCUPATION: *Farmer, merchant*

HOMETOWN: *Puerto López, Meta*

INTERVIEWED IN: *Villavicencio, Meta*

Jesús Cabrales left his family to live on his own when he was ten years old. After completing mandatory military service and working for an oil company, Jesús met his wife in 1999 and moved with her and her four-year-old son Felipe to a town called Puerto Príncipe[1] in Vichada province, which borders Venezuela. In February 2001, a few months after setting up their farm, the Colombian military launched Operation Black Cat, an offensive targeting FARC guerrillas and drug traffickers in the region. Jesús recounts that during the operation, members of the army prohibited locals from taking large quantities of food to their farms based on the assumption that they were supplying the guerrillas. As a consequence, he and his family left Puerto Príncipe for the city of Villavicencio in Meta province. In this narrative, Jesús describes how after returning to their farm in 2002, his family suffered new abuses and forced displacements at the hands of both the FARC and the Colombian army.

Names in this narrative have been changed at the request of the narrator.

---

[1] Puerto Príncipe is a false location employed here to protect the identity of the narrator.

I NEED PEACE SO THAT I CAN WORK

In 2002, about two weeks after we returned to Puerto Príncipe, four guerrillas arrived at my farm.[2] They said, "You big son of a bitch, what are you doing here?" I asked them, "Why are you talking to me like that?" They said that my wife and I were army informants, because when the army had come to the area during Operation Black Cat, we had left. And when people leave after the army arrives in villages, the guerrillas brand them as snitches. "Be grateful that we haven't killed you," they said.

After the guerrillas came to my house, I sent a letter to alias Negro Acacio, who was the commander of the FARC's[3] 16th Front, which operated in the area. In the letter, I asked if I could talk with him to see if the FARC would let me stay and work on my farm. I said that I didn't have anything to do with the army. I wrote the letter because I wanted to clarify my situation, whether it meant having to leave or being able to stay. Ten days after I sent the letter, some guerrillas showed up at my house and told me to go to a location along the river and wait for them to pick me up.

I didn't know if I was going to be killed, but I said bye to my wife Rosa as if I was never going to return. I told her where I had some money stored and who we had debts with, because after someone is killed, people always try to collect their debts. She told me not to go and I said, "I'm going to go because I haven't done anything." I thought it was very important to clarify my situation, because if not, I would have been even more exposed to them killing me at any moment.

---

[2] The Revolutionary Armed Forces of Colombia (FARC) and National Liberation Army (ELN) are Colombia's two main guerilla groups. Founded in the 1960s and claiming to represent the country's rural poor in the fight against Colombia's wealthy classes and U.S. imperialism, both groups commit widespread abuses against civilians, including killings, threats, and recruitment of child soldiers.

[3] The Revolutionary Armed Forces of Colombia (FARC) is the largest left-wing guerrilla group in Colombia.

I walked twenty minutes to the riverbank and four guerrillas picked me up in a motorboat. Three of the guerrillas were just kids, about fifteen, sixteen years old, and the fourth was around forty years old. In part I was afraid of them, because guerrillas and paramilitaries have no conscience, but I was also calm because I knew I hadn't done anything wrong. Four hours later, the boat pulled over on the riverbank, and from there I walked two hours until I arrived at a farm that belonged to a peasant. The guerrillas had me wait at the farm for two days. They didn't think that I was going to run away because I had no reason to do so; what I wanted was to meet with Negro Acacio. I thought, *I'm fine up until now, nothing's happened to me.* Then they picked me up at two in the morning and took me on an eleven-hour hike deep into the jungle. The guerrillas always walk around at night without any light. They have eyes that can see at night, but I could barely see anything. I tripped over things and a branch almost took my eye out.

At one in the afternoon, we arrived at the guerrilla camp, which was made up of lots of tents with two or three people in each one. There were tons of very well-armed guerrillas there. They hadn't chopped down any trees because the trees block army planes from seeing them. I was taken to talk to Negro Acacio. He was black, very tall, and had a closely shaven head. Just the two of us sat on a fallen tree trunk and talked. First he stood up on the trunk, and then he sat down next to me.

He was very polite and wasn't ever aggressive. He told me, "Brother, we have information about you. Beginning with the fact that you recently arrived in the area, and we always distrust recently arrived people because we don't know where they come from. And when the army arrived, you disappeared. There were lots of people from the army on your farm, so we got the feeling that maybe you were an informant."

I told him, "Look Commander, the truth is that the army arrived at my farm and robbed my chickens and my chainsaw. We went to get the chainsaw back from them and they told me that they'd put me in jail. I sent you the letter because you are the ones who rule here and we have property here, and we need to not have any problems with anyone and to live in peace. I have my home and I have my family and I need peace so that I can work."

He responded, "Okay, you can work." I wasn't surprised that he let me work, because when you haven't done anything wrong, you always walk around sure of yourself. Then again, you never know with the guerrillas, because they're taught to kill.

After he met Negro Acacio, Jesús and Rosa started working on their farm again, which had coca,[4] cattle, pigs, and chickens. Over the next several years they invested about 90 million pesos[5] in constructing seven houses on the farm, which grew to be more than 700 hectares. Jesús and Rosa also purchased a house in the city of Villavicencio, the capital of Meta province, and had a daughter named Eliana in 2004.

THE CIRCUS TENT COLLAPSES

By 2008, when my wife's son Felipe was twelve years old, a FARC guerrilla commander showed up at my farm and said, "Why don't we take your son with us one of these days?" I said, "No, no, not him, you're not taking him." The commander responded, "If you don't let us take your son we're going to have to have you leave. We'll have to banish you from here, because people are either with us or they're against us."

From that point on the guerrillas hassled me and humiliated me. They would hold meetings in the village and pull me out in front of everyone and say, "This guy has links with the army. There are some farm owners who may wake up dead." What they meant was that at any moment they could go to my farm and kill me. The guerrillas were furious with me because I wouldn't let them recruit Felipe. They had recruited kids from other farms in the area, and many parents hadn't resisted because if you did they could kill you.

---

[4] The leaves of the coca plant are the raw material used in making cocaine.

[5] About U.S.$45,000.

Around Easter Week in 2008 I went on a short trip. While I was still away, I talked by phone with a brother of mine who lives in Puerto Príncipe, and he told me that there was a rumor about me in town. When I got back to Puerto Príncipe, the local guerrilla commander told me that I couldn't go back to my farm, which was about seventeen kilometers away. The guerrillas wouldn't let me leave Puerto Príncipe to go to my farm, so I had to stay at a hotel in town.

After twenty-three days in town, two guerrillas knocked at my door at the hotel. They said that I had to go to a meeting in another village. I took a ten-minute motorbike ride, and when I got there, a female guerrilla told me, "Look brother, we're going to kill you now." They gave me a shovel and made me dig a hole. I dug the hole and prayed. I thought it was my grave. I stopped digging the hole, sat in it and told them, "If you're going to kill me, kill me." Usually when someone is going to be killed, they ask for forgiveness and say, "Ay, no!" Not me. God centered me at that moment.

I heard two shots, *pa-pa*, but knew that they hadn't hit me because I didn't feel any pain. I stayed completely still. One of the guerrillas came over to me and said, "Stand up, we were just testing you." They let me go and I ran back to town. It was like being born again. In town I asked the guerrillas if I could go back to work on my farm and they said I could.

When I got to my farm, two guerrillas showed up and gave me a note calling me to a meeting at the house of the village's Community Action Board.[6] I arrived at the meeting and there was a different guerrilla commander there. He said, "What the hell happened with you? There was a meeting and you didn't go." I said, "How could I have gone if I was in town and wasn't allowed to leave?" He said, "I don't give a shit! We're going to punish you!" I felt humiliated. I also felt scorned by the other farm owners in the area, because they had told the guerrillas that I hadn't gone to the meeting, even though they knew about my problem in town.

---

[6] Community Action Boards are small civil organizations that represent villages, communities and neighborhoods. Each board has a president who is elected to a three-year term.

The guerrillas punished me. They took me to a part of the jungle about seven or eight kilometers away from my house and told me I had to build almost forty meters of road for cars to go over. I had to chop down thick trees with an ax and cut three-meter-long pieces of wood. I would spend half a day chopping at the tree with an ax, and sometimes it wouldn't fall. The guerrillas would bring me food. I couldn't run away because I thought that if I had left before finishing the road, they would have killed me. If you don't comply with an order, they kill you. I was basically kidnapped.

I hung up a hammock from two trees and slept under a sheet of plastic. I was afraid. It's not safe to sleep in the jungle because there are panthers, tigers, snakes, and tarantulas. Huge ants would bite me, and the pain would last for eight hours. Thank God a snake never bit me because that would have killed me immediately.

My wife was pregnant at the time, but I didn't worry about her because I knew she had everything she needed at the house and that she took care of herself. I sent her letters with the people from the area who passed by, telling her that I was okay. I didn't think that the guerrillas were going to kill me, because I was complying with their orders. If they were going to kill me for any other reason, they would have already done it. I concentrated on the work that I had to do. I had to assimilate many things, and confront the problem that I had in front of me.

I wasn't making progress because I'm bad at chopping with an ax, and my back hurt. I'd been in the jungle for a month and a half when the guerrilla commander showed up and I told him that it would take me a year to finish the road on my own. The guerrillas thought I would never finish cutting the wood, so they gave me permission to hire a man with a chainsaw to cut it. The guerrillas cared more about the road than my punishment. So I hired someone with a chainsaw, and we chopped down the trees. I also hired some workers from the area to help me remove the wood and take it to where I was building the road, because I couldn't transport it by myself. After two months in the jungle, I finished building the road and went home. I didn't have to ask the guerrillas for permission. When I went back to my farm, my wife was there. I was skinny, skinny, skinny, with a long beard. I was unrecognizable; I looked like a clown.

After that, we felt like leaving. Then a guerrilla commander arrived at the farm again and began to insult me. I told him, "Men aren't humiliated, they're killed. If you want to kill me, kill me, but don't harass me." I'm very direct. I have to be black or white, not gray. The commander said, "You know what? Leave! I don't want to see you around here again."

When the guerrillas tell you to get lost or leave, it's an order, and I knew I had to obey the order. You only have one life. I fled with Felipe, my four-year-old daughter, and my wife, who was four months pregnant at the time. We only took our clothes and 18 million pesos[7] with us and left the farm under the care of a guy from the area. We fled through the jungle for almost two days. Fleeing through the jungle was like going to a circus, and the circus tent collapses. You know where you entered and you have to find the way to exit. The sun orients you. That's what the jungle's like.

HE POINTED THE RIFLE AT MY HEART

We went back to Villavicencio again and had our son, Jairo. When my son was born I enjoyed it internally, spiritually. I didn't get drunk with friends to celebrate or anything like that; my emotions are always internal.

I returned to Puerto Príncipe in July 2009 because the army set up a base there, which they hadn't had before, and because I didn't have any work in Villavicencio. I set up a shop selling supplies out of a house that belonged to a woman from town, and where another four guys were also living. My wife and kids stayed in Villavicencio. My plan was to work in the town of Puerto Príncipe while I recovered all of our motorized pumps, electricity generators, motorboat, and other personal belongings from our farm.

---

[7] About U.S.$9,000.

On the morning of August 3, 2009, the army entered the house I was staying in. The soldiers searched through all five of the rooms. I didn't know what they were looking for. An army captain was standing in the doorway with his hands stretched out holding the doorframe and a rifle hanging on his chest. Serenely, I went up to him and said, "Captain, please show me the search warrant, because you need a search warrant to enter a house." He said, "Stay there you big son of a bitch." He didn't show me any search warrant; he came closer to me and pointed the rifle at my heart. The barrel was five centimeters from my chest and he had his finger on the trigger.

I told him, "Are you going to kill me or what? If you're going to kill me, kill me." He backed up and shot at my feet. The bullet hit the floor and a shard of something from the floor shot up and wounded my right leg. The soldiers who were searching through the rooms came out when they heard the shot. I had my back to them and they hit my neck and threw me face down on the ground. Then the captain told the soldiers, "Grab that son of a bitch and tie him up because he's very dangerous."

The soldiers entered one of the rooms and took out a piece of rope. They took me out to the road in front of the house and tied my hands behind my back very tightly. My hands tingled. I was lying face down and the soldiers and captain put their boots on my back. I felt really angry and discriminated against.

A lot of townspeople crowded around because they had heard the shot. Some started to say, "Let him go, he's not an animal." The captain left me with some soldiers and went to continue to search the house. About fifteen minutes later he came back and told me, "Stand up!" I couldn't stand up because I was tied and told him, "Come and stand me up." He said, "Alright you big son of a bitch, I'll stand you up, but with a kick!" That's when he kicked me in my leg and burst open all the ligaments in my knee.

Then the captain told the soldiers, "Tie this son of a bitch up and drag him!" The soldiers tied my feet together with a piece of nylon and dragged me down a gravel road. They dragged me for about ten meters, until the townspeople started to intervene. The people told the captain, "He's not an animal! There's no reason to drag him."

The captain said, "Don't butt in unless you want the same fate as this guy! You don't even know who this guy is." A woman responded to the captain, "We've known this guy for more than ten years and he doesn't bother anyone. We know who he is and are willing to give testimony about what you're doing to him." When the captain saw the reaction of the townspeople, he had the soldiers grab me, lift me up, and throw me into their pickup truck as if I were a dog. Then they took me to a wooden house the army used on the edge of town. I felt a lot of anger against the army. And when I feel angry, I'm not afraid, I don't feel pain; I don't feel anything.

KIDNAPPED

I was in a room in the wooden house sitting on a chair with my hands tied behind my back. The captain arrived and told me that he had found a pistol in my room. I told him, "You have no balls, you big son of a bitch. You're covering up what you did." I was furious because I had never seen the pistol and thought that they were going to do a false positive[8] in order to cover up what they'd done to me. I thought to myself, *I'm going to have to spend five or seven years in jail because it'll be my word against his, and his word has more weight than mine.*

After about ten minutes they took me out into a hallway in the house and I saw a pistol lying on the ground next to a chair. The captain was filming the hallway with a video camera and told me to sit in the chair. I told him, "I'm not going to sit on that chair. The only way you'll get me to sit on that chair is by shooting me and killing me." I didn't want to sit

---

[8] Jesús uses the term "false positive" here in the general sense of the army framing an innocent person for the purpose of increasing their "positive" results in fighting illegal groups. In what has become known as the "false positives" scandal, army members murdered civilians, dressed them to resemble guerrillas or members of criminal groups, and reported them as combatants killed in action. For more information, see the glossary entry for false positives.

in the chair next to the pistol because they were recording me with video. Then the captain focused the camera on the pistol and began to read me a document accusing me of belonging to an armed group. The captain had called me a guerrilla one time, and a paramilitary another; he didn't even know which one I was.[9] I wasn't worried because I knew that I didn't have any links and that he wouldn't be able to prove it.

I asked the captain, "Why are you branding me as a guerrilla or as a paramilitary? In the end you can't even say whether I'm a guerrilla or paramilitary or not." I spoke to the camera he was recording with and said that I didn't have links with any guerrilla or paramilitary groups. Then, the soldiers brought me back to the room.

About five minutes later my friend from town named Mariela arrived at the wooden house with Ricardo, one of the guys who I lived with. I could hear Mariela and Ricardo outside, telling the captain that I didn't have anything to do with the pistol and that the pistol belonged to a paisa[10] who had left it in the house in exchange for a debt that he owed. Ricardo and Mariela told the captain to let me go and the captain told Ricardo that he was also under arrest. The captain put Ricardo in the room I was in, but released him within two hours.

I was tied up like a dog, worse than an animal. Around ten at night a corporal came into the room where I was being held. He told me, "Jesús, we need you to do us a favor. We need you to sign a document recognizing your good treatment by us so we can send it to the colonel."[11] I didn't sign the document. The corporal came back ten minutes later and told

---

[9] Right-wing paramilitary groups began to form in Colombia in the early 1980s with the purported aim of fighting left-wing guerrillas. Backed by the military, landowners, drug traffickers, and political and economic elites, they murdered tens of thousands of civilians.

[10] Paisa is a term that refers to a person from Antioquia province.

[11] The Office of the UN High Commissioner for Human Rights reported in 2010 that it had received information about alleged cases of illegal detention by the Colombian army and that "in some of these cases, victims suffered cruel or degrading treatment, even torture, and were released only after they were forced to sign a declaration that they had been well treated."

me, "Stand up, the captain needs you." I got up and went out to where the captain was sitting in a big wooden chair. The captain said to me, "So you're really tough, are you? Are we going to do this the hard way or are we going to do it the easy way?" I asked him, "What's the hard way?" He said, "The hard way is that I have the video, I have the camera, I have the power, I have the pistol. I have the whole setup to put you in jail." I said to him, "And what's the easy way?" He said, "The easy way is for you to sign the document of good treatment and I'll let you go."

But it was late at night, and I knew that if I signed the paper and they let me go, the army would kill me or disappear me[12] later that night. They could let me go at ten at night, kill me, dress me up with camouflage and a gun, and do a false positive. I thought it was more likely for them to kill me outside of the base than inside. I was under their responsibility in the base; if they killed me outside, it wasn't going to appear like their responsibility.

I said, "Captain, I need you to do me a favor and untie my hands because what you're doing to me is illegal. I'm going to leave here and file a complaint and they're going to kick you out of the army." He untied my hands and took me back to the room. But as tired as I was that night, I couldn't sleep because of the immense pain in my hands. My hands swelled up horribly, and were purple, purple, purple.

The captain and corporal came into my room at six in the morning and asked me to sign the document. I said, "I'll sign it, but you have to let me go." I signed because I felt safer during the day and had to attend to my business in town. He said, "Fine, I'll let you go." They were filming me when I signed the document and handed it over to the corporal. As the corporal walked away, the captain handed the video camera over to a soldier and said to me, "You big son of a bitch, now I'm going to show you I have balls." I ran up to the corporal and grabbed the document I had signed and ripped it into pieces in front of his face. I said, "Look," and I threw all the pieces of paper onto the ground except for one piece that I kept in my hand.

---

[12] Jesús is referring to the practice of abduction or detention, followed by the concealment of the victim's fate or whereabouts, and often ending with the murder of the victim.

When I did that, the captain said, "Grab that son of a bitch and tie him up hard and we'll see how he feels." The soldiers grabbed me, tied my hands up tightly again, and put me back into the room.

That day, Mariela came to visit me again, and I sent a message with her to the vice president of the Community Action Board in Puerto Príncipe, telling him that I needed to talk with him.

It got to be four in the afternoon. I'd needed to go to the bathroom since early in the morning but they hadn't given me permission. I told them, "I'm going to shit right here in my clothes." After I said that they put me in the bathroom. Afterwards, I said to the corporal, "Corporal, there's no arrest warrant against me. I'm kidnapped here. If I spend another hour here and you don't let me go, I'm going to denounce all of you. You can only have me here for twenty-four hours, and you have me kidnapped here."

At around five in the afternoon on August 4, the army let me go. The vice president of the Community Action Board from Puerto Príncipe arrived at the wooden house right before I was released. We both signed the document of good treatment so that they would let me go, because I needed to work. But the vice president told the corporal, "What you've done to him is bad."

I went directly to the health center in Puerto Príncipe, spoke with the man in charge there, and asked him to examine me. He said that he wasn't a doctor, but that he could give me a certificate saying that I said that I'd been mistreated by army members. He wrote the report and then I went to the Community Action Board in Puerto Príncipe. The board leaders told me to write a report about what had happened and that they'd sign it for me. I went to talk with the townspeople to see if they would sign the report, but nobody wanted to sign.

PURE LIES

I called Rosa and told her that I had had problems with the army commander, that he had hit me and dragged me and injured my leg. My family was worried.

About two days later, at around six at night, I went into the house where I had been staying in Puerto Príncipe and heard somebody in the back yard. I went to look and saw some soldiers knocking down the wood fence in the back. The front door was locked with a padlock so I escaped out the window. The soldiers must have been watching me when I entered the house. After that incident I started staying in a hotel in Puerto Príncipe.

On August 11, seven days after I'd been released, the army took a young man to the house where they had taken me. They took him to the same room, put a blanket over him and gave him a real beating. They busted up his ribs and nose. When he was released, he came to look for me, and I took photos of him. When the townspeople saw him, they also looked for me and about 120 people signed the report I had written describing what had happened to me.

I went through the town collecting signatures, and as I was collecting them, a soldier came up to me and asked, "When are you going to leave?"

The next day the vice president of the Community Action Board was shot twice in the arm when he was driving on a motorbike in a rural area. The army was about three minutes away from where he was shot. The vice president always had to travel around the area, and because of that, the army says that he's a guerrilla. Pure lies. After he was shot, he told me at the hospital that he had also received verbal threats from the army before, telling him that he was a guerrilla informant and that he had to leave Puerto Príncipe.

I took the shooting of the vice president as a signal that I had to leave. I made two copies of the report I had written of the incident— one to leave in Puerto Príncipe and one to bring with me. I couldn't leave Puerto Príncipe over land, because there are about seven army checkpoints along the road, and I thought that they would disappear me. So I sold my motorbike and Mariela sent a girl to buy me a ticket on the small plane out of Puerto Príncipe. There were two flights on August 18, the day I was going to leave. I had the girl put my name down for the flight I wasn't going to take, and buy a ticket under another name for the flight I was going to take.

The day of the flight I waited at the hotel, which was about seventy meters away from the landing strip. Ten minutes before the plane was going to take off, I walked with my bag to the landing strip. As I was walking, I saw the same captain who had detained me coming from the opposite direction in a truck. He saw me walking with my bag and came to a screeching halt about thirty meters away from me. I walked past the truck and laughed at him. He didn't do anything because there were a lot of people around.

I got to the plane and there was a corporal I had never seen before standing there. He said to me, "You're going to travel?" I said, "Yes." He said, "What's your alias?"[13] So I said to him, "Why do you have to say that to me? If you know I have an alias, why don't you arrest me? If you have control, have a uniform, and have authority, why don't you arrest me? Or do you want to risk the same fate as the captain and have me denounce you? Because I can do that to you." He let me get onto the plane and I left for Villavicencio.

WE'RE IN A LABYRINTH

When I got home in Villavicencio and saw my wife and kids, it was as if nothing had happened. My wife is pretty unemotional. She's not one of those people who says, "Ay! What happened?" No, no, no. She said, "What's up? How's it going? Tell me what happened." And I told her. I felt relieved to see my kids, because my kids are my life.

On August 19 I went to the Attorney General's office in Villavicencio and filed a complaint against the captain. I handed over photos of my leg and arms and also of the young man who had been beaten at the house. The photos showed my leg and arms completely bruised.

When I got to Villavicencio I couldn't work because of the injuries. I had to rehabilitate my hands. My neck, my spine, and my leg are still in-

---

[13] Most members of armed groups in Colombia have an alias that they are known by.

jured. Two of my vertebrae are out of place. I still have the scars on my legs, arms, and hands from when they dragged me. When the captain kicked me, he broke all the ligaments in my knee. I could barely walk and barely sleep. Now my knee pops out of place when I walk. I have to bandage it up.

If the captain had apologized to me, I wouldn't have denounced him. But he didn't apologize. So I filed a complaint, and I won't retract it. I'll continue even if he orders someone to kill me. He attacked my integrity and my morality when he said in front of everyone that I was a guerrilla or paramilitary. And what ruins you most is when they attack your morality.

A person's values are what he's worth. If you don't have values, you have nothing; you don't have dreams. And your dreams are your reality, because your dreams make you who you are. If you don't have dreams and can be won over easily, your principles end. Everyone has to find his own way to survive in the Eastern Plains. If you choose one side, trouble comes from the other; and if you don't choose any side, it'll come just the same. We're in a labyrinth, a labyrinth of knowing how to survive.

My life is in danger, because if what the captain did to me is eventually uncovered, there are a lot of people behind him who would also be affected. The army captain is still active. Nothing has happened with the investigation. The Attorney General's office hasn't even called me or the other witnesses.

I feel really angry inside. If you're a captain, you have power; if you're a general, you have force; if you're a lieutenant, you have arguments to justify anything. But I don't want revenge. I wasn't born to kill anyone.

ALBERTO CARRASCO

AGE: 73
OCCUPATION: *Former rancher*
HOMETOWN: *Mariquita, Tolima*
INTERVIEWED IN: *Bogotá*

Many historians trace the roots of today's conflict in Colombia to a period known simply as La Violencia, a time of partisan unrest which lasted roughly from 1948 to 1958. The violent conflict between the Conservative and Liberal parties during that period left between 200,000 and 300,000 people dead, and as many as two million displaced.

Alberto Carrasco was a young child when La Violencia broke out, and had to flee with his Liberal family from Conservative territory in Boyacá province. More than fifty years later, Alberto had to flee again; this time, he was forced from his cattle ranch in Meta province by leftist guerrillas of the FARC, the country's largest rebel group, born of the Liberal guerrillas of the 1950s.

Names in this narrative have been changed at the request of the narrator.

IF YOU WEREN'T BRAVE
YOU HAD TO PRETEND TO BE

I don't get nervous when I see dead people—not since I was about ten years old, when I had to yank a pack of mules over a hundred and fifty bodies during La Violencia.

I was born in Pacho, Cundinamarca province in 1938. My mom died when I was two years old, and my dad remarried that year and took me and my stepmother to live in Otanche, Boyacá province, where he had a farm. My dad was a Liberal. In that area, most people were Conservatives and there were only a handful of Liberals—about five or six families including mine. There was a Conservative armed group called "chulavitas," and Liberal guerrilla groups were called "chusma." Back then you had to be with one or the other.

I studied a little bit, but mostly I helped my dad on the farm and with his cattle trading. One day in April 1948, we were piling corn into a shed when we heard on the radio that Jorge Eliécer Gaitán, the Liberal Party politician,[1] had just been killed in Bogotá. My dad said, "Oh crap. Now we're in for it." After Gaitán was killed, a war started between Liberals and Conservatives, and there was terrible violence. There were many dead on both sides.

My dad was afraid we'd be rounded up and killed, so he sent a boy to give a note to Saúl Fajardo, who had organized a small Liberal guerrilla group in those parts. The note asked for Fajardo's group to help get the Liberal families out of Otanche. Fajardo sent about three hundred men armed with homemade weapons to help us into Liberal territory. The most powerful weapon they had was a hand-cranked shotgun.

The night Fajardo's men arrived, it was raining. My dad loaded up the mules with everything he could, and then I left with him and my stepmother and the other families.

To protect us, the Liberal guerrillas put us and five other families in the middle of their men. There were about two hundred men walking in front of us and another hundred men behind us. I walked leading a pack of five mules; the road was rutted, and I remember slipping and falling in the mud and the mules passing over me.

---

[1] Jorge Eliécer Gaitán (January 23, 1903–April 9, 1948) was a populist Liberal Party politician who was assassinated when he was running for president in the 1950 elections. His death sparked the onset of La Violencia.

Eventually we arrived near a village called Humbo. The guerrillas got word that almost two hundred chulavita policemen had been sent to Humbo to set up a roadblock because they'd heard that Saúl Fajardo's people were going to be passing by. The guerrillas went ahead while the families stayed back in the woods, hiding with the mules.

We heard the gunfire. It was terrible—*ta, ta, ta, ta, ta*! When things calmed down, the guerrillas came back for us and we set out again. But we had a problem, because the mules would back up as soon as they smelled the dead and saw the bodies—there were dead policeman on the ground, dressed all in white. So I had to yank the mules while someone else hit them from behind so that they'd pass over the bodies. That night, we had to pass over about a hundred and fifty bodies.

I couldn't show any fear because if I did, my dad would spank me and call me a coward. So if you weren't brave you had to at least pretend to be. There was one boy there, Álvaro, who was twelve or thirteen, and he was crying. His dad whipped him and said, "This sissy coward!"

We walked all night over the mountains until we got to a village called Llano Mateo. It was a Liberal town, and there were armed men all over the place to protect us, so there was no threat of the chulavitas or the Conservatives coming. We felt safe there.

I BECAME A BUTCHER INSTEAD

Thank God I have a noble spirit and I didn't become twisted by all that I'd seen. Someone else who lives through that, by the time they're fifteen years old, they can turn into the world's biggest guerrilla. Instead, I became a butcher and a cattle trader, like my dad. Since I was little, I'd always tagged along with my dad to buy and sell livestock. I also went with him to the slaughterhouses to butcher the cattle. Back then it was all done by hand. You'd knock down the cow and stab it in the jugular. Once it was dead, you'd lay it down with its legs in the air and you'd start skinning it and removing the different cuts.

By the time I was fifteen I was already working in slaughterhouses in La Dorada, Caldas on the Magdalena River, where my family moved to after Llano Mateo. My dad had four children with my stepmother but my father and stepmother separated in about 1953, and my dad and I moved to Mariquita, Tolima.

In 1959, when I was twenty-one, my dad decided to leave Mariquita, but I stayed behind. By then I had a good cattle business going, buying and selling. It was there that I met my wife Marieta, who I married in 1961. For me, Mariquita is my hometown because that's where I got married, where I made my home, and where my three daughters were born.

By 1980, things in Mariquita weren't going well because people stopped paying their debts. I'd sell fifty or sixty head of cattle on a weekend and people wouldn't pay. So my family and I came to Bogotá and set up a restaurant where we served set-menu lunches. There were days we could sell four hundred lunches, but we didn't make much money off it because we were naïve and the workers would steal from us.

Around that time, I started traveling to the Eastern Plains and checking out the cattle business there. I went to Villavicencio and I liked that city; there was a lot of movement and the cattle business was good there. So I said to my wife, "Mi'ja,[2] let's sell this restaurant. This isn't for us. Let's go to Villavicencio." We lasted in Bogotá about a year and a half altogether, and finally we left in 1983.

I set up a butcher shop in Villavicencio and things went well. Then I opened another shop, and another. I ended up having nine butcher shops in Villavicencio. Marieta was the administrator and I was in charge of buying the cattle.

In 1990 I started going to Vistahermosa, a cattle town in the south of Meta province, which was about three or four hours from Villavicencio when the road wasn't paved yet. I liked the region; it was peaceful

---

[2] A contraction of "mi hija," (in English, "my daughter"), which is used affectionately for female friends and relatives.

and the cattle were good. In 1993 I bought my first ranch there. Then I bought two more. My family and I still lived in Villavicencio but we traveled back and forth to the ranches.

The area was filled with FARC guerrillas, and they started charging vacunas.[3] They'd come around to the ranches collecting, and if I didn't have the money they'd say, "When can you have it?" and I'd say, "In a week or two," and in two weeks they'd come back for the money. It started off easy.

DON ALBERTO, WE DON'T WANT
TO TAKE YOUR HEAD OFF

One day in 1996, Marieta and I were on our way back from Villavicencio going to one of the ranches. It was very early, about 5:30 a.m., when we saw five guerrillas in uniform near the entrance to the ranch. They signaled for us to stop, and then they told me that Manuel, the administrator of my ranch, was stealing cattle from other farms. I'd heard in town that people had been complaining about it, and that it was apparently true. One of the guerrillas said to me, "Don Alberto, get that guy out of here. Otherwise we'll have to kill him here on your ranch."

I went to talk to Manuel and gave him the message. He got angry and denied it. I said, "Look, the guerrillas want you out." He was gone in a week.

Soon after, the FARC started charging not just the regular vacunas, but also for the cattle that was brought into the area for fattening. When I brought in cattle, they charged 50,000 pesos[4] per truckload. And when I took them out to sell, they charged another 50,000 pesos. If you didn't pay, they'd take your cattle.

---

[3] Vacunas, literally "vaccines," are extortion payments.

[4] About U.S.$50 at the time.

In 1998 the FARC safe haven started.[5] The government pulled out all the police and the army, and soon after, the guerrillas set up a roadblock in front of where the Vistahermosa army base had been. Before the safe haven we still had to deal with the guerrillas, but there was more respect because the army could always come in. But once the safe haven started, the guerrillas were everywhere. They started demanding that ranchers give them cattle, and every year they'd take three or four from each ranch. Who could say no?

Soon after the start of the safe haven, the paramilitaries showed up, and they were always clashing with the guerrillas. The paramilitaries would take cattle too; they were thieves just as much as the guerrillas were. It was really screwed up.

I ended up working just to pay them both. Whenever I went to my ranches from Villavicencio I had to go with my pockets full of cash. I'd get to the town of Castilla, about forty-eight kilometers from Villavicencio, and there'd be the first group of paras[6] on the road. They'd say "Oh, so you're going to the ranch?" They knew my ranch was in a guerrilla-controlled area. "Behave yourself," they'd say, and they would ask for a "donation." I'd have to give them 100,000 or 200,000 pesos.[7] Then in San Martín, it was the paras, but a different group, so I had to give more. Then in San Juan de Arama, it was the guerrillas. They would say, "Oh, so you've come from chatting with the paras have you? You behave yourself, Don Alberto. We don't want to have to take your head off." And they would also demand money.

---

[5] In 1998, the government of then-president Andrés Pastrana granted the FARC a rebel safe haven as part of peace talks between the rebels and the government. The area was 42,000 square kilometers, encompassing the municipalities of Vistahermosa, La Uribe, and La Macarena in Meta province, and San Vicente del Caguán in Caquetá province.

[6] "Paras" is conversational shorthand for paramilitaries. Right-wing paramilitary groups began to form in Colombia in the early 1980s with the purported aim of fighting left-wing guerrillas. Backed by the military, landowners, drug traffickers, and political and economic elites, they murdered tens of thousands of civilians.

[7] About U.S.$70 and U.S.$140 at the time.

I had to see a lot of dead people in those days. People got so used to seeing them that we called the cadavers "murracos," which means "dolls." It was common to hear that the guerrillas had killed ten or twenty people or that the paras had committed a massacre. You couldn't be afraid all the time. You just kept going.

One time I was on the road with a twenty-eight-year-old godson I have from Mariquita. We saw two people standing on the road and we stopped. I knew one of the men, Ramón. There in the middle of the road were four bodies lying head to head, like a plus sign. Ramón told me they were four brothers, and that the paras had killed them for supposedly being guerrillas. I said, "Well let's get them out of the way. What else can we do?" I grabbed one by the arms and Ramón grabbed his legs, and we put them one by one on the side of the road. My godson was a nervous wreck.

The next day my godson and I were on our way to a village called Bodega de San Juan when we saw two bodies in the ditch by the side of the road. Their mouths were wide open. My godson screamed, and I said, "Oh, the murracos. They won't do anything to you." I'm not afraid of the dead.

There was a guy who had worked for me, taking care of one of my ranches. He was very fond of me. His wife left him and so he quit the ranch and left town. The next I knew he had joined the paramilitaries. Around 1999 he sought me out and told me to be careful because his commander had handed out a list of everyone who had to be killed. He showed it to me. "Look, you're third on the list," he said. "I'm telling you because I'm your friend." After that, I didn't stop going to the ranches. I just didn't go as often.

55 MILLION PESOS AND
YOU SIGN OVER THE DEED

One day in 2001, five or six guerrillas came the ranch. One of them said to me, "Don Alberto, how's it going? We've come to make you a proposition." I said, "What is it?" He said, "We need you to plant coca[8] here. You put up the land and we'll give you a percentage." I said, "I don't know anything about growing coca. I only know cattle and pigs." The guerrilla said, "We'll keep talking," and then they left.

Two weeks later, a different group of guerrillas showed up. One of them said, "We've come to ask you what you've decided about the business deal." I replied, "No, I don't want to get involved in that." He said that in about two or three weeks someone was going to come by who wanted to buy the ranch. By that time, I had already sold one of my farms to a drug trafficker who wanted to put in an airstrip. The paramilitaries and the guerrillas were making it too hard to do business.

A few weeks later, two men showed up at the ranch. They were dressed in civilian clothes but they were armed with shotguns. One of them said, "How much is this ranch worth?" I said it was worth a minimum of 200 million pesos[9] because it was thirty hectares. He said, "Look, you have to leave here, but so that you don't leave empty handed, I'll give you 55 million pesos[10] for the land and everything on it." I didn't have so much cattle on the ranch anymore because things had become so complicated with the pressure from the guerrillas and the paramilitaries, but there were still fifty cows, forty sheep, and ten horses. The man said, "I've got 55 million pesos and you have to sign over the deed. This money is so you'll leave." Then that bastard said, "Use it for the bus fare."

I had to accept the deal. It was clear that if I didn't, they'd kill me or my wife, or one of my daughters. So that's how the deal was. Thirty hectares for 55 million pesos. Just the livestock alone was worth more than that.

A few days later I had to go to the public notary office and sign the deed over to another man. I was so angry that day. I also had to abandon another thirty-five-hectare ranch that I had.

---

[8] The leaves of the coca plant are the raw material used in making cocaine.

[9] About U.S.$90,000 at the time.

[10] About U.S.$24,000 at the time.

LOOK DOWN AND SUFFER FROM THE COLD

Ever since we sold the ranches in 2001, Marieta and I have been suffering, moving from one place to the other. We left Villavicencio for the city of Armenia, then from Armenia we went to Medellín, and now we're living in Bogotá with one of our daughters in a high-rise apartment building. Our eldest daughter lives in Spain and the other lives in Villavicencio. It's very hard on us here because we don't do anything all day but look down and suffer from the cold. I miss being in the countryside, or at least in a small town where you can go down to the coffee shop and chat with your friends and negotiate a head or two of cattle.

Now the government says they're going to help people like me get their land back, even if we'd been forced to sign the deeds over.[11] I recently learned that a friend of mine is now the mayor of Vistahermosa, where I'd had my ranches. He had also been forced to sell his ranches there. I called him and asked him about the land issue, and he said, "Yes, come here and file the report right away."

I went about two weeks later. My wife and daughters didn't want me to go to Vistahermosa and I said, "Why can't I go? Things there are calm now."[12] I still had a lot of friends there, though of course a few of them had been killed. When I got there, I asked about one of my friends and I was told he was dead. But then I asked about someone else and found out he was fine and had a ranch nearby, and in a little while I was surrounded by friends. But I didn't go to the ranches. That's still not safe.

---

[11] In June 2011, Colombian President Juan Manuel Santos signed the Victims and Land Restitution Law, which sets up special administrative and judicial procedures aimed at returning millions of hectares of stolen and abandoned land to displaced people.

[12] In February 2002 then-president Pastrana declared an end to peace talks with the FARC and to the safe haven established in Meta and Caquetá provinces. Government forces stepped up their military campaign against the guerrillas, driving them into the less-populated mountains and jungles of Colombia. Most paramilitary groups participated in the government-sponsored demobilization process between 2003 and 2006. Nevertheless, in 2010 the municipality of Vistahermosa registered a homicide rate seven times higher than the national average.

I filed the complaint in Vistahermosa and came back to Bogotá. Government officials initially told me that I should have my ranch back by the middle of 2012. But now they say it turns out the ranch is part of what is supposed to be a forest reserve, and that complicates things. Let's see what happens. The mayor of Vistahermosa told me that once I get everything in order, he'll buy my ranch.

I lived so well there, trading livestock with everyone, having a beer there in Vistahermosa; it makes me nostalgic for those times. But I don't want to go back there. With the money we get for the ranch, my wife and I would like to buy a little house, a place that's ours in a small town where it's warmer, where we can set up a shop or some sort of business and have our own things again.

RAMÓN SANTAMARÍA

AGE: 34

OCCUPATION: *Former boat driver, cocaine lab manager*

HOMETOWN: *Pereira, Risaralda*

INTERVIEWED IN: *Medellín, Antioquia*[1]

We first met Ramón Santamaría when he was begging for money on one of Medellín's main avenues. Sitting on the sidewalk in tattered clothes with his wife, three young children, and pet rabbit, they looked like a typical Colombian family freshly displaced from the countryside. In a nearby coffee shop, Ramón recounted how FARC guerrillas had just driven his family from their farm in Vichada province. He also described his previous life as a cocaine lab manager, during which he formed close working relationships with both the FARC and a paramilitary group.

The narrator's name has been changed at his request.

SCUM OF THE HOUSE

I was born in Pereira, Risaralda province, in 1977. I never met my mom—she left me with my grandmother when I was a baby—and I

---

[1] Both Pereira and Medellín are false locations employed to protect the narrator's identity.

don't even know who my dad is. I grew up with six younger sisters, and I was the scum of the house. I'll never forget—my sisters were all given nice sneakers and I was given rubber moccasins. No one loved me there.

When I was fourteen, a friend of mine from school said, "Let's go pick coca."[2] I agreed, and I went with fourteen other boys from Pereira to the jungles deep in the Amazon. There wasn't anything close by.

The first days picking coca were hard. I got malaria and my hands bled. We worked for the guerrillas[3] and were paid 4,000 pesos[4] per arroba[5] of coca, which was a lot of money back then. Getting far away from my family was the best thing I've done in my life.

After a year and a half, I went up to a town called Puerto Carreño, in Vichada province. I bought a little boat and a twenty-five horsepower motor, and I went to live in a nearby town on the Orinoco River. I met my wife there in 1993, when I was sixteen years old. Her mom ran a store where I'd go to parties and get drunk.[6] I sweet-talked her and we won each other over.

THE MERMAID OF DEATH

By around 2000, when I was twenty-three, I'd started working for the autodefensas.[7] I managed five coca-processing labs for the commander Ma-

---

[2] The leaves of the coca plant are the raw material used in making cocaine.

[3] The Revolutionary Armed Forces of Colombia (FARC) is the largest left-wing guerrilla group in Colombia. Founded in the 1960s and claiming to represent the country's rural poor in the fight against Colombia's wealthy classes and U.S. imperialism, the FARC commits widespread abuses against civilians, including killings, threats, and recruitment of child soldiers.

[4] About U.S.$7 in 1991.

[5] An arroba is a unit of weight used in some Spanish-speaking countries, whose exact measurement can vary depending on region.

[6] In Colombia, food and supply stores can often double as bars.

[7] Autodefensas means "self-defense groups," and is another term that is used to refer to paramilitary groups. Right-wing paramilitary groups began to form in Colombia in the early 1980s with the purported aim of fighting left-wing guerrillas. Backed by the military, landowners, drug traffickers, and political and economic elites, they murdered tens of thousands of civilians.

caco.[8] Planes would come at night and drop huge black bags called "percherons" that were filled with coca, and I would go in a tractor and collect them.

All of us who processed the coca in the area were given a tattoo on our chests of a woman called "the mermaid of death." The tattoo says, "If death comes, it's welcome." We all had to have it to be able to enter the area where the labs were. It was our ID card there.

The labs had to be underground so that the government helicopters wouldn't detect them. I was the boss, so I'd send about sixteen workers into the lab, turn on the electricity generators and microwave ovens, and go outside. It was hell in there: they'd be closed in for twenty-four hours with the microwave ovens turned on. Up to three or four workers could die each month from breathing in so much ether, acetone, and chemicals. If they died, they got thrown into the river. It was normal there where I lived. To die is normal. You don't die because you want to, but because God says, "Pack your bags and leave."

In twenty-four hours we'd produce ten or twenty kilos of cocaine called "fish scales"—pure, pure, pure—which was sent to the United States. I'd make about 4 million pesos[9] a month. The autodefensas paid me fairly.

They also killed without mercy. I had a farm that was at a strategic point, right on the Orinoco River, and the autodefensas would take people there to kill them. Many of the victims were peasants who were killed for being guerrilla informants. The autodefensas also did "social cleansing" of the thieves from nearby towns. They'd take them to my farm and kill them for stealing. No one could hear the shots, the chainsaws, or the bellowing there.

---

[8] Carlos Mario Jiménez, alias Macaco (in English "Macaque," a type of monkey), commanded the Central Bolívar bloc (BCB) of the United Self-Defense Forces of Colombia (AUC) paramilitary coalition.

[9] About U.S.$2,000 in 2000.

The autodefensas would tie them up there and shoot them in the head, or chop their heads off with a chainsaw as if they were cutting a tree in half. As long as they paid me, I'd drag fifteen or twenty cadavers to the river, take them out in my boat and throw them in the river. I had to, because if I didn't, they'd kill me. At first it was shocking when I had to take three or four heads in my hands, but in the end, after seeing so many dead people, it was normal—like seeing a bug get killed. You get used to everything.

Sometimes I'd also have to shoot people in the head. Either I killed them, or the autodefensas would have killed me. Maybe in other people's worlds it's not normal, but for me it was. It didn't shock me. If I had to kill someone, I'd kill him.

But I was never capable of burying anyone; I never had the heart to. I preferred to throw them in the river so that the fish would eat them. I was afraid to bury them, to throw dirt on their body. Even if I got covered in blood, I preferred to throw them in the river, where they'd sink, and bye bye. But to know that I would have to sleep close to where someone was buried—I wasn't capable.

Around 2005, Macaco turned himself in to the authorities[10] and the FARC entered the area. The guerrillas killed a lot of people, but fortunately, I wasn't one of them. The autodefensas turned themselves in, but they didn't hand over their labs or weapons. So around that time, I started to work for the guerrillas in the same labs that Macaco had run. At that time, I was living well. I had a huge farm, my money and my food. I had three children who could run around, and I could dive in to swim in the Orinoco River, which is the most beautiful thing in Colombia.

---

[10] The government sponsored a demobilization process for paramilitary groups between 2003 and 2006 in which more than 30,000 people participated in demobilization ceremonies. There is substantial evidence that many of the people who demobilized weren't paramilitaries, and that some factions of the groups remained active. Macaco entered the government's Justice and Peace demobilization program, which offered paramilitaries responsible for atrocities five-to-eight-year prison terms in exchange for demobilizing, confessing to crimes, and providing reparations to victims.

IT SMELLS THE SAME

In late 2010, a FARC informant came to Ramón's house and told him that the guerrillas were coming to kill him. Ramón suspects he was targeted either for refusing to take up arms as a guerrilla, for knowing too much about the guerrillas' operations, or for having produced impure cocaine in his lab. He packed some clothes, and within twenty minutes of speaking with the informant, Ramón was in his boat fleeing upriver. He went with his wife and three children, who were twelve, nine, and five years old at the time. By land and river, his family arrived in the city of Medellín.

In Vichada I had money and a lot of power, but it was devil's money. I couldn't put a peso in the bank. If I had gone to the bank in Puerto Carreño, I would have been put in jail, because supposedly I was a peon who worked for a day's wage. I invested all my money in capital—I bought machinery and motors—but I lost everything and now I live in absolute poverty.

Here in Medellín, when I have enough money, I pay for a night at a hotel in the neighborhood where all the whores are, and the very devil himself. It's the worst hole in Medellín. But that's the only place we can live because it's the cheapest, and where they rent to families with kids. The hotel costs 15,000 pesos[11] a night. If I don't make enough in a day, we go to a park, I lay out some blankets, and put my wife and kids to sleep. I sit there watching out for them the whole night. I have to.

I can't get work here because I'm thirty-four, didn't graduate from high school, and I'm toothless. I get up at seven in the morning, grab my rabbit, Quique,[12] and sit on the sidewalk to ask for money and leftovers. Quique is Venezuelan. The day the guerrillas went to kill me, we were escaping by motorboat and I found him five kilometers up river on the bank. He goes everywhere we go. We adore Quique. Quique is Quique.

---

[11] About U.S.$7.50.

[12] Pronounced KI-kay.

Some people help out and give us 50, 200, 1,000, 10,000 pesos.[13] But there are a lot of people that tell you, "Go and work, son of a bitch," or, "Go and work, you degenerate. Aren't you embarrassed to be begging there?" Some will give you food, some will treat you badly; it's all hypocrisy. The most I've made in one day is 20,000 pesos.[14] Now that it's been raining, I make about 4,000 pesos[15] a day.

When you're in such a horrible situation, you learn how to value life. Life is the most beautiful thing there is. Here in Medellín, I wouldn't be able to kill. I used to kill anyone, and for me, it was like killing a pig. A human, a pig, you open up the belly and it smells the same.

---

[13] About 3 U.S. cents, 10 cents, 50 cents, and $5, respectively. 50 pesos can buy a mint in Colombia.

[14] About U.S.$10.

[15] About U.S.$2, which buys a basic lunch at a restaurant in Colombia.

THE PATH
I'M FOLLOWING

Urabá

Tucked under Panama in the northwestern extreme of South America, Urabá has been at the center of Colombia's conflict for more than three decades due to its fertile lands, banana industry and strategic drug and arms trafficking routes to the Caribbean Sea. When descending by plane into Apartadó, the unofficial capital city of Urabá, one sees an endless green sea of banana trees. The region, which encompasses swaths of Antioquia and Chocó provinces that surround the Gulf of Urabá, exports some 70 million boxes of bananas annually. For decades, the FARC and EPL leftist guerrilla groups extorted huge sums of money from Urabá's banana companies and fought each other for influence over the industry's trade unions, often murdering workers from rival collectives. In 1994 FARC guerrillas gunned down thirty-four suspected supporters of the rival EPL's political movement at a barbeque in a working-class neighborhood of Apartadó, in what has become known as the La Chinita massacre.

In 1995, right-wing paramilitaries under the command of former army scout Carlos Castaño launched a major incursion into the region.

According to former paramilitary leaders, their campaign received the support of banana companies, cattle ranchers, politicians and military officers, including the commander of the local army brigade, General Rito Alejo del Río. Nicknamed the "Pacifier of Urabá," Del Río currently faces trial for the decapitation of a peasant during a joint military-paramilitary operation. By 1996, Urabá's homicide rate topped 300 killings per 100,000 inhabitants, more than five times the national average. A year later, Carlos Castaño would form a paramilitary federation known as the AUC, and replicate the Urabá model of paramilitary dominance throughout the country.

The paramilitary expansion in Urabá and beyond was financed in part by the Cincinnati-based multinational banana company Chiquita Brands International, which pleaded guilty in U.S. court to having paid U.S.$1.7 million to the AUC in Urabá and Santa Marta—another banana-producing region—between 1997 and 2004.

Paramilitaries and their business allies stole tens of thousands of hectares of land from displaced Afro-Colombian, indigenous and mestizo communities in Urabá, much of which they subsequently converted into African palm oil plantations, cattle ranches, and timber forests. AUC leader Vicente Castaño, brother of Carlos Castaño, recognized in a 2005 media interview, "We have [African] palm crops in Urabá. I myself got the businessmen to invest in those projects." Mayors, notaries, and officials from the government's land reform agency participated in the usurpation of nearly 42,000 hectares of land in Urabá, according to government investigations. Between 2008 and 2011, at least ten displaced people seeking land restitution in the region have been murdered. New paramilitary groups, which maintain a strong presence in the region, are believed to be responsible for many of the attacks.

LEONOR GIRALDO

AGE: 72
OCCUPATION: *Farmer*
HOMETOWN: *Beté, Chocó*
INTERVIEWED IN: *Curvaradó, Chocó*

Right-wing paramilitary expansion in northwestern Colombia in the late 1990s included the forced displacement of thousands of Afro-Colombians and mestizo peasants from their homes along the Curvaradó and Jiguamiandó river basins in northern Chocó province. In 2000, the government adjudicated the Afro-descendant communities of Curvaradó and Jiguamiandó roughly 100,000 hectares of collectively titled land.[1] But as displaced families attempted to return to their territories in the early 2000s, they found them still dominated by paramilitary groups and covered with large-scale African palm oil plantations and cattle ranches. In order to recover their land, they set up "humanitarian zones" in the region with the help of a Colombian NGO, the Comisión Intereclesial de Justicia y Paz (Inter-Church Justice and Peace Commission). These fenced-in communities banned the entry of all armed actors, including state security forces, in an effort to clearly demarcate the inhabitants' status as neutral civilians. In 2003, the Inter-American Court

---

[1] Law 70 of 1993 recognizes the right of Afro-Colombian communities to collectively own and occupy their ancestral lands. The law provides that the collective territories are to be "non-transferable, imprescriptible, and non-mortgageable."

of Human Rights, an international judicial institution, requested that the state of Colombia grant special protection to the humanitarian zones and adopt measures to protect the life and personal integrity of all the members of the Curvaradó and Jiguamiandó communities.

Since founding the humanitarian zones and advocating for the eviction of the business interests occupying their lands, several community leaders have been murdered. Colombia's Attorney General's office has accused African palm oil companies of having conspired with paramilitaries to seize part of the communities' lands. In 2009, a court ruling ordered palm companies and other private citizens to return the land to the Curvaradó and Jiguamiandó communities. As of this writing, the communities are still struggling to recover their collective territories.

We met with Leonor Giraldo at her home in Camelias, a humanitarian zone off the Curvaradó River. She and her husband were among the first people to settle in Camelias in the 1960s, where she raised a family of eight children in the remote Afro-Colombian community. When paramilitaries, allegedly allied with the Colombian security forces, invaded the region and committed a series of killings in 1996 and 1997, Leonor and her family sought refuge in the jungle. She recounts her family's constant flight over the subsequent years, until they regrouped with other displaced families to form humanitarian zones and reclaim their lost land.

Names in this narrative have been changed at the request of the narrator.

PEOPLE KILLED THE DOGS SO THEY WOULDN'T BARK

In October 1996, the paramilitaries[2] entered Brisas, which is a river port on the other side of the Curvaradó River. It was a Sunday, and there was going to be a soccer match in Brisas. The paramilitaries shot six of the people who were going to play, including my godson. It was the first massacre in the area.

---

[2] Right-wing paramilitary groups began to form in Colombia in the early 1980s with the purported aim of fighting left-wing guerrillas. Backed by the military, landowners, drug traffickers, and political and economic elites, they murdered tens of thousands of civilians.

The paramilitaries took off after the massacre, and the majority of the people who lived in the area started leaving. Hundreds of families left. But those of us who had roots there said that it wouldn't happen again, and we stayed. I stayed with my husband, my two youngest daughters Tamara and Íngrid, who were sixteen and ten years old at the time, and my one-year-old granddaughter. The rest of my kids left for Quibdó and the Beté River.

In the beginning of 1997 things were still pretty calm. There were rumors that paramilitaries had committed massacres in other places, but we said that the paramilitaries wouldn't come to where we were living.

Then the other attack came in early 1997. That day, my family and I were at home. I was putting rice out into the sun to dry, and my granddaughter was close by. Suddenly we heard, *Pra! Pa, pa, pa, pa, pa*! The paramilitaries were shooting in neighboring communities. I grabbed my little granddaughter, my husband José got a bag from the house and put a blanket and mosquito net in it, and we started running away from where the shooting was coming. My sixteen-year-old daughter Tamara was pregnant with her first son at the time, and she couldn't run well because her belly was really big. I ran and ran and ran, and my granddaughter held onto my neck. She looked like a little parakeet.

We ran for about thirty minutes until I caught up to my daughter Íngrid at a neighbor's house. I was about to faint; I couldn't run anymore, and my body was shaking. I gave Íngrid my granddaughter and kept on walking. Eventually we arrived in the village of Caño Claro, where we had to cross over a river on a bridge made out of a fallen tree. I couldn't walk across it because my body was shaking, so I had to get down and wrap my arms and legs around the tree in order to cross.

We got to an area called El Guino and took refuge there with six other families in the jungle, among the trees, under the sun and rain. During our time in the jungle, we slept underneath the roots of huge trees called bambas, which have roots above ground. When we heard shots we'd leave for another place with the other families. Sometimes we'd move up to twice a week, and sometimes we'd stay in a place for a month without moving.

We ate by sneaking products from our own farms. We had left our houses filled with rice, and there were chickens, pigs and coconut trees there. So when we didn't hear bullets for a day or two, three or four men would go to a house to look for food. One or two of them would hide and watch out as the other two crawled to the house to get the rice, knock down some coconuts, or grab some chickens. Then they'd go back to the bush where we were staying. On the days when we didn't hear bullets, some people would also go to fish in streams.

During that time, every rooster was a dead rooster. Because if it sang, the paramilitaries would know there were people there and they'd come looking for us. So all of the roosters went into the cooking pot. People also killed the dogs so that they wouldn't bark. We prayed to God in heaven that he wouldn't let anything happen to us, and we always had the hope and faith that we wouldn't die in the jungle.

SOMETHING WAS MOVING UNDERNEATH US

While we were in the jungle, Tamara gave birth to her son in a little hut that my husband had made there. I've been a midwife for more than twenty years, so my daughter gave birth with me, but badly. She was a first-time mother, and it was a very difficult birth. She was left very, very drawn. For a week after she had her son, she couldn't manage on her own. She wouldn't eat unless I sat her down to eat, and if I didn't give her the bedpan, she wouldn't pee.

About two weeks after my grandson was born, we heard the paramilitaries shooting and had to run again with the six other families. We had to cross over a river on a tree trunk, but my daughter and I weren't capable of crossing with her son. So a man from one of the other families put the baby's little legs in his pants pocket and crossed him over the bridge.

Another time we were running because the paramilitaries had entered an area along the Jiguamiandó River basin called La Paloma. We climbed up a hill and went down into a flat area. It got dark and we stayed the night there. My husband hung up the mosquito net between two rocks and we cut up some palm leaves, put them on the ground and laid a blanket on top. That night, a rainstorm fell that was sent straight from God in heaven. So I sat up, took my two grandchildren and put them underneath my skirt in order to cover them. I was shaking with cold. The rainstorm ended at about two or three in the morning, and I finally lay down to sleep. During the night, my husband told me to stop moving around so much, but I thought something was moving underneath us.

The next morning, we took down the mosquito net. My husband picked up the wet blanket and went to pick up the leaves, when he screamed, "Ay! A snake! We slept on top of a snake!" There was a huge coiled Mapaná snake on the ground, about two meters long.[3] The other men who were with us killed it with machetes.

WE COULD SEE THE SMOKE AND FLAMES

We lived in the jungle for six months until the NGO Paz y Tercer Mundo (PTM) and the church from Riosucio, Chocó got us out and we went to a village on the Jiguamiandó River called Bella Flor Remacho. We lived there with other families from the Curvaradó and Jiguamiandó rivers who had also come out of the jungle. We planted a crop of rice, but the day we were going to harvest it, the paramilitaries came. We heard shooting and we all started running, and left everything behind.

As we crossed the river by boat, we could see flames burning in the nearby town of Nueva Esperanza. Within an hour, between running and walking, we arrived with ten other families to the village of Caño Seco. And from Caño Seco we could see the smoke and flames in our village of Bella Flor Remacho. After we'd fled, the paramilitaries had also gone there and burned down the town center.

The paramilitaries left after two or three days, things kind of calmed

---

[3] Mapaná is a venomous snake found in the tropical lowlands of northern South America and is known in English as a lancehead.

down, and my family planted another crop of rice in Caño Seco. We made a little shack and we'd all pile in and sleep on the bare floor: my husband, daughters and grandchildren.

We stayed in Caño Seco for almost a year, until again there were rumors that the paramilitaries were coming. The Community Council[4] of Jiguamiandó met and decided that the elderly people who couldn't run and the people with lots of kids should go to the municipal center of Murindó.

So along with five other families, we walked for two days to Murindó. The river was flooded, so in some parts we had to walk with the water up to our waists. From the town center of Murindó we went to a little town called Bartolo, which was a four-hour walk. There, we lived in a house that the government had built, and we planted food crops. The mayor of Murindó was very supportive of displaced people because he's the son of a peasant, he's poor, and he's also suffered in life. Every week he'd buy about four thousand plantains, seven arrobas[5] of fish, and a cow to divide up among the community.

COMPLETELY COVERED WITH AFRICAN PALM

Supported by a Colombian NGO called the Inter-Faith Justice and Peace Commission, in 2003 Leonor and other displaced families started creating "humanitarian zones" along the Curvaradó and Jiguamiandó river basins. By 2008, after living in nearby humanitarian zones, Leonor and her family finally returned to their land in Camelias.

In 2008, community members created a humanitarian zone in Camelias

---

[4] Law 70 of 1993, which recognizes the right of black communities to own and live on collectively titled ancestral lands, requires each community to create a Community Council as its administrative body in order to adjudicate the collective property.

[5] An arroba is a unit of weight used in some Spanish-speaking countries, whose exact measurement can vary depending on the region.

with the support of the Inter-Faith Justice and Peace Commission. It was declared nationally and internationally a zone exclusively for the civilian population. The humanitarian zone where the community lives is three hectares. At first, five families came to Camelias. My husband came first with our kids, built a little shack and planted rice. I came to Camelias about two months after the first people had arrived.

At the time, Camelias was completely covered with African palm. But as people started returning to work in Camelias, wherever they went to plant corn or rice, they'd cut down the African palm. And God was with us, because a virus fell upon the palm and it started dying, and dying, and dying, until the palm was destroyed.

The people returned to their territories, but with a lot of threats. Here in Colombia, people who assert their rights and speak the truth, die. In 2008, the paramilitaries killed a leader in the Caño Manso community named Gualberto Hoyos, and in 2010 they killed a leader named Argénito Díaz from the Llano Rico humanitarian zone. The only thing we're not hearing now is the sound of gunshots, but the war hasn't ended; it continues just the same.

I live here with my husband, two sons, and two grandchildren. Tamara and Íngrid live in a nearby town. I was born in agriculture and I'm still in agriculture. My husband and I go out and work together, planting food crops on our land.

What motivates me to get the land returned to us is the future of my grandchildren, so that they have a place to work. We don't want this territory to be for businesses; we don't want to sell it, or invade it with large-scale projects. We want to work ancestrally, and for our autonomy to be respected as a community. The businessmen work by throwing chemicals on the land, mixing it up with a tractor and all that, so the land deteriorates. This land doesn't need that, and we don't work that way. Whatever you put in the land, it will produce without the need to give it poison. Mother Earth is an inheritance. That's what we live off and survive off.

FERNANDO ENAMORADO

AGE: *34*

OCCUPATION: *Farmer, land activist*

HOMETOWN: *Necoclí, Antioquia*

INTERVIEWED IN: *Montería, Córdoba[1]*

We met with Fernando Enamorado in a hotel room in the city of Montería. As we spoke, his government-assigned bodyguard watched the door outside. With remarkable calm, and with heavily slurred speech due to surgeries on his tongue and teeth, Fernando described how he almost lost his life in an assassination attempt in 2010.

Fernando grew up in a small village in the municipality of Necoclí, in the Urabá region of northern Colombia. From the age of nine, he lived on the run from paramilitaries and guerrillas. Then, in 2006, during the paramilitaries' demobilization process, Fernando returned to Necoclí and started leading displaced families in their efforts to recuperate stolen land from paramilitaries and their allies. His land activism made him a target for a neo-paramilitary group in the region that had inherited the demobilized paramilitary organization's wealth and criminal operations. In October 2010, gunmen tracked him down in Apartadó and shot him in

---

[1] Montería is a false location employed for the narrator's safety.

the face, armpit and shoulder. Today, Fernando lives in hiding because he received information that there is a 300-million-peso[2] reward for his assassination.

NOT EVEN THE BIRDS SANG

I'm from a little village in Necoclí called Ecuador, where there are fifty-six houses surrounded by two rivers. One afternoon in November 1994, when I was seventeen, I was playing soccer in a field when the army showed up. The soldiers searched everyone at the field and asked us if we had seen the guerrillas.[3] I said, "They passed by about four days ago." I wasn't worried about reprisals because the guerrillas who came by would tell us that, if the army asked, we should say we'd seen guerrillas, but inflate their numbers. If there were about four guerrillas, I told the army there were one hundred. The soldiers told us, "Don't be afraid of us. Be afraid of the people coming behind us. Because they're coming chopping off heads." But it didn't worry me because I wasn't involved in anything.

One morning about eight or nine days later I was in my house getting ready to go out to cut down some plantains. It was a cold and silent day; not even the birds sang. I sensed something was going to happen.

I went to collect plantains, and at around seven in the morning I saw a man dressed in camouflage in the distance. I felt that something bad was happening, so I hid in an irrigation channel underneath a little bridge. Two more uniformed men passed by. They went to the gate in the fence around my house, which was about six meters from where I was hiding. More uniformed men showed up until there were about fifteen people standing at the gate. I heard them laughing about the people

---

[2] About U.S.$168,000.

[3] The Revolutionary Armed Forces of Colombia (FARC) and National Liberation Army (ELN) are Colombia's two main guerrilla groups. Founded in the 1960s and claiming to represent the country's rural poor in the fight against Colombia's wealthy classes and U.S. imperialism, both groups commit widespread abuses against civilians, including killings, threats, and recruitment of child soldiers.

they'd already killed that day. They bragged about how they had killed a man by drowning him in a pool of water. They said three or four of them had stood on top of him so that he couldn't get up, and they laughed about how he'd struggled as they were killing him. They also said they'd chopped someone's head off and played soccer with it.

I snuck away because I thought that maybe they'd sense me there. I walked about a kilometer down the irrigation channel, went into the jungle and found my cousin Emiro hiding there. I was talking with him when another cousin named Leoncio arrived. He was scared. Leoncio told us he'd been bathing in a river when he saw some uniformed people passing by above him, and then he heard someone shout, "Don't kill me! Don't kill me!" Leoncio said he heard the sound of a blow and then nothing more, and then he ran into the jungle, where he found us. Emiro and I asked where it had happened, and Leoncio said, "A plantain field next to the main road." Emiro said, "It must have been my dad," and we took off running through the jungle to the plantain field. There, we found his dad, my uncle Abel. His head had been chopped off; it was attached by a little piece.

We were all in shock, and Emiro fainted. Leoncio and I picked him up, and I said, "Let's go! Those people could come back and find us here!" We ran back into the jungle carrying Emiro by his feet and hands, and we found our grandparents and uncles hiding there in the bush.

Sixteen people were killed that day; they all had their heads chopped off. I guessed it had been the paramilitaries that the army had warned us about.

Three days later, the people who had committed the massacre held a meeting in a nearby village, where they identified themselves as paramilitaries.[4] I was working that day, and by the time I got to the meeting it had already ended. But an uncle of mine had gone, and he told me that

---

[4] Right-wing paramilitary groups began to form in Colombia in the early 1980s with the purported aim of fighting left-wing guerrillas. Backed by the military, landowners, drug traffickers, and political and economic elites, they murdered tens of thousands of civilians.

a paramilitary named Kiko López said my entire family was in the guerrillas. Kiko was from a neighboring village. The guerrillas had killed his dad, so he and his three brothers had joined the paramilitaries. Kiko said that he was going to finish off all the men in our family.

I had one cousin who had links with the guerrillas, but it was just him. And because of him, the paramilitaries said that all of our family were guerrillas. My family thinks that it was Kiko who killed my uncle Abel. On the day of the massacre, some community members had seen Kiko identify my uncle in a neighbor's house and take him to where he was killed.

None of the men in my family went to my uncle's funeral the day after the meeting. It was just the women and other people from the village. The men stayed in hiding.

A few months after the paramilitary massacre in his village, Fernando moved to the nearby city of Apartadó, where he worked on a banana plantation. The majority of the male members of Fernando's family also left the village, but his parents stayed behind. In 1995, following the murder of his older brother in the nearby town of Chigorodó, Fernando returned to the village, which was still dominated by the paramilitary commander Kiko.

KIKO USED TO LAUGH AS HE KILLED PEOPLE

One Sunday during the rainy season in 1997, I was at my friend's house, cleaning the revolver that we went hunting with. We had finished cleaning the revolver and had it wrapped in a cloth on top of table, when we saw Kiko standing right in front of us. He must have cut the wire fence surrounding the house and entered without us realizing. Kiko was short, fat, and dark-skinned, and he was dressed in blue jeans and a red shirt. He had a rifle, and a pistol tied to his leg. Kiko grabbed my friend's revolver, loaded it with bullets, and kept it in his hand. He didn't say anything and we didn't say anything to him. All three of us looked at each other. Kiko had the bad habit of not looking at you directly in the face; he would look at you out of the corner of his eye. I thought, *My God, could it be that this guy is going to kill us right here?* Neighbors had told me that Kiko laughed as he killed people.

My friend's wife had just had a baby, and there was a jar of baby food on a shelf. Kiko told me, "Hey, put that jar on top of the post over there." There was a post about fifty meters away outside the house. The houses in the countryside are open, so there wasn't a wall separating the yard from the room we were in. I was afraid because I thought that he was going to shoot me, but I put the jar on the post and came back to the house.

Kiko handed the revolver to my friend, took out his own pistol, and shot at the jar six times, but he didn't hit it. Then he said to my friend, "Now it's your turn." He was laughing and laughing. My friend shot at the jar twice and didn't hit it either. So Kiko took the revolver away from my friend and passed it to me. I didn't want to hit the jar and appear to be a guerrilla with good aim, so I just raised my hand and shot. I hit the post, and the jar fell!

Kiko put his pistol against my chest, called me a guerrilla and insulted me. I had the revolver in my hand and I put it up against his stomach. He looked down, lowered his weapon and said, "Okay, we'll leave it like that." Then he got on his horse and left.

After that, I would hide when I saw him passing by the main road next to our house. Kiko rode around on a horse that made a strange sound, so I knew whenever he was coming.

Two months after the incident with Kiko, I got work in the village taking people across a river by boat. One morning, I was taking people across the river when I saw Kiko at the other side of the river, coming back drunk from a party at a cockfighting ring. He got in the boat, and I crossed him to the other side of the river. During the crossing, he had his head lowered, looking at me. I didn't look at his face; I looked at his hands. Finally, he got off at the other side of the river, and he pushed the boat away with his foot. When he lowered his hand to his belt, I saw his intentions, and I dove into the water and swam to the bottom. He shot at me three times. The people on the riverbanks yelled at him and took the pistol away from him.

After that happened, people told me it was better that I leave, because Kiko was going to kill me. So, four days later I went to work on a farm in a nearby town called La Toyosa, where one of my aunts lived.

I stayed there for four months until I ran into a friend from my village on a bus. He told me that the paramilitaries had killed Kiko. One night, Kiko had been drinking at the town bar. At four in the morning, as he was leaving, he told the people in the bar that he would kill the first person he came across. A twelve-year-old kid was riding on a mule when Kiko came across him and he killed him. The presidents of the Community Action Boards[5] from four villages in the area went to a higher-ranking paramilitary commander and complained that Kiko had killed the boy. The paramilitaries investigated who the boy was and found out that he came from a poor family who didn't have anything to do with the guerrillas and wasn't suspected of anything. Finally, two paramilitaries shot and killed Kiko in a nearby village.

I'M NOT CUT OUT FOR THE WORK YOU DO

El Alemán,[6] one of the top paramilitary commanders in the country, came to run the area in 1998. He wanted to recruit me because at that time I was the secretary of the village Community Action Board. At the end of that year he sent six guys to my house and they told me, "The boss wants you to work for him." I asked, "Who's the boss?" They said, "The number one." I asked, "But who?" They didn't want to tell me, so I said, "If you don't tell me, I'm not going to work for a person that I don't know." They

---

[5] Community Action Boards are small civil organizations that represent villages, communities and neighborhoods. Each board has a president who is elected to a three-year term.

[6] Freddy Rendón Herrera, alias El Alemán (in English, "the German") was a top leader of the United Self-Defense Forces of Colombia (AUC) national paramilitary coalition, and commanded the Élmer Cárdenas bloc.

said, "It's El Alemán." I had heard people mention El Alemán before but I had never personally met him. So I said, "Tell El Alemán that I'm good where I am, thank God."

At the time I was planting tomatoes, corn, yucca, plantains, and rice. I told them, "I live off what I plant and what the land produces. I'm not cut out for the work that you guys do. I don't like to be ordered to unjustly kill a person who did nothing to me or to society." The guys said, "Fine," and they left.

About a month later, El Alemán showed up at my house with some 150 men. He was with two tall, pretty, white monas,[7] and he was wearing a green sweater. He had pistols tied to his legs.

We stood outside the house and he asked what my reason was for not wanting to join, if it was money or what. I told him, "When I go to work I don't ask, *How much money will I be paid?* If the work serves society and I have to work for no money, I'll do it. I don't like to take any side. I like to help communities." I've always been like that; I've liked community work since I was young.

El Alemán kept his head bowed and stared at the ground while he kicked the dirt in the yard. I told him, "If I join you, you're going to order me to kill, and I wouldn't be capable of that. So what would you do? Kill me." I said it calmly because I don't get scared in the moment that something is happening; I get scared after. He said that he respected my decision, but that he hoped it didn't go beyond that. I don't know what he meant by that.

I felt cornered, because by that time everyone I had grown up with was working for El Alemán. I even had some family working for him. Everyone went around with a walkie-talkie, a pistol, and a rifle. The paramilitaries would pay them 800,000 pesos[8] per month. From the little that my family could sell from my farm, we only made about

---

[7] In Colombia, mona is a term used to refer to a blonde or light-skinned person.

[8] About U.S.$460 in 1999.

120,000 to 160,000 pesos[9] each month. When my friends were paid, they'd show up and invite me out to parties. They'd show me how much easy money they made and tried to convince me to join the paramilitaries, but I'd say no. But of the ten or twelve people from my village who joined the paramilitaries, all are dead now except for one, and he's in jail. Because after staying in the area for five or six months and being trained, they were sent to Chocó province, where the guerrillas killed them.

I became afraid to stay in Necoclí because I thought that maybe the paramilitaries would take reprisals against me for not wanting to join them. So I went to Apartadó again in February 1999 and started to work on a banana plantation. Every day that we went to the plantation, we'd count at least one or two dead people there on the road to the farm, or at the entrance. There was a dispute between the guerrillas and the paramilitaries for control of the area and the banana workers, and both groups took people to the road to kill them.

Fernando quit his job at the banana plantation in 2003 when he realized that the FARC was looking for him. At that time, they suspected that he was collaborating with the paramilitaries. He went on to pick coca in the Bajo Cauca region of Antioquia and Tierralta, Córdoba, but in 2006 he had to flee from the paramilitaries once again, and returned to his village in Necoclí.

THE PLAN WAS TO FACE UP TO THEM

I returned to live with my parents in the village of Ecuador in the beginning of 2006, when I was twenty-nine years old. I didn't have a partner or children. With all my moving around it was hard. No one was going to put up with that.

---

[9] About U.S.$70–$90 in 1999.

The paramilitary commander El Alemán turned himself in at the end of that year as part of a demobilization process for the paramilitaries.[10] After the paramilitary demobilization, there were less paramilitaries, but they were still there and they continued patrolling at night. Eighty-five percent of the people who demobilized from El Alemán's paramilitary bloc weren't paramilitaries. They were peasants and people from town who the paramilitaries paid so that they would pretend to be paramilitaries at the demobilization ceremonies. But the real paramilitaries didn't turn themselves in; they didn't demobilize.

A lot of people who had been displaced from the area started coming back. But I saw that they didn't enjoy their rights to health care, free education, humanitarian aid, and housing subsidies because they didn't know about them.[11] In November 2007, a two-year-old girl from my village died because her parents didn't have the money to get her medical attention. If the parents had had a document saying that they were displaced, they could have gone to the hospital and not been charged anything. About three hundred people went to the girl's funeral. After the girl was buried, I stood on top of a tomb in the cemetery and I felt the sadness and need in the faces of the members of the community. So right after, I told the displaced people from the area to get me their documents, photocopies of their IDs, and the registration of their kids. I collected all the documentation, went to the town of Necoclí, had a meeting with the

---

[10] El Alemán and a faction of his Élmer Cárdenas bloc partook in a demobilization ceremony in August 2006. This was part of the government's demobilization program for the AUC paramilitary coalition, in which more than 30,000 supposed fighters participated in demobilization ceremonies and pledged to cease criminal activity between 2003 and 2006.

[11] Displaced people who register with the government are entitled to certain types of state aid.

coordinator of Social Action[12] and presented him with all of the cases so they would be included in the government registry of displaced people. I'd been displaced like three times by then, but I myself was never accepted in the registry.

Eventually, I represented families from nine villages who were mostly victims of paramilitaries. People would give me 100 pesos for a coffee, or 1,000[13] when they could. We would have raffles and such to raise money to make photocopies.

Some of the families could go back to their land and others couldn't. Between 1994 and 2001 in the majority of the Urabá region—in the municipalities of Chigorodó, Mutatá, Dabeiba, Necoclí, Arboletes, San Juan de Urabá and San Pedro de Urabá—the paramilitaries had gone directly to people's homes. They would put a pistol on the table and ask the person, "Well, are you going to sell me your farm or is your widow going to sell it to me cheaper?" Some people would sell for between 50,000 and 100,000 pesos[14] per hectare, which was very cheap. If you didn't sell to them, they'd come back to kill you in two weeks. Then they would take your chickens and cattle and sell them, and then they would burn down the house.

The families used to have farms of up to twenty hectares. There'd be one or two thousand hectares in each village, but then the paramilitaries came and knocked down all of the fences between the farms and made one big farm.

The paramilitaries converted most of the stolen land in Necoclí into pastures for cattle. African palm crops that produce palm oil were planted in other places in Urabá, like Belén de Bajirá. Sometimes the very owners of the land would have to go to work for the people occupying their land, just so they could get paid for a day's work. Thank God my parents never

---

[12] The government entity entrusted with coordinating assistance to the displaced population, to the poor, and to victims of violence. Social Action was replaced by the Department for Social Prosperity in 2012.

[13] About 5 U.S. cents and 50 cents, respectively.

[14] About U.S.$64 to $128 in 1994, and $22 to $44 in 2001.

sold our farm to the paramilitaries. The paramilitaries hadn't taken any of the land in my village. I imagine it's probably because it flooded a lot there, so maybe it didn't serve their purposes.

At first, the association of displaced people I worked with wasn't asking for land back because we were afraid to talk about it. Back then, we were only making certain claims to the rights of displaced people; for example, we demanded that the government give families humanitarian aid.

But one day around July 2008, I heard on the radio that there was a group of people in Mutatá, Antioquia that was directly occupying land that had been stolen by paramilitaries. There was a number to call for anyone who had land problems. That's when I called Benigno Gil. Benigno was a displaced person who had lost 700 hectares to the paramilitaries, and he was leading the land occupations.

I went to join him on his farm that he was trying to recover in Mutatá. There were people there from all of Urabá. I spent two months there with them and got to know Benigno really well. I was part of his security and he didn't go anywhere without me. We organized and called ourselves the Peasants' Table. Then we decided to spread out, and I was put in charge of farm occupations in the northern part of Urabá.

I sent a letter to a radio station telling them to advertise a meeting at the community center in Necoclí. More than seven hundred people showed up; the crowd barely fit in the building. I introduced Benigno and some other land leaders. Benigno said that the people had to lose their fear and return to their land that the paramilitaries had taken away. That same day, people voted for me to represent them in the land occupying process. I didn't get paid to do it, but at the time I also worked on other people's farms in the village two or three days a week.

Between a hundred and a hundred and fifty of us would go to someone's farm with land titles in hand. The owners couldn't go alone, because if you started to make the claim by yourself, you'd disappear. We would tell the administrator of the farm to please leave, because the farm wasn't his. Some would leave and some would resist and say that the land was theirs. In the central part of Urabá, many of the businessmen have false land titles. In Urabá, all of the state entities are still co-opted by the paramilitaries. Nobody in the area liked us, neither the army nor the police.

We each had a machete, a rucksack on our shoulder, a pillow, a blanket, and a hammock. During the day we'd clean up the village, widen the paths, and fix the bridges. At night we'd be on the lookout, with two-hour shifts each.

We'd stay at a farm for one or two months, and when we saw that there weren't problems, we'd leave ten people behind. And then we'd go to other farms. People saw that we were getting results in recovering land, and more and more displaced farmers got involved. Toward the end of 2008, we were able to recover about 1,000 hectares of land.

In October that year, I went back to occupying Benigno Gil's farm with more than sixty other people. One night, at around 8:30 p.m., two members of the Peasants' Table called and told us that about eight trucks were coming in our direction. The Peasants' Table members were twenty-five minutes away on another farm. They said that the trucks looked like they belonged to paramilitaries, because who else was going to have that many trucks? Four days earlier, Benigno had met with an army colonel from the area who had given him his number and told him to call right away if anything happened. So we called the army, which had a base about fifteen minutes away. Then we started to see the lights of the trucks coming towards us. Everyone got scared, but the plan was to face up to them, to stand together in front of them and see what they wanted. After standing for fifteen minutes, an army truck came. When it arrived, the other trucks stopped. Then shortly after, the trucks turned around.

About two weeks later the mayor of Mutatá sent some two hundred riot police to remove us by force. They said that we were squatters and they sent Benigno to jail for the night. The rest of us left and went to another farm that the Peasants' Table was occupying. My friends called Benigno the next morning and he said that he had been released from jail and that he was fine. He said he was going to Apartadó to file a complaint in the Attorney General's office.

In November 2008, I led forty people in the occupation of a farm in a forest area in northern Urabá called the Filo del Caballo. It's an area controlled by Giovanni, a top regional paramilitary commander of the group called the Urabeños.[15] They had cocaine labs there. One afternoon when we were playing cards at the farm, six paramilitaries dressed as civilians with revolvers and pistols came to talk to me, saying that Giovanni had sent them. One of them said that if we thought we were tough, they were tougher than us. I said, "Your boss didn't pay for the farm that we're on. We're going to go onto the farms that you all didn't pay for." But they were nervous because the army showed up around there and Giovanni's people thought we called them.

A week later I called another leader from the Peasants' Table to see how things were going. He told me that Benigno had been killed the day before in Chigorodó.

I didn't say anything about it to anyone, so people wouldn't get scared. But I was afraid, and I didn't sleep that night, wondering what would happen next, if they would come for me too. I was also worried that the people participating in the occupations would become discouraged. And I was sad about losing a friend.

When you get involved in this sort of movement, the other members become your family. You build up trust, you share personal things with them, and you spend more time with the group members than with your own family. After his death, I was down for a long time.

THAT'S WHEN THE PERSECUTION BEGAN

There was a meeting in Medellín scheduled for January 8, 2009, where the different displaced persons' groups from Necoclí, Mutatá, and Turbo would form the Association of Victims for the Restitution of Land and Assets in Urabá (Asovirestibi). So on January 5 I left the farm we were

---

[15] The Urabeños are a neo-paramilitary group that formed after older paramilitary groups had demobilized. Giovanni's real name was Juan de Dios Úsuga David.

occupying in Filo del Caballo and got a ride in a public car to Necoclí, where I planned to stay for a couple of days before going on to Medellín. On my way to Necoclí, two paramilitaries stopped the car and told me to get out. Everyone in the car looked at each other because they thought that the guys were going to kill me. No one said anything.

I wasn't afraid at that moment and got out of the car. I was thirsty, so with the paramilitaries watching me, I walked over to a little store by the side of the road and bought a soda. Then, two more guys showed up. One of them called Giovanni on his cell phone and said, "Boss, we have the target here." He walked away and talked on the phone for a while longer. Then he came back and passed me the cell phone. Giovanni told me to keep quiet because people had been "fucking around with the land" too long. He said that he didn't want any more bloodshed in Urabá, and that I shouldn't just take it as an empty threat, because they had already killed Benigno.

I didn't respond. I just passed the cell phone back to the paramilitary, who said to me, "Brother, I'm going to give you some advice. Don't come back here. The order that we had was to kill you in front of the people on the farm." Then they let me go. Later that day, I called my friends at Filo del Caballo and they told me that the paramilitaries had arrived at the farm that morning at six, a half-hour after I had left there.

I didn't go to the meeting in Medellín. I laid low and went back to work on my parents' farm, but I didn't withdraw from the association. That's when the persecution began. The paramilitaries started to follow me. The day after I arrived in my village, they put a paramilitary dressed as a civilian at the entrance to the village and another one at the exit. They sat there watching everyone who went by. They knew when I came and went, and who I talked to. Over the next few months, they watched everything I did.

One day in April, I heard on the news that the authorities had captured Don Mario, one of the leaders of the paramilitaries in the area.[16] I thought that his arrest would be a problem because Don Mario had been staying close to the farm where my family lived, and that the paramilitaries might think I was the informant who'd given information to the police, which wasn't true.

The next day I was in a car heading to a meeting of displaced people at a village in Necoclí, when a community leader there called me and said, "There are some guys here asking for you." He said that they'd been waiting for me all day, and that they'd stopped every car that arrived to see if I was in it. He told me not to go to the village, and I didn't.

I called two of the other Asovirestibi leaders and they told me to leave Necoclí because the paramilitaries might kill me. So I immediately left for Apartadó, without packing any clothes or anything. I slept in a little room in the back of the Asovirestibi office there for about a month and a half. Then I went to live on a farm there that belongs to Carmen, the leader of Asovirestibi. She and her husband paid me to work on their farm, and I lived off of that. I stayed there for about six or seven months.

THE PROPHECY

At the time, the police were offering a reward for information about Giovanni, his brother Otoniel, and El Indio.[17] So I gave information to a police colonel in Apartadó about where the three of them moved around. I also gave them information about where a cocaine processing lab was located, and the police went and burned it down. I wanted the money, but I was never given a reward. My thinking was also that if the security

---

[16] Daniel Rendón Herrera, alias Don Mario, is the brother of El Alemán and a former leader of the AUC paramilitary coalition and Urabeños neo-paramilitary group.

[17] At that time, both Otoniel and El Indio were also leaders of the Urabeños neo-paramilitary group.

forces caught those commanders, many displaced people could return to their land again.

Someone took a photo of me when I was talking to the police and sold the photo to Giovanni. I found out because some paramilitaries showed the photo to someone I know in Urabá.

Giovanni started searching heaven and Earth for me. My mom called me on a Sunday in January 2010 and said that the paramilitaries had gone to her house. They told her they were going to kill me because I'd given information to the police, and that they regretted not having killed me the year before.

The next afternoon, my aunt, who lives in Apartadó, called me and told me that some guys had passed by her house on a motorcycle four times. So I called one of the leaders of Asovirestibi and told him what was happening. He called a government official in Bogotá, who then called a police colonel in Urabá.

The police picked me up and took me to live in the police station in Chigorodó[18] so that I'd be protected. I lived in a jail cell. I could walk around the station, but I didn't go out onto the street unless I was with three or four SIJIN agents. One of the policemen at the station told me to watch out, because there were a lot of policemen there who worked for the BACRIM.[19] He said that they'd know about everything I said at the station.

When I was living at the station, some DAS agents were sent from Bogotá to evaluate my level of risk, to see whether I deserved protection measures from the Interior Ministry's protection program.[20] I was

---

[18] Chigorodó is about twenty-four kilometers away from Apartadó.

[19] BACRIM, which stands for "Emerging Criminal Gangs," is the official name the Colombian government uses for neo-paramilitary groups.

[20] The Department of Administrative Security (DAS) was the government's national intelligence service. It was dissolved in 2011, following various scandals concerning illegal surveillance and collaboration with paramilitaries. Before being closed, DAS agents often conducted "risk evaluations" to determine whether individuals could benefit from the government's protection program.

rejected; they decided that my level of risk didn't warrant protection.

Then after almost three months, around April 2010, I left the station. I got tired of living there; I couldn't even go out onto the street by myself. The police escorted me to Mutatá, and from there I drove to Medellín in Carmen's car. Two weeks after I arrived in Medellín, I found work in construction. The contractor I was working for was a good guy. I explained my situation to him, and he had me work at different sites so that the paramilitaries wouldn't find me.

While I was in Medellín, other leaders from Asovirestibi were killed. The death of Albeiro Valdés in May was an especially hard blow for me, because I had accompanied him to occupy his farm and we worked together there.

On Thursday, October 21, a car arrived in Medellín that the Interior Ministry had approved for me as part of my protection scheme.[21] It wasn't bulletproof, but at least I didn't have to take public transportation. They finally approved it because of the deaths of the other leaders from Asovirestibi.[22]

The next day I left work at nine, and two guys were waiting for me in front of the building where I was working. One of the guys took out a gun and tried to fire it, but it wouldn't go off. I took off running, went back into the building, and escaped.

On Saturday, I left for Apartadó, where my sister Arelis lived, and arrived that night. On Sunday I hired a driver, because the Interior Ministry doesn't let protected people drive the cars they're provided with. Arelis suggested I go to church that day so I went to an Evangelical church. A woman there told me a prophecy. She stood behind me, put her hands

---

[21] Colombia's Ministry of Interior and Justice (now just Ministry of Interior) runs the government program that provides protectionary measures—including bodyguards, cars, cell phones, and bulletproof vests—to threatened individuals including human rights defenders and trade unionists.

[22] Albeiro Valdés Martínez was killed on May 10, 2010, and Hernando Pérez was killed on September 19, 2010.

on my head, and talked close to my ear. She said, "You've gone through a lot of difficult things, and they will continue happening, but God will protect you. You're walking, and you'll trip and fall, and you'll get back up again." That was the prophecy.

I ALREADY SURVIVED THIS ONE

On Monday night I ate dinner at my sister Arelis's house and my other sister Elsy was also there. When I saw that it was getting dark outside, I told them, "I'm going to go because it's getting really late." Whenever I left a place, I'd look to see who was around. But as I left my sister's house I didn't look around because I was looking for Carmen's number in my cell phone. I walked to the car where the driver was waiting for me, and opened the car door. When I sat down in the passenger seat, I felt the shot in my face. Blood came out of my mouth and showered the front of the car. I immediately remembered the words that the woman had told me at church the day before.

I was shot again and again. I acted as if I were dead and stayed silent. The driver opened the car door and got out. The gunmen must have thought that the driver was armed, so they took off running. The driver also ran away.

I was conscious. I didn't feel anything because the impact of the bullets numbed my flesh. I hit the horn so that the driver would come back. Neighbors started to crowd around the car, and began shouting that I was alive. I kept honking so that the driver would come, because I knew that the guys were going to come back to finish me off.

Finally the driver came back with my sister Elsy, who got in the car and hugged me. She held my head with her hand because my mouth was filling up with blood. As the driver took us to the hospital, my sister told me to say something to her. I could hear, but I couldn't talk, so they thought I was dead. At the time, I wasn't afraid of dying. I wasn't having difficulty breathing, and I remembered what the woman had told me at church: "You'll get back up again." I thought, *God willing, I already survived this one.* When I got to the hospital, they laid me down on the stretcher, and I fainted.

I stayed in intensive care for three days. There were two police officers at the entrance to my hospital room because there was fear that the gunmen were going to come back to finish me off.

I had to be transferred to the hospital in Rio Negro, outside of Medellín. I don't remember arriving there. The gunmen had shot me in my shoulder, my armpit, and my face. The bullet had exited underneath my jaw, knocked out eight teeth and split my tongue in two pieces. I stayed in the hospital for about two months. During that time, the doctors performed a lot of operations on me—I've had twelve surgeries now—and I only ate pure liquids. It was difficult in the beginning, because I went for those two months without speaking. Now, my lower teeth don't fit with my upper teeth, and my jaw and teeth hurt when it's cold outside.

I'M FOLLOWING A PATH

A relative of mine has a friend who works for the paramilitaries, and he told my mom that when Giovanni realized that I hadn't died, he offered a 50 million-peso[23] reward to anyone who killed me. I was afraid, especially because I'd learned that the SIJIN in Apartadó had found my photo on the cell phones of captured paramilitaries.

Today I live in an apartment in Montería with two bodyguards, my girlfriend Rosa, and her eleven-year-old daughter. I met Rosa before the attack, when I was working in construction in Medellín. After I was shot, she visited me in the hospital, and I got together with her in January 2011. I told her that if she was going to commit herself to this kind of life, we'd have to keep moving around. She's committed. She said that it didn't matter to her because she loves me.

I live off the gas money that the Interior Ministry gives me for the

---

[23] About U.S.$28,000.

new bulletproof SUV they assigned me, which is 1,500,000 pesos per month.[24] My bodyguards help me out a lot. We split the rent and groceries, and sometimes, when I don't have a peso to fill up the tank with gas, they pay for it.

What I've begged of God is that the paramilitaries don't do anything to my parents. My mom and dad still live on the same farm in Necoclí. Around June 2011, a relative told me that Giovanni had given the order to kill my dad. But Giovanni supposedly found out that my dad was sick and that he was about to die, and he decided that they should just wait for him to die.

I filed a complaint with the Attorney General's office, but I didn't tell my mom and dad about the kill order. My dad has high blood pressure and he's already furious with the paramilitaries.

At the time Rosa was about five months pregnant, and our first child was due that November. I thought having a child would give my girlfriend and I some tranquility. But that November, another member of Asovirestibi, Alejandro Padilla, was killed.

The police reported Alejandro's death as a traffic accident. But someone who saw Alejandro get killed called me the day after and said that two men had been waiting for Alejandro on a bridge. He said that they'd stopped him, thrown his motorcycle off the bridge and started to beat him with planks of wood. The next day Alejandro was found dead on the bridge.

I called the media and went on television saying that it hadn't been a traffic accident, but that Alejandro had been beaten to death. That same afternoon, two paramilitaries went to my parents' house and told my mom that if I kept talking on television, they were going to kill her and my dad. My son was born a few days later.

On January 1, 2012, the police killed Giovanni in Acandí, Chocó. That's made things more complicated for me. Now I've heard that the

---

[24] About U.S.$840.

reward for my death is up to 300 million pesos[25] because the Urabeños think that I, and other land leaders, tipped off the police about where Giovanni was.

Nine leaders of Asovirestibi have been killed. I don't know what will happen to me. I got involved in the land issue, but it wasn't consciously; I'm following a path, and I don't know where it's going or where it came from. I've given my life to defend the rights of other people, and I don't regret it.

---

[25] About U.S.$168,000.

APPENDICES

I. THE COLOMBIAN CONFLICT AND ITS ACTORS

By Winifred Tate

Colombia is best known to many Americans as a major source of illegal drugs, particularly cocaine, for the U.S. market. It is less widely known that Colombia is enmeshed in the longest running internal armed conflict in the Western hemisphere. Since the 1960s, the major actors in this conflict have included left-wing guerrillas attempting to take over the government, state security forces defending the existing political and economic power structures, and paramilitary groups allied with the military. In the past two decades these forces have evolved significantly, and the illegal drug trade has shaped them all.

For much of the past century, two parties—Liberals and Conservatives—have dominated Colombian political life. While in many ways the parties have been indistinguishable, with little difference between their economic and political platforms, they inspired intense allegiances that some scholars compared to a religious identity. In the winner-take-all political system established by the 1886 Constitution, the president appointed governors who in turn appointed mayors. Elected legislative assemblies, subject to strict review by national politicians,[1] fostered the kind of strong patron-client relationships among politicians and communities that encouraged back-room dealing and violence.

Political violence escalated throughout the 1930s, despite a strong economy fueled by high coffee prices and a U.S. indemnity payment for its intervention in support of Panama's secession from Colombia in 1903. Liberals accused Conservatives of wanting to physically liquidate the poor; the Conservatives in turn accused Liberals of allegiances they considered objectionable, with Communists, Jews, Protestants, and Masons.[2]

La Violencia, as the partisan violence of the 1940s and '50s is known, erupted with the April 9, 1948 assassination of Liberal populist Jorge Eliécer Gaitán in downtown Bogotá. Gaitán had formed his own third party in 1933, the National Revolutionary Leftist Union (UNIR), and was the front-runner for the 1950 presidential elections. Although the assassin was caught and lynched on the street, the sponsor of the crime remains unknown. Enraged Liberals began a three-day riot, known as el Bogotazo, resulting in the almost total destruction of downtown Bogotá. In an effort to parlay the general unrest into a revolutionary movement, Communist and Gaitanista leaders created "revolutionary juntas" in Bogotá and small-town radical strongholds (most notably Barrancabermeja and Puerto Berrío), but failed to galvanize cohesive support.

La Violencia dominated political life. During one debate, a Conservative shot and killed a Liberal on the floor of Congress. In the Colombian countryside, however, the conflict was much more severe. The main agents of Conservative rural terror were the pájaros (literally, "birds"), assassins who traveled throughout the country carrying out the dirty work of local political barons and urban, elite sponsors,[3] and the Chulavitas, peasants recruited from the Boyacá district of Chulavita to replace Liberal policemen dismissed from their positions by Conservative politicians. Liberal guerrillas commanded by men with noms de guerre like Sangre Negra (Black-blood) and Capitán Venganza (Captain Vengeance) also patrolled the Colombian countryside targeting political opponents. Much of the violence involved torture and bloody public displays; killers developed elaborate mutilation techniques. Land conflict, particularly in areas of lucrative coffee production, fueled the struggle: coffee provided approximately 80 percent of the foreign-exchange revenues for the Conservative government,[4] and the three most violent provinces (Caldas, Antioquia and Tolima) produced two thirds of Colombian coffee and 60 percent of the deaths during this period. During La Violencia, an estimated 200,000 to 300,000 people were killed.

La Violencia de-escalated with Colombia's only modern military dictatorship, when General Rojas Pinilla, with significant civilian support, took power in 1953. Five years later, the traditional parties reestablished their power by removing Rojas and instituting a power-sharing agreement known as the National Front. By alternating power between the two traditional parties and maintaining the system of political appointments whereby presidents appointed governors, who in turn appointed mayors, no third-party participation was allowed, nor any electoral choice offered among candidates. Some historians say the power-sharing agreement marked the end of La Violencia; however, political killings continued and periodization is subject to debate.

THE FORMATION OF MARXIST GUERRILLA GROUPS

Colombia's largest and oldest guerrilla group traces its origins to La Violencia, when peasant self-defense forces fled government and Conservative militia persecution into unsettled lands, a process later described as "armed colonization."[5] Their leaders were larger-than-life figures in the model of Robin Hood, combining armed robbery with peasant resistance. Although weakened by amnesty offers from the government which enticed many leaders into civilian life, and battered by overwhelming counterinsurgency campaigns, these armed enclaves survived into the 1960s as "independent republics" operating outside the control of the central government. Guerrilla leaders, radicalized by the military campaigns against them, declared themselves the Southern Bloc and issued a national agrarian platform in a meeting on July 20, 1964. Two years later, at the second national conference of guerrilla groups, the leadership adopted a Marxist platform and announced the birth of the Revolutionary Armed Forces of Colombia (FARC). For the next two decades, the FARC remained a loose federation of poorly organized armed peasant groups.

The next generation of guerrilla organizations emerged in the 1960s and '70s. Students, union organizers, and other activists were inspired to take up armed opposition by the examples of colonial liberation movements across the world, and by the Cuban revolution closer to home. Despite impassioned—and sometimes lethal—sectarian disagreements among these groups in Colombia, the myriad armed radical organizations that mushroomed throughout this period generally shared central elements of a political vision: one in which revolution was imminent, wealthy politicians completely blocked any possibility of national development, and a monumental political crisis was brewing.

One of the most important of these groups, the National Liberation Army (ELN), was the brainchild of a small group of Colombian students with close ties to progressive Catholics. These students had traveled to Cuba and vowed to recreate the Cuban revolution in Colombia upon their return. The ELN's first combat operations began on January 7, 1965, with sixteen combatants. By the early 1970s, the group was almost completely annihilated by a series of successful counterinsurgency operations.

A smaller guerrilla group, the People's Liberation Army (EPL), also formed with Communist aspirations: the EPL emerged from the Communist Youth and the Marxist Leninist Communist Party (PCML), a legal political party that sided with the Chinese during the Sino–Soviet split.

Members of yet another group, the dissident political movement called the National Popular Alliance (ANAPO), formed their nationalist guerrilla force in the early 1970s. The April 19 Movement (M-19) took their name from what they viewed as electoral fraud that prevented the ANAPO's candidate from assuming the presidency on election day, April 19, 1970. The group specialized in dramatic symbolic gestures; for their first official act, in 1974, they stole the sword of colonial liberator Simón Bolívar from a Bogotá museum, vowing to return it when real democracy returned to Colombia (although the sword was then lost). Other actions included stealing milk to give to the poor, the nighttime theft of weapons from the army's northern Bogotá arsenal, and taking fourteen ambassadors as hostages during a dinner party at the Dominican embassy.

THE MILITARY, PARAMILITARY GROUPS,
AND THE NARCOTICS TRADE

Throughout the 1960s and 1970s, the Colombian military remained small, with a budget of less than 2 percent of the country's GDP, and its combat operations were minimal. In part this reflected its distinct role in Colombian society; historically, Colombia's military had been a marginal force, fractured under the authority of regional bosses until well into the twentieth century. In exchange for their ongoing nonintervention in electoral politics, understood as political neutrality, the military was granted authority to design and implement national security policy largely independent of any civilian oversight. Originally known as the Lleras Doctrine, from the 1958 speech to the armed forces by then-president-elect Alberto Lleras, this historic trade-off was instrumental in Colombia's lack of defined policy regarding its national security.[6] In areas where the guerrilla presence increased, the army often opted to avoid direct confrontation, but train and arm local civilians as "paramilitary" forces, which had been legally authorized in 1968. These legal paramilitary forces often overlapped with illegal death squads that began operating with local military support in the 1970s, such as the American Anti-Communist Alliance (AAA), active in the Magdalena Medio region.

Colombia's role in the illicit narcotics trade began to impact all of these groups during the 1980s. In that decade, the Medellín and Cali family-based cartels, refining coca paste produced in Bolivia and Peru and shipping it to U.S.-based retailers, came to control a billion-dollar cocaine industry. Drug traffickers began buying large parcels of land as a means of money laundering and gaining political influence. According to one estimate, as many as six million hectares changed hands between 1985 and 1995, in what some analysts called a "reverse agrarian reform."[7] Once they became owners of vast haciendas, drug traffickers needed protection from guerrillas, whose primary fundraising techniques involved boleteo (extortion), vacunas ("vaccination" against guerrilla attack), and, increasingly, kidnapping wealthy rural landowners. Landowners, even those outside of the drug trade, and drug traffickers funded "self-defense" forces, providing training, weapons, and salaries, and coordinating operations with local military commanders who shared a counterinsurgency agenda. The self-defense groups attacked guerrillas and their perceived supporters, including peasants, community activists, religious leaders, and opposition politicians promoting agrarian reform.

Political reforms began to allow broader electoral participation, but violence targeting politicians escalated. A series of laws in the late 1980s increased local control over state financial resources, and allowed the popular election of mayors and other local officials who had previously been appointed to their posts. Guerrillas and their demobilized members participating in peace talks in the 1980s and 1990s created new political parties, including the Patriotic Union (the UP, founded by the Colombian Communist Party and the FARC in 1985, during the guerrillas' ultimately unsuccessful talks with the government), and the M-19 Democratic Alliance, which was instrumental in the referendum resulting in a new Constitution in 1991. At the same time, paramilitary forces, including gunmen linked to military intelligence and to narcotics trafficking operations (particularly the Medellín cartel), killed thousands of activists and other first-time participants in Colombia's electoral system, including numerous UP mayors, several members of Congress, and two UP presidential candidates. Additionally, the FARC and other guerrilla groups periodically attempted to sabotage elections by declaring armed strikes, threatening candidates, and sometimes assassinating them.

GUERRILLA EXPANSION

In the 1990s, the Colombian guerrillas increasingly relied on criminal activities to fund their military and political operations. This was not entirely new: throughout their history, Colombian guerrillas had relied on kidnapping and extortion to fund many of their operations. The ELN, for example, had been able to rebuild its organization in the 1980s thanks in part to ransom and extortion payments—a German multinational construction company, Mannesmann Anlagenbau AG, admitted paying more than $2 million in 1985 for ransom during the building of the Caño Limón pipeline along the Venezuelan border (long an ELN stronghold), and the ELN claimed to receive more than $20 million in total ransom during the construction project.[8] During the 1990s, guerrilla groups, particularly the FARC, dramatically increased this sort of criminal activity. Colombia led the world with the number of kidnappings; more than 3,700 people were reported kidnapped in 2000, with 57 percent attributed to the guerrillas. During so-called pescas milagrosas, ("miraculous fishing" expeditions), guerrillas set up improvised roadblocks and conducted mass kidnappings based on the presumed wealth of their hostages. According to Colombian governmental statistics, the FARC and the ELN received approximately U.S.$1.2 billion in ransom between 1991 and 1998.

Additionally, changes in Colombia's role in the illegal narcotics trade played a significant role in the FARC's expansion during the 1990s. For the first time, Colombia became a major producer of coca, the raw material for cocaine, which grew in mountains and remote lowland jungle regions, many of which were historic strongholds of the FARC. Initially, the FARC was solely involved with taxing coca production by small farmers, but progressively moved up the production chain, taxing intermediaries, trading cocaine for weapons, and reportedly trafficking cocaine in Brazil and Mexico, until revenue from the drug trade provided the majority of the FARC's revenues, with estimates ranging from $100 million to $200 million a year.[9] The FARC used this money to more than quadruple their forces—they numbered approximately 18,000 by the end of the 1990s—as well as to build substantial urban militias.[10] A series of exceptionally daring raids on military barracks, such as the November 1, 1998 attack by 1,200 guerrilla troops on the remote jungle capital of Mitú, led many analysts to conclude that the FARC had adopted the tactics of a standing army. Some claimed the FARC controlled 40 percent of the country, although few noted that this territory was the largely uninhabited southwestern flooded jungle lowlands; guerrilla "control" would have been more accurately described as free range in abandoned outlying regions. The FARC's military expansion also included the use of land mines and improvised gas cylinder mortars that have killed hundreds, and possibly thousands, of civilians, though exact numbers are almost impossible to calculate. One infamous gas cylinder mortar attack, occurring in Bojayá, Chocó province on May 2, 2002, killed 79 people and displaced more than 5,750.[11]

THE AUC: FROM REGIONAL RENEGADES TO POLITICAL OPERATORS

Paramilitary forces expanded their military operations and political agenda during the 1990s as well. In part, this resulted from changes in the structure of the narcotics trafficking industry; as the heads of the Medellín and Cali cartels were killed or jailed in the early 1990s, a new generation of regional traffickers and warlords emerged. The leaders of this new generation, such as Salvatore Mancuso and Jorge 40, worked with paramilitary traffickers who had come up through the cartel hierarchy, such as Don Berna and the Castaño brothers. At the same time, the Colombian government created a new legal structure for rural defense forces, known as the Convivir, which were enthusiastically supported by former President Álvaro Uribe during his tenure as governor of Antioquia (1995-1997). Officially launched in 1994, the Convivir often served as front organizations for paramilitary groups. Following numerous complaints of participation in human rights abuses, a 1997 Constitutional Court ruling maintained that they were legal, but prohibited them from collecting intelligence for the security forces and from possessing military-issued weapons.[12]

That same year, paramilitary leaders, including charismatic spokesman Carlos Castaño, announced the creation of a new national coordinating body, the United Self-Defense Forces of Colombia (AUC). The AUC proclaimed a national command structure to represent and organize regional groups, and issued a statement announcing a campaign of military offensives into new regions of the country "according to the operational capacity of each regional group." Newly created "mobile squads"—elite training and combat units—carried out these operations, targeting the civilian populations of these areas in hundreds of massacres, often with the close coordination and logistical support of local military commanders. The first operation after the implementation of this plan was the July 1997 massacre in Mapiripán, Meta, when, from July 15-20, some two hundred gunmen from the AUC took control of Mapiripán, killing dozens of people and throwing their dismembered bodies in a river. After the massacre, AUC chief Carlos Castaño promised "many more Mapiripáns." The AUC went on to commit more than 240 massacres between 1997 and 2002, according to the Human Rights Observatory of the office of the Vice President. Paramilitary gunmen targeted civilians and presumed guerrilla sympathizers in guerrilla strongholds, pushing them into remote rural areas and breaking the supply networks of local residents previously willing to provide insurgents with food, gasoline, and other refined products.

During this period, paramilitary forces transformed themselves from regional renegades to political operators respected in many quarters, and valid interlocutors worthy of sitting at the negotiating table with the government. This metamorphosis involved an increase in violence alongside a substantial public relations campaign, aimed at changing public perceptions at home and abroad. Paramilitary leaders attempted to gain political legitimacy with the public through sophisticated websites, frequent media interviews, and the creation of NGOs. Additionally, many sectors of the country's security forces tolerated and supported Colombian paramilitaries even while they functioned as armies with their own doctrine, chain of command, iconography (such as uniforms, emblems, and hymns), sophisticated weaponry, and regulations governing social life in the regions where they operated. Colombian commentators during this period referred to paramilitary groups as the "armed wing" of the official state security forces—in many regions, better equipped and trained than the military due to resources from narcotics trafficking, and seen as more successful in counterinsurgency operations.

EXPANDING STATE SECURITY WITH INTERNATIONAL AID

In the late 1990s, the Colombian security forces began a significant expansion, first under the Pastrana administration (1998-2002) and accelerated by the following Álvaro Uribe government (2002-2010). From 2000 to 2007, the number of standing troops increased by 45 percent, growing from 275,000 to almost 400,000; five divisions expanded to seven, and numerous elite special units were created (including the roving mobile brigades, high mountain battalions, and anti-terrorist special forces units). During this period, the defense budget increased dramatically, from 3.4 percent of the GDP in 2000 to 6.3 percent in 2007 (approximately U.S. $7 billion).[13] Much of this transformation was encouraged by the U.S., which began an ongoing series of aid programs with the passage of Plan Colombia, in 2000. The initial package directed approximately 80 percent toward military aid, much of it for training and equipping counternarcotics units of the Colombian military. The U.S. delivered helicopters to improve troop mobility, shared intelligence, and provided equipment and training to increase Colombia's human-intelligence-gathering and technological-surveillance capacity. During his administration, President Uribe also increased police coverage to all municipalities, and attempted to bring permanent local military outposts into many areas. Beginning in 2004, U.S. advisors helped coordinate a major counterinsurgency campaign called Plan Patriota, targeting guerrilla forces in the south.

By the latter half of the first decade of the twenty-first century, guerrilla groups were significantly weakened by military and paramilitary attacks. President Pastrana had been elected in 1998 on a peace platform, but following widespread criminal activity in a large demilitarized zone in southern Colombia, and the February 2002 FARC hijacking of a domestic civilian airline, the government abandoned its peace negotiations with the guerrilla group. The FARC's most senior leader, founder Manuel "Sureshot" Marulanda, died of natural causes in 2008, and a series of military strikes killed a number of senior leaders (Raúl Reyes in 2008, Mono Jojoy in 2010, and Sureshot's successor, Alfonso Cano, in 2011). The number of FARC troops declined from an estimated high of 20,000 in 2002 to 8,000 in 2010. The ELN's estimated membership of 5,000 combat troops declined to 1,500, concentrated primarily along the border with Venezuela and in southwestern Colombia.

In the face of these setbacks, both the FARC and the ELN returned to traditional guerrilla tactics. More recently, they have been reported to be developing strategic alliances with criminal groups, forcibly recruiting children to replenish their ranks, and carrying out sporadic attacks in regional strongholds. To this day, the ELN and FARC continue to attack with land mines, gas cylinders, and car bombs, and commit massacres against civilians.

PARAMILITARY DEMOBILIZATION

In 2002, President Uribe began to promote peace talks with the AUC leadership. Under the auspices of the Catholic Church, the group's first formal agreement to disband was signed by the government and five of the major AUC leaders on July 15, 2003.[14] The first collective demobilization of paramilitary fighters occurred in November 2003; by the end of 2006, more than 32,000 people had participated in collective demobilization ceremonies, pledged to cease criminal activity, and entered reintegration programs. The government effectively amnestied the vast majority of those who demobilized, and never investigated their crimes. According to national and international observers, the process was profoundly flawed; many commanders were believed to have retained weapons and continued to wield power, even after the demobilizations. A number of the people who took part in demobilization ceremonies were local, unemployed men paid to participate in the place of paramilitary fighters. The government also implemented special legislation known as the Justice and Peace Law (2005), which offered AUC members already convicted or facing prosecution for severe crimes a single reduced sentence of five to eight years in exchange for confession, and a 2006 Constitutional Court ruling strengthened the requirements of the confession process.

In 2008, President Uribe extradited fourteen top paramilitary leaders to the United States, where they faced trials for drug trafficking; since then, many more have been sent to trial in the U.S. Due to extradition and the following prosecutions for drug-related crimes, many prosecutions of human rights offenses by Colombian justice officials were effectively suspended. Analysts criticized the demobilization process as contributing to impunity in Colombia by not fully investigating paramilitary crimes.

Additionally, the paramilitary demobilization process failed to ensure the return of land and other goods obtained through violence. Since taking office in 2010, President Juan Manuel Santos has passed legislation aimed at returning stolen and abandoned land to displaced persons. This has been a challenge due to paramilitaries' strategic land appropriation, in which they maintained possession to increase their wealth and security, repopulating rural regions with people loyal to them while creating sanctuaries for their business interests, including drug trafficking and ranching. (In contrast, although guerrillas occasionally appropriated land, they are more likely to abandon it for tactical reasons. They rely on stolen goods, even cattle and vehicles, as liquid capital to fund their military operations.) President Santos's land program faces sizable challenges—the country's land tenure structure is extremely complex, and threats against returning families and restitution leaders are common.

Since demobilization, significant links between paramilitary forces and the national and regional political elite have been exposed. Confessions by demobilized paramilitary leaders and investigations by justice officials, journalists, and academics revealed extensive links between politicians, business leaders, and military officers extending over the past two decades. In 2006, the Supreme Court launched one of the largest of these investigations, probing the paramilitary ties of members of Colombian Congress in the so-called parapolítica scandal. By 2011 more than 120 current and former legislators had come under investigation, and more than forty had been convicted. Testimony by demobilized paramilitaries has implicated 916 members of the armed forces. Approximately one-third of Colombia's mayors, governors, and congressmen have also been implicated.[15] Investigations remain ongoing.

A NEW GENERATION

Despite their expansion and efforts at professionalization, the state's official security forces have also faced large scandals and allegations of recent abuse. In 2006, the same year the parapolítica scandal broke, journalists and other investigators revealed the widespread torture of military recruits during training, as well as the massacre of a police anti-narcotics unit by an army patrol in the pay of drug traffickers. Also, the first allegations of falsos positivos (false positives) came to light. "Positivos" had come to refer to military commanders' relentless demands for high body counts, or "positive" results. "False positives" involved young, often poor men who were disappeared, murdered, and then presented by military units as members of illegal armed groups killed in combat. The Office of the U.N. High Commissioner for Human Rights estimates that more than 3,000 people may have been victims of extrajudicial executions by members of state forces, and that the majority of cases were committed by the army between 2004 and 2008. Another set of journalistic and judicial investigations during the Uribe administration revealed widespread and illegal surveillance of Supreme Court magistrates, journalists, rights defenders, and government critics by Colombia's domestic intelligence agency (DAS). In 2011, the DAS director from 2002-2005 was convicted of conspiracy for having put the intelligence agency at the service of the AUC and for his role in the paramilitaries' murder of a social activist in 2004.

Most recently, human rights groups and other analysts have documented the emergence of reorganized paramilitary forces, which the government calls "emerging criminal bands" (BACRIM), and pointed to this development as evidence of the larger failure of the demobilization process to diminish paramilitary power.[16] In numerous provinces, former mid-level paramilitaries have organized death-squad operations to protect economic projects, particularly the illegal drug trade. Although they fall far short of the levels of collaboration with the state military seen during the time of the AUC, these paramilitary successor, or neo-paramilitary, groups do benefit from the tolerance and collusion of some members of the security forces. Their criminal networks are largely detached from the hierarchical military structure that characterized the AUC, and have yet to articulate political demands, although many analysts argue that they significantly impact political and economic life in a number of regions.[17] According to Colombian police estimates in late 2011, BACRIM groups had 5,700 members but independent analysts and NGOs put the number closer to 10,000. In many regions, journalists report criminal alliances between guerrilla forces and neo-paramilitary groups. Analysts continue to struggle with how to assess the impact of neo-paramilitary forces on Colombian political life, and the groups' ongoing power; unlike the older paramilitaries, the newer organizations may be less significant for their specific command structures than for the enmeshment of illegal and legitimate economic interests, and the continuing use of violence to enforce particular interests. What is clear is that, like their predecessors, neo-paramilitary groups commit widespread abuses—including murders, massacres, rape, and forced displacement—against the civilian population.

Winifred Tate is assistant professor of anthropology at Colby College and the author of the award-winning book Counting the Dead: The Culture and Politics of Human Rights Activism in Colombia. *She has been researching political violence, illicit economies and community activism in Colombia since the late 1980s.*

II. THE UNITED STATES, COLOMBIA, AND THE DRUG WAR

By Adam Isacson

The United States' engagement in Colombia dates back at least to the 1950s, when Colombia sent a battalion to fight in the Korean War, and grew amid Cold War concerns over potential communist expansion in the Americas. The most intense period, however, began in the 1980s, as the country's booming drug trade became a main target of the Reagan and Bush administrations' War on Drugs. The drug war, and later the War on Terror, came to guide U.S. policy toward Colombia for the ensuing decades.

These policies went through several iterations. In the first, from the late 1980s to the mid-1990s, the focus was defeating the Medellín and Cali drug cartels that dominated the world trade in cocaine; most cocaine was consumed in the United States. The George H.W. Bush administration launched the Andean Initiative, the first regional package of anti-drug aid to exceed U.S. $100 million per year for a single group of countries. Nearly all of this aid went to Colombia's police; the armed forces (army, navy, and air force) resisted involvement in counter-drug operations that they viewed as a distraction from the country's guerrilla wars. This period of U.S. assistance ended not just with the Clinton administration's initial unwillingness to continue the Bush administration's aid commitments, but with the 1993 killing of Medellín boss Pablo Escobar and the 1994 capture of the Cali cartel's leadership—neither of which had any impact on supplies of cocaine entering the United States.[18] In fact, the inflation-and-purity-adjusted price of a gram of cocaine on U.S. streets actually fell—indicating supply met demand even better than before—both before and after the cartels' takedown.[19]

During the 1994-1998 administration of Colombian President Ernesto Samper, whom the U.S. government shunned due to allegations of cartel support for his campaign, Washington, then under President Clinton, engaged almost exclusively with Colombia's National Police. The War on Drugs remained the Clinton administration's priority, but with the demise of big cartels, U.S. strategy shifted from capturing kingpins to eradicating coca plants. U.S. policymakers reasoned that coca bushes, grown by poor farmers in remote areas, were the one link along the cocaine production chain where the product was openly visible. Colombia agreed to a U.S. plan to spray coca-producing areas with herbicides dispersed from aircraft, a method that Bolivia and Peru have refused to adopt. This program, which continues, has since fumigated nearly 2.5 million hectares of Colombian territory.

By the late 1990s, it became clear that this strategy was failing. Coca production increased so much that Colombia displaced Peru and Bolivia as the world's number-one grower of coca leaf. To the alarm of Clinton administration officials, coca profits were going not to cartels but to guerrilla and paramilitary groups, which quadrupled in size over that decade.[20] Amid concerns about cocaine production, and claiming that Colombia risked becoming a "failed state," Clinton administration officials urged the government of Andrés Pastrana (1998-2002) to adopt a comprehensive security, governance, and counter-drug strategy.

PLAN COLOMBIA

By late 1999, Bogotá had come up with a framework that it called Plan Colombia: Plan for Peace, Prosperity, and the Strengthening of the State. It envisioned U.S. $7.5 billion in new investments in security, rural development, counter-drug, and institution-building efforts, of which U.S. $3.5 billion would come from foreign donors.

The United States immediately embarked on the contribution of most of the military, police, and coca-eradication aid. In 2000, the Clinton administration proposed (and the Republican-majority Congress quickly passed) a package of U.S. $1.3 billion in assistance to Colombia, including over $400 million in aid to Colombia's neighbors. Three quarters of this outlay, the first of several for Plan Colombia, was in military and police aid. Over the next several years the U.S. government would grant Colombia equipment including more than ninety helicopters, two dozen spray planes, and cargo and surveillance aircraft, while helping to establish new units in Colombia's armed forces and training over 70,000 soldiers and police. Its participation in Plan Colombia represented the first time since the Cold War that Washington had provided significant aid—and the first instance of substantial counter-drug aid—to Colombia's military. (Colombia's police, which had received nearly all counter-drug aid before, received a significant but smaller share of Plan Colombia aid.)

This shift troubled many in American and Colombian human rights communities. Allegations of torture and extrajudicial executions began to surface, and Colombia's armed forces were widely accused of aiding and abetting the paramilitaries' ongoing scorched-earth campaign against civilians who lived in guerrilla-controlled areas, massacring thousands of people and displacing hundreds of thousands more every year.

The Democratic Party minority in the U.S. Congress shared these concerns, and added conditions to foreign-aid budget legislation designed to tie U.S. aid to the Colombian military's human rights performance. A provision known as the Leahy Law, named for sponsoring Senator Patrick Leahy (D-Vermont), banned aid to military units worldwide that abuse human rights with impunity.[21] Though it applies to aid across the globe, Colombia is one of the only countries in which the Leahy Law has been implemented, triggering temporary cutoffs to several army and air force brigades there. Another Colombia-specific set of conditions freezes a portion of military aid every year until the U.S. State Department can certify, among other requirements, that the Colombian military is cooperating with criminal investigations of human rights crimes in the civilian judicial system. These conditions, enforced more vigorously after the Democratic Party regained majority control of U.S. Congress in 2006, held up tens of millions of dollars of military aid on several occasions. The Leahy and Colombia-specific conditions did not stop Colombian military abuses. They did, however, encourage historic trials of senior officers for human rights crimes, and they forced the U.S. government to acknowledge and prioritize the poor human rights record of a country it supported with so much financial and military aid.

In Plan Colombia's early years, officials sought to keep the focus of aid on counter-narcotics, and, due to reluctance to take on a major new counterinsurgency mission, to avoid involvement in Colombia's larger fight against guerrillas and paramilitaries. The strategy, then, began by establishing an army, Counter-Narcotics Brigade, to secure fumigation in the southern province of Putumayo. However, the mission expanded in the wake of the September 11, 2001 attacks in the United States and the February 2002 collapse of peace talks between the Colombian government and the FARC. In the next iteration of U.S. assistance, "counter-terror" military aid, which no longer focused only on drugs, began to flow into Colombia. Despite the Leahy and Colombia-specific human rights conditions in U.S. law, post-9/11 U.S. assistance went to military units, particularly in the Colombian Army, who were later discovered to have committed large numbers of extrajudicial executions of civilians—in many cases, attempting to falsely inflate the numbers of armed-group members killed in combat.

As the government of Álvaro Uribe came into office in August 2002, the United States helped it carry out a country-wide offensive against guerrilla groups, principally by supporting a program to protect the Caño Limón-Coveñas oil pipeline, advising a thorough reorganization of the armed forces, providing intelligence, and supporting an ambitious military offensive—Plan Patriota—that sent nearly 20,000 Colombian troops into traditional FARC strongholds in southern Colombia. The deeply conservative President Uribe, meanwhile, moved to make Colombia the United States' closest ally in a region where the Bush administration's image was plummeting. Uribe's government was one of very few in the region to support the 2003 invasion of Iraq, and contingents of Colombian military and police personnel traveled to Afghanistan to discuss counter-insurgency techniques with local forces. President Uribe was also among the few foreign leaders to visit President George W. Bush at his Texas ranch; in early 2009, days before Bush left office, Bush invited Uribe to the White House to receive the Medal of Freedom, the United States' highest civilian honor, alongside Britain's Tony Blair and Australia's John Howard.

By the mid-2000s, the success of the offensive was mixed. Guerrilla groups had been weakened, and security had improved. But the effort to reduce drug production—the principal focus of U.S. aid to Colombia—had yielded little. Also, local operations in guerrilla strongholds had not brought a presence of civilian government entities; the armed groups were pushed out temporarily, but soldiers found themselves governing alone in so-called recovered territories.

CONSOLIDATION

U.S. strategy shifted somewhat after 2006, in part because the Democratic Party retook the majority of both houses of the U.S. Congress and began to change aid appropriations, focusing on non-military judicial, development, and humanitarian aid. Fumigation declined by about 40 percent; responsibilities for maintaining expensive aircraft shifted to Colombia's budget; and aid for judicial reform, rural development, and assistance to displaced populations more than doubled. U.S. policymakers began emphasizing trade—a free trade agreement was signed in 2006. Though signed by both presidents, however, the agreement's legislative ratification was delayed for five years as the Democratic majority in the U.S. Congress objected to continued failure to investigate and prosecute thousands of killings, threats and other attacks against trade unionists that had made Colombia the world's most dangerous country for labor activism.

Meanwhile, a framework known as Consolidation came to replace Plan Colombia. Instead of launching offensives or spraying the crops of impoverished coca growers—activities that continued, but with less intensity—Colombia's National Territorial Consolidation Plan aimed to establish a presence of civilian government services in vast, historically neglected areas. Colombian planners, assisted by the U.S. Southern Command and the U.S. federal government's USAID, chose several regions of Colombia where soldiers would establish a security perimeter and civilian agencies would provide basic services to neglected populations.

By the time the Obama administration took power, Consolidation had become the principal framework for U.S. aid, which was steadily decreasing amid the closing out of Plan Colombia and the post-2007 economic crisis. Consolidation's funding increased as other programs such as fumigation and aircraft maintenance decreased or were turned over to Colombia's budget, and made some progress in the La Macarena zone in Meta province in southern Colombia. Here, coca cultivation fell sharply and the FARC lost its control of town centers. However, Consolidation had not received as much investment elsewhere, where it proceeded slowly and received less attention from the new government of Juan Manuel Santos (who took office in 2010). Even in La Macarena, especially in rural areas, the security situation remained quite difficult, and the Colombian military was still the main government presence in the zone.

In total, between 2000 and 2011, the U.S. government gave Colombia assistance valued at U.S. $8 billion, making Colombia the world's sixth-largest recipient of U.S. aid during that period. Three quarters of this funding went to Colombia's armed forces and National Police. Toward the end of this period, more aid went to civilian institutions and development programs, but Colombia's security forces have remained at the center of recent U.S. engagement.

A decade after the launch of Plan Colombia, most observers recognized that it had contributed to important successes in reducing insecurity and, after 2007, the production of illegal drugs. But most non-governmental analysts also acknowledged that this success had been deeply flawed, partial, and difficult to replicate elsewhere. The Plan Colombia years saw the Colombian military involved in severe human rights violations, particularly the "false positives" scandal—in which soldiers allegedly killed an estimated 3,000 civilians, presenting many of them to officials as armed-group members killed in combat. A series of other scandals—"para-politics," the DAS wiretaps, and other corruption allegations—indicated that government institutions that worked effectively and honestly remained an urgent, unmet need. Significant drops in coca cultivation began only in the latter part of the 2000s, after fumigation declined. Colombia remains the world's leading cocaine producer and is tied with Peru as the largest coca-leaf producer.[22] While the FARC and ELN guerrillas were reduced in number and pushed to more marginal areas, they remained very active, averaging more than two attacks per day nationwide. Additionally, a new generation of paramilitary groups, most led by former mid-level

AUC paramilitary bosses, had proliferated throughout the country. Several measures of insecurity, such as kidnappings, massacres, urban homicides, and extortion, began to rise after 2008. This owed to shifts in guerrilla tactics, competition between the new paramilitary groups, and a sense of "strategic drift" as the Colombian government focused on President Uribe's failed bid for a third term in office. In effect, the U.S.-supported security effort had reached the limits of what a mostly military plan could do.

Plan Colombia and its successor policies showed what a "war" on drugs and drug production could achieve—but it also showed the limits of this kind of strategy. By 2012, Colombia remained Latin America's top military-aid recipient. But with lengthy, complicated wars in the Middle East and violence on the rise in Mexico and Central America, Washington's gaze had largely turned elsewhere, and military assistance had dropped below 1999 levels.

Adam Isacson is a senior associate for regional security policy at the Washington Office on Latin America (WOLA). He joined WOLA in 2010, after fourteen years working on Latin American and Caribbean security issues with the Center for International Policy.

III. FOUR MILLION AND COUNTING: FORCED DISPLACEMENT IN COLOMBIA

By Nadja Drost

Forced displacement is at once the most widespread and the most invisible of the ordeals that Colombians have suffered as a result of the country's conflict. Over the past two decades, violence and armed conflict have forced some four million Colombians to flee their homes, giving Colombia the largest population of internally displaced people in the world. Instead of tent camps or massive international humanitarian operations, however, displaced Colombians find refuge in schools, the homes of relatives, or in makeshift shacks in sprawling urban slums.

Between 1997 and 2011, the Colombian government registered 3.9 million displaced persons.[23] The Colombian NGO Consultancy for Human Rights and Displacement (CODHES), estimates over five million—about 11 percent of Colombia's total population—have been displaced since 1985.[24] This estimate includes displaced persons not officially registered by the national government.

There are a host of reasons that forcibly uproot Colombians, but more than half of displaced families registered in the government system cite direct threats against them as their reason for leaving.[25] Other reasons include assassination attempts, the murder or forced disappearance of a family member, massacres, forced recruitment by an armed group, or living amidst combat or violence.[26] Additionally, 14 percent of families experience more than one displacement.[27] After leaving their homes, some displaced people are uprooted yet again when death threats follow them, or because they find themselves living amidst new violence.

Armed groups of all political backgrounds and ideologies have used displacement as a strategy to gain territorial control.[28] A 2010 survey found that, historically, 31 percent of Colombia's internally displaced registered in the government's system said they were uprooted by right-wing paramilitary groups; nearly 27 percent by the FARC; 2 percent by the ELN; and 15 percent by "an unidentified guerrilla group." Less than 1 percent blame security forces for their displacement.[29] Displacement takes many forms: armed groups may occupy a family or a community's land, issue orders for residents to leave, send death threats, or generate enough terror—by carrying out assassinations and massacres, for example—that residents flee.

By forcibly displacing entire communities as well as individuals, armed groups weaken civil resistance movements, disperse people who oppose their presence, and acquire valuable land—all of which increase their power.[30] Over the last three decades, displaced people have left behind 6.6 million hectares of stolen or abandoned land.[31] The development of large-scale agro-industrial and mining projects, which have sometimes been accused of using paramilitaries to clear land, have also been a driving force behind displacement.

The majority of the people who are displaced come from rural areas[32] and flee to major urban centers.[33] When they arrive, some stay with relatives or friends. Others stay in shelters run by the city government or by a church. Still others sleep in the streets and under bridges. Cities that receive large populations of displaced people, such as Bogotá,

Medellín, Cartagena, and Buenaventura, have formed extensive neighborhoods on their outskirts or hillsides made up almost entirely of displaced families. According to one study, almost 90 percent of displaced families nationwide lack decent housing.[34]

With rural job skills not easily adaptable to an urban environment, finding work can be difficult for displaced people. If they do find work, it is almost always in the informal sector, such as jobs as street vendors or domestic help.[35] Almost all displaced families live under the official poverty line, and three quarters of them live in extreme poverty.[36]

Displacement tends to affect society's most vulnerable populations, who become even more vulnerable after they are uprooted. Afro-Colombians and indigenous people, for example, make up a disproportionately high percentage of Colombia's displaced, according to rights groups. In 2009, the Constitutional Court urged the government to prevent displacement of indigenous peoples in particular, stating in its ruling that at least thirty indigenous groups in Colombia were in danger of extinction due to armed conflict and displacement.[37] The Court recognized that, in the case of indigenous groups, forced displacement affects not only their individual but also collective rights. Because indigenous groups' autonomy, identity, and cultural survival are so closely tied to their territory, forced removal from their land is particularly destructive.[38] The impact of forced displacement on women is not only disproportionate, but particular, as the armed conflict has put women at higher risk of sexual violence. Oxfam International estimates that one out of every five displaced women were forced to flee as a result of crimes related to sexual violence.[39]

Colombia has established an intricate system of laws and institutions to address the issue of forced displacement. National law recognizes a displaced person as anyone who has been forced to abandon his or her home or work because of threats or violations to life, personal freedom, or safety due to the internal armed conflict, breaches of human rights and international humanitarian law, general violence, or civil disturbances.[40] Those recognized as displaced have the right to immediate government aid, such as clothing, bedding and food, but surveys show that the great majority do not receive it.[41] They also have the right to placement in public schools and assistance with rent and health care. Most assistance to displaced populations is administered by the Department of Social Prosperity (formerly called Social Action), but a variety of other entities, such as municipalities and the offices of the local Human Rights Ombudsman, also attend to the various needs of displaced people. Humanitarian organizations such as the International Committee of the Red Cross, Oxfam, and others also give emergency aid to displaced families.

In order to receive government assistance, a person must first submit a declaration to the Department of Social Prosperity and have their status as a displaced person investigated and approved. This often involves stepping through many bureaucratic hoops and enduring a long wait: the wait between a person's application and the start of their first humanitarian aid can be from a few months to two years.[42] Those who don't register, however, can't access government aid. Under-registration is a chronic problem; a national survey mandated by the Constitutional Court of Colombia showed that 34 percent of internally displaced people were not registered with the government in 2008, either because they didn't know how to register, were afraid of becoming targets for retribution by those who had forcibly displaced them, or had their claims of forced displacement rejected by the government.[43]

Although internal displacement had already been considered a systematic problem by the 1980s, the Colombian state only started to develop a body of norms to address it in the following decade.[44] Development of Colombia's law on internal displacement— eventually passed by Congress in 1997—followed a 1994 visit to Colombia by the U.N. Special Rapporteur on internal displacement. Furthermore, the 1997 law benefited from many of the elements of Colombia's 1991 Constitution, which included mechanisms for the protection of human rights and displacement in particular.[45]

The law's implementation was severely flawed, and in 2004, the Constitutional Court found that a large part of the displaced population was being denied its rights, through action or omission, by several state entities. The Court ruled that the government's response to internal displacement amounted to an "unconstitutional state of affairs."[46] The ruling triggered the creation of the Monitoring Commission on Public Policy on Forced Displacement, to evaluate the government's compliance with its legal obligations to displaced peoples.[47]

In addition to the millions displaced within Colombia, there are an estimated 500,000 Colombians who have fled to neighboring countries, only a small minority of whom are registered as refugees.[48] In January 2011, the Office of the United Nations High Commissioner for Refugees (UNHCR) considered 171,136 people in Ecuador a "population of concern" which includes officially recognized refugees and asylum seekers. Almost all are Colombian. By 2011 Ecuador had granted just over 55,000 people refugee status.[49] Many externally displaced Colombians remain unaware of their right to seek asylum and receive assistance. Fear also prevents many from coming forward.[50] Even for those who do, lack of documentation proves a great challenge to obtaining official refugee status, without which many Colombians lack access to employment, housing, and education.

Understandably, many displaced people want to return home, and Colombia's law on internal displacement provides the right to do so with government support and protection. But most have not. Even with the support of the government, returns can be very difficult. Many families who decide to return find their homes and possessions destroyed, and their previous source of income, such as crops, gone. They may also return to renewed trauma and fresh threats against their lives. The success of returns is in many cases jeopardized by the continuing presence of armed actors in the area, who are often part of the same group responsible for the initial displacement.

In 2011, President Juan Manuel Santos signed the Victims and Land Restitution Law, which aims to give reparations to victims of the armed conflict and return stolen and abandoned land to displaced people.[51] The law—which came into full effect on January 1, 2012 and will be applied through 2021—has great potential to improve the lives of people wanting to return to the land they were forced to leave. According to Amnesty International, "It will allow for integral reparations for some of the survivors of human rights abuses committed during the armed conflict and for the return of millions of hectares of land stolen mainly by paramilitary groups, sometimes in collusion with the security forces."[52] President Santos's administration has declared its intention to return 2.5 million hectares to displaced people by 2015.

However, land restitution efforts, and their ultimate success, are challenged by ongoing conflict in many of the same areas slated for land return, where the criminal forces that drove away peasants still persist.[53] Leaders of displaced populations who have organized and advocated for land restitution do their work at particularly high risk: fifty were assassinated between 2005 and December of 2011, according to Codhes. Many human rights groups have expressed concerns that if displaced people returning to their lands can't expect any guarantees of security, many simply won't go home.

Nadja Drost is a Canadian multi-media reporter based in Colombia since 2009. She directed and produced the award-winning documentary Between Midnight and the Rooster's Crow *(2005). She is a 2012 Alicia Patterson Fellow.*

IV. TIMELINE: COLOMBIA SINCE LA VIOLENCIA

April 9, 1948—The assassination of populist presidential candidate Jorge Eliécer Gaitán sets off La Violencia, the civil conflict between Conservatives and Liberals.

1958—Establishment of the National Front, a power-sharing agreement that set up an alternating presidency between the Liberal and Conservative parties. Many historians point to the agreement as the end of La Violencia.

1964—Colombian government troops overrun the "Republic of Marquetalia," a Liberal and communist enclave led by Pedro Marín, aka Manuel Marulanda Vélez. The guerrillas regroup and form the Bloque Sur, or Southern Bloc.

1964—The Ejército de Liberación Nacional (National Liberation Army, ELN) is founded. Close ties are forged with communist Cuba.

1965—The Maoist Ejército Popular de Liberación (Popular Liberation Army, EPL) is founded.

1966—The Southern Bloc officially changes name to become the Fuerzas Armadas Revolucionarias de Colombia (Revolutionary Armed Forces of Colombia, FARC).

1968—Colombia passes Law 48, which effectively legalizes paramilitary activity.

Early 1970s—The M-19 urban guerrilla group is created. Begins kidnapping drug traffickers and their family members for ransom and develops support among the urban middle class and intellectuals.

1980—An M-19 commando storms a reception at the Dominican embassy in Bogotá, taking fifty people hostage. After sixty-one days the hostages are released in exchange for safe passage for the guerrillas to Cuba.

1981—The Muerte a Secuestradores (Death to Kidnappers, MAS) death squad is founded by the Medellín drug cartel. Its main purpose is to protect large landowners and cartel leaders from guerrilla attacks, extortion, and kidnapping.

1984—The Colombian government signs cease-fire agreements with the FARC, M-19, and EPL. The last of these agreements ends in 1990 when the military attacks the FARC's Casa Verde camp in Meta province.

1984—U.S. Ambassador Lewis Tambs coins the term "narco-terrorist" after the discovery of the Medellín cartel's Tranquilandia cocaine-refining complex in FARC territory, which contains nineteen laboratories and eight airstrips.

1985—As part of peace negotiations with the government, the FARC and the Colombian Communist Party found a legal political party called the Unión Patriótica (Patriotic Union, UP), with the support of leftist movements. Roughly 1,500 of its members— including two presidential candidates—are killed, in large part by paramilitaries. The party officially disappears in 2002.

November 6-7, 1985—M-19 takes over Bogotá's Palace of Justice, sparking a counter-siege by the Colombian army. Eleven Supreme Court judges and all but one of the guerrillas are killed.

1989—The "Extraditables," a group of drug traffickers led by Pablo Escobar, escalates its terror campaign demanding a ban on extradition.

January 18, 1989—In La Rochela, Santander the "Masetos" paramilitary group detain fifteen judges and investigators who had traveled to the area to investigate a paramilitary massacre. Only three of the detainees survive.

April 19, 1989—The government bans paramilitary groups by striking down the Law 48 of 1968.

August 18, 1989—Liberal Party presidential candidate Luis Carlos Galán is assassinated under orders from Pablo Escobar. UP party candidate Bernardo Jaramillo will be assassinated seven months later.

1990—President César Gaviria convokes the National Constituent Assembly. The M-19 sign a peace agreement with the government and participate in the process.

February 1991—The EPL negotiates amnesty with the Colombian government. It will become the Hope, Peace, and Liberty Party and present candidates for electoral office. In 1991, the party is given two seats in the National Constituent Assembly, which was engaged in drafting the new constitution. Many other demobilized EPL join paramilitary groups.

June 1991—After surrendering to state forces, Medellín drug cartel leader Pablo Escobar enters a prison known as La Catedral, or The Cathedral, which he had designed near his hometown of Envigado, Antioquia. One year later, after the government orders his transfer to another prison, Escobar escapes.

July 1991—The new Constitution, considered one of the most progressive in the world, grants historic rights to Colombia's indigenous peoples and Afro-Colombian communities, limits the power of the executive branch, and bans extradition.

1992—The United States redirects aid to Colombia away from the Colombian army, and toward the police, air force, and navy in an attempt to better target anti-drug operations rather than counterinsurgency.

December 1993—Pablo Escobar is killed on a Medellín rooftop by Colombian security forces, with U.S. assistance.

1994—U.S. Congress begins requiring by law that aid to Colombia be certified by the Secretary of State as "primarily for counternarcotics activities," as opposed to counterinsurgency.

1994—Carlos, Fidel, and Vicente Castaño found the Autodefensas Campesinas de Córdoba and Urabá (ACCU), the immediate precursor to the AUC.

February 11, 1994—A government decree establishes the "Special Vigilance and Private Security Services" (known as CONVIVIR), private security groups intended to fight guerrilla activity. Many human rights groups trace the roots of modern paramilitary groups to the CONVIVIR.

July 1996—Farmers in Putumayo begin a protest against government eradication of their coca crops after U.S. officials demand that Colombia use stronger herbicides and change their methods for calculating the success of counternarcotic offensives.

September 30, 1996—The "Leahy Law" is enacted, which places human rights conditions on U.S. aid to the Colombian military.

1997—The United States places the FARC on its list of Foreign Terrorist Organizations.

1997—Regional paramilitary groups unite under the umbrella of the Autodefensas Unidas de Colombia (United Self-Defense Forces of Colombia, AUC), establishing a presence in much of the country. Carlos Castaño is the visible leader of the group.

February 1997—The Colombian military carries out "Operation Genesis" in Urabá, which human rights groups and local communities allege was coordinated with paramilitary groups. Hundreds of Afro-Colombians are displaced.

July 15-20, 1997—Paramilitaries in Mapiripán, Meta kill dozens of people in the Mapiripán Massacre. Despite eight telephone calls by a local judge seeking help, the army and police do not react until the paramilitaries have left Mapiripán.

December 1997—Congress lifts ban on extradition.

1998—Shortly after his inauguration, President Andrés Pastrana opens peace negotiations with the FARC, following through on a major campaign promise. The negotiations would eventually include a government troop pullout from a 42,000-square-kilometer safe haven for the FARC.

October 18, 1998—ELN blows up an oil pipeline in Machuca, Antioquia, causing an explosion that kills eighty-four people.

February 16-18, 2000—400 uniformed paramilitaries enter El Salado, Bolívar and commit the El Salado massacre. For two days, paramilitaries force residents out of their houses and to the local micro-soccer court, where they are tortured and murdered. Sixty people are killed in the massacre.

July 2000—U.S. President Clinton signs Plan Colombia, a major aid package to Colombia mostly directed to the military for counternarcotics operations.

January 17, 2001—Approximately eighty paramilitaries round up dozens of residents of Chengue, Sucre, and kill the men by crushing their heads with heavy stones and a sledgehammer. The event comes to be known as the Chengue massacre. Months before, local authorities had warned military, police, and government officials of a planned paramilitary massacre.

2001—The United States places the AUC on its list of Foreign Terrorist Organizations.

February 20, 2002 —Pastrana's administration breaks off peace negotiations with the FARC when a FARC team hijacks a plane on its way to Bogotá and kidnaps the leader of the Senate Peace Commission.

February 23, 2002—The FARC kidnaps presidential candidate Íngrid Betancourt, and her campaign manager Clara Rojas. The two become part of a group of hostages that include politicians and members of the military, which the FARC aims to exchange for jailed rebels.

May 2, 2002—Approximately eighty people, including forty-eight children, die after the FARC launch a cylinder gas bomb against a church during a clash with paramilitaries in Bojayá, Chocó. Nearly 6,000 people are displaced.

August 2002—President Álvaro Uribe takes office, promising to crack down on guerrillas and improve security nationwide.

September 2002—The U.S. Department of Justice indicts and requests the extradition of Carlos Castaño and Salvatore Mancuso, top AUC leaders.

2002—Hoping to negotiate an agreement to block U.S. extradition, paramilitary leaders approach the Uribe administration, and negotiations begin between paramilitary leaders and the Colombian government. The paramilitaries declare a cease-fire in December, though it is often breached.

2003—The Colombian government begins the process of demobilizing the paramilitary groups in the AUC. Members are demobilized either individually or as part of a paramilitary bloc. More than 30,000 people undergo demobilization, pledging to stop criminal activity and enter a reintegration program.

January 2004—The Colombian Constitutional Court orders the state to reform its policies and improve measures addressing internal displacement.

April 16, 2004—Top AUC leader Carlos Castaño is killed by rival paramilitaries, which include his brother Vicente Castaño.

June 21, 2005—The Uribe administration secures Congressional passage of the Justice and Peace Law, for paramilitary members who have been convicted of or face investigation for serious crimes. The law allows these individuals to receive reduced sentences for their confessions and demobilization, but is criticized for providing a short time frame for investigations resulting from confessions, and for failing to provide strong consequences for omitting information about crimes and accomplices.

2006—The Colombian Supreme Court begins an investigation into the influence of paramilitaries in Colombian Congress, known as "parapolitics," resulting in subsequent investigations of more than 120 members of Congress and public verbal attacks on the Court by President Uribe. Nearly all of the lawmakers investigated are members of President Uribe's coalition. More than forty are ultimately convicted.

May 2006—The Colombian Constitutional Court reviews and strengthens the Justice and Peace Law, requiring full and complete confessions, and allowing for the revocation of sentence reductions for failure to comply with certain requirements.

June 5, 2006—Colombia's Peace Commissioner reports to the U.S. Embassy about the appearance of ten to thirty "new emergent anti-communist criminal groups" in the wake of the AUC demobilization. Later labeled "emerging criminal groups" (BACRIM), these neo-paramilitary groups, led largely by former AUC commanders, will grow to 5,700 members across the country by 2011.

August 15, 2006—Official end of AUC demobilizations.

November 22, 2006—President Uribe and President Bush sign the U.S.-Colombia Free Trade Agreement. Ratification of the treaty is delayed in U.S. Congress due to concerns over anti-union violence.

Early 2007—Confessions begin for those who applied for benefits under the Justice and Peace Law.

March 2007—Chiquita Brands International, based out of Cincinnati, pleads guilty in U.S. court to having paid U.S.$1.7 million to the AUC in Urabá and Santa Marta—both banana-producing regions—between 1997 and 2004. Chiquita Brands claims that the money was to protect its employees and facilities from AUC attacks.

February 4, 2008—Millions of Colombians take to the streets throughout the country to protest against the FARC and their practice of kidnapping.

March 26, 2008—Pedro Antonio Marín, alias Manuel Marulanda Vélez, the top leader and founder of the FARC, dies of natural causes.

May 13, 2008—An unprecedented period of paramilitary confessions under the Justice and Peace Law is cut short when Uribe decides to extradite almost all of the paramilitary leadership to face drug charges in the U.S.

July 2, 2008—A military rescue operation frees Íngrid Betancourt and fourteen other hostages from FARC captivity.

September 2008—The discovery of bodies of executed civilians, reported by the army as members of illegal groups killed in action, begins the "false positives" scandal. Subsequent investigations find that army troops regularly carried out these types of murders to increase body counts, and many have since been brought to trial.

January 2009—A Constitutional Court ruling states that at least thirty indigenous groups in Colombia are in danger of "cultural or physical extermination" due to armed conflict and displacement.

February 4, 2009—The FARC massacres seventeen members of the Awá indigenous group in Nariño province.

February 2009—*Semana* magazine, Colombia's leading newsweekly, reveals that the country's national intelligence agency (DAS) has been engaged in the illegal surveillance of Supreme Court judges, journalists, trade unionists and critics of the Uribe government.

August 2010—President Juan Manuel Santos takes office.

January 2011—The Urabeños group kill two students from an elite Bogotá university on vacation in Córdoba province, bringing the problem of neo-paramilitary groups to the national spotlight. The National Police Chief publicly recognizes such groups are the largest source of violence in the country.

June 10, 2011—President Santos signs the Victims and Land Restitution Law, which aims to return land to Colombia's internally displaced population and provide reparations to victims of human rights and international humanitarian law violations.

October 12, 2011—U.S. Congress signs the U.S.–Colombia free trade agreement.

October 31, 2011—President Santos officially closes the DAS after a series of scandals including collaboration with paramilitaries and illegal surveillance of political opponents, human rights activists, judges, and others.

November 4, 2011—Alfonso Cano, top leader of the FARC, is killed by the military during an operation in Cauca province.

March 23, 2012—An activist seeking land restitution and his fifteen-year-old son are disappeared and murdered in Urabá, allegedly by the Águilas Negras neo-paramilitary group, raising serious concerns about implementation of the Victims and Land Restitution Law.

V. GLOSSARY

Afro-Colombians—Refers to Colombia's Afro-descendant population, the second largest in Latin America. Afro-Colombian communities are concentrated on the Pacific and Atlantic coasts, and represent an estimated 10–25 percent of Colombia's population.

arroba—A unit of weight used in some Spanish-speaking countries, whose exact measurement can vary depending on region.

Asociación Nacional de Usuarios Campesinos (ANUC)—An agricultural workers' union, ANUC was founded in 1968 as an engine for the rural poor to advocate for land reform and political representation.

AUC (Autodefensas Unidas de Colombia / United Self-Defense Forces of Colombia)—An umbrella organization of regional paramilitary groups that formed in 1997 and officially concluded its demobilization in 2006. The paramilitary coalition committed hundreds of massacres, forcibly disappeared tens of thousands, and displaced more than a million Colombians.

coca—The plant from which cocaine is produced. It is also used by indigenous groups in the Andean region as a medicinal and spiritual plant.

coca paste—An intermediary product in the production of coca into cocaine, extracted when the coca leaf is crushed and mixed with kerosene and other chemicals.

Community Action Board—Small civil organizations that represent villages, communities and neighborhoods.

CONVIVIR (Cooperativas de Vigilancia)—A national program of rural security cooperatives established in 1994 as "Special Vigilance and Private Security Services," and later known as CONVIVIR. Through the program, individuals could petition the government for a license to arm themselves, especially in areas with a strong guerrilla presence where the government could not guarantee public safety. A November 1997 Constitutional Court ruling banned CONVIVIR from collecting intelligence for security forces and from possessing rifles, machine guns and other restricted weapons. Human rights groups allege that CONVIVIR often served as front organizations for paramilitary groups, and former paramilitary commanders have admitted that they controlled many CONVIVIR militias.

CTI / Technical Investigation Corps—An entity attached to the Attorney General's office and charged with providing investigative and forensic support in criminal cases.

ELN (Ejército de Liberación Nacional / National Liberation Army)—Colombia's second largest left-wing guerrilla group. The ELN engages in the killing of civilians, forced displacement, kidnapping, the use of antipersonnel land mines, and the forced recruitment and use of child soldiers.

Envigado Office—An organized crime group based in Medellín that provides assassination services and maintains ties to paramilitary groups and their successor organizations.

"false positive"—The murder of a civilian by the military for the purpose of increasing the troop's body counts. The deceased is made to look like a guerrilla or a member of a criminal group, and is reported as killed in action. A "false positives" scandal that eventually uncovered hundreds of these killings erupted in 2008. Colombia's Attorney General's office is investigating more than 2,800 extrajudicial killings by state agents, most of which were committed by the army between 2004 and 2008.

Family Welfare (Instituto Colombiano de Bienestar Familiar / Colombian Institute of Family Welfare)—A government agency charged with protecting children and guaranteeing their rights.

FARC (Fuerzas Armadas Revolucionarias de Colombia / Revolutionary Armed Forces of Colombia) —Colombia's largest left-wing guerrilla/insurgency group, it was founded in the 1960s by guerrillas who fought in La Violencia and began as an association of peasant self-defense groups. The group commits widespread abuses against civilians, frequently uses antipersonnel land mines and indiscriminate weapons, and is often involved in killings, threats, forced displacement, and recruiting and use of child soldiers.

forced disappearance—The arrest, detention, abduction, or deprivation of liberty by state agents or persons acting on behalf of the state or with state acquiescence, followed by the concealment of the whereabouts or fate of the person.

fumigation (of coca crops)—A method of aerial spraying of chemical herbicides aimed at killing coca and other illegal crops which began in Colombia in the 1990s. Since fumigation can affect such broad areas, it has raised concerns about food destruction, water contamination, cattle illness, and skin infections.

"ghost plane" (avión fantasma)—A name given by civilians to the Douglas AC-47 "Spooky," a U.S.-made Vietnam-era airplane retrofitted for use in the Colombian Air Force.

guerrillas—Members of any one of the several left-wing insurgent groups that have formed in Colombia. The Revolutionary Armed Forces of Colombia (FARC) and National Liberation Army (ELN) are the two largest guerrilla groups in Colombia. Founded in the 1960s and claiming to represent the country's rural poor in the fight against Colombia's wealthy classes and U.S. imperialism, both groups commit widespread abuses against civilians, including killings, threats, and recruitment of child soldiers.

Incoder (Instituto Colombiano para el Desarrollo Rural)—Formally known and organized differently as INCORA, the government institution in charge of agricultural policies, rural development and property.

Informants' Network / Red de Cooperantes—A network of civilian informants established by President Uribe with the aim of collecting information about the FARC and other insurgent groups. Informants usually receive small payments for tips, but these can increase if the information leads to arrests or the prevention of a guerrilla attack.

Inspector General's Office / Procuraduría General de la Nación—The state office that conducts most disciplinary investigations of public officials and monitors criminal investigations and prosecutions, and other state agencies.

internally displaced person—Colombian law recognizes an internally displaced person as anyone who has been forced to abandon their home or work because of threats or violations to life, personal freedom, or safety due to the internal armed conflict, breaches of human rights and international humanitarian law, general violence, or civil disturbances. By 2011, official statistics from the Colombian government reported nearly 3.9 million internally displaced persons in the country since 1997.

Justice and Peace Law—A 2005 demobilization law that allowed paramilitaries convicted of or facing investigation for serious abuses to receive significantly reduced sentences in exchange for confessing to their crimes, ceasing criminal activity, and providing reparations to victims. As initially passed by Congress, paramilitaries would have faced few consequences if they failed to meet these conditions. However, a 2006 ruling by the Constitutional Court tightened its requirements, which helped lead to hundreds of investigations into paramilitary collaborators in Colombian politics and the military. By April 2012, paramilitaries had confessed to more than 50,000 crimes under the law, yet special Justice and Peace prosecutors have obtained just seven convictions.

Liberal and Conservative parties—The two main opposing political parties in Colombia until the turn of the twenty-first century. Their opposition can be traced back to the 1840s, when Liberal support came from a landed, merchant elite, and Conservative support largely favored by the Catholic Church.

M-19—A predominantly urban guerrilla group. The group took their name from the date of the 1970 presidential election that its founders claimed was stolen from the National Popular Alliance (Alianza Nacional Popular, ANAPO) candidate.

miliciano—A name for a member of a guerrilla group who typically dresses in civilian clothes and provides information and support to other guerrillas.

National Reparations Fund—A fund that holds land and other assets turned over by paramilitaries under the Justice and Peace Law.

neo-paramilitary groups / paramilitary successor groups / BACRIM—Groups that began to emerge after the end of AUC demobilization in 2006 and continued or restarted many of the criminal activities that the demobilized paramilitaries no longer ran, engaging in abuses against civilians such as extortion, threats, rapes, murders, massacres, and forced displacement. A majority of their leaders are mid-level AUC commanders. The government labels them BACRIM (emerging criminal gangs at the service of drug trafficking). Neo-paramilitary groups do not have the strict hierarchical structure of the previous generation of paramilitary groups and have yet to form a single coalition similar to the AUC. Paramilitary successor groups include the Rastrojos, Paisas, Urabeños, and some go by the name Águilas Negras (Black Eagles).

N.N. / **"no name"**—From the Latin *nomen nescio*, the morgue registration of a corpse without identifying documents, which is likely to go unclaimed.

Ombudsman's office / **Defensoría del Pueblo**—The government office, created by the 1991 Constitution, responsible for promoting and defending human rights and international humanitarian law.

panela / **panela water**—A food item made of boiled sugarcane juice, sometimes dissolved in water.

paramilitaries / **autodefensas**—Right-wing groups that began to form in Colombia in the early 1980s with the purported aim of fighting left-wing guerrillas. Backed by the military, landowners, drug traffickers, and political and economic elites, paramilitaries have murdered tens of thousands of civilians, including peasants, leftist politicians, human rights defenders, and trade unionists.

paramilitary demobilization—The process between 2003 and 2006 by which more than 30,000 supposed members of paramilitary organizations pledged to abandon paramilitary groups and stop criminal activity. The vast majority of people who demobilized were effectively pardoned for paramilitary membership and were not investigated for other crimes. There is substantial evidence that many of the participants were not paramilitaries, and that a portion of the groups remained active. While many combatants did abandon paramilitary activity, analysts have concluded that the failure to investigate and dismantle paramilitaries' criminal, financial, and political networks, as well as insufficient efforts to combat demobilization fraud and verify the identities of people demobilizing, contributed to the growth of paramilitary successor groups.

parapolitics—Refers to the scandal exposing extensive links between paramilitaries and Colombian politicians. More than 120 former and current members of Congress have come under investigation for paramilitary ties, and more than forty have been convicted as of 2011. Hundreds of mayors, governors, and councilmen have also been implicated.

Personería—A municipal entity charged with monitoring human and citizens' rights, ensuring that government bodies such as the police and military act within the law and the Constitution. They pass complaints received from citizens to the Inspector General's office (Procuraduría) for investigation. The heads of Personería offices are known as personeros.

Rastrojos—A neo-paramilitary group, the Rastrojos' roots can be traced to the armed wing of the Norte del Valle drug trafficking cartel, located in southwestern Colombia.

red zone—An area known for persistent guerrilla activity and intense armed conflict.

Social Action (Accion Social / Presidential Agency for Social Action and International Cooperation)—Until 2012, the state entity charged with coordinating social programs, aid, and resources to vulnerable populations, including internally displaced persons and victims of the conflict. Social Action was replaced by the Department for Social Prosperity in 2012.

tutela / acción de tutela—A legal tool originating in the 1991 Constitution, a tutela allows citizens to file for judicial injunction against public authorities and private parties who they claim have violated their constitutional rights.

Urabeños—A neo-paramilitary group that inherited the disbanded AUC's criminal activities in Urabá, and expanded their operations throughout the country. Led by former mid-level AUC leaders, the Urabeños are the direct descendants of Carlos Castaño's armies.

vacuna—Literally translated into English as "vaccine," a *vacuna* is the name for extortion payments demanded of civilians by armed actors.

The Violence / La Violencia—The name given to the 1948-1958 civil conflict between Liberals and Conservatives. Experts have called La Violencia "one of the largest armed mobilizations of peasants in the hemisphere," and historians have estimated that it killed 200,000 people and internally displaced as many as two million.

ENDNOTES

1   Park, James. *Rafael Núñez and the Politics of Colombian Regionalism, 1863-1886.* Baton Rouge: Louisiana State University Press, 1985.

2   Perea, Carlos Mario. *Porque la sangre es espíritu: Imaginario y discurso político en las élites capitalinas 1942-1949.* Bogotá: Iepri, 1996.

3   Many developed well-known nicknames; among the most famous was El Cóndor in Valle del Cauca; his evolution from mild-mannered cheese salesman and Conservative Party lackey to paid assassin was the subject of the Colombian classic novel, *Cóndores no entierran todos los días,* and the movie of the same name. Pecaut compared them to arditi, private groups that accompanied Italian fascism, and Eric Hobsbawm compared them to the Sicilian Mafia.

4   Chernick, Marc. "Economic Resources and Internal Armed Conflicts: Lessons from the Colombian Case" in Arnson, Cynthia J. and Zartman, I. William, eds. *Rethinking the Economics of War: The Intersection of Need, Creed, and Greed.* Washington: Woodrow Wilson Center and Johns Hopkins University Press, 2005.

5   Molano, Alfredo. *Siguiendo el corte: Relatos de guerras y de tierras.* Bogotá: El Ancora Editores, 1989.

6   Pardo Rueda, Rafael. *De primera mano: Colombia 1986-1994, Entre conflictos y esperanzas.* Bogotá: Cerec and Grupo Editorial Norma, 1996; and Isacson, Adam. *Amending the "Pact:" The Shifting Civil-Military Balance in Álvaro Uribe's Colombia,* manuscript. Center for International Policy, Washington DC, 2005.

7   Reyes Posadas, Alejandro, with Amaya, Liliana Duica. *Guerreros y campesinos: el despojo de la tierra en Colombia.* Buenos Aires: Grupo Editorial Norma, 2009.

8   Chernick, 2005.

9   See Richani, Nazih. *Systems of Violence: The Political Economy of War and Peace in Colombia.* SUNY Press, 2002. There is great debate around these figures. Some place the FARC's total earning as high as $900 million or $1 billion a year, though this seems highly improbable given the size of the Colombian economy, the total illegal export earnings and the position of the FARC in the overall illegal economy.

10 Chernick, Marc. "Negotiating Peace Amid Multiple Forms of Violence: The Protracted Search for a Settlement to the Armed Conflicts in Colombia" in Arnson, Cynthia ed. *Comparative Peace Processes in Latin America.* Stanford University Press and Woodrow Wilson Center Press, 1999; and Arenas, Gustavo García and Roesel, Mónica, eds. *Las verdaderas intenciones de las FARC.* Santafé de Bogotá: Corporación Observatorio Para La Paz: 1999. For an earlier record of FARC positions during negotiations in the 1980s, see: Arenas, Jacobo. *Correspondencia secreta del proceso de paz.* Bogotá: Editoral La Abeja Negra, 1989.

11   Centro de Memoria Histórica. *Guerra sin límites (War Without Limits)*. Bogotá: Centro de Memoria Histórica, 2010.

12   See Human Rights Watch. *Colombia's Killer Networks*. New York: Human Rights Watch, 1995; and Washington Office on Latin America. *Losing Ground: Colombian Human Rights Defenders Under Attack*. Washington: WOLA, 1997.

13   Isacson, Adam. "Enmendando el 'Pacto': El cambio en el equilibrio civil-militar en la Colombia de Álvaro Uribe" in FLACSO. *Influencias y Resistencias. Militares y Poder en América Latina*, 2010.

14   International Crisis Group. "Demobilizing the Paramilitaries in Colombia: An Achievable Goal?" Brussels: ICG, August 2004.

15   Otis, John. "Court tell-alls tie the elite to paramilitary killings" in *Houston Chronicle*, May 20, 2007; and Romero, Mauricio, ed. *Parapolitica: La ruta de expansion paramilitar y los acuerdos politicos*. Bogotá: Corporacion Nuevo Arco Iris, Cerec, Asi, 2007. The web site Verdad Abierta (http://www.verdadabierta.com/web3/) has been established by Colombian investigative journalists with international funding to compile information about the process (last accessed June 17, 2012). Claudia Lopez's 2010 edited volume, *Y refundaron la patria*.

16   International Crisis Group. "Colombia's New Armed Groups." Washington: Latin America Report No. 20, May 10, 2007; Human Rights Watch. "Letting Paramilitaries Off the Hook." New York: HRW, January 2005; "Preocupante aumento de bandas armadas en Colombia." *Semana*, November 26, 2008. HRW report in 2010, "Paramilitaries' Heirs: The New Face of Violence in Colombia."

17   International Crisis Group. "Cutting the Links Between Crime and Local Politics: Colombia's 2011 Elections." Washington: Latin America Report No. 37, 25 July 2011.

18   Although Colombia continues to have numerous smaller drug-trafficking organizations—including the guerrillas and paramilitaries—the era of big, nationally dominant, monopolistic cartels ended with the 1994 arrest of the Rodríguez Orejuela brothers, who ran the Cali cartel, and the death of Pablo Escobar, the Medellín cartel's kingpin, the previous year.

19   The numbers from the UNODC 2009 World Drug Report are 1990: $421; 1991: $343; 1992: $263; 1993: $251; 1994: $232; 1995: $275; 1996: $217; 1997: $208; 1998: $189; 1999: $193.

20   Only three countries in the world grow coca in any significant amount. In short, the cartels' fall catapulted Colombia from the third to the top spot, as cartels were replaced by armed groups and small narco gangs that did not have the cartels' capacity to grow the crop in other countries, then bring it to Colombia for processing into cocaine.

21   The text of the Leahy Law prohibits aid to foreign security-force units whose members are credibly alleged to have committed gross human rights abuses without effective measures to investigate and prosecute those responsible. How to determine "unit,"

"credibly alleged," "gross" abuses, and "effective measures" has been the subject of entire reports and many years of occasionally nasty discussion between human rights groups, congressional staff, and U.S. officials. As the law has evolved, embassies are required to keep a database of individuals and their units who are "credibly alleged," and to ensure that no aid goes to these units.

22   For cocaine estimates, see Office of National Drug Control Policy. "Cocaine Smuggling in 2010." January 2012. http://www.whitehouse.gov/sites/default/files/ondcp/international-partnerships-content/20_january_cocaine_smuggling_in_2010_for_posting_on_ondcp_webpage_2.pdf.

      For coca estimates, see Oficina de las Naciones Unidas contra la Droga y el Delito (UNODC). "Perú: Monitoreo de Cultivos de Coca 2010." June 2011. http://www.unodc.org/documents/crop-monitoring/Peru/Peru-cocasurvey2010_es.pdf and Oficina de las Naciones Unidas contra la Droga y el Delito (UNODC). "Colombia: Monitoreo de Cultivos de Coca 2010." June 2011. http://www.unodc.org/documents/crop-moni toring/Colombia/Colombia-cocasurvey2010_es.pdf.

23   Observatorio Nacional del Desplazamiento Forzado. *Análisis de la tendencia del desplazamiento forzado*. Diciembre 2011.

24   CODHES (Consultoria para los derechos humanos y el desplazamiento). *¿Consolidación de qué? Informe sobre desplazados, conflicto armado y derechos humanos en Colombia en 2010*. March 2011.

25   Comisión de Seguimiento a la Política Pública sobre Desplazamiento Forzado (Follow-up Commission on Public Policy on Forced Displacement). *Third national survey on the verification of rights of the displaced population*. October 2010.

26   Ibid.

27   Comisión de Seguimiento a la Política Pública sobre Desplazamiento Forzado (Follow-up Commission on Public Policy on Forced Displacement). *El reto ante la tragedia humanitaria del desplazamiento forzado: Garantizar la observancia de los derechos de la población desplazada*. Volume 2, April 2009.

28   Ibáñez, Ana María. *El desplazamiento forzoso en Colombia: un camino sin retorno hacia la pobreza*. Universidad de los Andes, presentation at Bancaria Convention, 27 August 2009.

29   Comisión de Seguimiento a la Política Pública sobre Desplazamiento Forzado (Follow-up Commission on Public Policy on Forced Displacement). *Third national survey on the verification of rights of the displaced population*. December 2010.

30   Ibid.

31   Comisión de Seguimiento a la Política Pública sobre Desplazamiento Forzado (Follow-up Commission on Public Policy on Forced Displacement). *Third national survey on the verification of rights of the displaced population. Summary of preliminary findings regarding rural goods*. October 2010.

32   Salamanca, Luis Jorge; Gómez, Fernando Barberi; and Gómez, Clara Ramírez. *The Humanitarian Tragedy of Forced Displacement in Colombia.* 2009.

33   Albuja, Sebastián and Ceballos, Marcela. "Urban displacement and migration in Colombia" in *Forced Migration Review*, Issue 34, February 2010.

34   Salamanca, Luis Jorge; Gómez, Fernando Barberi; and Gómez, Clara Ramírez. *The Humanitarian Tragedy of Forced Displacement in Colombia.* 2009.

35   Ibid.

36   Ibid, and Ibáñez, Ana María. *El desplazamiento forzoso en Colombia: un camino sin retorno hacia la pobreza.* Universidad de los Andes, presentation at Bancaria Convention, August 27, 2009.

37   Auto no. 004/09, Constitutional Court of Colombia, January 2009.

38   Ibid.

39   "Sexual Violence in Colombia: Instrument of War." Oxfam Briefing Paper, September 2009, p. 3.

40   Law 387 of 1997.

41   Salamanca, Luis Jorge; Gómez, Fernando Barberi; and Gómez, Clara Ramírez. *The Humanitarian Tragedy of Forced Displacement in Colombia.* 2009.

42   Albuja, Sebastián and Ceballos, Marcela. "Urban displacement and migration in Colombia" in *Forced Migration Review*, Issue 34, February 2010.

43   Comisión de Seguimiento a la Política Pública sobre Desplazamiento Forzado (Follow-up Commission on Public Policy on Forced Displacement). *El reto ante la tragedia humanitaria del desplazamiento forzado: Garantizar la observancia de los derechos de la población desplazada.* Volume 2, April 2009.

44   Viana, Manuela Trindade. "International Cooperation and Internal Displacement in Colombia: Facing the Challenges of the Largest Humanitarian Crisis in South America" in *Sur. Revista Internacional de Direitos.* Volume 6, Number 10, p.p. 138-161, 2009.

45   Fadnes, Ellen and Hordt, Cindy. "Responses to Internal Displacement in Colombia: Guided by What Principles?" in *Refuge*, Volume 26, Number 1, 2009.

46   Viana, Manuela Trindade. "International Cooperation and Internal Displacement in Colombia: facing the challenges of the largest humanitarian crisis in South America" in *Sur. Revista Internacional de Direitos.* Volume 6, Number 10, p.p. 138-161, 2009.

47   Salamanca, Luis Jorge; Gómez, Fernando Barberi; and Gómez, Clara Ramírez. *The Humanitarian Tragedy of Forced Displacement in Colombia.* 2009.

48   White, Ana Guglielmelli. *In the shoes of refugees: providing protection and solutions for displaced Colombians in Ecuador.* Office of Government Relations, Episcopal Church, Washington, DC and the UNHCR Policy Development and Research Service, August 2011.

49   UNHCR. *Global Trends 2010*. June 20, 2011.

50   UNHCR. *Global Needs Assessment Pilot Report: Refugee Realities*. October, 2008.

51   Human Rights Watch. "Colombia: Victims Law a Historic Opportunity." June 10, 2011. http://www.hrw.org/news/2011/06/10/colombia-victims-law-historic-opportunity.

52   Amnesty International. "Colombia: Victims Law an Important Step Forward but Questions Remain." June 3, 2011. http://www.amnesty.org/en/for-media/press-releases/colombia-victims-law-important-step-forward-questions-remain-2011-06-03.

53   Drost, Nadja. "Santos' Land Bill" in *Women, War and Peace*. PBS. November 1, 2011. http://www.pbs.org/wnet/women-war-and-peace/features/santoss-land-bill/.

ACKNOWLEDGMENTS

This book would not have been possible without the support of many people and organizations who contributed time, advice, and wisdom to this endeavor. We would like to acknowledge the generous support for this project from Stephen Brady, Don and Janie Friend, Betsy Karel, Julie McGowan, Amy Rao and Darian Swig.

We are grateful to the organizations that provided guidance in finding narrators and collecting their stories: Centro Integral de Rehabilitación de Colombia (CIREC); Asociación Nacional de Afrocolombianos Desplazados (AFRODES); Fundacion Humanitaria Nuevo Amanecer; Fundación Víctimas Visibles; Escuela Nacional Sindical; Movimiento de Víctimas de Crímenes de Estado; Asociación Tierra y Vida; Comité Cívico por los Derechos Humanos del Meta; Hebrew Immigrant Aid Society (HIAS); Comisión Intereclesial de Justicia y Paz; Proyecto Justicia y Vida; Latin American Working Group (LAWG); Peace Brigades International; Pastoral Social of Ipiales; Luis Sztorch at the UNHCR office in Pasto, and the Asociación de Institutores de Antioquia (ADIDA).

Our deep appreciation to Nadja Drost, Adam Isacson, and Winifred Tate for the wisdom and knowledge they generously contributed in their essays.

We extend our heartfelt gratitude to Stephen Ferry for his insight, advice, friendship, and for providing the cover photograph.

Our families and friends have been invaluable in their support.

Sibylla is especially grateful to her husband Oliverio Caldas, without whose encouragement she could not have made this book. For her dear sister Raquel Feigenbutz, and for Teresita Lleras, María Pabón and Pilar Amaya, thank you for being willing to listen. To Paula Allen, thanks for planting the seed. To her beloved parents, Marianela and Jacob Brodzinsky, Sibylla offers her eternal love and gratitude.

Max would especially like to thank his parents Amy and Harry Schoening for their boundless support and love.

ABOUT THE EDITORS

SIBYLLA BRODZINSKY is a journalist who has spent more than twenty years writing about Latin American politics, human rights, and social issues in publications including the *Economist*, the *Christian Science Monitor*, and the *Guardian*.

MAX SCHOENING is a researcher in the Americas division of Human Rights Watch. He has written extensively about human rights issues in Colombia, and lived there during the making of this book.

The VOICE OF WITNESS SERIES

Voice of Witness is a non-profit book series, published by McSweeney's, that empowers those most closely affected by contemporary social injustice. Using oral history as a foundation, the series depicts human rights crises in the United States and around the world. *Throwing Stones at the Moon* is the tenth book in the series. The other titles are:

SURVIVING JUSTICE
America's Wrongfully Convicted and Exonerated
Compiled and edited by Lola Vollen and Dave Eggers
Foreword by Scott Turow

These oral histories prove that the problem of wrongful conviction is far-reaching and very real. Through a series of all-too-common circumstances—eyewitness misidentification, inept defense lawyers, coercive interrogation—the lives of these men and women of all different backgrounds were irreversibly disrupted. In *Surviving Justice*, thirteen exonerees describe their experiences—the events that led to their convictions, their years in prison, and the process of adjusting to their new lives outside.

VOICES FROM THE STORM
The People of New Orleans on Hurricane Katrina and Its Aftermath
Compiled and edited by Chris Ying and Lola Vollen

Voices from the Storm is a chronological account of the worst natural disaster in modern American history. Thirteen New Orleanians describe the days leading up to Hurricane Katrina, the storm itself, and the harrowing confusion of the days and months afterward. Their stories weave and intersect, ultimately creating an eye-opening portrait of courage in the face of terror, and of hope amid nearly complete devastation.

UNDERGROUND AMERICA
Narratives of Undocumented Lives
Compiled and edited by Peter Orner
Foreword by Luis Alberto Urrea

They arrive from around the world for countless reasons. Many come simply to make a living. Others are fleeing persecution in their native countries. But by living and working in the U.S. without legal status, millions of immigrants risk deportation and imprisonment. They live underground, with little protection from exploitation at the hands of human smugglers, employers, or law enforcement. *Underground America* presents the remarkable oral histories of men and women struggling to carve a life for themselves in the United States. In 2010, *Underground America* was translated into Spanish and released as *En las Sombras de Estados Unidos*.

OUT OF EXILE
The Abducted and Displaced People of Sudan
Compiled and edited by Craig Walzer
Additional interviews and an introduction by
Dave Eggers and Valentino Achak Deng

Millions of people have fled from conflicts and persecution in all parts of Sudan, and many thousands more have been enslaved as human spoils of war. In *Out of Exile*, refugees and abductees recount their escapes from the wars in Darfur and South Sudan, from political and religious persecution, and from abduction by militias. They tell of life before the war, and of the hope that they might someday find peace again.

HOPE DEFERRED
Narratives of Zimbabwean Lives
Edited by Peter Orner and Annie Holmes
Foreword by Brian Chikwava

The sixth volume in the Voice of Witness series presents the narratives of Zimbabweans whose lives have been affected by the country's political, economic, and human rights crises. This book asks the question: How did a country with so much promise—a stellar education system, a growing middle class of professionals, a sophisticated economic infrastructure, a liberal constitution, and an independent judiciary—go so wrong?

NOWHERE TO BE HOME
Narratives from Survivors of Burma's Military Regime
Compiled and editedby Maggie Lemere and Zoë West
Foreword by Mary Robinson

Decades of military oppression in Burma have led to the systematic destruction of thousands of ethnic-minority villages, a standing army with one of the world's highest numbers of child soldiers, and the displacement of millions of people. *Nowhere to Be Home* is an eye-opening collection of oral histories exposing the realities of life under military rule. In their own words, men and women from Burma describe their lives in the country that Human Rights Watch has called "the textbook example of a police state."

PATRIOT ACTS
Narratives of Post-9/11 Injustice
Compiled and edited by Alia Malek
Foreword by Karen Korematsu

Patriot Acts tells the stories of men and women who have been needlessly swept up in the War on Terror. In their own words, narrators recount personal experiences of the post-9/11 backlash that has deeply altered their lives and communities. *Patriot Acts* illuminates these experiences in a compelling collection of eighteen oral histories from men and women who have found themselves subject to a wide range of human and civil rights abuses—from rendition and torture, to workplace discrimination, bullying, FBI surveillance, and harassment.

INSIDE THIS PLACE, NOT OF IT
Narratives from Women's Prisons
Compiled and edited by Ayelet Waldman and Robin Levi
Foreword by Michelle Alexander

Inside This Place, Not of It reveals some of the most egregious human rights violations within women's prisons in the United States. In their own words, the thirteen narrators in this book recount their lives leading up to incarceration and their experiences inside—ranging from forced sterilization and shackling during childbirth, to physical and sexual abuse by prison staff. Together, their testimonies illustrate the harrowing struggles for survival that women in prison must endure.